The New York Times

WILL SHORTZ WANTS YOU TO SOLVE CROSSWORDS!

The New York Times

WILL SHORTZ WANTS YOU TO SOLVE CROSSWORDS!
200 Easy to Hard Puzzles

Edited by Will Shortz

ST. MARTIN'S GRIFFIN 🔊 NEW YORK

DIFFICULTY KEY

Easy: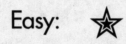

Medium: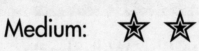

Hard:

ACROSS

1 Green gem used in Chinese carvings
5 Noisy bird
10 Mimicked
14 Mountain goat
15 Actor Davis of "Grumpy Old Men"
16 Enclosure for a pet bird
17 Expensive neighborhood in 43-Across
19 Istanbul resident
20 Acts of the Apostles writer
21 Co-creator of Spider-Man
23 Doctor's request before a throat examination
26 Some gym wear
27 The Beatles' "___ Road"
30 Understand
32 Impress and then some
33 "Just the facts, ___"
34 Nickname for 43-Across
36 Chill out
39 Boxer Tyson
40 More robust
41 Self-referential, in modern lingo
42 Cheer at a bullfight
43 Theme of this puzzle
44 ___ hygiene
45 Joe Biden's state: Abbr.
47 Oozy road material
48 Gas and coal
49 Rub elbows (with)
52 Firebugs
54 Boxing combos
56 Applies, as influence
60 Backside
61 43-Across stadium

64 Not wacko
65 Emancipated
66 Song for a diva
67 "So what ___ is new?"
68 Orchestra woodwinds
69 Amount owed

DOWN

1 Triangular sails
2 Drive the getaway car for, say
3 Hand out cards
4 "I beg your pardon"
5 $$$
6 Cigar remnant
7 "___: NY" (cop show spinoff)
8 Is sick
9 Whip marks
10 "Hurry or you'll miss out!"
11 43-Across patriot who went on a "midnight ride"
12 Snowy ___ (marsh bird)
13 Hockey feints
18 "Fine by me"
22 Fictional captain who said "Thou damned whale!"
24 Horrified
25 Shoe lift
27 Bullets and such
28 What some bondsmen offer
29 Popular food in 43-Across
31 Big Bang ___
34 Nonetheless, briefly
35 Vase
37 And others: Abbr.
38 Dames

41 Rubber item next to a computer
43 Squander
46 Course between appetizer and dessert
48 Devious
49 Basketball game that involves spelling
50 Shaquille of the N.B.A.
51 Highly successful, in Varietyese
53 Peruses
55 Belgrade native
57 Opposite of well done
58 Windy City daily, with "the"
59 Trick-taking game played with 32 cards
62 Prefix with natal
63 Tiny

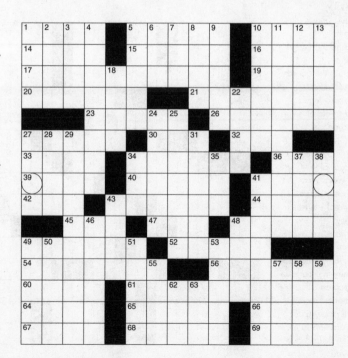

by Ian Livengood

ACROSS

1 Verizon FiOS and EarthLink, briefly
5 Feet, in slang
9 Leadership positions
14 Face on a coin of A.D. 64
15 "Git!"
16 Online outlay
17 *Abrupt reversals of opinion
19 Get stuck (in)
20 Madagascar mammal
21 Grits, essentially
23 *Uninjured, after "in"
26 *Hoosegow
29 Card game for two
30 Red and white stoppers?
32 Doozy
33 Singer Julius of early TV
35 Styptic pencil targets
36 *Scandal damage control
39 *Across-the-board
41 Les ___-Unis
42 Overprivileged 6-year-old of children's lit
44 Ship records
45 Virginia Woolf's "___ of One's Own"
46 Play charades
49 *Ghostly figures
51 *Kind of insurance policy
54 Blowouts
56 What steam coming out of the ears may signify in a cartoon
57 Lineup on a computer screen
59 One packing up the answers to the seven starred clues, maybe
62 Chop to bits

63 Sunbathe too long
64 Language spoken around Loch Ness
65 U.P.S. alternative
66 Whirl
67 Creepy look

DOWN

1 Amount received, as of cash
2 Actress Gomez
3 First layer of furniture protection
4 Absorb
5 Web access inits.
6 Jolly exclamation
7 Tunneling rodents
8 Garnering a "meh," say
9 Prefix with -tropic
10 Bygone Ford van
11 Figure invoked in casinos

12 E-mail or letter: Abbr.
13 "Ain't ___ Sweet" (song classic)
18 It's "Black" once a year: Abbr.
22 Ed Sullivan and others, informally
24 Beige-ish
25 Mini ___
27 Hollywood's Sommer
28 Sign of industrial decay
31 Explosion sound
33 1983 David Bowie #1 hit
34 Ovid's "___ Amatoria"
35 "Daughters" rapper
36 Cartoon frames
37 Texter's "Then again . . ."
38 Wayfarer

40 Arm or leg
43 Make a mess of
45 Volcanic spew
46 Losing side in a 2000 Supreme Court ruling
47 "Monty Python" comic John
48 Roof worker, of a sort
50 County NE of London
52 Pep rally cry
53 NBC newsman Richard
55 Recedes
57 Global economic oversight org.
58 Inc., in France
60 D-backs, on scoreboards
61 Home of "The Situation Room"

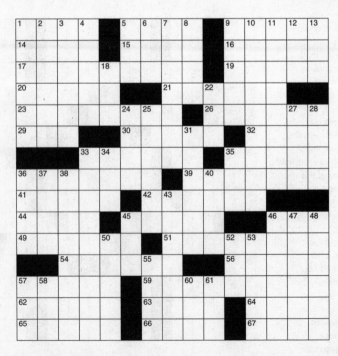

by Jean O'Conor

ACROSS

1 Peak
5 Bolivian capital
10 Animal house?
14 Italy's shape
15 Addis ___, Ethiopia
16 Temporary calm
17 More than awesome
18 Purchase for an all-nighter
19 ___ fixe
20 Like a sweet story
23 White House grp. that meets in the Situation Room
26 "Revenge of the ___" ("Star Wars" subtitle)
27 Jet-black
28 Fortuneteller's card
30 "Yeah, right!"
33 Like an unbelievable story
36 Circle measure: Abbr.
40 Suave or Prell
41 Two-character David Mamet play
43 Magazine whose cover has a red border
44 Like a hilarious story
46 Hubbub
47 Deluxe sheet fabric
48 Japanese fish dish
52 Valentine's Day flower
55 Adriatic or Aegean
56 Like a hilarious story
60 Listing on eBay
61 Mountain-climbing tool
62 "Iliad" warrior
66 Marcel Marceau, for one
67 Military group
68 "The Twilight ___"
69 Ball-___ hammer
70 Shoelace problems
71 Jeweled Fabergé objects

DOWN

1 "Honest" president
2 Nightstick carrier
3 "Me?," to Miss Piggy
4 ___ A Sketch
5 Neighbor of Maui
6 Cancel, as a launch
7 Asian noodle dish with peanuts
8 Take ___ (acknowledge applause)
9 Drag queen in "La Cage aux Folles"
10 Go up
11 Sound transmission
12 John who was the first American to orbit the earth
13 Poem for the dearly departed
21 Legally prohibit
22 Boxing official
23 Bikini blast, briefly
24 Give a quick greeting
25 Additive to coffee
29 "Coffee, Tea ___?"
31 Snooty sort
32 Eskimo home: Var.
34 The Olympic rings, e.g.
35 Earsplitting
36 Facts and figures
37 The "F" and "B" of Samuel F. B. Morse, e.g.: Abbr.
38 Comics orphan
39 ___ cum laude
42 German steel city
45 Underwater missile
46 "___ better to have loved and lost . . ."
48 Pinch pennies
49 Loosen, as 70-Across
50 "Come up and ___ sometime"
51 Biceps-flexing guys
53 Dizzying designs
54 Boxcars, with dice
57 Show of affection from a dog
58 Open ___ of worms
59 Good, long look
63 Easy run
64 Lee who directed "Crouching Tiger, Hidden Dragon"
65 Ballot marks

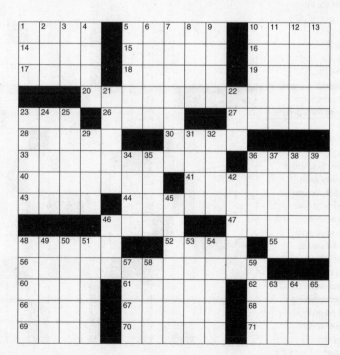

by Andrea Carla Michaels

ACROSS

1 Upholstery materials
8 Caddy alternative
11 Great Leap Forward leader
14 Pale eye shade
15 Candidates for rehab
17 Who you appear to be
18 Honor . . . and #5 on a list by 40-/46-Across of the 500 greatest songs of all time
19 Frozen product with blueberry and chocolate chip flavors
21 Give a dime on the dollar
22 Fulfillment . . . and #2 on the list
28 Gem of a girl?
29 Belly ache?
30 Lessens
34 With 40- and 46-Across, mossless? . . . and #1 on the list
36 River to the Caspian Sea
38 Prohibition, for one
39 Center of gravity?
40 See 34-Across
43 Subdivision part
44 Old French coin
45 One who says "loo" instead of "john"
46 See 34-Across
48 University div.
50 Advertisers' awards
53 Almost never
54 Casual greeting . . . and #4 on the list
57 Kind of knife
60 Excursion
61 Pretend . . . and #3 on the list

64 Things felt in a classroom?
69 Goes full tilt
70 Site of the Missouri State Fair
71 Dr. for the neck up
72 Place to get off: Abbr.
73 Time spent with a psychiatrist

DOWN

1 Quick swim
2 Best pitcher on the team
3 Debussy's "La ___"
4 Torso muscles, for short
5 Gin berries
6 Martial art
7 Martial arts actor Steven
8 Honey container
9 Actor Vigoda
10 Vigor
11 Part of it might consist of dashes
12 Go up, as eyebrows
13 Bone: Prefix
16 Chiropractor's target
20 Witch, e.g.
22 Puzzling no more
23 For one
24 Start, as a hobby
25 Grosse ___, Mich.
26 Hatcher of Hollywood
27 Land on the Persian Gulf
31 Hold membership
32 One going for the big bucks?
33 Glossy cloth
35 Wall St. trader
37 Some N.F.L. blockers: Abbr.

41 SeaWorld sight
42 Pleasant accent
47 Heap
49 Sticks in a nest
51 Fiona in "Shrek," e.g.
52 Evening bash
55 Successors
56 2010 releases from Apple
57 Ill temper
58 Sign
59 Word after 60-, 75- or 100-
62 Point to pick
63 Org. with air and water standards
65 Carrier to Oslo
66 New Haven scholar
67 Vegas casino
68 ___ Pedro

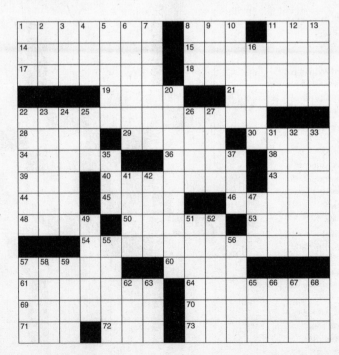

by Peter A. Collins

ACROSS

1 Uneasy feeling
6 Timekeeper
11 Madrid Mrs.
14 "Understood," to a radioer
15 Drug company that makes Valium
16 Rooster's mate
17 Randy Travis or Travis Tritt
19 Chicken ___ king
20 Tennis great Andre
21 "Wing" for Dumbo
22 Airline that doesn't fly on the Sabbath
23 Finished
24 Minivan since the mid-'90s
27 Material in an underwear waistband
29 Sinks to the bottom, as silt
30 '60s draft org.
31 "___ first you don't succeed . . ."
33 Seaboard
34 Drummer for the Who
37 Mexican houses
40 Slangy assents
41 Free TV spot, for short
44 Attribute (to)
47 Overall profit
49 Arizona N.B.A.'er
51 Tehran's land
52 Amaze
53 College transcript no.
54 Period when a computer is functioning
56 Abbr. on a sale item's tag
57 Clark Kent and Lois Lane's paper
59 Make a sharp turn back
60 Binge

61 Uneasy feeling
62 Hurricane's center
63 Swarms (with)
64 "Long time ___!"

DOWN

1 Pinball parlors
2 Humongous numbers
3 Lizards sometimes kept as pets
4 Past, present and future
5 Crafts' partner
6 Weep
7 One who can't catch a break
8 Groups of eight
9 Alternative to cash or check
10 Lead-in to plop or plunk
11 Song syllables in the title of a 1964 hit
12 Takes a breather
13 Brokerage worker
18 Classic 1955 Jules Dassin heist film
22 John who sang "Rocket Man"
25 One-___ (old ball game)
26 Without any profit
28 Connects
32 "___ will be done" (Lord's Prayer phrase)
34 Singer Carpenter
35 Restaurant posting
36 Words after a yell of "Police!"
37 Flip over, as a boat
38 Apt pig Latin for "trash"
39 ___ of God (epithet for Attila the Hun)

41 Leftovers after peeling
42 Shorthaired cat
43 Actress Bening of "American Beauty"
45 Galoot
46 Run out, as a subscription
48 Jordache jeans competitor
50 Oregon's capital
55 Scheme
57 Summer hours: Abbr.
58 Band with the 1983 hit "Owner of a Lonely Heart"

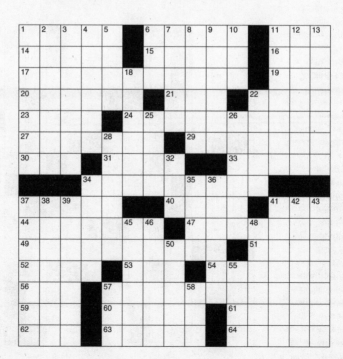

by Alan Arbesfeld

ACROSS

1 Aesop animal
4 Frisbee, e.g.
8 Notable watchmakers
13 Abbr. in two state names
14 Mattress giant
15 Ship of 1492
16 It makes gray go away
17 Make off with some raffle tickets?
19 Loosen, as a knot
21 "Give ___ whirl"
22 Lake creators
23 Make off with some kitchenware?
27 "Great blue" wader
28 Washes away
32 Italian exile island
34 Shredded
37 Scene of gladiatorial combat
38 "That stinks!"
39 Make off with some vehicles?
41 Sports V.I.P.
42 Luau greeting
44 Lot in life
45 Word repeated in "___ will be ___"
46 Washington city in apple-growing country
48 Confederacy foe
50 Make off with some cash?
55 Attraction for a butterfly
58 Big guns in D.C. lobbying?
59 Open, as a jacket
60 Make off with some gym equipment?
64 Actress Lupino
65 Also-ran
66 First lady between Bess and Jackie
67 Circus safety precaution
68 O. Henry work
69 Cauldron or sword in "Macbeth," say
70 Test for an M.A. applicant

DOWN

1 Make sense
2 Decline
3 Pad of drawing paper
4 Fed. overseer of the Controlled Substances Act
5 Vex
6 Container for a draft of ale
7 Desert bloomers
8 Fitness facility
9 British royal name since 1917
10 Llama herder of old
11 Winder on a watch
12 Wise off to
14 Rodeo wrestling target
18 Possess
20 Big retailer of home accessories
24 Dog in Oz
25 Book publisher Alfred A. ___
26 Pitching stats
29 Doing the job of an attack ad
30 A deadly sin
31 Gullible ones
32 Shopping venue with the options "Books" and "Toys & Hobbies"
33 She gets whatever she wants in "Damn Yankees"
35 Color TV pioneer
36 Devour eagerly
39 Woman's sleeveless undergarment, informally
40 Actress Russo
43 Type who wears tight-fitting jeans and thick-rimmed glasses, maybe
45 Cold war capital
47 One of two of Henry VIII's six
49 Not idle
51 Form tight curls in
52 "Horrible" Viking, in the comics
53 Downy duck
54 Sudden outpouring
55 Woes
56 Mob gone wild
57 "Assuming that's true . . ."
61 Ironically humorous
62 Payer of many dr. bills
63 Helpful hint

by Lynn Lempel

ACROSS

1 With 69-Across, childish taunt . . . and a homophonic hint to the answers to the asterisked clues
5 Monastery head
10 Angry, resentful state
14 First James Bond movie
15 Italian scientist after whom an electrical unit is named
16 Carbon compound
17 Turkish honorific
18 Kind of personality, in broadcasting
19 Hairstyle that's rarely seen on blonds and redheads
20 *Elated
23 Egyptian boy king
25 Masthead figures, for short
26 References in a footnote
27 "I give!"
29 One who goes a-courting
32 *Believing in nothing
35 With 40-Across, tip off
39 Major Fla.-to-Calif. route
40 See 35-Across
41 Spanish years
42 Relinquish
43 *Inflammation of gum tissue
45 Spying aircraft
47 Journalist ___ Rogers St. Johns
48 Houston baseballer
51 Item of sports equipment sometimes seen on top of a car
53 Yea's opposite
54 *Eensy-weensy beach garments

59 Chicken ___ (dish)
60 Man of steel?
61 Told a whopper
64 Olympic sword
65 France's Val d'___
66 "In that case . . ."
67 Joins in holy matrimony
68 "lol, u r so funny" and others
69 See 1-Across

DOWN

1 Pharmaceutical-approving grp.
2 Grp.
3 Separated, as a horse from its carriage
4 Horse with more than one color
5 Steer clear of
6 Water pipes

7 Unexciting
8 "Miss ___ Regrets"
9 Covering pulled out during a rain delay
10 Stick it in your ear
11 Not suitable
12 Talent
13 Dental thread
21 Part of a shoe with a tap
22 Here, to Henri
23 Old Greek garment
24 Join
28 Low, hard hits
29 Children's author R. L. ___
30 Pegasus appendage
31 Play's opening
33 "O, beware, my lord, of jealousy" speaker
34 Lower part of the leg
36 Make stronger and deeper

37 "And there you have it!"
38 Alternative to true-false or multiple-choice
44 Self-absorbed
46 Politico Paul
48 Off-kilter
49 Michael of R.E.M.
50 Cornered, as a raccoon
51 Women's hybrid tennis garment
52 Toys with tails
55 Bits of sand
56 Audio equipment giant
57 Alpine goat
58 Tennis's Nastase
62 WNW's opposite
63 Mexican couple

by Daniel Raymon

ACROSS

1 Pet adoption org.
5 Campfire remains
10 Trim, with "down"
14 Gradually remove, as a foal from its mother's milk
15 Cinnamon pattern, in toast
16 God whose name is a homophone of a zodiac sign
17 Humble reply to a compliment
18 Two units, in 56-Across
20 Test for Ph.D. seekers
21 Two-time Cy Young winner Lincecum
22 "You can count on me"
23 Three units, in 56-Across
27 Coral producer
28 Partner of desist
29 World's fair, e.g.
31 Facebook button
32 Jobs announcement of 2010
33 John McCain and Kurt Vonnegut, once, for short
37 Five units, in 56-Across
40 "Wowzers!"
41 Brutish sort
42 Battery units
43 Potter's oven
44 Small paving stones
45 Foe of Cobra, in comics
49 Three units, in 56-Across
52 Early afternoon time
54 What horizontal head shakes signify
55 Low island
56 Four units, in 56-Across
59 Santa __, Calif.

60 A few poker chips, maybe
61 Relative of a giraffe
62 Windfall
63 Honey
64 MetLife Stadium athlete, for short
65 B&Bs

DOWN

1 Drinks from a bottle, maybe
2 Kate's groom in "The Taming of the Shrew"
3 1980s toy craze
4 Whatever number
5 Reach for the stars
6 Hindu teacher
7 Bomb's opposite
8 Drop a fly ball, e.g.
9 School zone sign
10 Poet Neruda
11 On __ (doing well)
12 Cry before "set"
13 Legally prohibit
19 Plan for losers, informally?
21 Stun gun
24 It was originally first on the Roman calendar
25 Roman god of horses
26 Word before change or revenge
30 Kissing in a crowd, e.g., in brief
31 Droop
32 Poker declaration
33 Prefix with type
34 One whose success is well-earned?
35 Monsoon period
36 Ones taking the 20-Across

38 Who said "It's not bragging if you can back it up"?
39 Trailer park people, for short
43 Topple (over)
44 "Cut that out!"
45 Spoil
46 Vacuous
47 Volkswagen compact
48 "The Wind in the Willows" character
50 Bid at the last second, as on eBay
51 Meg and Paul
53 It's next to fluorine on the periodic table
57 It's over your head
58 Pilgrimage to Mecca
59 Slugger's stat

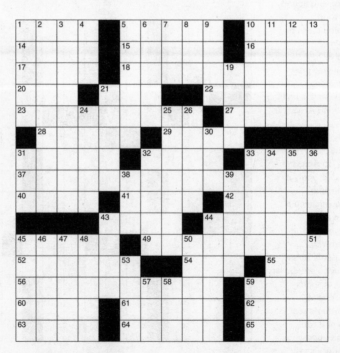

by Joel Fagliano

ACROSS

1 Gabs, gabs, gabs
5 One jumping to conclusions, say
11 Piece of gig gear
14 Eve's mate
15 Like Swiss mountains
16 "___ whillikers!"
17 Prefix with potent
18 Tiny bagel flavorers
20 Fairy tale bullies
22 Pasture
23 Delete with a cross
24 Two in craps
26 Cycle after wash
27 Christmas tree
28 Laudatory poem
29 Makeshift bookmark
30 Spanish bears
32 Put bubbles in
35 Ones getting all A's
40 Keynote address presenter
41 Adjust, as sails
43 Like stencils and missing persons
46 Happy ___ clam
49 Org. on a toothpaste box
50 12-inch sandwiches
51 Room decoration with a pattern
54 Subj. concerned with booms, crashes and panics
55 Sack
56 Music devices with earbuds
57 Obsolescent Kodak product
60 & 62 Doing great . . . or where to find 18-, 24-, 35-, 51- and 57-Across?
63 Ultimatum words
64 "There's nothing ___!"

65 12 oz. and others
66 Special Forces caps
67 Some Dadaist pieces

DOWN

1 Eight-time N.B.A. All-Star ___ Ming
2 Upbraid
3 Old TV's Captain ___
4 Smile that's not a warm smile
5 Fell off the wagon, say
6 "Don't Bring Me Down" grp.
7 Fruit to bob for
8 Plumbing, largely
9 "Orinoco Flow" singer
10 Hi-___ image
11 Early toddlerhood
12 Gorgon with venomous locks

13 Keep bothering
19 Demanding immediate attention
21 Help-wanted letters
24 Calif. air hub
25 It makes bread rise
26 Learning by recitation
29 Mom's mate
31 Shaved ice treat
33 W.W. II command area: Abbr.
34 Opposite of urban
36 Magnetite and others
37 "Totally awesome!"
38 Hidden exit
39 Lose forward traction
42 Spoil
43 Moon jumper, in "Hey Diddle Diddle"
44 Take back, as testimony

45 Scents
47 Smears with gunk
48 Purchase from the iTunes Store
51 Cracker
52 Nimble
53 Important blood line
55 Unadorned
58 ___ blind
59 W.W. II vessel
61 Sgts.' superiors

by Jean O'Conor

ACROSS

1 Digging . . . or word after "digging"
5 Santa ___, Calif.
9 Penne, e.g.
14 "Me neither"
15 Geishas' wear
16 Synthetic fiber
17 Research that may be outdoors
19 "Lemon Tree" singer Lopez
20 Org. recommending regular checkups
21 Function
22 Camera adjustments
24 "I'm with you!"
26 Variable spring period
28 Some cheers
29 Something not to be spared, in a saying
31 A .08% reading may lead to it, for short
32 Casey with a radio countdown
34 Not suitable
36 What employers tap to get employees
39 There are five on China's flag
41 Alternatives to Slurpees
42 San Francisco's ___ Hill
43 One of 154 for Shakespeare
46 Prisoner's sentence
50 Fortunate sort
52 Late bloomer
53 Lit
54 Fink
56 "Yuck!"
57 Magician's assistant in an audience, say
58 Supposed inventor of baseball . . . or a hint to 17-, 26-, 36- and 50-Across
61 Hollywood's Davis
62 Wicked

63 Vulcan mind ___
64 Source of Indian black tea
65 Ready to come off the stove
66 "Got it"

DOWN

1 Severe disrepute
2 "I haven't the foggiest!"
3 Bringer of peace
4 Medium for Van Dyck or van Gogh
5 Counterparts of columns
6 High wind?
7 Word said with a salute
8 Request
9 Helen Keller's portrayer in "The Miracle Worker"
10 "This way" indicator
11 Attacked anonymously
12 Stiffen through nervousness
13 Ring king
18 Couple
23 ___ Poke (candy)
25 Holocaust hero Schindler
26 Fixing, as the bottom of a skirt
27 Press ___ (media packet)
29 General on Chinese menus
30 Part of H.M.S.
33 Auto safety feature, redundantly
35 Flight destinations
36 Attire for scientists
37 Bandage brand

38 Like some mil. officers
39 NBC show since '75
40 Messes up, as the hair
44 "___ to Joy"
45 Dozed (off)
47 27 Chopin works
48 Entertain lavishly
49 Half of Stevenson's "strange case"
51 ___ Kinte of "Roots"
52 The Braves, on scoreboards
54 Many an archaeological site
55 Like Napoleon, before Elba?
57 Org. with balls and strikes
59 ___-lacto-vegetarian
60 Big inits. in music

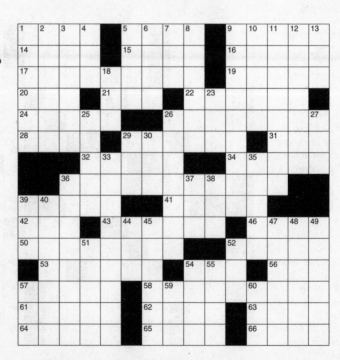

by Zhouqin Burnikel and Don Gagliardo

ACROSS

1 For real, in slang
6 Day-___ paint
9 2008 candidate with the slogan "Change we can believe in"
14 Supreme Court justice Samuel
15 Tech giant with the catchphrase "You've got mail"
16 English royal house before Stuart
17 "Come on, stop being such a wimp!"
18 Wheedle
20 Backup strategy
21 Push roughly
22 "Au revoir, ___ amis"
23 Course that's a cinch
25 Investments for old age, for short
27 Largest inland city in California
30 Org. for the Redskins, but not the Reds
32 5K or 10K
35 Grazing area
36 "A penny saved is a penny earned," e.g.
38 Two-legged creature
39 Illegal torching
41 Old Russian space station
42 Minor failing
43 "Kama ___" (ancient love guide)
44 Case of the blahs
46 PC hookup
47 Door turner
48 "Life of Pi" director Lee
49 Nasty looks
51 Letters of invitation?
53 Serves meals to
55 Eggs in fertility clinics
57 Gets closer to
59 Pretty poor grade
63 Like some premium roasts

65 Garlicky sauce
66 Note an alto is unlikely to hit
67 Even score
68 Basic belief
69 Stylishly streamlined
70 Urban grid: Abbr.
71 A cube has 12 of them

DOWN

1 Reading light
2 Carrier to Israel
3 Actress Gershon of "Bound"
4 ___ Store (source of many 99¢ downloads)
5 Kingpin
6 Bloated
7 Simple things to pick . . . or what 5-, 11-, 29- and 38-Down have?
8 Ersatz butter
9 Riverbank frolicker
10 "Nothing ___ net"
11 Lump that moves when you swallow
12 Distinctive Cindy Crawford feature
13 Clumsy boats
19 Satan's doing
24 Turf
26 Diva's delivery
27 Hooch container
28 Any "Seinfeld" showing, now
29 "Colorful" city bordering Newark, N.J.
31 Office plant
33 Onetime Joker portrayer ___ Romero
34 Perfect settings
37 "You said it, brother!"
38 Dinner and a movie, say, with someone you don't know
40 Spheres
45 "___ it or lose it"
48 Mimicry pro
50 Glimpsed
52 Style of T-shirt that does not have a round collar
54 ___ Park, Colo.
55 Former New York Times publisher Adolph
56 Bit of headgear raised at the wedding altar
58 Stage presentations
60 ___ John Silver
61 Title beekeeper in a 1997 film
62 Takes the bench
64 Word usually ignored in alphabetization

by Ian Livengood

ACROSS

1 Chowder ingredient
5 Go fish
10 "Dear" advice-giver
14 Opera set in Egypt
15 Pricey watch
16 Hacienda room
17 Product of colliding weather systems
19 Lowlife
20 Extra-powerful engine
21 Mr. ___ (Peter Lorre role)
22 What some strummers strum, informally
23 Fainting fits, e.g.
25 Grinders
27 Carve in stone
29 Manage
32 "Bonanza" brother
35 1982 Fleetwood Mac hit whose title is sung three times after "Come on and"
39 Altar constellation
40 Tolkien creature
41 Coupe, e.g. . . . or a hint to 17- and 64-Across and 11- and 34-Down
42 Breach
43 Expert
44 Really enjoys
45 "All ___ are off!"
46 Annoy
48 McEntire of country
50 Rustic accommodations
54 Cheap booze
58 Digging
60 Meara of comedy
62 More than elbow
63 Weenie
64 Annual tennis tournament played on clay

66 "Bye now"
67 Do without
68 "Dies ___" (hymn)
69 Bowlful for Bowser
70 Admittance
71 At sea

DOWN

1 Flings
2 Began to smoke
3 Dig, so to speak
4 Children's game in which players "knuckle down"
5 Kennel sound
6 Usual figure
7 Melancholy
8 Slow, musically
9 Laud
10 Give one's word
11 Behind the scenes
12 Feeling down
13 Thanksgiving dish

18 Shed
24 Vowel sound represented by an upside-down "e"
26 Teen follower
28 Happening with lots of laughs
30 Sitter's headache
31 Goes on and on and on
32 Bucket of bolts
33 How many times Laurence Olivier won a Best Actor Oscar
34 Metaphor for a sharp mind
36 Mormon Church inits.
37 Forbidding, as an expression
38 Sullen sort
41 Angry, with "off"

45 Aromatherapy purchase
47 Kind of doll
49 Claptrap
51 Faux pas
52 Noted bankruptcy of 2001
53 Hägar the Horrible's dog
55 Switch from amateur status
56 Eye parts
57 Article of faith
58 Ancient Andean
59 Dog on TV's "Topper"
61 M.I.T. grad, often: Abbr.
65 Coquettish

by Jacob McDermott

ACROSS

1 "What ___ in the 5-Down!"
6 Poetic black
10 Head of an office
14 Run out, as a subscription
15 Record for later viewing
16 Leaf gatherer
17 "Theme From Shaft" composer, 1971
19 Comparable (to)
20 One of three for an out
21 "For here ___ go?"
23 "___ Misérables"
24 "Toodles!"
25 Part of a project just before the end
28 Therefore
30 Feeder school for Oxford and Cambridge
31 "Blech!"
34 Intersects
36 Cheese in a red wheel
39 Degree of importance
41 Throb
44 10th grader, informally
45 Hogs
47 6–3, e.g., in tennis
48 Cancún coin
51 Blacksmith's block
53 Condiment that can remove crayon marks
56 Women's magazine with a palindromic name
60 Aged
61 "___ we forget"
62 Goner's declaration
64 Ark builder
66 Intense look
68 New Age singer from Ireland

69 Makes a misstep
70 Complement of Disney dwarfs
71 Midterm, for one
72 Price to pay
73 Lock of hair

DOWN

1 Group of preferred party attendees
2 Spaghetti or ziti
3 In pieces
4 Old Testament prophet
5 Locale for an Adam's apple
6 When a plane is due, for short
7 Rifle attachment
8 "Der Rosenkavalier," for one
9 Crunch maker

10 So-called "mansiere," essentially, in a "Seinfeld" episode
11 Team in "Moneyball"
12 "Nothin' but blue ___"
13 Have a feeling
18 Playboy founder Hugh
22 Choose
26 Alternatives to Slurpees
27 Tilling tools
29 Down Under bird
31 Letters at the start of a destroyer's name
32 Old Pontiac muscle car
33 The Fonz's sitcom
35 Whirls
37 Had supper
38 N.Y.C. presenter of 8-Down, with "the"

40 "The Cosby Show" son
42 Reveal
43 Wreath in Waikiki
46 They're good at taking orders
49 NBC weekend fixture, for short
50 "Hang on . . ."
52 Accountant's book
53 Impressionist Claude
54 Solo
55 Houston ballplayer
57 Depart
58 Lolls (around)
59 Idyllic places
63 Classic computer game set on an island
65 Sombrero, e.g.
67 Ballpark fig.

by Jim Peredo

ACROSS

1 "Huh?"
5 Mrs., in Majorca
8 ___ blanche
13 Top of the line
14 Use a surgical beam on
16 Be of use to
17 Wii
19 Money makers
20 Farther away, quaintly
21 One-celled organism
22 Birdie beater
23 Oui
25 Chevy S.U.V.'s
28 All's partner
29 Very eager to see something
30 Send in
33 Org. for Wizards and Magic
36 We
40 Rep.'s counterpart
41 Onionlike vegetables
42 No. 2
43 Start of a musical scale
44 Portfolio contents
46 "Whee!"
52 Téa of "Jurassic Park III"
53 Actress Zellweger
54 Abbr. after a series of equations, maybe
57 Commonplace
58 Wee
60 Weird
61 They aren't returned
62 Impudent
63 Suffix with road and hip
64 Works in a gallery
65 Selects, with "for"

DOWN

1 Candlelike, say
2 Rail rider
3 Soon, quaintly
4 Stereotypical cowboy name
5 Attacks à la "Ghostbusters"
6 Baltimore footballer
7 Easy ___
8 Tried to seduce
9 Zoo feature
10 Long-limbed
11 Championship
12 Someone ___ (not mine)
15 "In the Valley of ___" (2007 film)
18 Not found in many stamp collections, say
23 Steams (up)
24 Not bad
25 Military base tune
26 "A Death in the Family" novelist
27 Instrument used to play 25-Down
30 Charlotte of "The Facts of Life"
31 Yellowstone grazer
32 AWOL chasers
33 Red feature of Ronald McDonald
34 Total failure
35 Antenna users
37 They're often archived
38 Scholarship criterion
39 Thomas with a sharp pen
43 1997 Nicolas Cage thriller
44 Like the philosophy "Out with the old, in with the new"?
45 Former home of the Mets
46 Detectives' helpers
47 Put back to the beginning
48 "___ the One That I Want" (song from "Grease")
49 Funny Bombeck
50 Classic German camera maker
51 ___ circle
54 Bon mot
55 While preceder
56 Barely passing grades
59 Team size in beach volleyball

by Dan Schoenholz

ACROSS

1 Plays a part onstage
5 Ebony
10 What a definition defines
14 Opening for a coin
15 The "U" in UHF
16 Jai ___
17 Theater critic Walter
18 Wage increase
20 Carpet layer's calculation
22 ___ syrup
23 Dog doc
24 Journalist's credential
26 Wage increase
28 Frightened by shots
29 Golda of Israel
30 Inclined (to)
31 Characteristic
35 Takes home, as an income
36 "Observant of you to notice the error!"
38 Luster
41 South Korea's capital
42 Work of ___
45 Rat (on)
46 Panda's favorite plant
48 Gladden
50 1960 John Updike novel
53 Swiss peak
54 Prolonged attack
56 Genuine
57 It may be composed to accompany a movie
60 Unfreeze
62 ". . . happily ___ after"
63 Kitchen gadget for apples
64 Zippo
65 Mama's counterpart
66 Flood
67 "You sure got that right!"

DOWN

1 Pose, as a question
2 Become less cloudy
3 Flood
4 Cause of gray hair and worry lines, some say
5 Vehicle that may have a farebox
6 Long-necked animal in a petting zoo
7 Book of atlas
8 Betting game with dice
9 Communism theorist Marx
10 Cry from a nursery
11 Best Actor for "Hamlet," 1948
12 Makes hand over fist
13 Ones who've got something to lose?
19 "Get ___ Ya-Yas Out!" (Rolling Stones album)
21 Kutcher of "Two and a Half Men"
24 Links org.
25 One who delights in starting fires, informally
27 Far Eastern housemaid
32 Commercials
33 Skater's surface
34 Chinese principle
35 Cream-filled pastry
36 Moolah
37 Ernest of the Country Music Hall of Fame
38 One way to serve clams or rice
39 Terrific, in slang
40 Ran out, as time
42 President Lincoln
43 Dish of meat wrapped around a filling
44 Ship's unit of weight
47 Sicilian volcano
49 PC key for problem situations
50 Postgame wrap-up
51 Ancient Greek marketplace
52 Flat-crowned cap
55 AOL and MSN
58 One of the Gershwins
59 Before, poetically
61 Looking sickly

by Gary Cee

ACROSS

1 *Relative of an orange
8 *Tropical storm
15 Eroded
16 Certain steroid
17 Disappointment
18 "The Mary Tyler Moore Show" co-star
19 Procter & Gamble's first liquid laundry detergent
20 Plenty ticked off
22 Back in history
23 *Lingerie material
25 Race with lots of passing
27 New Orleans pro team
31 Feeling one's ___
35 Sonata maker
37 *Act deferentially
39 Best rating at Moody's
40 *French fries topper
42 Dedicated verse
43 *Like an eager beaver
45 Friend of Hamlet
47 City in Nevada
48 Alcoholic's recourse
49 Former Israeli P.M. Ehud
52 *Food, slangily
56 Decline
59 The blahs
63 "If you ask me," in blog comments
64 Radio pioneer
66 Surveillance pickup
68 Genie's master
69 Op-ed pieces
70 *Root used in some energy drinks
71 Language that's the source of the words answered by this puzzle's starred clues

DOWN

1 Nutrient-rich cabbages
2 Organs men don't have
3 Lead, for one
4 Four times a day, in an Rx
5 Some, in Santiago
6 No. in chemistry
7 Sound of music
8 Dominant ideas
9 Song in the Alps
10 Often-counterfeited luxury brand
11 ___ Pinafore
12 Wife of Charlie Chaplin
13 Universal donor's type, informally
14 Villain in the 2009 "Star Trek" film
21 Plant with a heart
24 The Wildcats of the Big 12 Conf.
26 "That hurt!"
28 Egyptian symbol of life
29 Thought: Prefix
30 ___ King Cole
32 Yours, in Paris
33 Foofaraw
34 Neighbor of Nor. and Fin.
35 Major swag
36 Jerk hard
37 Actor Russell
38 October gem
39 What the number of birthday candles indicates
41 Sexy
44 Big bunch
46 Sleuth, in slang
48 Making public
50 Cabin or cottage
51 1998 De Niro crime thriller
53 Vegas request
54 Signs
55 In decline
56 Slate, e.g.
57 Indonesian tourist mecca
58 Fiber-rich food
60 800, in old Rome
61 "I know! I know!"
62 Landlocked African land
65 Some B&N wares
67 Large vat

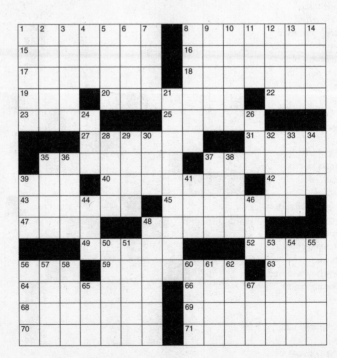

by Zhouqin Burnikel

ACROSS

1 Man-goat of myth
4 "Make it snappy," on an order
8 Smartly dressed
14 Media inits. since 1958
15 Guys' counterpart
16 Mike Nichols's comedy partner ___ May
17 Abba-inspired hit musical
19 Is unable to
20 Loud, as a crowd
21 Sign before Virgo
23 Gillette razor brand
24 River of the underworld, in myth
25 Movie starring Lon Chaney Jr., with "The"
28 Footnote abbr.
30 ___ of Wight
31 "Now I get it!"
34 Suffix with buck
36 "Since ___ My Baby" (1965 Temptations hit)
40 Washington rally of 5/14/00
44 Push
45 False god
46 Timid
47 Office worker just for the day
50 Makes bales on a farm
52 Dogpatch matriarch
56 Tibetan priest
60 Even, after "in"
61 Math's highest degree?
62 Baseball's Hammerin' Hank
63 Many a corporate plane
65 Classic advertising slogan . . . and a hint to 17-, 25-, 40- and 52-Across

68 Very advanced, computerwise
69 Test
70 Mal de ___
71 Al and Al Jr. of auto racing
72 Puerto ___
73 Suffix on juice drinks

DOWN

1 Mountain cats or sneakers
2 Miles ___ (not even close)
3 Leonard who played Mr. Spock
4 Medium in bio labs
5 "Uncle ___ wants you"
6 Boxer Muhammad
7 "The Lord is my shepherd . . . ," e.g.
8 Wooden ducks
9 Pie ___ mode
10 Long, thin cigar
11 Mottled horse
12 Huge, in poetry
13 Adjust the margins again
18 Opposite of mini-
22 Brit. record label
25 Artist Joan
26 Japanese soup noodles
27 Meagerly
29 Barnum's circus partner
31 Friend of François
32 "I Will Follow ___" (1963 #1 hit)
33 Mont Blanc, e.g.
35 White House financial advisory grp.
37 Surgery sites, for short
38 Educ. facility

39 "___ will be done . . ." (Lord's Prayer phrase)
41 "Hmmm . . ."
42 Honolulu's home
43 Sir's counterpart, informally
48 Bird mimics
49 One calling the kettle black, in a saying
51 Metal waste
52 ___ Picchu (Incan site)
53 Had dinner at home
54 Light fogs
55 Official language of Cambodia
57 Scent
58 Made a cow call
59 Tennis's Agassi
62 Bullets, BB's and such
64 Co. that makes A.T.M.'s
66 1011, in old Rome
67 McDonald's Big ___

by Ed Sessa

ACROSS

1 Place for washing instructions, often
6 Houdini feat
12 Free TV ad, for short
15 Wack
16 One end of a pencil
17 Grain beard
18 1990 Kevin Costner film
21 Reason for an R rating
22 Urban ordinance that might apply to a late-night party
23 1990 Nicolas Cage film
27 November exhortation
28 "Nice!"
29 Mont Blanc, e.g., to locals
30 Flu symptom
31 "___ Boys" (Alcott novel)
32 "___ Maria"
33 Drilling sites
34 18-, 23-, 51- and 56-Across?
38 One of two used facetiously in Mötley Crüe
41 "Oedipus ___"
42 Combat
45 Attendees
46 Ballet bend
48 DVD player button
50 Bushels
51 1967 Dustin Hoffman film
53 Not a club for big shots?
55 "Get the Party Started" singer
56 1989 Robin Williams film
61 Part of E.T.A.: Abbr.
62 "As you wish"
63 For all ___
64 Neighbor of Homer

65 In public
66 Misses at a bullfight?: Abbr.

DOWN

1 Pot top
2 Santa ___ winds
3 "Walk Like an Egyptian" band, with "the"
4 Purposely obfuscate, in a way
5 Ogle
6 "That's nasty!"
7 ___ Lanka
8 Quick refresher
9 Where sailors go in port
10 Lapwing
11 Mythological lover boy
12 "The Dying Swan" ballerina
13 Cardigan, e.g.

14 What an information booth has
19 Volleyball action between a bump and a spike
20 Is honest (with)
23 Paper with "Marketplace" and "Money & Investing" sects.
24 ___ Jima
25 Privileged one
26 K–5, schoolwise
30 Adversary
32 A.B.A. member
33 Betty Crocker product
34 Ran out, as in front of traffic
35 Vienna's land: Abbr.
36 Not a copy: Abbr.
37 Go off course
38 Kampala resident
39 "Tartuffe" writer

40 "Get Shorty" novelist Elmore ___
42 Most diluted
43 Play part
44 Hwy.
46 One of the friends on "Friends"
47 Like the pre-Easter season
48 Decrees
49 Ill's father
51 Scout unit
52 Abbr. on mail to a soldier
54 ___ facto
57 R.S.V.P. part
58 Hog's home
59 What a caddy may hold
60 What "aye" means

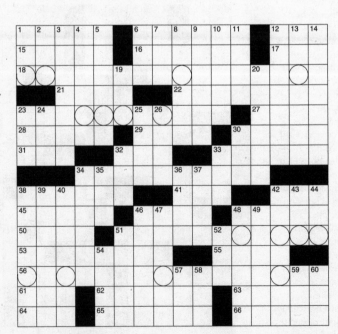

by Peter A. Collins

ACROSS

1 Actor Pitt
5 Do a voice-over for, as a foreign-language film
8 Cube or sphere
13 Gave a hand
15 Cute ___ button
16 More than fat
17 ___ Hawkins Day
18 Places where only guys go
20 Food preparation cutting technique
22 And so on and so forth: Abbr.
23 Eisenhower, affectionately
24 Cleaning tool
27 School charges?
28 School basics
32 Thailand, formerly
33 Bronco great John
34 "Let's go!" . . . or a hint for the ends of 20-, 28-, 41- and 52-Across
39 Sneezing sound
40 Regrets
41 Look of infatuation
44 Muslim leader
48 53-Down grad: Abbr.
49 Ruckus
50 Mexican dish sometimes described as "hot"
52 Fancy dress affairs
55 In the opposite order
58 Gullet parts
59 Dodge
60 "Barbara ___" (Beach Boys hit)
61 Waste carrier
62 John who succeeded William Henry Harrison
63 Bellum's opposite
64 Small songbirds

DOWN

1 Short-legged hound
2 Theater district
3 One who's hooked
4 Clears with a scraper, say
5 "___ Yankees"
6 Secondhand
7 Stagecoach robber
8 Wizards
9 Instrument used to set the pitch for an orchestra
10 Novelist Tolstoy
11 Suffix with capital or Marx
12 ___ Moines, Iowa
14 Bug spray ingredient
19 One of an Indian minority
21 Part of a play after intermission, maybe
24 Whine
25 Said aloud
26 College subj. with experiments
29 Breakfast meat
30 Fingernail file
31 "Evil Woman" grp.
32 Watched protectively
34 Clickable symbol
35 Pres. Jefferson
36 Soak, in dialect
37 Wed. preceder
38 West: Sp.
39 18, e.g., as a minimum for voting
42 French river
43 Snare
44 Turkish inn
45 African land whose name consists of three state postal abbreviations
46 Completely wrong
47 Counterpart of Mmes.
51 School basics
52 Yield
53 Annapolis inst.
54 Tailless cat
55 One who might care for a sick cat
56 Wall-climbing plant
57 Where L.A. is

by Susan Gelfand

ACROSS

1 Deposed leader of 1979
5 Suffix meaning "city" in some European place names
9 Shih ___ (diminutive dogs)
13 With 59-Across, where [circled letters] came from
15 Like a drive-thru order
16 "For ___ jolly good fellow"
17 When repeated, consoling words
18 Charge for currency exchange
19 Once, old-style
20 Child actress who appeared with [circled letters]
23 Biol., e.g.
25 Creator of [circled letters]
26 Palm, as a playing card
28 Golf's Ernie
29 Dodge models until 1990
30 Possible answer to "How'd you hurt yourself?"
33 Site of four sold-out 1972 Elvis Presley concerts, for short
36 Swamp growth
37 Base runner's attempt
38 Wool lover
39 Go astray
40 Not so outgoing
41 Painter Picasso
42 ". . . or ___ gather"
43 Some Wisconsin farms
45 What [circled letters] wanted to do
48 Bunch
49 Means of escape for [circled letters]
52 It's cast

53 Time to give up?
54 Jazz's Blake
57 Wayward G.I.
58 Therefore
59 See 13-Across
60 Be inclined (to)
61 Suffix with prank
62 Observer

DOWN

1 Lush
2 "Come again?"
3 Had an evening meal
4 Frau's mate
5 What a gyroscope may provide
6 Forum robes
7 "It's ___!" (birth announcement)
8 Avon commercial sound
9 One's wife, informally
10 Free-fall effect, briefly
11 "Back in the ___"
12 Suffice, foodwise
14 With 41-Down, composition of a trail followed by [circled letters]
21 New Deal inits.
22 Cheerleader's cheer
23 Best Original ___ (award for the film with [circled letters])
24 Rising star
27 Spanish hero El ___
31 Checking charge
32 One using an otoscope
33 Locale of an 1864 Civil War blockade
34 Fifth-century pope with the epithet "the Great"

35 Costume for [circled letters] on Halloween
37 They're "hung out" by professionals
38 Scratch
40 Anon
41 See 14-Down
42 Warrior's aid
44 Adams of "The Fighter"
45 Traffic cone
46 Late thumb-turning critic
47 Stamp collector's fastener
49 "Animal House" house
50 Rob of "The West Wing"
51 "Little Latin ___ Lu" (1966 hit)
55 Freezer stock
56 Suffix with slogan

by Kevin Christian

ACROSS

1 Treaty
5 Muslim leader
9 Office notes
14 Sore, as from overexercise
15 One-named Nigerian singer of "The Sweetest Taboo"
16 Pass into law
17 *Suddenly slam on the brakes
19 Expand, as a building
20 ___ moss (gardening purchase)
21 Previously, in old usage
23 Dallas hoopster, informally
24 Corporate jet manufacturer
26 *Top 40 music world
28 Fundamentally
30 Means of music storage
31 Tie the ___ (wed)
32 Was gaga about
35 Kennel bark
36 *"NYPD Blue" or "Miami Vice"
38 Fraternity "T"
41 Strongman of the Bible
42 Porkers
43 Deluxe Cuban cigar brand
46 Eight-armed sea creature
49 *Tricky tennis stroke
52 Paul of "Mad About You"
53 Like many workers, after age 65: Abbr.
54 Gauge showing r.p.m.'s
55 Sunrise direction
56 Ancient Greek public square

58 Spy activities . . . or a hint to the answers to the six starred clues
62 O'Brien of late-night TV
63 Preowned
64 ___ Mountains (Eurasian range)
65 Struck with a bent leg
66 Rules and ___
67 Fire lover, briefly

DOWN

1 Faux ___ (blunder)
2 Circus performance
3 *Stolen car destination, maybe
4 Prepare for printing
5 Beatty/Hoffman bomb of 1987
6 Chairman whose figure overlooks Tiananmen Square

7 11-Down extra
8 D.C.'s subway system
9 Goulash, e.g.
10 "___ of discussion!"
11 Emmy-winning AMC series set in the 1960s
12 Gas rating
13 Kitchen centerpieces
18 Yemen's capital
22 Vice president Agnew
24 Like some poorly applied makeup
25 Source of many Sicilian explosions
27 Cow's chew
29 Reveille's counterpart
33 Brit. military award
34 "Yikes!"
36 Where to get a taxi
37 Mutual of ___

38 *Opening segment in a newscast
39 Fit of fever
40 Stalin's land, in brief
41 Nurse a beverage
42 Raise, as with a crane
43 Means of music storage
44 Setting for TV's "Portlandia"
45 Definitely a day to run the A.C.
47 Church beliefs
48 Glum drop
50 Come to pass
51 "___ were the days . . ."
57 Arctic explorer John
59 Relax, with "out"
60 3, 4 or 5 on a golf course
61 ___-mo replay

by Ian Livengood

ACROSS

1 Tennessee team, for short
5 Acknowledge as true
10 Pole or Czech
14 Admit openly
15 Often-maligned relative
16 ___ mind
17 Blue-skinned race in "Avatar"
18 With 50-Across, it's represented by 15 squares in an appropriate arrangement in this puzzle
19 Some Monopoly purchases: Abbr.
20 French pupil
22 Grandpa on "The Simpsons"
23 Boot
24 Live it up
26 N.F.L. player with a black helmet
28 Hebrew month when Hanukkah starts
30 Richard Branson's airline company
33 Hundred Acre Wood resident
34 Place to hear fire and brimstone
38 Personal question?
39 Washing machine contents
41 David of "The Pink Panther"
42 Rear half of a griffin
43 Writer Katherine ___ Porter
44 Barely adequate
45 Iams competitor
46 1943 penny material
48 Suffix with meth- or prop-
49 What you might buy a flight with
50 See 18-Across

53 Place with complimentary bathrobes
56 Pronoun for Miss Piggy
57 Rodeway ___
58 Past the expiration date
61 Ship sinker
63 Pep up
65 "Not my call"
66 Words of encouragement
67 Calls it quits
68 Weatherproofing stuff

DOWN

1 Revolver with the letters N-E-W-S
2 Speed skater's path
3 Make-out session spot
4 Spin, as an office chair
5 It might be bummed
6 Basketball player who starred in "Kazaam"
7 Commoner

8 Police stun gun
9 "I ___ you one"
10 Barber, at times
11 Medical directive
12 With, on le menu
13 Item under a jacket, maybe
21 At any time
23 Nefarious
25 Roulette bet
27 ___-garde
28 Caffeine-laden nuts
29 "Not gonna happen"
31 Comment made while crossing one's fingers
32 Pitchers' hitless games, in baseball slang
35 Experienced through another
36 The first Mrs. Trump
37 Shakespeare's Antonio and Bassanio, e.g.
40 Judge

42 Reclined
47 British sailors
49 One of the friends on "Friends"
51 No-show in a Beckett play
52 Certain belly button
53 Tuxedo shirt button
54 St. Peter was the first
55 B.A. part
58 Cabo's peninsula
59 Lots
60 Thing often of interest?
62 Hawaiian dish
64 Blanc or Brooks

by Joel Fagliano

ACROSS

1 Pat down, as pipe tobacco
5 Trade
9 Carpenter's file
13 Grammy winner McLachlan
14 Heading on a list of errands
15 Salt lake state
16 1959 hit by the Drifters
19 Stock market index, with "the"
20 Collaborative Web project
21 Helpers
22 What children should be, and not heard, they say
24 Pudding or pie
27 1970 hit by Eric Clapton
32 Barbie and others
34 180 degrees from WNW
35 Close by
36 Letter after pi
37 Belly muscles, for short
40 Magazine with an annual "500" list
42 ___-la-la
43 Forever and ever
45 "___ in apple"
47 Nutso
49 1978 hit by Journey
53 Something to scribble on
54 "Hurry!," on an order
57 11- or 12-year-old
60 Therefore
62 One may be under a blouse
63 What the artists of 16-, 27- and 49-Across are doing (in reference to the last words of their hits)?
67 "___ and the King of Siam"
68 On the Adriatic, say
69 Brings in, as a salary

70 Piece of fly-casting equipment
71 Roseanne, before and after Arnold
72 Exercise that may involve sitting cross-legged

DOWN

1 California/Nevada border lake
2 "Can anybody hear us?"
3 Feb. follower
4 "Close call!"
5 Bram who created Dracula
6 "Alas!"
7 Billboards, e.g.
8 Certain lap dog, informally
9 Gloat
10 Slightly
11 Kemo ___ (the Lone Ranger)
12 ___ ed. (gym class)
13 Norms: Abbr.
17 Nobel-winning author André
18 Fisherman's tale
23 Org. for the Bears and Bengals
25 "But of course, amigo!"
26 Garden of ___
28 Fed. air marshal's org.
29 Locale for an 1863 address
30 "B.C." creator Johnny
31 A waiter carries plates on it
32 Sketched
33 Cry before "I know!"
38 Worms, to a fisherman
39 Not at all nutso

41 Network with an "eye" for entertainment
44 Dakar's land
46 Pearly Gates sentinel
48 Alias letters
50 Anderson of "WKRP in Cincinnati"
51 "That's so funny I forgot to laugh"
52 Rim
55 ___ football
56 Fail's opposite
57 Bygone Kremlin resident
58 Cabernet, for one
59 Feminine suffix
61 Follow, as orders
64 Arrest
65 Fed. property manager
66 Philosopher ___-tzu

by Amy Johnson

ACROSS

1 With 1-Across, toy train
5 Set of values
10 Half of cuatro
13 ___ mark (#)
14 Texas city
15 Messenger ___
16 Introductory drawing class
17 Old game consoles
18 Early Tarzan Ron
19 Not found
21 With 21-Across, "I'll believe it when I see it!"
23 With 23-Across, CBer's opening
26 With 26-Across, #1 hit for the Mamas & the Papas
27 ___ Doone (cookie brand)
28 Prefix with center
31 Jobs at Apple
32 Six-pointers, in brief
33 Med. exam involving an injection into the forearm
36 "Washingtons"
37 With 37-Across and 37-Across, a holiday song
39 Lead-in to girl
42 Tots
43 ___ Records
46 Play lazily, as a guitar
48 Rap's Dr. ___
49 Thai or Taiwanese
51 With 51-Across, town crier's cry
53 With 53-Across, "Nothing's changed"
55 With 55-Across and 55-Across, real-estate catchphrase
58 Real nerve
59 ___ Records
60 Montana's capital
62 "The lady ___ protest too much"
65 "Perfect" number
66 Part of a train headed to a refinery
67 Drama award since 1956
68 The "E" in E.S.L.: Abbr.
69 Drenches
70 With 70-Across, #1 hit for Billy Idol

DOWN

1 With 1-Down and 1-Down, lively Latin dance
2 With 2-Down, "Ver-r-ry funny!"
3 Stable employees
4 Buckeye
5 Sup
6 "Shut yer ___!"
7 Title for Goethe
8 "Green thumb" or "purple prose"
9 Universe
10 German city rebuilt after W.W. II
11 Temporarily away
12 Agrees
14 With 14-Down, like some talk shows
20 Play in the N.H.L.
22 Being pulled
23 Diner inits.
24 Curtain holder
25 Made tighter, as a knot
29 With 29-Down, nursery rhyme starter
30 Debatables
34 "As an aside," in chat lingo
35 Big inits. in C&W
37 First lady before Michelle
38 ___ bin Laden
39 Jock
40 1976 horror film whose remake was released, appropriately, on 6/6/06
41 Copying exactly, as a sketch
43 1970 John Wayne western
44 Baseball's Ripken
45 &
47 Collection of legends
50 Hardly ever
52 Farm letters?
54 With 54-Down, food gelling agent
56 Spanish pot
57 Bottle part
61 "Illmatic" rapper
63 With 63-Down, title boy in a 2011 Spielberg film
64 With 64-Down and 64-Down, Fat Albert's catchphrase

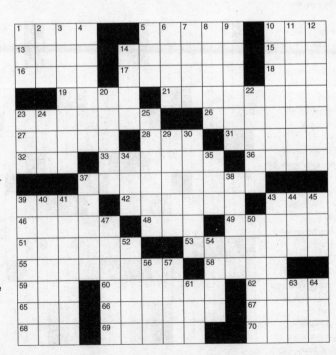

by Tim Croce

ACROSS

1 Scotch ___
5 Stare dumbfoundedly
9 Simba's best friend in "The Lion King"
13 Nyet : Russian :: ___ : German
14 More than some
15 Engine
16 Jamaican sprinter nicknamed "The Fastest Man on Earth"
18 Story for storage
19 Polynesian kingdom
20 Nothing daring in terms of offerings
22 Ostentatious displays
24 Sounded like a horn
25 Washtub
27 Indian dress
28 Mediterranean and Caribbean
30 Winter pear
32 Having painterish pretensions
36 Golf course target
37 PC outlet
39 Had supper
40 Firebug's crime
42 Lovett of country music
43 Title beekeeper in a 1997 film
44 "Dies ___" (hymn)
46 Brand of dinnerware with a Scandinavian design
48 Bandleader Glenn
51 Roger who played 007
53 Service charges
57 Apple tablets
59 "Dig?"
60 Heralded, as a new era
62 Rum drinks for British sailors
63 Subway support
64 Companion of the Pinta and Santa Maria
65 Cravings
66 Pig's grunt
67 "General Hospital," e.g.

DOWN

1 Letter-shaped fastener
2 Fable writer
3 Nightspots for cocktails and easy listening
4 Mysteries
5 Yak
6 Baseball's Matty or Jesus
7 D.C. types
8 "___, Brute?"
9 Sore loser's cry
10 Fragrance of roses
11 France's longest river
12 Shaped like a rainbow
15 Teen hanging out among shoppers
17 Dozes
21 "The ___ Daba Honeymoon"
23 Brothers and sisters, for short
26 Aristocratic
27 Bawl out
28 Place that might offer mud baths
29 Pointy part of Mr. Spock
31 007, for one
33 Rush Limbaugh medium
34 Sault ___ Marie, Mich.
35 "___-haw!"
37 Turmoils
38 500 sheets
41 Structures in the Gulf of Mexico
43 Annual tournaments . . . or a description of the starts of 16-, 20-, 37-, 53- and 60-Across?
45 Terrier's sound
47 Roulette bet that's not rouge
48 Hot and humid
49 River of Grenoble, France
50 Divulge
52 Minneapolis suburb
54 It replaced the franc and mark
55 Actor Morales
56 Body part that's often bumped
58 Partner of Crackle and Pop
61 "Benevolent" club member

by Zhouqin Burnikel and D. Scott Nichols

ACROSS

1 Cowboy chow
5 Distresses
9 Word from the Arabic for "struggle"
14 Simpson who said "Beneath my goody two shoes lie some very dark socks"
15 & 16 Preparing to pop the question, say
17 Cash dispensers, for short
18 "___ first you don't succeed . . ."
19 What a star on a U.S. flag represents
20 Subject of the book "Revolution in the Valley"
22 Beset by a curse
23 Pinocchio, periodically
24 Snarling dog
25 Poisonous
28 Person who works with dipsticks
33 Not much, in cookery
34 Powerful org. with HQ in Fairfax, Va.
35 Shine, commercially
37 People in this may have big ears
42 Shot ___
43 "Criminy!"
44 Actress Watts
45 Sioux shoe
49 Metaphor, e.g.
50 "Whazzat?"
51 Employs
53 Meal with Elijah's cup
56 Journalist of the Progressive Era
61 Kick out
62 Vogue alternative
63 Starting score in tennis
64 Techie sorts
65 From the top
66 Managed, with "out"
67 Unable to hold still
68 Speaker's place
69 Like Lindbergh's historic trans-Atlantic flight

DOWN

1 Glitz
2 Meter maid of song
3 Gomer Pyle's org.
4 Legendary lizard with a fatal gaze
5 Japanese dog breed
6 Notify
7 Pastures
8 Brother of Cain and Abel
9 Book after Deuteronomy
10 Person getting on-the-job training
11 Snopes.com subject
12 Upfront stake
13 Monopoly card
21 Specialty
24 Cartoonist Addams
25 Pack down
26 Detestation
27 ___ knife
29 Japanese mushroom
30 Grand ___ (wine of the highest rank)
31 Eskimo home
32 Stick together
36 Theater award since 1956
38 Word repeatedly sung after "She loves you . . ."
39 "___ amis"
40 Opposite of exit
41 Deals at a dealership
46 Partner of balances
47 Girl's show of respect
48 Cell centers
52 Twists, as facts
53 Gaming giant
54 Smooth
55 Lighten up?
56 Quaff for Beowulf
57 Bone next to the radius
58 Gorilla pioneering in sign language
59 Knievel of motorcycle stunts
60 Make over

by Patrick Blindauer and Andrea Carla Michaels

ACROSS

1 Slyly spiteful
6 The "D" of PRNDL
11 Easy-to-chew food
14 Mutual of ___ (insurance giant)
15 Aid in detecting speeders
16 ___ Direction (boy band)
17 John Cusack thriller based on a Grisham novel
19 "Golly!"
20 Inviting
21 "Gimme ___!" (start of an Iowa cheer)
22 Southward
23 "___ Misérables"
24 Santa's little helper
26 Snouts
28 Newly famous celebrity
32 ___ date (make some plans)
35 Tuna container
36 Lying on one's back
37 Conductors of impulses from nerve cells
39 Grazing area
41 Judicial statements
42 Fought like the Hatfields and McCoys
44 Abbr. after a lawyer's name
46 Lose traction
47 Stipulation that frees one of liability
50 Minor difficulty
51 Bit of butter
52 "He said, ___ said"
55 Praise
57 Nautical record
59 Nautical unit of measure
61 Swiss peak
62 Part of a ski jump just before going airborne

64 Bronx ___
65 Pop concert venue
66 Strong, seasoned stock, in cookery
67 Japanese money
68 Military cap
69 Run-down, as a bar

DOWN

1 Atoll composition
2 Tell jokes, say
3 Oxygen suppliers for scuba divers
4 Spicy Southeast Asian cuisine
5 Show that's bo-o-oring
6 Unmoist
7 Indian nobleman
8 "Can't say"
9 Sundry
10 Suffix with crock or mock
11 Toy that hops
12 All over again
13 Ball-___ hammer
18 Shoelace end
22 Hate, hate, hate
25 "Words ___ me!"
27 Macho sort
28 Quick but temporary fix
29 Prepare for prayer
30 Voting against
31 What library patrons do
32 How the cautious play it
33 Mates who've split
34 Mention in passing
38 Aug. follower
40 Inits. on a rush order
43 State openly, as for a customs official
45 Drink, as of ale
48 Tight necklace

49 Fills with personnel
52 Disgrace
53 ___ in on (got closer to)
54 "E" on a gas gauge
55 Indolent
56 ___ vera
58 Trait transmitter
60 Factual
62 File extension?
63 Grain in Cheerios

by Gary Cee

ACROSS

1 Now, in Acapulco
6 Like a college course labeled "101"
11 551, once
14 One using Yelp or TripAdvisor, perhaps
15 Prefix with biology
16 Suffix with planet or fact
17 Overcome an unpleasant misunderstanding
19 Fall mo.
20 Bit of crew equipment
21 ___ tai
22 Actor Milo
24 Left-brain activity
29 "Anderson Cooper 360°" channel
30 Asimov and Newton
31 March honoree, for short
34 "And ___ bed"
36 "The Wonder Years" teen, for short
38 2004 film featuring Dustin Hoffman
42 Half a bikini
43 Accompanying
44 Final approval
45 Anderson Cooper, e.g.
48 Midpoint: Abbr.
49 Reason to see a rheumatologist
54 Instrument played by George Harrison
55 Gulf state: Abbr.
56 Loony
58 ___ Paulo, Brazil
59 "The Lord of the Rings" setting . . . or a feature of 17-, 24-, 38- and 49-Across?
64 Young Darth Vader, to friends
65 Filmmaker Morris
66 He-Man's sister
67 Initials of fashion
68 Oracles
69 Point toward

DOWN

1 Instruction to play with the bow
2 Special-request flight meal option
3 Cheri formerly of "S.N.L."
4 "The Crying Game" actor Stephen
5 Sheet music abbr.
6 Joy formerly of "The View"
7 Failed in a big way
8 "___ Na Na"
9 Common pasta suffix
10 Mexican beer
11 Thingamajig
12 Royalty payers, say
13 Collar attachment
18 Certain Fed
23 Reggae precursor
25 Org. with Lions, Tigers and Bears
26 ___'acte
27 Thumb a ride
28 Escapes injury
31 Fam. member
32 Allies of the Trojans in the "Iliad"
33 What pad Thai is often cooked in
34 Bake, as eggs
35 Not closeted
37 Letters on brandy
39 Old draft category for civilian workers
40 Italian wine area
41 Cartoon boy who can be described by an anagram of his name
46 It runs the 'L'
47 Mercury counterpart
48 Native Canadian
49 Test, as ore
50 Mary or Elizabeth
51 Cough drop brand
52 Like some legal proceedings
53 Kama ___
57 Word said while pointing
60 Dander
61 Dr. ___
62 Spanish 57-Down
63 Tuna type

by Kevan Choset

ACROSS

1 Top
5 ___ Lingus
8 Sleeping sickness transmitter
14 Film ___ (movie genre)
15 Multiplatinum album with the 2002 hit "Ain't It Funny"
16 Met productions
17 Star of 64-Across
19 Dancer Ginger
20 2004 World Series "curse" beaters
21 Exchange blows
23 Summer drink
24 Henry Ford's son
25 Number of 17-Across in 64-Across
27 Putdown
29 Shakespeare's "___ Like It"
30 Explosive
33 "___, meeny, miney, mo"
35 Sand
38 Catchphrase of 25-Across
43 Out of kilter
44 "___ Lisa"
45 Bread with seeds
46 Paint palette accompanier
50 Artist Bonheur
52 Gadget for 25-Across
55 Check for odors
59 ___ Mahal
60 Part of an interstate
61 Quite the party
62 Small garage capacity
64 Campy 1960s hit sitcom
66 Spin
67 "Xanadu" band, for short
68 "Don't look ___!"
69 Fellow
70 Ex-G.I.'s grp.
71 Gifts at Honolulu International Airport

DOWN

1 Tennis's Agassi
2 Murmured
3 Watches, as a store
4 Wipes clean
5 Comet competitor
6 Nightmarish street, in film
7 Martini & ___ vermouth
8 Hebrew scrolls
9 Like Corvettes and Mustangs
10 Brain scan, for short
11 Money manager
12 Famed New York restaurateur
13 Elizabethan earl
18 Dressed (up)
22 Links org.
25 Rubik who invented Rubik's Cube
26 Bear or Berra
28 180° turn, slangily
30 Bygone carrier
31 "This instant!"
32 Some airplanes
34 "Tasty!"
36 Old-fashioned Christmas trim
37 Summer shirt
39 Ancient Greek instrument
40 Yawn inducer
41 British musician Brian
42 Ropes in
47 Still awake at 1 a.m., say
48 Generous one
49 Darlin'
51 20 Questions category
52 Tempest
53 Vietnam's capital
54 Israeli desert
56 Angered
57 Physicist Enrico
58 Honors in style
61 Pack away
63 Cool dude, in jazz
65 Keebler baker, supposedly

by Roy Leban

ACROSS

1 Mongrel dogs
5 Color of honey
10 On the road
14 Meltable food item
15 One of the Flintstones
16 Salad cheese
17 Keyboard key
19 Go smoothly
20 No Mr. Nice Guy
21 Joint with a cap
22 View in northern Italy
23 Cantankerous
25 Throw off track
27 Dates
29 16-Across is preserved in it
32 "Surely you ___!"
35 Geronimo, e.g.
39 Powder holder
40 Que. neighbor
41 Theme of this puzzle
42 Fraction of a joule
43 The year 56
44 Toughen, as glass
45 O.T.B. postings
46 First president to marry while in office
48 Dovetail
50 Memory gaps
54 "Enough!"
58 Clubmates
60 "Quickly!"
62 Imam's faith
63 Door sign
64 Where thunderstorms may occur
66 Teeming
67 Iraq's ___ Triangle
68 Mary Kay rival
69 Manipulative one

70 Bakery supply
71 Make (one's way)

DOWN

1 Hearst magazine, familiarly
2 Gastric woe
3 Played over
4 Most quickly
5 Saddler's tool
6 Do some work on a dairy farm
7 Strawberry ___
8 Toaster, or roaster
9 Autumn toiler
10 Fling
11 Popular
12 On
13 Swerves at sea
18 Cousin of a harp
24 Long (for)
26 Genesis son

28 Board game turn
30 Encyclopedia reader from A to Z, say
31 Caviar, essentially
32 Bump hard
33 It's a sin
34 Painting of flowers, e.g.
36 Barbary beast
37 Secretive sort
38 Lady of Troy
41 Stadium rollout
45 Electrical principle
47 Parade day
49 Make dirty
51 Fresh-mouthed
52 Suffix with Roman
53 Spot for sweaters
55 Oil source
56 Wouldn't stop
57 Touch up

58 Lima's land
59 W.W. II enemy
61 Gives zero stars to
65 Torched

by Barry C. Silk

ACROSS

1 Swimming units
5 Not tight
10 Possess
14 Geometry calculation
15 City on the Missouri
16 Asia's ___ Sea
17 Laurel or Musial
18 VCR button
19 Pastrami purveyor
20 Actor Quaid transgressed
23 Giant Hall-of-Famer
26 Not as much
27 Condoleezza Rice's department
28 Bongos
30 Two-striper in the Army: Abbr.
32 Draft org.
33 Frontiersman Boone did some carpentry
38 Bridge
39 St. Nick
40 Capital on a fjord
44 Actor Hickman showed boredom
47 Fuel economy stat.
50 Non-earthlings, for short
51 Asinine
52 Move on all fours
54 Hydrofluoric ___
57 Exxon product
58 President Ford stared fiercely
62 As a czar, he was terrible
63 Home of the University of Maine
64 ___ Romeo (sports car)
68 Olympic sled
69 Assign to, as blame
70 Potting material
71 Popular jeans
72 Fencing weapons
73 Very large

DOWN

1 ___ Cruces, N.M.
2 "But is it ___?"
3 Vegetable that rolls
4 Hourglass contents
5 Greene of "Bonanza"
6 Black cats, to the superstitious
7 Caravan's stop
8 "___ a Lady" (Tom Jones hit)
9 Diner sign
10 Lacked, briefly
11 Sporting venues
12 Gentlemen's gentlemen
13 Omits, in pronunciation
21 Ultimatum ender
22 Man or Wight
23 ___ and ends
24 Links hazard
25 Albacore or yellowfin
29 Intellect
30 Hit with a ticket
31 Thespian production
34 Future D.A.'s exam
35 Ayes' opposite
36 Cape ___, Mass.
37 Low in spirits
41 Hose problem
42 ___ the Hyena
43 Praiseful poems
45 Place to make a wish
46 Assistant
47 Montreal university
48 Advance look, informally
49 It may have a remote-activated door
53 Declines
54 "Home ___," Macaulay Culkin movie
55 Tippy craft
56 Numbered clubs
59 Latest news, slangily
60 Stagehand
61 Sprinter's event
65 Singer Rawls
66 Tiniest amount to care
67 "Cakes and ___" (Maugham novel)

by Holden Baker

ACROSS

1 Mrs. Loopner player
7 Tells a bedtime story
14 Free drinks set-up
16 Mr. Blues player
17 Tickler of the ivories
18 Figured out, as secret writing
19 Show that debuted 10/11/1975, for short
20 Buffet table heater
22 Hail Mary, e.g.
23 King, in Cádiz
24 Bard's nightfall
25 Wearies
28 Syr. neighbor
29 Weekend Update anchor
34 Les États-___
35 Literary piece
36 Wretched
37 Longstanding 19-Across opener
40 Kuwaiti leaders: Var.
41 Take a swing
42 Old Venetian official
43 Announcer for 19-Across
44 Org. for Mariners
45 Lachesis and Clotho, in myth
46 Ground breaker
47 Ottoman ruler
48 University mil. group
52 Terrible trial
54 Network of 19-Across
57 Mistakenly
59 New York's ___ Bridge
61 Samurai tailor player
62 Medal giver
63 Naps, for señores
64 Ms. Conehead player

DOWN

1 Police
2 ___ arms
3 Genuine
4 Old cable TV inits.
5 Nile birds
6 Foul
7 Ms. Roseanne Roseannadanna player
8 Keep an ___ (watch)
9 Dog breeder's assn.
10 Withdraw from, as a case
11 Kind of water
12 Sailing ropes
13 Bookie's figure
15 Hwy.
21 Looked like
23 Tend to, as a barren lawn
25 Kentucky Derby drink
26 True inner self
27 Springboard performer
28 Phrase of commitment
29 Intimidate
30 The best of times
31 Under way
32 Power glitch
33 Actress Sommer and others
35 Surgeon's locales, quickly
36 Dripping
38 To and ___
39 Collar
44 Mr. Escuela player
45 Catlike
46 Big to-do
47 Von Richthofen's title
48 Barbecue fare
49 R.E.M.'s "The ___ Love"
50 Prefix with conference
51 Vineyards of high quality
53 Biblical suffix
54 Benchmark
55 La ___ Tar Pits
56 Foot ailment
58 String after Q
60 Close a show

by Mike Torch

ACROSS

1 Unravel, as a cord
5 Hand support
9 Fissures
14 Christmas season
15 To be, in Toulon
16 Messages via MSN.com, e.g.
17 "___ small world!"
18 Extended family
19 Backside
20 Old-fashioned
23 Nonverbal O.K.'s
24 Author Harper ___
25 Amer. soldiers
28 Result of a hung jury, maybe
31 Fit ___ fiddle
34 Fess up (to)
36 Driver's lic. and such
37 +
38 Fundamental
42 ___ liquor
43 Two halves
44 "All in the Family" spinoff
45 The whole ball of wax
46 Mt. Rushmore material
49 "Law & Order" fig.
50 Shipwreck signal
51 Instrument hit with a hammer
53 Petty
59 Lethal snake
60 Yankee nickname starting 2004
61 Workbench attachment
63 "Doe, ___, a female . . ."
64 Sagan or Sandburg
65 Glimpse
66 It might be 18 oz. on a cereal box
67 Safe sword
68 ___ the wiser

DOWN

1 Memo letters
2 Justice ___ Bader Ginsburg
3 By the same token
4 Long (for)
5 Ebb
6 "Finally!"
7 Tehran's land
8 What usurers do
9 Gas up again
10 Spitting ___
11 Weapon of 59-Across
12 Wee
13 Underhanded
21 After a fashion, informally
22 Really good time
25 Alpha, beta, ___ . . .
26 Perfect
27 Wee
29 Turn red, as a strawberry
30 Wedding vow
31 Not silently
32 Luxury leather
33 Liability's opposite
35 Cousin ___ of "The Addams Family"
37 School fund-raising grp.
39 Like the Vikings
40 Genetic stuff
41 Change, as the Constitution
46 Fun park car
47 Tune out
48 Walk like a little 'un
50 It fits into a nut
52 First, as a name
53 Lymph bump
54 "Yeah, sure"
55 Open fabric
56 Amount not to care
57 Soybean paste
58 Armchair athlete's channel
59 Pop-top's place
62 Storm's center

by Gregory E. Paul

ACROSS

1 ___ Brockovich, Julia Roberts title role
5 Mex. misses
10 Tom, Dick or Harry
14 1998 N.L. M.V.P. from Chicago
15 Sports hiree
16 Former Sen. Bayh of Indiana
17 See 35-Across
20 Ladies of Lisbon
21 Crowbar, e.g.
22 "I've Got ___ in Kalamazoo"
23 Soccer ___
25 See 35-Across
30 Geniuses' group
31 12/24 or 12/31
32 Golfer Ballesteros
34 Samuel's teacher
35 This puzzle's theme, succinctly
39 Gen-___ (boomer's kid)
40 Shakespeare's stream
42 Hood's gun
43 Rhone tributary
45 See 35-Across
49 Cold war inits.
50 "___ No Mountain High Enough" (1970 #1 hit)
51 Underground Railroad user
54 Least drunk
58 See 35-Across
61 Follower of inter or et
62 "Marat/Sade" playwright
63 Statement to a judge
64 Chicken cordon ___
65 Cosmetician Lauder
66 Teamster's rig

DOWN

1 A.B.A. members' titles
2 Lecherous sort
3 "Beauty ___ the eye . . ."
4 Famous name in hot dogs
5 Japanese beetle, e.g.
6 Isle ___ National Park
7 Small amounts
8 90° from down: Abbr.
9 Any ship
10 Unbeatable foe
11 Tel ___, Israel
12 Luxuriant locks
13 M.I.T. grad., often
18 Bowser's identification
19 Diva Gluck
23 "Outta my way!"
24 Prime S.S.S. classification
25 Probe, with "into"
26 Bagel choice
27 Major mattress maker
28 Nettled
29 Each's companion
30 "___ culpa"
33 Bard's before
36 Soufflé needs
37 Asian goat
38 Holder of claimed property
41 ___ riche
44 Persian governors
46 Hand-me-down
47 Supposed founder of Taoism
48 Nucleic acid sugar
51 Strike defier
52 Vegetate
53 Gallic girlfriend
54 Fit of pique
55 Creator of Perry and Della
56 Goblet feature
57 Bangkok native
59 Have a tab
60 Jazz's Montgomery

by Jay Leatherman

ACROSS

1 Wood for Woods
5 Where to set books
10 Community service group
14 Queue
15 Four-bagger
16 Pipe problem
17 Writer Wiesel
18 Breathing
19 Unnerve
20 Hopping mad
23 Mother hog
24 Chafes
25 Tear-jerking sentiment
27 In good spirits
30 Obliterate
32 Wrestling maneuvers
33 Lose-weight-fast plan
37 Antipollution org.
38 About half of crossword clues
39 "Gotcha!"
40 Step just before publishing an article
43 Outranking
45 Sheets, tablecloths, etc.
46 Annual event at 43-Down Stadium
47 Frugality
50 Fed. watchdog since 1971
51 Motorists' org.
52 Change defeat into victory
58 Egyptian pyramids locale
60 Itinerary
61 One with a duster
62 Hawaiian strings
63 Tribal leader
64 Like good wine
65 Urge on
66 Visionaries
67 Prying

DOWN

1 Musical symbol
2 1953 Leslie Caron film
3 The "U" in I.C.U.
4 Visibly embarrassed
5 "Not too ___"
6 The 18 in a round of 18
7 Send out
8 ___ Strauss & Co.
9 Complimentary ticket
10 Santa's little helper
11 Tether
12 Musical instrument for the nonmusical
13 Distorts
21 Owned jointly by you and me
22 Sprint
26 One of the Kennedys
27 Person who's often sent compliments
28 Indian tribe with kachina dolls
29 Spirit
30 W.W. II German general Rommel
31 Sound off
33 Morse ___
34 Denny's alternative
35 Roof overhang
36 Next
38 They may sit in a glass at night
41 He could "float like a butterfly, sting like a bee"
42 Boost
43 See 46-Across
44 Ferry operator
46 Wedding helpers
47 Get ready to run, in baseball
48 Three-line poem
49 Demolishes
50 Bewhiskered swimmer
53 Film part
54 In the raw
55 Shakespearean villain
56 Fizzles out
57 Whirlpool
59 Cigar waste

by Lynn Lempel

ACROSS

1 Held a session
4 Crustaceans eaten by whales
9 Arcade flubs
14 Each
15 Kind of ink
16 Former TWA honcho Carl
17 Ill temper
18 2003 Tom Cruise movie, with "The"
20 Children's song refrain
22 Mint or chive
23 Mound dweller
24 In memoriam phrase
28 "Quién ___?" ("Who knows?"): Sp.
29 Creamsicle color
33 When doubled, a dance
36 Blue eyes or curly hair, say
39 Like many college dorms, now
40 Lean right, at sea
44 Diva's delivery
45 Copier need
46 "You, there!"
47 Hanker for
50 Greek consonants
52 What Bo-Peep did
58 RR stop
61 Workers' welfare overseer: Abbr.
62 Looie's underling
63 Van Gogh biography
67 Refinable rock
68 Put down
69 Atelier prop
70 Pa. neighbor
71 Alternative to plastic
72 Colorado's ___ Park
73 Otherworldly visitors, for short

DOWN

1 Pitchman's pitch
2 Hilltop home
3 Shoe stiffeners
4 Electrical power unit
5 Genetic letters
6 Cards with photos, for short
7 Certain print, briefly
8 Surgical beam
9 Lumberjack's call
10 Hosp. area
11 Tomb raider of film, ___ Croft
12 Comparison connector
13 Foul mood
19 Cornstarch brand
21 "___ been real!"
25 River of Aragón
26 Eat like a king
27 Snack in a shell
30 Wyle of "ER"

31 Richard of "Chicago"
32 Whirling water
33 Decked out
34 Take on
35 Sales tag words
37 "Am ___ believe . . . ?"
38 Oncle's wife
41 Follow closely
42 Paddler's target
43 NATO headquarters site
48 Housetop laborer
49 Gas brand in Canada
51 ___ Na Na
53 Birdie score, often
54 N.F.L. coach called "Papa Bear"
55 Wear down
56 "Snowy" bird
57 Suffers from sunburn

58 Retaliation for a pinch
59 Hefty horn
60 Quickly, in memos
64 China's Lao-___
65 Adherent's suffix
66 Agent's due

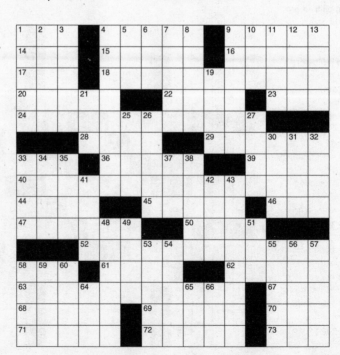

by Kurt Mengel and Jan-Michele Gianette

ACROSS

1 Put up, as a picture
5 ___ salts
10 Restaurant acronym
14 Fit for drafting
15 Mamma's mate
16 Shore bird
17 Headliner
18 Strand, as during a blizzard
19 Give a nudge, so to speak
20 "Take a chill pill"
23 CD predecessors
24 Conservative pundit Alan
25 Old copy machine, briefly
28 Pea's place
29 Exams for future attys.
33 Female in a flock
34 Whistle-blower on a court
35 Error
36 Out of it, as a boxer
40 Embedded
41 Witch
42 Stephen of "The Crying Game"
43 When some news airs
44 Like hearts and diamonds
45 Great time
47 Treated a lawn, perhaps
49 Winning tic-tac-toe row
50 Finally accept
57 Gave the boot
58 Pep up
59 Wax-coated cheese
60 Big rig
61 Singer Lopez
62 El ___ (Pacific Ocean phenomenon)
63 Ship's speed unit
64 Tennis champ Monica

65 Recipients of the cries seen at the starts of 20-, 36- and 50-Across and 7-Down

DOWN

1 "Bonanza" son
2 Opposed to
3 In order
4 Scramble, as a signal
5 Grand stories
6 Small indentation
7 "We were just talking about you"
8 Voiced a view
9 1975 Barry Manilow #1 hit
10 "Sure, why not"
11 Toss
12 Gymnast Korbut
13 Common movie house name ending

21 G.I.'s address
22 Excavation find
25 TV, radio, etc.
26 Words of refusal
27 Whimpers
28 Word before capita or annum
30 Integra maker
31 Adjusts, as a piano
32 Went after
34 Reel's partner
35 Ryan of "When Harry Met Sally"
37 Performed a routine perfectly
38 Mr. ___
39 Ate
44 Stop working at 65, say
45 Baseball's Jackson and others
46 Bargain-basement

48 Drops feathers
49 Old Dodges
50 Wine holder
51 Field team
52 Quick note
53 Philosopher Descartes
54 Peculiar: Prefix
55 Powdered drink mix
56 Med. care choices

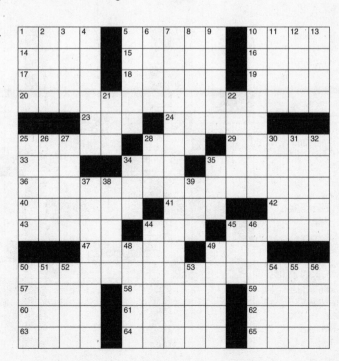

by Jim Hyres

ACROSS

1 "Jaywalker" of late-night TV
5 C sharp equivalent
10 ___ Spumante
14 Worse than bad
15 Something coffee has
16 Golda of Israel
17 Leaves for cooking
18 About 39 inches
19 Scottish hillside
20 Coming attractions shot at a mobile home park?
23 It may be passed on the Hill
25 ___ Speedwagon
26 ___ work (road sign)
27 Full-length films shot at a day spa?
32 To any extent
33 Chafes
34 Lariat
35 Late civil rights pioneer Rosa
37 Gillette razor
41 "___ on Down the Road"
42 Throat malady
43 Film segments shot at an arsenal?
48 Ice cream sundae, e.g.
49 Eggs
50 Anka's "___ Beso"
51 Documentaries shot at a vacation paradise?
56 Did laps, say
57 Modern reading material
58 "Sorry about that!"
61 Fountain of jazz
62 Water ride
63 Expert
64 Iditarod entry
65 Like most manuscripts
66 On

DOWN

1 French article
2 "Deliver Us From ___," 2003 film
3 Nip before a tuck?
4 Table spread
5 Interest of a knight in shining armor
6 Without
7 Trent of the Senate
8 From the U.S.
9 Skater Lipinski
10 English novelist Eric
11 Unruffled
12 Jeweled coronets
13 "___ my case"
21 River to the Caspian
22 Don of morning radio
23 Many miles away
24 Roman statesman and writer
28 Spot of land in the Seine
29 Goofed
30 Diving bird
31 Superstation letters
35 Scorecard number
36 "___ was saying"
37 U.S./Eur. divider
38 Auditions
39 Counts in the gym
40 Lhasa ___ (dog)
41 Words to Brutus
42 Surgery reminder
43 Embroidery yarn
44 Make fizzy
45 Rear-ended, e.g.
46 "Beat it!"
47 Brought forth
48 Kitchen measures: Abbr.
52 Skillful
53 Skillfully
54 Egg drop, e.g.
55 "Animal House" attire
59 For
60 "How's it hangin', bro?"

by Sarah Keller

ACROSS

1 Tiff
5 Go out on the ocean
9 Bogged down
14 Letter before kappa
15 Longest river of Spain
16 "___ fired" (Trump catchphrase)
17 Classic holiday entertainment
20 In whatever way
21 Swing that rips the leather off the ball
22 "Waking ___ Devine" (1998 film)
23 Co. photo badges, e.g.
24 W.W. II female
26 Expectorate
28 Houston major-leaguer
30 Crouches
34 Amo, amas, ___ . . .
37 Morays
39 Dickens's ___ Heep
40 Shock
43 Three to one, e.g.
44 Nick and ___ Charles of "The Thin Man"
45 44-Across's dog
46 Lagoons' surroundings
48 Sleek fabric
50 "Too bad!"
52 Mos. and mos.
53 Clemson competes in it: Abbr.
56 Fit ___ fiddle
59 Horse feed
61 20 Questions category
63 "The Thin Man," for one
66 Bygone airline
67 Corner chesspiece
68 Sacked out
69 Sound made while sacked out
70 I's
71 Chess ending

DOWN

1 Biblical mount
2 Hit with a hammer
3 Lawyers: Abbr.
4 Dashboard dial, for short
5 Brine
6 Network of "Lost"
7 Nettles
8 Many movie houses
9 Magical aura
10 Letters of debt
11 Undo
12 Art Deco master
13 Monopoly card
18 Has the oars
19 Emulates Eminem
25 King of Thebes, in myth
27 Headdress that's wound
28 Head of the Huns
29 Actor Edward James ___
31 Is under the weather
32 Stretched tight
33 Former Queens stadium
34 Magician's opening
35 Castle protector
36 Choir voice
38 Leave the straight and narrow
41 Leader's cry, said with a wave
42 Where to hang derbies and fedoras
47 Volvo rival
49 "But there ___ joy in Mudville . . ."
51 Look steadily
53 Itsy-bitsy creature
54 West Pointer
55 Bonnie's partner in crime
56 Nile slitherers
57 Good, close look
58 Florence's river
60 Walk with difficulty
62 Mosque V.I.P.
64 Hearing aid
65 British john

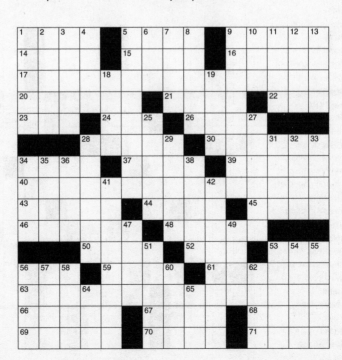

by Jay Livingston

ACROSS

1 Poisonous plants
7 Letters for Letterman
10 "Right now!"
14 Discordant
15 Cry heard in a bullring
16 Small jet maker
17 Place to test aerodynamics
19 Isaac's eldest
20 Bakery gizmo
21 One of the Lennons
22 Broadway background
23 Hoopster Archibald
24 Kukla or Ollie, e.g.
28 Give it a go
30 Employ more employees
31 Glass marble
34 Clutch
37 Chinese author ___ Yutang
38 Placing (and a hint to the first words of 17-, 24-, 47- and 60-Across)
41 Stool pigeon
42 Out of style
43 Dull drills
44 2,000 pounds
46 Telepathic letters
47 Skinny Minnie
51 Funnyman Sandler
55 Offbeat
56 Some shortening
57 Brazilian soccer legend
58 Amorphous mass
60 Author's success
62 "La Bohème" heroine
63 Bit of sunshine
64 Practical
65 Direction wagon trains headed
66 Alias
67 Nebraska river

DOWN

1 Greeted, as the New Year
2 Central New York city
3 "Water Lilies" painter
4 Mario of the Indianapolis 500
5 Hipster
6 Like half-melted snow
7 Arthur ___ Doyle
8 It's not 100% this or that
9 French seasoning
10 Is in dreamland
11 Aviator in search of bugs
12 Battery size
13 Robert Morse Tony-winning role
18 PBS benefactor
22 Potluck get-togethers

25 Face, slangily
26 Some cyberreading
27 Looks after
29 Give an answer
31 1960s–70s dos
32 Goliath
33 Vestibules
34 Dogfaces
35 Hosp. staffers
36 Count of candles on a cake
39 "___ in there!"
40 Come to terms for less jail time, say
45 Gossip unit
46 Ultimately becomes
48 Dickens's "___ House"
49 Cushy course
50 Know-how
52 Blue-and-white earthenware
53 Alaskan native

54 Singer Haggard
58 Upscale auto initials
59 Practice tact, perhaps
60 Playtex offering
61 Immigrant's subj.

by Gail Grabowski and Nancy Salomon

ACROSS
1 All excited
5 Unexpected sports outcome
10 Small salamander
14 Earring site
15 John who was once known as the Teflon Don
16 "That's clear"
17 Houston Astro, for one
19 Stare
20 Met production
21 Chart toppers
23 Dot-com's address
25 Ump's call
26 Actors not playing major parts
34 "Quiet, please!"
35 Disdain
36 Father Christmas
37 Sounds of relief
39 Keep after
41 ___ Piper
42 Bad way to run
44 Pigpens
46 Caribbean, e.g.
47 In the driver's seat
50 What to call an officer, maybe
51 Hither's partner
52 Where to get taxis
58 Comparison shopper's quest
62 Norway's capital
63 Not bad in result
65 Mix (up)
66 Laser printer powder
67 Diva Horne
68 Spinning toys
69 Winter falls
70 Historic periods

DOWN
1 Brand for Fido
2 Trail mix
3 Double-reed instrument
4 Get ready
5 "Yuck!"
6 Experts in vote-getting
7 Flower stalk
8 Jazz singer James
9 Attaches, as a rope
10 Bedtime drink
11 Actor Morales
12 Cried
13 Golf ball props
18 Field protectors
22 Holds close
24 ___ Ness monster
26 "Naughty, naughty!"
27 "Yeah"
28 Perch
29 It's a fact
30 Navel type
31 Biscotti flavoring
32 Girder material
33 "I did it!"
34 Swedish auto
38 Tailor's tool
40 Wet, as morning grass
43 Make a sweater
45 Rudely push
48 Pre-edited versions
49 Allow
52 Purchase price
53 Regarding
54 Radar image
55 It follows 11
56 First 007 film
57 One-dish meal
59 Suggestive look
60 School for a future ens.
61 J.F.K. postings
64 Mins. and mins.

by Marjorie Berg

ACROSS

1 Showman Ziegfeld
4 Shakespearean character who calls himself "a very foolish fond old man"
8 Traveler's baggage handler
14 Mary's boss on "The Mary Tyler Moore Show"
15 Writer Sarah ___ Jewett
16 Bogged down
17 Beer festival mo.
18 Musical staff symbol
19 Wanderers
20 Nickname for author Ernest
23 Prunes, once
24 France's Belle-___
25 Vegetarian's protein source
28 Abominable Snowman
29 Classic New York City eatery
32 Amtrak facility: Abbr.
34 Cartoonist Drake
35 Summer along the Seine
36 Paul McCartney in the Beatles
40 Not in stock yet
42 "So that's it!"
43 Milne's "The House at ___ Corner"
45 Anka's "___ Beso"
46 Fanny Brice radio character
49 Burst of wind
53 Greek peak
54 Card below quattro
55 Postal scale marking
56 This puzzle's theme
60 Photo assignments
62 "It's ___" ("I'm buying")
63 A couple of chips, maybe
64 Dawn goddess
65 ___ Martin (cognac brand)
66 Brenda of country music
67 Geological wonder
68 Madrid Mmes.
69 Wind up

DOWN

1 Disk type
2 Place
3 Yield
4 Scottish boating spots
5 ___ Stanley Gardner
6 What Procrit may treat
7 Uses another roll on
8 Symbol of troth
9 Sufficient, in poetry
10 Ex-senator Alfonse
11 Filled in a coloring book
12 I.R.S. exam: Abbr.
13 Sour cream container amts.
21 Not quite right
22 "Super!"
26 Big bash
27 ___-friendly
29 Lawyer created by 5-Down
30 Areas between shoulders?
31 Slugger Slaughter
33 Rewards for waiting
36 Popular clown at kids' parties
37 Teachers like to hear them
38 Long, drawn-out excuse
39 One end of a bridge
41 Scoundrel
44 "Egad!"
47 Louts
48 More acute
50 Not up to it
51 Sift
52 Tried out
55 Minds
57 To be, to Henri
58 Boris Godunov, e.g.
59 Madame Bovary
60 Droop
61 Ruby or emerald

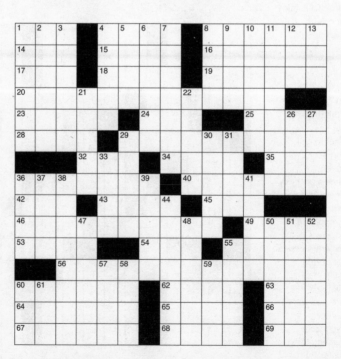

by Sarah Keller

ACROSS

1 Hunger twinge
5 Unpaid group of 7-Down
9 Sound heard hourly from Big Ben
14 Bassoon's little cousin
15 Nobelist Wiesel
16 Passenger
17 Bagpiper's wear
18 "___ Well That Ends Well"
19 Warn
20 Dutch cheese
21 Union: first stage
23 Label again, as a computer file
25 Put away for a rainy day
26 Money in South Africa
28 St. Francis' city
33 React like a threatened dog
36 Land on the Arabian Peninsula
39 Home for Adam and Eve
40 Put a cap on
41 One in a union with 37-Down
42 Lieu
43 "It's a sin to tell ___"
44 G.O.P. foes
45 Birthplace of the Renaissance
46 Interfere (with)
48 ___ of Sandwich
50 Voting no on
53 More profound
57 Union: second stage
62 100-meter race, e.g.
63 Precursor of the "Odyssey"
64 Reside (in)
65 Director Preminger
66 Washer cycle
67 Pizzeria fixture

68 City of waltzes, to natives
69 "Ciao!"
70 Overly bookish sort
71 Scent receiver

DOWN

1 Doc Holliday's game
2 Reside (in)
3 Actor Lloyd ___
4 Union: third stage
5 Overwhelm with sound
6 Jazzy Fitzgerald
7 See 5-Across
8 Physicist who pioneered alternating current electricity
9 Whooping birds
10 Site of Jack and Jill's spill
11 Prefix with -logue

12 Griffin who created "Jeopardy!"
13 Art Deco designer
22 "Terrible" czar
24 Brewer's ingredient
27 Damfool
29 Union: last stage
30 Genesis of an invention
31 Flippered mammal
32 ___ 500
33 Not shut quietly
34 Pharaoh's river
35 Surrounded by
37 One in a union with 41-Across
38 Cathedral recess
42 Beget
44 Post-Mao Chinese leader
47 NASA vehicle
49 The 3 or 5 in 3 + 5 = 8

51 Claw
52 "Uncle!"
54 Sunbather's spot
55 ___ Park, Colo.
56 Beaujolais's department
57 Lass
58 Kazan who directed "On the Waterfront"
59 Hue
60 Comfort
61 ". . . happily ___ after"

by Wesley Johnson

ACROSS

1 Stamp or coin collecting, e.g.
6 Artist Chagall
10 Men-only
14 "Fidelio," for one
15 Margarine
16 Frau's partner
17 Shouts of triumph
18 Rivers of comedy
19 "Green Gables" girl
20 Clueless reply
23 Hightail it
24 Statistics calculation
25 Camera type, briefly
27 Highway access
30 Squelch
34 Romances
36 Bump off
38 Skylit lobbies
39 Clueless reply
42 McQueen of "Bullitt"
43 52 cards
44 Brazilian soccer great
45 Con artists, slangily
47 Lose control on the highway
49 G-man or T-man
50 Pipe part
52 Continental currency
54 Clueless reply
60 Autobahn auto
61 Bound
62 Game for peewee batters
64 Brit's baby buggy
65 Brontë governess
66 New York Harbor's ___ Island
67 Rice wine
68 Monopoly acquisition
69 Edited out

DOWN

1 Supertrendy
2 Brightly colored fish
3 Pleasant place, metaphorically
4 Slugfest
5 Arafat of the P.L.O.
6 Voodoo spell
7 Outfielder Moises
8 Royal domain
9 Purchased apartments
10 Beatles command, baby, in "Twist and Shout"
11 Dollywood's state: Abbr.
12 Florence's river
13 Got bigger
21 Intoxicating
22 G.I.'s neckwear
25 Nothing-but-net sound
26 Numbers game
28 State of mind
29 Evergreens
31 Slugfest
32 Fine cotton fabric
33 Lightened (up)
35 Uses a shortcut
37 Head/shoulders connector
40 "Doggone!"
41 Powder lover
46 Ready for mailing, as an envelope
48 Checked for prints
51 "That's hogwash!"
53 Moscow money
54 Mushroom toppers
55 Ambience
56 Bismarck's home: Abbr.
57 Cabby's client
58 Newspaper's ___ page
59 Writer Wiesel
63 Psychedelic of the '60s

by Nancy Salomon

ACROSS

1 Take hold of
6 Anatomical pouches
10 "___ Excited" (Pointer Sisters hit)
14 Severity
15 Melville novel
16 Alcove
17 First president born outside the original 13 colonies
19 Easy tennis shots
20 Retirees, often
22 A Chaplin
23 Norma ___, Sally Field Oscar-winning role
24 Mentally sharp
26 Revolution time?
28 Ewe's mate
31 Often ___
32 Long time
35 Airhead
37 April 15 org.
38 B team
42 Driveway covering
43 Leslie Caron title role
44 Fleming who created 007
45 Shaquille of the N.B.A.
47 Kind of camera: Abbr.
49 Catch sight of
53 Kind of acid
55 Yellowstone Park animal
58 "Mazel ___!"
59 They're neither nobility nor clergy
63 Horse's hue
64 Bad way to be held by a judge
65 007 foe
66 Scheme
67 Suffered defeat, slangily
68 "I'd hate to break up ___"
69 MS. enclosure
70 Zellweger of "Bridget Jones's Diary"

DOWN

1 Lawnlike
2 Hearty steak
3 List for a meeting
4 Songs for one
5 Before, with "to"
6 World Cup sport
7 Mine, in France
8 Stallion, once
9 Actress Braga
10 Coast features
11 Frank Zappa's daughter
12 Sympathy-arousing excuse
13 Approves
18 Gun lovers' org.
21 One of the Gabors
25 S.A.T. company
27 Stimpy's pal on TV
29 Aleve competitor
30 "Mamma ___!"
33 Like some old-fashioned lamps
34 "___ won't!"
36 Prefix with angle
38 Mop wielders
39 Foam material
40 "Treasure Island" author's inits.
41 Suffix with labyrinth
42 Bridge weight unit
46 Retort to "Am too!"
48 Decorated anew
50 Place for pollen
51 Entree with a crust
52 Actress Mimieux
54 Poker pieces
56 Actor Cariou
57 Relatively cool sun
60 "To Live and Die ___"
61 Certain TV's
62 French head
63 Nutritionist's fig.

by Kevan Choset

ACROSS

1 Antisub weapon, slangily
7 Boarded up
11 Atty.'s title
14 Composer Debussy
15 Hawaiian fish, on menus
16 Thanksgiving, e.g.: Abbr.
17 1984 campaign slogan
19 ___ polloi
20 Descartes's "therefore"
21 Graceful woman
22 Folk singer Joan
23 Actresses Ireland and St. John
24 1980s White House nickname
25 The "E" in Alfred E. Smith
29 Classic drugstore name
32 Animated Disney heroine of 1998
33 Main artery
36 Sign before Virgo
37 Song from "Anything Goes"
40 Ordinal suffix
41 Dens
42 Ryan of "The Beverly Hillbillies"
43 Rotary phone user
45 Pump figures
47 Family girl
48 Bring back to court
50 Samsung or RCA product
52 In a way, slangily
53 Brewer's kiln
57 Boise's state: Abbr.
58 1975 #1 disco hit
60 It can hold its liquor
61 John Lennon's "Dear ___"
62 Mideast market
63 Hurricane center
64 Frankenstein's helper
65 Come into view

DOWN

1 Farm division
2 Talk like a drunk
3 Nail to the wall
4 Stephen King canine
5 Sidewalk stand quaff
6 Storied monster, in tabloids
7 Suspect
8 Angels' strings
9 "No way!"
10 Oscar statuette, mostly
11 Green Mountain Boys leader
12 Clog or pump
13 20 questions, say
18 Course outlines
22 Go rounds in a ring
23 Lions' "kingdoms"
24 "The Apprentice" TV genre
25 War correspondent, in modern lingo
26 Prefix with task
27 Hawaii's nickname
28 Slangy refusal
29 MapQuest offering: Abbr.
30 Sierra ___
31 Home Depot competitor
34 Bruins great Bobby
35 Italian dish cooked in broth
38 Berne's river
39 Woman's support system?
44 Roman 54
46 Buster of Flash Gordon serials
48 Columnist Mike
49 Unwanted computer message
50 Center of activity
51 June 6, 1944
52 Trudge
53 Élève's 11
54 Miles away
55 Smeltery refuse
56 Radial for a Jaguar, e.g.
58 Memo-opening letters
59 Descartes's "sum"

by Adam Cohen

ACROSS

1 Inclement
6 "Let me know if ___ help"
10 "Damn Yankees" siren
14 Mrs. Kramden of "The Honeymooners"
15 Grp. that outlasted the Warsaw Pact
16 Sacred bird of the pharaohs
17 Rock bottom
18 Gator's cousin
19 Captain for 40 days and nights
20 Wisconsin pro footballer
23 Craze
24 Wedge-shaped inlet
25 Reconstruction outsider
32 Length of 14 2/3 football fields
35 George Bush's home state
36 Fashion magazine
37 Airport flight info: Abbr.
38 Wine cask
39 Can.'s southern neighbor
40 Trucker's rig
42 Freeway sign with an arrow
44 Consider
45 Golden Gloves participant
48 Big inits. in long distance
49 Opposite of absorb
52 Center of Mt. St. Helens
58 Crèche figures
59 Brilliant star
60 Play much too broadly on stage
61 Stewpot
62 26- or 55-Down
63 Joe of the Yankees

64 Hammer's end
65 "Auld Lang ___"
66 Underhanded sort

DOWN

1 Send to the gallows
2 Morning waker-upper
3 "___ cock-horse to Banbury Cross"
4 Biology or chemistry
5 Rupture
6 Old Peruvian
7 Actor Grant
8 Perched on
9 Diet food catch phrase
10 Connection
11 Penetrating wind
12 Fibber
13 Close-grained wood
21 One of TV's Simpsons

22 Undercover org.
26 Russia's ___ the Great
27 Bedroom community
28 Activity for which "it takes two"
29 Stickum
30 ". . . or ___!" (threat)
31 Paper purchase
32 Small plateau
33 Any thing
34 Holy man of Tibet
41 From Tuscany, e.g.
42 Sci-fi creatures
43 Company bigwig
44 "Yeah, sure!"
46 List ender
47 Wading birds
50 Workplace for the person named at the end of 20-, 25-, 45- or 52-Across
51 Half of octa-

52 Place between hills
53 Look at long . . . and with longing
54 Prying
55 ___ the Terrible
56 Org. helping people in need
57 Smell
58 Implement in a bucket

by Gary Steinmehl

ACROSS

1 Angelic music maker
5 Think ahead
9 San Diego baseballer
14 Parkay product
15 Capital of Italia
16 Instruments used in orchestra tuning
17 Pronto
20 Sack material
21 ". . . or ___ just me?"
22 Dallas-to-Duluth dir.
23 Place to hear snorts
24 Family M.D.'s
26 Adds or deletes text
28 Pronto
32 E. Lansing school
34 "Platoon" setting
35 Hoodwink
36 French roast
37 Snatches
40 Lahr who played the Cowardly Lion
41 Smooth-barked tree
43 Shoot the breeze
44 Promising words
45 Pronto
49 Skin layer
50 Head lines?: Abbr.
51 "20/20" network
54 Prince ___ Khan
56 Loony
58 Sweetums
60 Pronto
63 Area, weatherwise
64 Rebuke from Caesar
65 Latest thing
66 Calculus symbol
67 Haul in
68 Desire personified

DOWN

1 Roy ___, lead role in "The Natural"
2 Native Alaskan
3 Cook, as beans
4 Certain hotel amenity
5 Getting ready
6 Moviedom's Myrna
7 Mine, on the Marne
8 Sartre novel
9 Bonneville maker
10 Blood-typing system
11 Smaller now, in corporate-speak
12 Check, with "in"
13 Italian Renaissance art patron
18 Prego competitor
19 Rug rats
25 Lasting impression
27 Small-time
28 Lunch dish from the oven
29 S. S. Kresge, today
30 Whodunit hero Wolfe
31 Round Table title: Abbr.
32 Big name in faucets
33 Reliable source of income for a band
36 Suicide squeeze stat.
38 Innocent
39 Puts the pedal to the metal
42 Celestial Seasonings beverage
46 Part of a Latin I conjugation
47 Kind of
48 Pulitzer-winning writer James
51 Loud, as a crowd
52 "That's it!"
53 Hands over
54 Travels like a skyrocket
55 "___ Marlene," song of 1944
57 Web spot
59 Fair-sized garden
61 "Well, let me see . . ."
62 Tkt. office locale

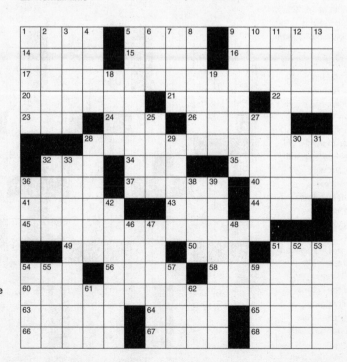

by Nancy Salomon

ACROSS

1 ___ Bearcat (classic car)
6 Muslim leader
10 Cover the driveway
14 Gdansk natives
15 "I Just Wanna Stop" singer ___ Vannelli
16 Manipulator
17 How often rent is usually paid
19 Perlman of "Cheers"
20 1950s prez
21 It's nothing at all
22 Herb with the Tijuana Brass
24 Oldtime crooner Julius
26 What a settlement avoids
28 Indian music
30 Difficult situations
34 "My Friend ___" (old radio/TV series)
37 Frozen waffle brand
39 Lovable ogre of film
40 Bellyache
41 What each of the longest words in 17-Across, 65-Across, 10-Down and 25-Down famously lacks
43 Online auction site
44 Mexican friend
46 MasterCard alternative, informally
47 Inquires (about)
48 Kodaks, e.g.
50 Crowd reaction
52 Jokes
54 " " " " "
58 Rocket propulsion
61 Pudding fruit
63 Blood-typing letters
64 Second-largest of the Hawaiian islands
65 Lone Ranger's cry
68 Writer Waugh

69 ___ synthesizer
70 Din
71 Small winning margin
72 Diarist Frank
73 Xenon and neon

DOWN

1 Go bad
2 Toy truck maker
3 Stomach malady
4 Golf ball raiser
5 A Gabor sister
6 Stravinsky or Sikorsky
7 North Dakota city
8 Picnic intruder
9 Angora fabric
10 Military hero's award
11 ___ Stadium (Queens landmark)
12 Suddenly change course

13 Part of Q.E.D.
18 Scanty
23 Young fellows
25 Breakfast beverage
27 Boardinghouse guest
29 Shocked
31 Wall St. figures
32 Plumbing problem
33 "The ___ the limit!"
34 Apple computer
35 Italia's capital
36 Seriously injure
38 Sock hop locale
42 Large-scale emigration
45 Underground deposits
49 Respiratory problem
51 Pointing
53 Observe furtively
55 Smiley of PBS
56 Fatter than fat
57 Tender areas

58 Fed. agent in finances
59 Saint's glow
60 Regrets
62 Seating section
66 Charged particle
67 Mauna ___ volcano

by Allan E. Parrish

ACROSS

1 Urban pollution
5 Booster, to a rocket
10 Winter home of the Chicago Cubs
14 Volcanic flow
15 Hang in the air
16 "We deliver for you" sloganeer: Abbr.
17 Ruthless personnel director
18 The Hunter
19 Genesis twin
20 Seasoned dancer?
23 Frequently
24 Austrian peaks, locally
28 Ancient writing material
31 Spacecraft to Jupiter
33 Missed by ___ (was way off)
34 Mantra sounds
35 Cockpit datum: Abbr.
36 Seasoned singer?
41 Missing button on an iPod: Abbr.
42 Monday night game org.
43 Extra, as a bedroom
44 The Washington Monument, e.g.
47 Emily Dickinson's home, in Massachusetts
49 Police weapon
50 Bridge authority Charles
51 Seasoned baseball player?
57 Portend
60 ___-ground missile
61 Anise-flavored liqueur
62 Sierra Club co-founder
63 ___-O-Matic (baseball game company)
64 Sitting on
65 Victories
66 Approval power
67 "Yo, ___!"

DOWN

1 Waste material
2 Passé skirt style
3 Breadmaking place
4 Quaint building decoration
5 Vowel sound in "puzzle"
6 Spanish constructions
7 Par ___ (how to send mail to France)
8 Atlas maker's subj.
9 White-tailed eagle
10 Nutritious breakfast cereal
11 Double curve
12 Resort
13 Tempe sch.
21 ___ Zimbalist Jr.
22 "Too-ra-loo-ra-loo-___"
25 Two-dimensional
26 Conger catchers
27 Possible answer to "Are we there now?"
28 Polly, who wants a cracker
29 Protozoan
30 Sign after Aquarius
31 Maker of Yukon SUV's: Abbr.
32 Communication for the deaf: Abbr.
34 Olive ___
37 Opposite of a ques.
38 Washington's ___ Stadium
39 Milo of "Barbarella"
40 Route that invites speeding
45 Pariahs
46 Rage
47 Main arteries
48 Peter Lorre role in eight movies
50 President Ford, informally
52 Free ticket
53 Round bread
54 Ballet attire
55 Popular shirt label
56 "Uh-uh!"
57 Autobahn auto
58 Yes, in Québec
59 Clamor

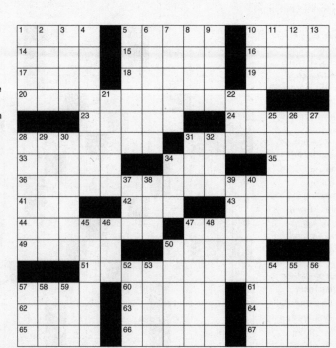

by Roy Leban

ACROSS

1 Borrow without intending to repay
6 College administrator
10 Eyebrow shape
14 Oak's source
15 Former attorney general Janet
16 Hawaiian feast
17 Terrific
18 Cupid's Greek counterpart
19 Ancient Peruvian
20 Part of a famous 1897 editorial
23 Author Fleming
24 Delete
25 Christmas drink
27 Christmas trimming
30 First 007 film
31 Tree's anchor
32 Ballet movement in which the knees are bent
35 Went out, as the tide
39 "Lord, is ___?"
40 Editorial, part 2
42 Swiss river to the Rhine
43 Analyze grammatically
45 Prefix with nautical
46 Thomas ___ Edison
47 Quickly, in memos
49 Spice in Christmas cookies
51 Christmas songs
54 River around the Île de la Cité
56 Attorneys' org.
57 Editorial, part 3
62 Prima donna
64 "Things aren't looking good"
65 City NNE of Paris
66 Detail
67 Greedy person's cry
68 Prudential competitor
69 Philosopher known as "the Stoic"
70 Observer
71 Vision of sugarplums dancing in one's head, e.g.

DOWN

1 Sly
2 Farming unit
3 Executes
4 Most serious
5 Complete
6 Lees
7 Like a ghost's howling
8 Ever and ___
9 More meddlesome
10 He KO'd Foreman in '74
11 Altercation
12 Tree that's the source of chocolate
13 Second-longest river of China
21 Kramden of "The Honeymooners"
22 "___ of God," 1985 film
26 Sailor, slangily
27 Misstep
28 Greek "I"
29 Film ___
30 Rudolph and team
33 Spring
34 Anger
36 Unguent
37 Roof overhang
38 Pull behind
40 Edison rival
41 Ancient Greek colony
44 ___ Paulo, Brazil
46 Artist's workplace
48 Take for granted
50 In one's birthday suit
51 Port of Spain
52 Have ___ to eat
53 Poe bird
54 Keep others awake at night, maybe
55 Upper atmosphere
58 Cry to a matey
59 Germany's Konrad Adenauer, Der ___
60 Bone near the radius
61 Stitching line
63 ___, amas, amat . . .

by Richard Hughes

ACROSS

1 Command to Rover
5 Feudal estate
9 Veronica of "Hill Street Blues"
14 Jai ___
15 Not taken in by
16 Stubborn as ___
17 British man-of-war
19 Bulgaria's capital
20 On a higher plane
21 Above everything else
23 Formerly, formerly
25 Nuns' garb
26 Knuckleheads
29 Neighbor of Francia
32 Landed
33 Yellow fruit
34 Nice winter coat
37 Man o' War
40 Dam-building org.
41 Comparatively close
42 "What's in a ___?": Juliet
43 It's gender
44 Kafka's "In the ___ Colony"
45 The Supreme Court, e.g.
48 Lowly worker
50 Place for things to get sorted out
53 Home in bed, ill
57 In other words
58 Portuguese man-of-war
60 Copier company
61 Natural balm
62 Three-point shot, in hoops slang
63 "Danse Macabre" composer Saint-___
64 Card catalog abbr.
65 Towel embroidery

DOWN

1 "Stop! You're killing me!"
2 Trees in an O'Neill title
3 "___ of Eden"
4 Opera script
5 They're not fair
6 Place to overnight
7 Jazz singer James
8 A. J., the racer
9 Rosh ___
10 One-celled creature
11 Civilian attire
12 "Middlemarch" author
13 Bounds' partner
18 Pair in a dinghy
22 "Casey at the Bat" writer Ernest Lawrence ___
24 Treat roughly
26 A bit cuckoo
27 Sainted Norwegian king
28 Capital near the ruins of the ancient city Pachacamac
30 Bowler's pickup
31 Indiana hoopsters
33 False start?
34 Friend of Kukla and Ollie
35 Alma mater of D.D.E.
36 Virginia dance
38 Brings to light
39 20%
43 A Rockefeller
44 Supplicate
45 Mideast princes
46 Gymnast Comaneci
47 Family girl
49 Sitcom that debuted in 1994
51 Town near Santa Barbara
52 Blanc and Brooks
54 Kind of need
55 Word with fee or ID
56 ___ Ed.
59 High ball?

by Nancy and Holden Baker

ACROSS

1 "A guy walks into a ___ . . ."
4 State Farm competitor
9 French artist Edgar
14 From ___ Z
15 Start of a weightlifting maneuver
16 ___ Gay (W.W. II plane)
17 Wail
18 1994 John Travolta film
20 Unordinary
22 Mended, as socks
23 Litter's littlest
24 Boob tube, in Britain
26 Damon of "Good Will Hunting"
28 O3
30 Suffix with Oktober
34 Swiss peak
35 Mouse catchers
36 Defense grp., 1954–77
37 Dentists' focus
39 Tire pressure measure: Abbr.
40 Varnish ingredient
41 The "E" of EGBDF
42 Sponsorship
44 "We Know Drama" cable channel
45 Actress Ward
46 British guns
47 McDonald's arches, e.g.
48 Place
50 Bridge guru Sharif
52 Friend of Betty and Veronica, in the comics
55 Wine server
58 "Queen of Hearts" vocalist, 1981
61 Neither's partner
62 Place to exchange rings
63 Boutiques

64 "Little" car in a 1964 top 10 hit
65 Bridle straps
66 Competitive, as a personality
67 Mind-reading ability, for short

DOWN

1 Low voice
2 Sitting on
3 British leader from whom the "bobbies" got their name
4 Former defense secretary Les
5 Line that extends for 24,902 miles
6 1960s–80s rock group Jethro ___
7 Short snooze
8 Fed. law enforcement org.
9 Toy race car adornment
10 Price to participate
11 Enter
12 Skin cream additive
13 Hourglass fill
19 Doing nothing
21 Last word from a director
24 Tournament favorite
25 Coast Guard rank
26 Pub buddies
27 Tylenol rival
29 Mexican revolutionary Emiliano
31 City neighboring Newark, N.J.
32 Bee injury
33 Kemo Sabe's sidekick
35 "___ kingdom come . . ."
36 Some S.A.T. takers

38 Refuse holder
43 Heavy hydrogen, e.g.
46 Witnessed
47 Perry Mason's profession
49 Stadium levels
51 High-I.Q. set
52 Open slightly
53 Govern
54 Commercial prefix with bank
55 "Halt!"
56 Goes bad
57 Plunge
59 Guinness Book suffix
60 "How come?"

by Allan E. Parrish

ACROSS

1 Biblical gift-givers
5 Tattle (on)
9 Knight's "suit"
14 "Ain't that the truth!"
15 Where to get off
16 Lorna of literature
17 Flier of coffee for long distances?
19 "___ luck!"
20 Big '60s dos
21 Flustered state
22 Fleet leader
25 1981 Julie Andrews movie
26 Martians, e.g., in brief
27 Author A. Conan ___
28 Bleep out
30 Surgery ctrs.
31 Steps out of France
34 Not completely closed
37 Loco
39 Sound heard in 17- and 58-Across and 11- and 24-Down
40 Grenade part
41 Kind of engr.
42 Hoofing it
44 "This ___ test"
45 Long arms?
47 Went like a shooting star
49 Ottoman governor
51 TV spots
52 Fearful feeling
54 Private gag
56 Corners
57 Alla ___ (music notation)
58 High school grads?
62 The one with 0 in 7–0
63 Not much
64 Craving
65 Bookkeeping task

66 1936 Jean Harlow title role
67 Pizazz

DOWN

1 Capt.'s superior
2 Te ___ cigars
3 "How about that?!"
4 Behind bars
5 Cousin of quadri-
6 Praise to the rafters
7 Empty promises
8 Word unit: Abbr.
9 Wings it
10 Tooth part
11 Milk?
12 Early stages
13 Brings up
18 Violinist Zimbalist
21 "Stick around!"
22 Clay for bricks
23 Miami stop on the P.G.A. Tour

24 Witticism from Sherlock Holmes?
25 Take care of
28 Sleeve ends
29 Clumsy sort
32 Tristan's love
33 Canonical hour
35 Intelligence or good looks, e.g.
36 "Set?"
38 Chem. or bio.
43 They may be graduated
46 Smoke and mirrors
48 Off-color
49 Perennial best seller, with "the"
50 Noted bankruptcy of 2001
52 Ball's partner
53 Lacking lucre
55 "Back to you"
56 Dancer's dress

58 Essen assents
59 Electronic address
60 Turkish title
61 Cub Scout group

by Lee Glickstein and Nancy Salomon

ACROSS

1 ___ Antoinette
6 Tallies
10 Series of scenes
13 Actress Blake or Plummer
15 Not having a stitch on
16 Letter before sigma
17 Lump in the throat
18 "Calm down!"
20 Neighbor of Scot.
21 Dabbling duck
23 Years and years and years
24 "Move!"
29 One-named Art Deco master
30 Stephen of "The Crying Game"
31 Bear in constellation names
34 Cap or helmet
39 "Pay attention!"
43 Cared for a home while the owner was away
44 Pink wine
45 Hang back
46 Sail support
49 "Lookie there!"
56 Like many a wiseacre's comment: Abbr.
57 Part of F.Y.I.
58 Lots of laughs
60 "Oh, be serious!"
64 Car model with a musical name
66 Metalliferous rock
67 Done with
68 Passes, as a law
69 Auction motion
70 Farewells
71 "Savvy?"

DOWN

1 Crew member
2 Honor ___ thieves
3 Poconos or Tetons
4 Write-___ (some votes)
5 Manuscript receiver
6 White, in Mexico
7 Owing
8 Banned insecticide
9 Caribbean, e.g.
10 "This way" sign
11 Dishes for fancy meals
12 ___-turvy
14 Native seal hunter
19 "Golly!"
22 Breakfasted, e.g.
25 Parts of an udder
26 Stew
27 Go like mad
28 "If I ___ hammer . . .'"
31 "Yuck!"
32 Rock's ___ Speedwagon
33 Sutcliffe of the early Beatles
34 F.D.R. successor
35 Middle measurement
36 It may be puffed up
37 Sighs of contentment
38 Letter carrier's assignment: Abbr.
40 Hades
41 Golfer ___ Aoki
42 Heroic legend
46 Call to a calf
47 Blow ___ (become enraged)
48 Brawny
49 Not be able to swallow
50 When to celebrate el año nuevo
51 Schlepped
52 "Gimme ___!" (frequent Alabama cheerleader's cry)
53 Color specialists
54 "It's ___" ("There's no doubt")
55 ___-frutti
59 Cartoonist Thomas
61 High tennis shot
62 Some Christmas greenery
63 Doctor's quote
65 Scottish refusal

by C. W. Stewart

ACROSS

1 It's full of holes and traps
5 Gastric juices, e.g.
10 Remnant of a tattoo removal, maybe
14 Zone
15 Herb popular in Indian food
16 Staff note
17 Glam rocker's accessory
19 Jessica of "Fantastic Four" films
20 The "F" in the equation "F = ma"
21 Pat on the back, as a baby
22 Sleigh
23 Get up
25 Loathes
27 Usurer's victim
30 Throat condition
31 Parisian streets
32 Tiptop
35 Drained of color
38 "What ___ the odds?"
39 Dumps (on)
41 Guitarist's guitar
42 Succeed in life
44 It fills barrels
45 Freshly
46 Make believe
48 Espy
50 Like trees on a prairie
52 Hooch
54 "Mr. ___ risin'" (classic Doors lyric)
55 One always on the lookout for a deal
57 Hotel room posting
61 Wife of Osiris
62 Director's cry . . . or a statement about 17-Across and 11- and 29-Down
64 Longtime Yugoslav chief
65 Flood preventer
66 Surrounding glow
67 List ender
68 Play to the back of the audience
69 Longings

DOWN

1 Sailor's hook
2 Nabisco cookie
3 King who was the father of Cordelia
4 Moneybags types
5 Starting pitcher
6 Places to park
7 Saturate
8 New Look designer
9 Answer in anger
10 Overhead shots
11 Transparent packaging material
12 Color meaning "caution" on 13-Down
13 See 12-Down
18 Guitar ___ (hit video game series)
24 Oil-rich land
26 They're uplifting
27 Bummer
28 Money since 2002
29 Taco alternative
30 Coal bed
33 Extended family
34 Stereotypical tattoo
36 Company V.I.P.
37 Former speaker Gingrich
39 "Exodus" author
40 Long-gone bird
43 Kind of can
45 Eroded
47 Like caresses
49 Writer Pound
50 Beat, biblically
51 Take as a given
52 "Wonderful!"
53 Wedding band, maybe
56 Polite way to interrupt someone
58 Loyal
59 Pull in
60 Watering holes
63 "Get it?"

by Kevin Donovan

ACROSS

1 Stars and Stripes, e.g.
5 Places where lines meet
9 French greeting
14 ___ of Sandwich
15 Cause of a game cancellation
16 Unaccompanied
17 "Here he is now!"
20 Black card
21 Talks one's head off
22 French summer
23 Twinings selections
26 Sign before Virgo
27 Big Apple ave.
28 Be undecided
33 ___ Wednesday
34 Suds maker
35 Mounted, as a horse
38 Talking maybe a little too fast
40 Snapshot
43 Sgt. Snorkel's dog
44 Fable writer
46 No. on which a magazine's ad rates are based
48 Freudian one
49 Persist to completion
53 Prefix with center
55 Column's counterpart
56 Interstate entrance or exit
57 Fish after which a cape is named
58 Logic diagram
60 Long Island airfield town
64 Command center? . . . or where you might hear the starts of 17-, 28- and 49-Across
68 Nephew of Donald Duck
69 For whom the bell tolls, in a John Donne poem
70 Numerical prefix with -ber
71 Bygone Montreal ball club
72 Quiet exercise
73 Remove from the freezer

DOWN

1 Admit (to), with "up"
2 Reindeer herder
3 Geometry calculation
4 "My pleasure"
5 Black power hairdo, for short
6 Dunderpate
7 The "C" in N.Y.C.
8 Divided 50/50
9 Dirge
10 Schooner fill
11 Billet-doux
12 Join
13 Old message system
18 Wails
19 Dueling sword
24 Perched on
25 Deposed Iranian
28 "Roots," for one
29 ___ of Wight
30 Message on a shipping crate
31 Geologic time unit
32 Pigeon's sound
36 Big elevator manufacturer
37 ___ too soon
39 Droid
41 Wedding cake feature
42 Killer whale
45 Republican, Democratic, Green, etc.
47 "Luann" or "Blondie"
50 Knight time?
51 A score
52 End result
53 French place of learning
54 Mail receiver, in brief
59 Repeat
61 ___ Ness monster
62 Itsy-bitsy bit
63 Winter truck attachment
65 God, in Italy
66 Brain scan, for short
67 Bounding main

by Ken Bessette

ACROSS

1 Where to tie the knot
6 "Bearded" bloom
10 Captain Hook's henchman
14 Exotic jelly flavor
15 "___ a deal!"
16 Boston suburb
17 Is pessimistic
20 Waterborne youth group member
21 "I agree completely"
22 Follows orders
24 Ballpark worker
25 Stuffed mouse, maybe
29 Diving bird
31 Intergalactic traveler
32 ___ shui
34 Hellenic H's
38 Is optimistic
41 Eliot of the Untouchables
42 Taj Mahal site
43 Hobby knife brand
44 Bearded grazer
45 Springing bounce in tall grasses, as by an animal, to view the surroundings
46 Garbage
50 A dwarf planet, now
53 Makes use of
55 Binging
60 Is apathetic
62 March plaything
63 "Hurry!"
64 Frolics
65 Sapphic verses
66 Attack, as with eggs
67 Attack with rocks

DOWN

1 Dark ___
2 Elegance
3 Bite-size appetizer
4 Forum greetings
5 Masked scavengers
6 One Time?
7 Like a bad dirt road
8 "___ bin ein Berliner"
9 Tom Jones's "___ a Lady"
10 Job openings
11 Gift of the Magi
12 Come after
13 Key in
18 Shakespeare's Sir ___ Belch
19 Captain Queeg's creator
23 Year-end temp
25 "Love and Marriage" lyricist Sammy
26 Natural emollient
27 A lot of a car valet's income
28 Buttonless shirts, informally
30 "Disgusting!"
32 Get all steamy
33 Flub
34 24/7 auction site
35 PC whiz
36 Regarding
37 Halt
39 "Go, team!" screamer
40 Whistle-blowers
44 Neuter, as a horse
45 Walk of Fame embedment
46 Screwy
47 Steer clear of
48 Cook in a wok, maybe
49 Scrabble pieces
51 Opposite of express
52 Not suitable
54 Start of a play to the quarterback
56 Storyline
57 San ___, Italy
58 Nascar airer
59 In ___ (actually)
61 China's Lao-___

by Eugene W. Sard

ACROSS

1 "I saw ___ sawing wood . . ." (old tongue twister)
5 Lawn base
8 Finally
14 Outlaws
15 "I won! I won!," e.g.
16 Amp toter
17 What President Washington said upon winning the lottery?
19 Professor's goal
20 "I've got a mule, her name is ___"
21 Once around the sun
22 Hidden valley
23 What flagmaker Ross said . . . ?
28 Colonial Franklin, familiarly
29 Cheer to a matador
30 Just watched
33 What Miss Molly said . . . ?
39 End in ___ (draw)
40 In a huff
41 Captain who said "Eat your pudding, Mr. Land"
42 What Galileo said . . . ?
44 "I can't ___ satisfaction" (Rolling Stones lyric)
45 "___ shocked . . . SHOCKED!"
46 Collide
47 What the Big Bad Wolf said . . . ?
55 Figure skater's jump
56 Rocklike
57 Clamor
59 Overhaul
62 What Noah Webster said . . . ?
64 Aftershock
65 Shepherd's locale
66 Nylons
67 High-school honey
68 Directional suffix
69 Ready for business

DOWN

1 Flows out
2 Request at a medical exam
3 Viewpoint
4 Put to good ___
5 Porch protector
6 "Rock of Ages" accompaniment
7 Hair colorers
8 Picasso output
9 Little piggy
10 Actress Jessica
11 Rated NC-17, e.g.
12 Fathers
13 Wee
18 Hand-wringer's words
24 Monk's home
25 Traffic noises
26 Merrie ___ England
27 Command to Rover
30 ___ Miguel, largest island of the Azores
31 Part of N.C.A.A.: Abbr.
32 Actor Robbins
33 Commercial prefix with phone
34 Row
35 "You're ___ talk!"
36 Rent out
37 Trio after K
38 "___-hoo!"
40 Slanted type: Abbr.
43 Sis or bro
44 Lightheaded
46 Novelist Melville
47 Witches' blemishes
48 Put forth, as effort
49 Flood stopper
50 Transporter across the Andes
51 Not cut up
52 HBO's "Real Time With Bill ___"
53 Lottery winner's yell
54 Convalescent home employee
58 Biblical place of innocence
60 Hip, in the '60s
61 Delve (into)
63 "Sez ___?"

by C. W. Stewart

ACROSS

1 MacDowell of "Groundhog Day"
6 #41 or #43
10 These may be coddled
14 Nickel and dime
15 Home to most Turks
16 Maul or awl
17 Providential
19 Mr. Peanut prop
20 Vogue competitor
21 Not 'neath
22 Walked like a tosspot
24 Disco ___ of "The Simpsons"
26 Conclude one's argument
27 Nary a penny
33 Gymgoer's pride
34 Portfolio contents
35 Carrot or radish
37 Ending with bed or farm
39 Mai ___
40 Cass and Michelle, in '60s pop
41 Does something
42 Like cows, to Hindus
44 Hieroglyphics serpent
45 In close pursuit
48 Double reed
49 One of two in "boxcars"
50 Never-before-seen
53 Be in hock
55 Follow closely
59 Pope from 440 to 461
60 Adds up . . . like this puzzle's theme?
63 "We try harder" company
64 Up to the task
65 Bracelet site
66 Thought before blowing out the candles

67 Tide type
68 Significant ___

DOWN

1 Ibuprofen target
2 Coward of the theater
3 "Don't touch that ___!"
4 Play the market
5 Suffix with Brooklyn
6 When stolen, it stays in place
7 Tech caller
8 Covet thy neighbor's wife, say
9 Dislikes, plus
10 "Yadda, yadda, yadda"
11 Slap shot success
12 Auctioneer's last word
13 Iditarod entry

18 Some are proper
23 Upper-left key
25 Wart cause, in folklore
26 Hit the hay
27 Gunslinger's mark
28 "___ a Nightingale"
29 Everything that's left
30 Get to
31 "___ is an island"
32 Done for, slangily
33 Org. with dens
36 Cough medicine amt.
38 Really wow
40 Early 17th-century year
42 One with a carrot nose, maybe
43 Tricky turns
46 U.K. honour
47 Full range
50 What "there oughta be"

51 Strauss of jeans
52 Cohort of Clark
53 State with a panhandle: Abbr.
54 Show grief
56 Hieroglyphics cross
57 Archipelago unit
58 Sly glance
61 "Honest" prez
62 ___ Paulo

by David Pringle

ACROSS

1 Ooze
5 La ___, Milan opera house
10 One-spot cards
14 "Not guilty," e.g.
15 Jeopardy
16 Phileas ___, who went around the world in 80 days
17 Like 39-Across's fans on his induction day?
19 Plenty
20 Uses a stool
21 Spy Mata ___
23 Warmongers
26 H.S. junior's exam
28 Old horse
31 Away from the wind
32 Layers
34 Letter before omega
35 "___ Bitsy Spider"
36 Waved one's arms at, as a cab
37 Place to wager on the 28-Acrosses: Abbr.
38 Goes bad, as fruit
39 Notable Army inductee of 3/24/58
40 Military no-show
41 Part of a gearwheel
42 Flexible
43 Land of Lima and llamas
44 French "a"
45 Makes very happy
46 Balletic bend
47 ___ and feather
48 Simplicity
49 Legendary Chicago Bears coach George
50 Singer ___ Anthony
52 One who makes a good first impression?
54 Derrière
56 Last movie 39-Across made before his Army stint

62 Dunce cap, geometrically
63 1975–78 U.S. Open champ Chris
64 Finger's end
65 Novelist Seton
66 Artist who liked to paint dancers
67 Hard journey

DOWN

1 Place to refresh oneself
2 Building wing
3 Wriggly swimmer
4 Openers for all doors
5 Good name for a Dalmatian
6 Corporate V.I.P.'s
7 Noah's ___
8 "Ally McBeal" actress Lucy
9 Some computer software checks
10 Light years away
11 Army officer who met 39-Across in 25-Down
12 Self-esteem
13 Last Army rank of 39-Across: Abbr.
18 What the "H" of H.M.S. may be
22 Not too much
23 Much-photographed event after 39-Across's induction
24 City with a Penn State campus
25 Where 39-Across was stationed overseas
26 First Army rank of 39-Across
27 Like seawater

29 Waldorf-___ Hotel
30 First movie 39-Across made after his Army stint
32 Defeated soundly
33 Actresses Shire and Balsam
40 Clear to all
42 Word before group or pressure
49 What the "H" of H.M.S. may be
51 Neighborhood
52 Indian tourist city
53 Police hdqrs.
54 Record label of 39-Across
55 Long, long time
57 "___ had it!"
58 Photo image, briefly
59 Rowboat mover
60 Made-up story
61 Antlered animal

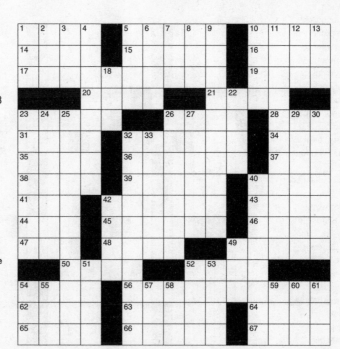

by David J. Kahn

ACROSS

1 Philosophies
5 Fiesta Bowl site
10 Tortilla sandwich
14 Bring in from the fields
15 ___ squash
16 Breezy greeting
17 Gallic girlfriend
18 Blasé group of directors?
20 5, 7, 9, etc., for juniors' dresses
22 Dallas-to-Des Moines dir.
23 Change
24 TV, radio, newspapers, etc.
26 Double or triple, say
28 Tourmaline, e.g.
29 Read quickly
31 Smokestack emission
32 Mormon state
34 "Pomp and Circumstance" composer
36 Traditional paintings
40 Spend an afternoon in a hammock, e.g.
41 Musical beat
42 Exam for a future atty.
43 It can get under your skin
44 Under way
45 "Lohengrin" lass
46 Slowing, in mus.
48 Get ___ arms
50 Head lines?
51 Helmets and such
55 Exclude
57 Notwithstanding the fact that, briefly
58 Messenger material
60 Kickback

62 Lovely hotel accommodations?
65 Addict
66 Eye drop
67 "Li'l" one in the comics
68 Refinery waste
69 Abbr. on a business sign
70 It may go off on you
71 Partners of haws

DOWN

1 Bank offerings, for short
2 Arsenic or antimony
3 Farm-grown labyrinth?
4 Methamphetamine
5 "Running" amount
6 Business subj.
7 Wake at dawn?
8 Primp
9 Player next to a tackle
10 Pit in its entirety?
11 Lasso
12 Lew who played Dr. Kildare
13 Mexican father
19 Where spirits run freely?
21 "___ boom bah!"
25 Film material
27 Kind of artery
28 Waters south of the South, e.g.
30 Hebrew leader?
33 Mooing group of cattle?
35 Each
37 Key passage?
38 Light in a light show
39 Unaccompanied
47 "___ Rhythm"

49 It's south of S.D.
51 Swiftness
52 Actor Cary of "Twister"
53 Bothered a lot
54 Caribbean vacation spot
56 Dentist's advice
59 Fit to ___
61 Pieces of work?
63 Schnook
64 Fumble

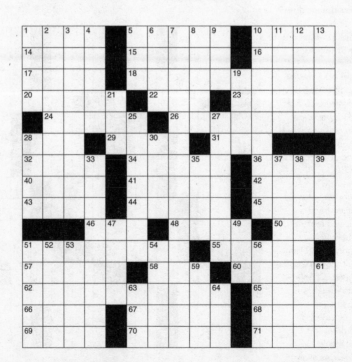

by Steve Salmon

ACROSS

1 Sea creature that sidles
5 Group of eight musicians
10 Underhanded plan
14 Greeting in Granada
15 Get up
16 Toy block brand
17 Andy's partner in old radio
18 *Sci-fi barrier
20 *Newspaper article lead-in
22 Quenched
23 Big name in audio equipment
24 Martial artist Jackie
25 Result of a belly flop
28 *When the curtain goes up
32 Quiet spells
33 Bed board
34 Turf
35 Kind of history
36 Word that can precede each half of the answers to each of the eight starred clues
37 Performed ballads, e.g.
38 President pro ___
39 Go after bucks or ducks, say
40 Outpouring
41 *Wrestling move that puts an arm around someone's neck
44 Less bold
45 Slick
46 Corduroy ridge
47 Measly
50 *Secret communication location

54 *Mars Pathfinder, for one
56 Rouse from slumber
57 Regarding
58 Western flick, in old lingo
59 Farm measure
60 Abound (with)
61 One of a reporter's five W's
62 Annum

DOWN

1 Punched-out part of a paper ballot
2 Capital of Italia
3 Plenty
4 *Diamond game
5 Like a lout
6 Hag
7 Become bushed
8 PC bailout key
9 Golfer's opening drive
10 Flexible
11 Cousin of an onion
12 Gawk at
13 Sondheim's "Sweeney ___"
19 Scratch on a diamond, e.g.
21 Amount printed in red ink
24 Nautical map
25 Slow-moving mammal
26 Blender setting
27 South American wool source
28 Move with one's tail between one's legs
29 Actor and rockabilly crooner Chris
30 Three-card hustle
31 Yard worker's tool
33 Impertinent
37 *Indy 500 venue

39 "Yikes!"
40 Hawk, as wares
42 Business that may have gone boom and then bust in the '90s
43 Pre-euro money in 2-Down
44 ___ d'
46 Eucharist disk
47 H.S. junior's exam
48 Cathedral recess
49 Tardy
50 Corner, as a king
51 10K or marathon
52 Gumbo ingredient
53 House of Lords member
55 Pep squad shout

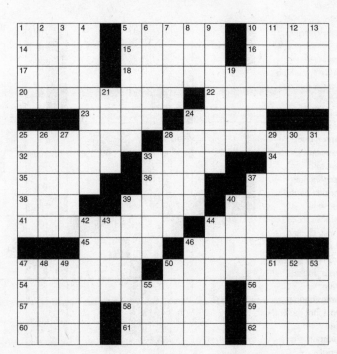

by Jeff Armstrong

ACROSS

1 Dress shirt closer
5 Four times a day, on an Rx
8 Person who doesn't put down roots
13 Had on
14 Acapulco article
15 State as one's view
16 Nitwit's swoon?
18 Nonsense, slangily
19 Torah holders
20 New York tribe defeated by the Iroquois
21 Exterior
22 Cartoon Chihuahua
23 On the house
24 Respect
25 Kind of eyes
27 Force (open)
28 Turn one way and then back
29 "A Tale ___ Cities"
30 Uncompromising sort
33 Regret some stupidity . . . with a hint to this puzzle's theme
37 Girls in the family
38 Watergate hearings chairman Sam
40 Univ. where "Good Will Hunting" is set
43 Suffix with neat or beat
44 ___ Conventions
45 Shabbily clothed
47 Rock star, e.g.
49 Speed (up)
50 Vinegar: Prefix
51 Pre-remote channel changer
52 R.E.M.'s "It's the End of the World ___ Know It"
53 Danger in dangerous waters

54 Spring in the air?
56 News groups
57 "Tastes great!"
58 "___ do for now"
59 Analyze the composition of
60 N.B.A. tiebreakers
61 Like some orders

DOWN

1 Promised to give up
2 Was attentive
3 Internet addresses
4 "Excellent!," in slang
5 Paper quantity
6 Type of 39-Down
7 Movie companion, maybe
8 Vibes not being picked up by anyone?

9 Painkiller since ancient times
10 "Uncle" of early television
11 Rages
12 Some tractors
16 Red River city
17 Houston hockey player
23 Doing credible work as a magician?
24 Mozart's "Madamina," e.g.
26 Verdon of "Damn Yankees"
27 Top exec.
30 Miner's tool
31 Hawaiian instrument, for short
32 Pulled apart
34 Gifts at Honolulu Airport

35 Push too hard, as an argument
36 Have it good
39 Belly part
40 Bad atmosphere
41 "
42 Steps (on)
44 Asian desert
46 Places in the heart
47 Contribution, as of ideas
48 Buildings near some cafeterias
51 Bout-ending slug
52 Mennen shaving brand
55 Shining

by Manny Nosowsky

ACROSS

1 See 48-Down
5 Stick in one's ___
9 Frank of the Mothers of Invention
14 Not loco
15 "___ and the King of Siam"
16 Decorate
17 Bess Truman or Barbara Bush
19 Snooped, with "about"
20 "You're ___ talk!"
21 Enclosure with a MS.
23 NNW's opposite
24 Hi-___ monitor
25 Question after the fact
29 Car bomb?
31 Old letter salutation
32 "God's Little ___" (Erskine Caldwell best seller)
34 Competitor of Dove or Camay
36 Prop for Picasso
40 Takes care of all possibilities
44 Pan-cooked brunch treat
45 Words after ". . . as long as you both shall live?"
46 "Mona ___"
47 Make the cut?
50 Funny DeGeneres
52 Grilling
56 "Shame on you!"
59 Crew's control?
60 One who indulges too much in the grape
61 French city famous for its mustard
63 Garbo of "Mata Hari," 1932
65 1990 Macaulay Culkin film
68 Ed of "Lou Grant"
69 The "U" in B.T.U.
70 Compete in the America's Cup
71 Bookcase part
72 Model Banks
73 Med school subj.

DOWN

1 In regard to
2 Where Bangor is
3 Put aside for later
4 Place for eggs
5 Iron Man Ripken of the Orioles
6 Genetic letters
7 ___ forth (et cetera)
8 Brother comic Shawn or Marlon
9 "Riders of the Purple Sage" author
10 Hullabaloo
11 Star's entourage
12 ". . . or ___ 1 for more options"
13 Peruvian peaks
18 Play with, as a Frisbee
22 Star Wars program, for short
26 Morays, e.g.
27 Hint
28 Fit to be tried?
30 More profound
32 U.N.C.'s athletic org.
33 Where streets intersect: Abbr.
35 "Sweet" age in ancient Rome?
37 Play by George Bernard Shaw
38 Superman's symbol
39 Meadow
41 Relatively low-temperature star
42 German river in a 1943 R.A.F. raid
43 Part to play
48 With 1-Across, infamous Ugandan dictator
49 Opposite of "At ease!"
51 Mother of Castor and Pollux
52 "Animal House" party costumes
53 Like winters in the Arctic
54 Ballroom dancer Castle
55 Foolish person, slangily
57 Braga of "Kiss of the Spider Woman"
58 Prepared to pray
62 She requested "As Time Goes By"
64 ___ Aviv
66 Bygone Russian space station
67 When a plane is due in: Abbr.

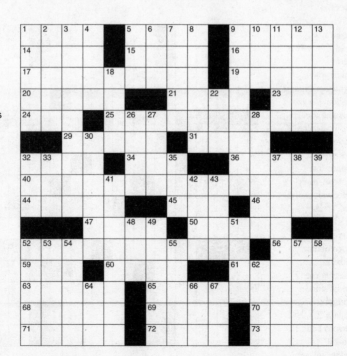

by Randall J. Hartman

ACROSS

1. Kaplan of "Welcome Back, Kotter"
5. Tally
10. Émile who wrote "Truth is on the march"
14. Is in hock
15. More than sore
16. Leave out
17. Ronald Reagan movie
20. Think tank products
21. Indy 500 inits.
22. Cuban boy in 2000 news
23. As a result
25. Chat room shorthand for "Here's what I think"
27. "Rule, Britannia" composer
30. Doris Day movie, with "The"
35. ___ Paulo, Brazil
36. Era-spanning story
37. Greg of "My Two Dads"
38. Honda with a palindromic name
40. Gradual decline
42. Cause of some food poisoning
43. 2001 title role for Audrey Tautou
45. Wren or hen
47. ___ Irvin, longtime cartoonist for The New Yorker
48. Rock Hudson movie
50. Not fem.
51. Deuce beater
52. Bonkers
54. "___ is human"
57. Sandy island
59. Football's Fighting ___
63. Barbara Eden TV series
66. ___ St. Vincent Millay
67. Old newspaper sections
68. Touch-and-go
69. Support staffer: Abbr.
70. Map detail
71. Have-___ (lower economic group)

DOWN

1. Mongolian expanse
2. Impressed and then some
3. "Venerable" monk
4. Bequeathed property
5. Colgate competitor
6. Equestrian competition
7. Bonkers
8. A world without 71-Across
9. According to
10. Of the animal kingdom
11. First Dodge with front-wheel drive
12. Minnelli of "Arthur"
13. Like ___ of bricks
18. Suffix with bull or bear
19. Didn't act up
24. Work ___ lather
26. Flaubert's Bovary, e.g.: Abbr.
27. B.M.I. rival
28. "Spider-Man" director Sam
29. It's no short story
31. ___ the Hutt of "Star Wars"
32. Ancient meeting place
33. Maxim's target audience
34. Pioneering 1940s computer
36. Annabella of "The Sopranos"
39. "It's on me!"
41. Subject of a 1976 film "ode"
44. Stand-in for "you" in "Concentration"
46. "Flying Down to Rio" studio
49. Captain of industry
50. Informal greeting at a breakfast shop
53. Grp. known as the Company
54. "___ yellow ribbon . . ."
55. Bookie's quote
56. Coastal raptors
58. P.M. periods
60. Dope
61. Sort (through)
62. Attention getters
64. Hosp. procedure
65. Ballpark fig.

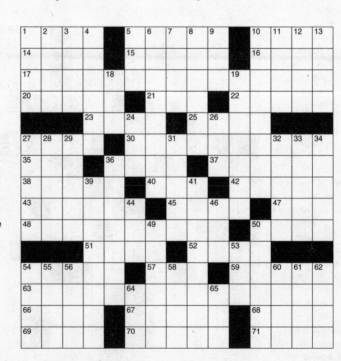

by Dave Mackey

ACROSS

1 "I didn't know I was speeding, officer," e.g.
4 Cover sheet abbr.
8 Hire
14 A mean Amin
15 Tropical food that is poisonous if eaten raw
16 Kind of solution
17 Pince-___
18 Girl's floral name
19 ___ Hollywood
20 "Charlotte's Web" actress on a hot day?
23 Like some pickings
24 Number of weeks in Julius Caesar's year?
25 Pickled veggie
28 "A Brief History of Time" author doing sales?
33 "Shucks"
34 DVR brand
35 With 45-Across, conger, e.g.
36 Like some consonants
40 Scarce
42 Bond girl Green of "Casino Royale"
43 Attorney General Holder
45 See 35-Across
46 "Porphyria's Lover" poet with a pan of ground beef on the stove?
51 One of the two characters in Dr. Seuss' "Fox in Socks"
52 Limbo need
53 Take ___ from
55 "Tom Jones" novelist playing baseball?
60 Most music is played in it

62 One-volume works of Shakespeare, e.g.
63 Ukr., until 1991, e.g.
64 "Same here!"
65 Pollster Roper
66 Not shoot straight
67 Neglects to
68 Official with a list
69 J.D. holder

DOWN

1 Comes across
2 10's, say
3 Rock's Limp ___
4 In a shouting match, perhaps
5 Skater Lipinski
6 Little nothing
7 One who's morally flawed
8 "Pardon the Interruption" network
9 Country that's over 50% desert
10 Max of physics
11 Person who has a way with words?
12 You, generically
13 "Better ___ . . ."
21 ___-3 fatty acid
22 Nothing
26 Bender?
27 "Holy moly!"
29 Dwindle, with "out"
30 Symbol after "I" on many a bumper sticker
31 "___ to a Kill"
32 Sign on a door
36 Corner office, e.g.
37 Sweet Swan of ___ (epithet for Shakespeare)
38 "Musetta's Waltz" opera

39 Scooter ___, Plame affair figure
41 Poem in which Paris plays a prominent part
44 Handmade
47 Applies
48 A.L. East athlete
49 CBS drama featuring LL Cool J
50 Puts the pedal to the metal
54 Symbol of the National Audubon Society
56 Loud, as a color
57 Plant holder?
58 Literary matchmaker
59 Kings of ___ ("Use Somebody" band)
60 ___ the Kid (N.H.L. nickname)
61 Eastern principle

by Erik Wennstrom

ACROSS

1 One of the three dimensions
6 Pro bono promo, for short
9 It may have many jets
12 Tight squeeze
14 Pirate portrayer of film
15 Keyboard key
16 "I was wrong . . . big whoop"
17 Abbr. accompanying 0
18 "___ luck?"
19 Pound, as potatoes
20 Milk, in a way
21 Nasties
22 Captain von ___ (musical role)
25 Overzealous
27 Some arm exercises
28 Something requiring little study
29 Sick
30 Mind
32 Mary of early Hollywood
33 Says, informally
35 Garden spot
38 Wetlands birds
40 "V" vehicle
41 Grab suddenly
43 Broadway's "Me ___ Girl"
44 Burrows, e.g.
46 Grab suddenly
47 Note
49 Carpenter ___
50 Annual literary award
51 ___ Carpenter
54 Horny devil
56 Psychoactive drug used in medicine
57 Insurance worker
58 Mainframe brain, for short
59 Nabisco offering
61 Cooking spray

62 Diane of "Numb3rs"
63 Perk for a pool party?
67 Dangerous sprayer
68 Soft cheese
69 Outstanding
70 Cowboy moniker
71 Chain part: Abbr.
72 Some close-ups

DOWN

1 Scale abbr.
2 Classified inits.
3 2012 rap Grammy nominee for "Life Is Good"
4 14-Down starring Jack Lemmon
5 Keeps one's mouth shut?
6 Beverage introduced as Brad's Drink

7 Maker of the LZR Racer suit
8 Loan letters
9 Football Hall-of-Famer Bart
10 Comic part
11 Bottomless pit
13 Triple Crown winner of 1934
14 Drive-in theater draw . . . with a literal hint to 4- and 21-Down
21 14-Down starring Frank Sinatra
22 Brewed beverages
23 Bob Marley, e.g.
24 Sean of "The Lord of the Rings"
26 Viva voce
31 A.L. East team, on scoreboards
34 Little fella

36 "Let's give ___"
37 Get rid of
39 Prefix with pathetic
42 Juno, to the Greeks
45 Brew whose name is an article of clothing when read backward
48 Star-studded show, with "the"
51 Utterly dead
52 Goggling
53 Dance version of a record, often
55 You may be fooled at its beginning
60 ___ de boeuf
62 Org. whose motto is "Fidelity, Bravery, Integrity"
64 Brewed beverage
65 Music writer Hentoff
66 R.N.'s are in them

by Patrick Blindauer

ACROSS

1 Term of address from a hat-tipper
5 Changes channels rapidly
10 Bumps off
14 Periodic table fig.
15 Staircase sound
16 Learn by ___
17 Roe source
18 Delhi language
19 Madeline who played Lili Von Shtupp
20 Southern town whose name is the longest example of 52-Across [on the left]
23 Words on either side of "what"
24 Satisfied sigh
25 Muhammad's resting place
26 Pats down
28 Request to a barber
30 "___ to mention . . ."
31 Like yesterday's bagels
32 Stockyard bellows
33 Get an eyeful
34 Midwest town whose name is the longest example of 52-Across [on the right]
37 Disney World conveyance
40 Leaf support
41 Warming periods
45 "Death Becomes ___"
46 Oaf
47 Female TV dog whose portrayers were all male
48 Where Yeltsin ruled
50 Be indisposed
51 Pod item
52 See 20- and 34-Across
56 Alaska ZIP code starter
57 Courageous one
58 Department
59 List-ending abbr.
60 Become one on the run
61 Fresh-mouthed
62 "___-starter" (résumé cliché)
63 Some score marks
64 Derry derrière

DOWN

1 Mountainous expanses
2 Crosswise
3 Result of iron deficiency, to a Brit
4 Manner of doing
5 Start and end of 3-Down, phonetically
6 Scheming Heep
7 Not buy, say
8 Lose brilliance
9 Minor battle
10 Ticked off
11 Persuading by flattery
12 Biofuel option
13 Able to see, hear, etc.
21 End of a seat seeker's query
22 Pro ___
27 Candidate for urban renewal
28 Moderated, with "down"
29 Leeway
32 Sleuth played by Lorre
33 Reactions to fireworks
35 Hawaiian, e.g.
36 An original eurozone member
37 Bathroom fixtures, slangily
38 Get back together
39 Weapons stockpile
42 Ambitious one
43 The "pigs" in pigs in blankets
44 Channel to the ocean
46 Org. in "Argo"
47 Petrol measures
49 Library unit
50 Like a whiz
53 Hill's opposite
54 Bow-toting god
55 ___ John's (Domino's competitor)

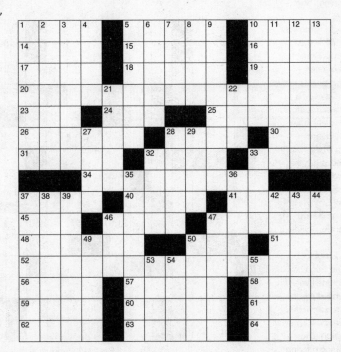

by H. David Goering

ACROSS

1 Delivery specialists, for short
4 Something groundbreaking
10 Tiny bit of kindling
14 Chinese calendar figure
15 Seagoing vessels
16 Refine
17 With 22-Across, fail to cope with difficult circumstances
20 ___ Diurna (daily Roman notices)
21 She, in Italy
22 See 17-Across
23 Tolkien's Dark Lord of Mordor
25 Belts boxers don't want to receive?
27 With 35-Across, highway sign meaning "slow down"
34 Fist-pounding sort
35 See 27-Across
36 Ritually torments
40 Unit of energy
41 British poet laureate ___ Day-Lewis
42 Whimsical outburst
43 Ingredient in an Arnold Palmer
45 With 51-Across, Monaco has the world's highest
50 The Yoko of "Oh Yoko!"
51 See 45-Across
53 Graceless landing, say
56 Hindu noblewoman
59 World Cup chorus
60 What the three sets of circled squares in this puzzle represent
63 Terse invitation
64 Too much
65 Poetic preposition

66 Some Groucho Marx humor
67 Tarnishes
68 Greek night goddess

DOWN

1 Black-and-white threats
2 Where people get loaded on a train
3 Center of a square, maybe
4 See 29-Down
5 Language learner's goal
6 Particle accelerator particles
7 Engine parts
8 Addressing
9 Old D&D co.
10 Sif's husband in myth
11 Eroded (away)

12 South America's ___ Trail
13 Plowman's command
18 Stitch
19 Express
24 Exposes a secret of
26 German direction
28 Old A. C. Gilbert toy
29 With 4-Down, reluctant questioner's opening
30 Eroded (away)
31 Actor Cage, informally
32 Early 10th-century year
33 California's ___ River
36 What was cool in the '50s?
37 Gone by
38 Nuke
39 Follower of brown. or auburn.

41 Hunting gear, informally
43 Golfer Poulter
44 Form a ring around
46 City in New Jersey or California
47 Dominican baseball family name
48 Showing ill humor
49 Like wet paint
52 County bordering Cambridgeshire
53 10 benjamins
54 Canticle
55 Exercises
57 Colgate product for men
58 "Me neither"
60 Hallucinogenic inits.
61 Composition of many a music library
62 Brit. legislators

by Timothy Polin

ACROSS

1 Dos + dos + dos
5 Utterly hopeless
11 "We ___ the 99%"
14 Dermatologist's concern
15 Capital on the Vltava River
16 ___ Heels (college team)
17 First name in folk
18 Like a raccoon's tail
19 Confessional confession
20 *What paper profits aren't
22 Checkout counter count
24 Counting-out rhyme start
25 Oil-rich nation invaded in 1990
26 Good dishes
29 Taste whose name means "savoriness" in Japanese
31 *Photo gear with variable focal lengths
34 Metro map points: Abbr.
38 Kind of clef
39 Like a fugitive
40 Hype up
41 Berate, with "out"
42 *Titularly
44 Lauder of cosmetics
46 Case for Scully and Mulder
47 Torch holder
50 Big Ben sound
52 To a great extent
53 *Sarcastic remark upon hearing bad news
58 Ashes holder
59 One passing out cigars, maybe
61 See 13-Down
62 "Shoot!"
63 "Seinfeld" woman
64 Hazmat-monitoring org.
65 Prefix in some French surnames
66 Bing Crosby or David Crosby
67 Condé ___

DOWN

1 Mark for life
2 See 7-Down
3 Tierra surrounded by agua
4 *Precious, brief time with a loved one
5 Butcher's wear
6 Like pickle juice
7 With 2-Down, book that includes the line "Conventionality is not morality"
8 Like a soufflé
9 Word before card or stick
10 Rote learning, to most people
11 Where hurricanes originate
12 "Spider-Man" director Sam
13 With 61-Across, physicist who studied supersonics
21 ___ plan
23 Drink garnish . . . or a hint to five letters in the answer to each starred clue
25 Casey of "American Top 40"
26 Executive branch V.I.P.
27 Tunnel, e.g.
28 I as in Ilium?
29 Rte. with a terminus in Key West, Fla.
30 Natural table
32 A-listers
33 Slim to ___ (poor odds)
35 "Mickey" vocalist ___ Basil
36 Empty, as a math set
37 Eyelid woe
43 Part of a dental visit
45 Act parts
47 Nine, in baseball
48 Wish evil on
49 Farm sounds
50 Hughes's Spruce Goose, e.g.
51 One with seniority
53 Olympic skater Michelle
54 Hippie's "Got it!"
55 Friendship org. of 1962
56 Phil who sang "Draft Dodger Rag"
57 Word from the hard-of-hearing
60 QB Manning

by Erik Wennstrom

ACROSS

1 It wraps scraps
9 Scratches, say
15 Unlocked, as a computer file
16 Saws
17 J
18 Apartment dweller, e.g.
19 Transvestite of song
20 Loud laughs
22 Third neighbor?
23 Cellphone feature
25 Backup singer's syllable
27 Eighth-day rite
28 Source of the phrase "brave new world," with "The"
31 Splitting headache?
33 Subj. of psychological experiments with inconclusive results
34 Dirty
36 Skater Harding and others
37 U
39 Downsized
42 Was overcome with embarrassment, in slang
43 Goat sound
46 Does perfunctorily, as a performance
48 Openly state
50 Letters on a stamp
51 Scand. land
53 Parts of an "Old MacDonald" verse
54 Mughal Empire rulers
56 Related
59 Parks in a bus
60 Beggars of a sort
62 X
64 Gettysburg Address, e.g.
65 Neat and trim
66 Trample
67 1994 film that spawned a TV series

DOWN

1 Collapse
2 Division rivals of the Rays
3 Quaint illumination
4 A flat is the same as this
5 Derisive response
6 Hip-hop devotee, in old slang
7 Baseball's Felipe
8 Gordon ___, "Wall Street" character
9 Fraternize, with "around"
10 Alternatives to saws
11 Y
12 "My bad"
13 "Another name for opportunity," per Ralph Waldo Emerson
14 Trypanosomiasis transmitters
21 Roll at a nursery
24 Accelerator particles
26 This way
29 Oscar-winning screenwriter for "The Social Network"
30 "___ the last rose of summer" (Thomas Moore poem starter)
32 Activity with dolls
35 Was up
37 O
38 Test the temperature of, in a way
39 Presses together
40 Negotiate
41 Tamed, as a stallion
43 Mediterranean resort island, to locals
44 Proposes a date to
45 Armand of "Private Benjamin"
47 "Just kidding!"
49 Dismissal
52 Strenuous college programs, for short
55 ___ lily
57 Light air
58 "The Sopranos" actress ___ de Matteo
61 Prefix with fuel
63 Location of the tragus

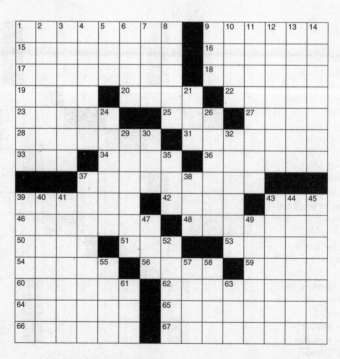

by Daniel A. Finan

ACROSS

1. ___ Mesa, Calif.
6. Legs on an insect or strings on a guitar
11. Decryption org.
14. Square dance group, e.g.
15. ___ curiae (friends of the court)
16. Done, to Donne
17. Author Zora ___ Hurston
18. Sells in the stands
19. Insult, slangily
20. Norwegian import in the dairy case
23. Windsor's locale: Abbr.
24. Bit of ink, for short
25. "Aw, hell!"
26. Some book jacket blurbs
28. Links
33. Not so risky
35. Youngest 600-homer man, informally
36. You can hardly believe it
41. Oscar winner Jannings
42. Inappropriate for the easily offended, say
45. Bit of equipment for an outdoor kids' game
51. Help (out)
52. Electronically scored duel
53. Western treaty grp.
55. ___-Blo fuse
56. What 20-, 28-, 36- and 45-Across are
62. Cranberry locale
63. Carlos Danger, e.g.
64. Lavatory sign
65. ___ Taylor (clothier)
66. Beatnik's percussion
67. Ring-tailed primate
68. ___ judicata
69. "S.N.L." bit
70. Northern Scandinavians

DOWN

1. Scams
2. Where Polynesia is
3. Go from square one
4. Blow the whistle, so to speak
5. "This is only ___"
6. Can't help but
7. E.M.T. part: Abbr.
8. Ped ___
9. Aussie rockers with a knickers-clad lead guitarist
10. Potluck choice
11. Spouse's refusal
12. Earth movers?
13. Literary sleuth ___ Lupin
21. Do a supermarket task
22. Ending of many an e-mail address
27. French seasoning
29. Grammy-winning Eric Clapton tune
30. ___ diavolo
31. Potter or Klink: Abbr.
32. Valhalla ruler
34. Cambodian currency
37. Marseilles Mrs.
38. Bro, for one
39. Flapper's do
40. Struggling at the plate, say
43. Amasses, as debt
44. Sales pros
45. Party room fixture
46. "The Internet in your pocket" sloganeer, once
47. Fakes
48. Sedge locale
49. Many
50. "Well, ___-di-dah"
54. Participant in 1-Down
57. Chews the rag
58. Zero-star fare
59. Rotgut buyer, perhaps
60. To whom Brabantio says "Thou art a villain"
61. Fit for drafting

by Sarah Keller

ACROSS

1 Napkin, e.g.
5 Licensing grp.
8 Like Goodwill goods
12 Figure on the ceiling of the Sistine Chapel
13 Oil vessel
15 Warm, say
16 Provider of two- and four-yr. scholarships
17 Equaled altogether
18 It may be "aw"-inspiring
19 What the circled letter in this answer represents, homophonically
22 What the circled letter in this answer represents, homophonically
24 Refrigerant inits.
25 Some football linemen: Abbr.
26 Cotillion V.I.P.
27 Traffic control org.
29 Final dramatic notes of the "1812 Overture"
31 Scopolamine and sodium pentothal, e.g.
33 Classic camera
34 Joe
37 Some seizures, for short
38 Typhon was trapped under it, in Greek myth
39 Something a picker picks
41 Table d'___
42 What the circled letter in this answer represents, homophonically
45 Relief might follow it
46 Et ___ (footnote abbr.)
47 What the circled letters in this answer represent, homophonically
54 Bryn ___

55 Bobby in a 1971 #1 hit
56 Chits
58 One with a pretty strong hunch?
59 Hoops great Baylor
60 Not loopy
61 Liable to clump
62 Taylor who sang "Tell It to My Heart"
63 Prehistoric terror, informally

DOWN

1 Hostilities
2 Simple vow
3 "Walkin' After Midnight" singer, 1957
4 Act opener
5 Bar offerings
6 Chew (on)
7 Nixed
8 Let float from the dollar, say
9 Suddenly took interest in
10 Take in
11 Like some humor
13 Seals's partner in 1970s music
14 Dense desserts
20 Main line
21 View from Vatican City
22 Washed up
23 Like Timbuktu
24 Star
28 Money in the bank, e.g.
30 Trendy "superfood"
32 Burger's successor
34 "Whew!"
35 French article
36 Dance club figs.
39 Big or full follower

40 Disgustingly large, as an amount of money
43 Bill blocker
44 Antipoverty agcy. created under L.B.J.
47 "Star Wars," e.g.
48 "Star Wars" critter
49 Where Troy Aikman was a QB
50 Pop's ___ Pop
51 Foreign refusal
52 Big laugh
53 Simple number
54 4-Down's item
57 Driver's license info

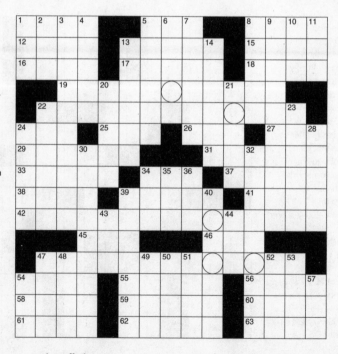

by Jeff Chen

ACROSS

1 Testimony spot
6 Nursing school subj.
10 Defeats regularly, in slang
14 Muscular strength
15 30 Rock's architectural style
16 Female mil. unit created 5/15/42
17 Like a patient person's attitude
19 Analogy words
20 Flying Cloud of old autodom
21 Take the top off of, in a way
22 Stray from the subject
29 Rooney ___, star of "The Girl With the Dragon Tattoo"
30 Browses, in a way
31 Place to wallow in mud
32 Quick ballroom dance
35 Relating to the calf
37 Mideast monarchy
42 Passion
43 Term of address for a 2-Down
44 Model Carangi
47 One of almost 20 French kings
49 Fishing rod, flies, lures, etc.
50 Without delay
54 Where some ex-major-leaguers play
55 ___ Taylor (clothing retailer)
56 Company that once owned the trademark "Escalator"
57 Not corroborated
64 Cork's locale
65 Component of brass
66 Words of compassion
67 Progeny

68 Rash feeling?
69 See 61-Down

DOWN

1 Vane dir.
2 Member of la familia
3 Purchase from Pat Sajak
4 Last figure on an invoice
5 Tower over
6 Scanners, webcams, etc.
7 Super ___ (old game console)
8 Do superbly on
9 Shoe part
10 Short, in a way
11 Laps against
12 Floating
13 "Star Trek" character who says "Aye" a lot
18 Modernist's prefix

21 Failing inspection, say
22 Some pickups
23 Island with Yokohama Bay
24 Like many presentations
25 Statements in a legal case
26 Alpine land
27 Irrefutable
28 Some "Hair" hairdos
33 Sci-fi author Ellison
34 "___ the seventh day . . ."
36 "Cute" sound
38 Month in l'été
39 Where Duff Beer is poured
40 ___ Sea (now-divided waters)
41 ___ a one
44 Toys known as Action Men in the U.K.

45 Headed for sudden death, perhaps
46 Aim high
48 Swipe, as a purse
51 Shocked, in a way
52 Tolkien creature
53 Negro leagues star Buck ___
57 Assault weapon named for its designer
58 Minor complaint
59 Post-apartheid ruling org.
60 Chem. or biol.
61 With 69-Across, beach markings . . . 14 of which are hidden vertically and horizontally elsewhere in this puzzle
62 'Fore
63 ___ Plaines, Ill.

by Jonathan Gersch

ACROSS

1 Stop threatening
12 "How to Marry a Millionaire" actress
15 One's initial response to this clue, perhaps
16 Police dept. broadcast
17 Suspended avian home
18 While, in brief
19 Campaign pro
20 Bamboozled
21 ___ de Guerre (French military award)
23 What shepherds may shepherd
25 Superior home?: Abbr.
26 Actors James and Scott
27 Kind of jet
29 Web opening
30 Deterrent to swimming
33 Three-time N.H.L. M.V.P.
34 ___ trap
38 Audition rebuff
42 "Or what shall a man give in exchange for his ___?": Mark 8:37
43 Sea urchin delicacy
44 Many opera houses have them
45 Throw off
47 Dimwit
49 Lhasa ___
51 Worked (up)
52 Biltmore Estate state: Abbr.
56 Pooch, in Paris
57 Mantles
59 "Ti ___" (Italian lover's declaration)
60 Owner of Moviefone
61 Site of W.W. II's first amphibious landing
64 Number of colori on the Italian flag
65 Commercial figure holding six beer mugs
66 Singer known as La Divina
67 Extremely tight

DOWN

1 Homer's Muse
2 Discombobulate
3 Two-time Olympic running gold medalist ___ Gebrselassie
4 Bolivian president Morales
5 Place ___ Concorde
6 Quick combination
7 It may be full of dirt
8 Math ratios
9 Ancient theaters
10 Moroccan city known as the Athens of Africa
11 Moneybags
12 One being passed in a race
13 Black fly, e.g.
14 Roadside fixture
22 Rogue
24 German wine made from fully ripe grapes
26 PC key
28 Reminisce about
29 Much of central Eur., once
30 Circular parts
31 Head overseas
32 Animal whose young is a calf
33 Be obliged
35 Size up
36 High, rocky hill
37 N.S.W. locale
39 "O'Hara's Choice" novelist
40 Inebriate
41 Ford last produced in 1986
46 In the midst of, poetically
47 The Blue Demons of the N.C.A.A.
48 Verdi opera
49 Hoy día
50 Gobs
51 Was equipped for summer heat, as an auto
53 "That's enough!"
54 Ruben ___, Phillies Gold Glove-winning shortstop
55 Class starter
56 Sound of derision
57 Family head
58 Agronomy and metallurgy: Abbr.
62 ___-Aztecan (language family)
63 Historical period

by Stu Ockman

ACROSS

1 With 67-Across, man whose 1930 salary was $80,000
5 Gives off
10 Seventh anniversary ruiner?
14 Treats, as a sprain
15 Like some sprays
16 One's part?
17 Nickname for 1-/67-Across
20 Peace and quiet
21 Injures
22 Bro's sib
23 Whittle
24 Deerstalker, e.g.
27 It's the law
30 Eleanor : F.D.R. :: Bess : ___
33 Obama's birthplace
35 School for James Bond
36 Be really annoying
38 Man whose 1930 salary was $75,000
41 Snowy wader
42 Writer James
43 Faucet annoyance
44 Kenny Rogers's "___ Believes in Me"
45 Battlers at sea
48 Naval rank: Abbr.
49 Newcastle Brown and others
50 Pre-barbecuing mixture
52 Deplorable
55 Repay
60 Quote from 1-/67-Across on why he outearned 38-Across
62 One of the Jackson 5
63 It lights up when it's excited
64 Guitarist Clapton
65 Go into the wild blue yonder
66 Runs rampant
67 See 1-Across

DOWN

1 Memory units
2 Be sore
3 "Beauty is in the eye of the ___ holder": Kinky Friedman
4 Bluegrass duo?
5 Up in arms?
6 QB Stafford
7 "What can ___?"
8 Treat, as a hide
9 Not adept in
10 Time piece?
11 Go to ___ on
12 Attired
13 Sexual attraction, with "the"
18 One-piece garments, informally
19 Precede
23 Gave up by giving up control
24 Crosses one's fingers, perhaps
25 "Good grief!"
26 Word repeated when consoling someone
28 Units of brilliance?
29 Its capital is Nuku'alofa
30 Le ___, France
31 Rathskeller order
32 A.C.C. team, informally
34 Purpose
37 Surveyor's unit
39 Vicina della Francia
40 Listens up, quaintly
46 Chestnut-colored flying mammal
47 Litigant
49 Zeal
51 The "emptor" in "caveat emptor"
52 Best sellers
53 Home of the U.S.'s largest cities whose names start with X and Z
54 Pro ___
55 Lender's offering: Abbr.
56 It's elementary
57 Big silver exporter
58 Mathematical physicist Peter who pioneered in knot theory
59 Philharmonic grp.
61 "Inconstancy falls off ___ it begins": Shak.

by Erik Agard

ACROSS

1 Fig. mentioned in Miranda warnings
4 Feudal V.I.P.
8 Made ends meet?
14 Your substitute?
15 Arabian Peninsula land
16 Lead dancer in a ballet company
17 Exonerated boxer who is the subject of a Bob Dylan song
20 Exceedingly
21 Tennis's Agassi
22 Capt. : Navy :: ___ : Army
23 Grazeland?
24 Young 'uns
25 Drops
27 Transition
29 ___ and the Waves ("Walking on Sunshine" band)
31 Superman's dog
33 2008 recipient of govt. largesse
34 Piercing gaze
35 Ingredient in a witch's potion
39 Address for a G.I.
40 Weighted fishing nets
41 Walt Disney World's ___ Lagoon
45 Name dropper, often?
46 Get extra value from
48 "___ a Spell on You" (1956 hit)
50 Nevada birthplace of Pat Nixon
51 Resident of an elaborate underground "city"
52 Hidden valleys
53 Farm females
55 Minor-leaguer whose team is named after a Coney Island roller coaster

59 Orangutan locale
60 Land with a harp on its coat of arms
61 ___ lane
62 Measure of a man?
63 Falls into decay
64 Revolutionary icon

DOWN

1 Tenderfoot
2 Hustling is the same as cheating, according to these authorities
3 Where to work out
4 Its code uses just G, T, A and C
5 Four of a decathlon's 10 events
6 Enforced silence
7 Giant Ferris wheel on the Thames

8 Easily passed
9 Terre in the eau zone?
10 Border
11 Name in old graffiti
12 Be sassy, with "off'
13 Autumnal hue
18 Uses sock puppets to talk to a therapist, say
19 Voting against
25 Is suitable for
26 Ogling wolfishly
27 Med. readout
28 Vast treeless area
30 Go up, up, up
32 "That being said," in textspeak
36 Mess hall queue
37 Green, juicy fruit

38 Ending for a record-breaker
41 Certain teachers
42 Unctuous
43 Enlightening experience
44 Ambassador from the Holy See
46 Certain teacher
47 Onetime sponsor of what is now Minute Maid Park
49 Part of an affair to remember?
52 Latch (onto)
54 Portentous nights
56 Air Force ___
57 It means "white" in Hawaiian
58 Instant

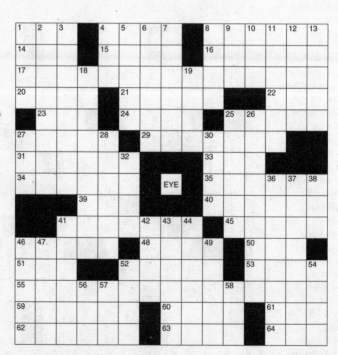

by Timothy Polin

ACROSS

1 Craigslist offering
4 Company with a spokesduck
9 It's gathered during recon
14 Baseball club designation
15 Keynote speaker at the 1984 Democratic National Convention
16 1940s–60s P.M.
17 "Laugh-In" comic
19 "Is Shakespeare Dead?" writer
20 ___ on it (agree)
21 "Chitty Chitty Bang Bang" author
23 Telesthesia, e.g.
25 ___ Disney Resort (original name of Disneyland Paris)
26 Kingdom on old Asian maps
29 Bestow
32 ___ law
36 Daytime host starting in 2012
38 Like the Perseid meteor shower
40 1994 World Cup country
41 Nuts
43 2014 World Cup city
44 Outlets for some small pumps
46 Punk rock icon
48 Twist
49 Also, in Arles
51 Rightmost column
52 Broad sashes
54 Drain
56 One of two acting brothers
61 Drive dangerously, in a way
65 Rival for Federer
66 Noted groom of 10/20/1968
68 City 15 miles from Rome
69 Runs in place
70 Matterhorn, e.g.
71 Precept
72 Life partner?
73 Confident crossword solver's implement

DOWN

1 Amphorae, e.g.
2 It can be a curse
3 ___ Fresh (Tex-Mex restaurant chain)
4 Stuntmen's woes
5 "Sounds dandy!"
6 Take the booby prize
7 King of the gods, in Egyptian myth
8 Bestow
9 Bury
10 Sequel to "Twilight"
11 Cuisine with tom yum soup
12 CNN anchor Burnett
13 Breathing space?
18 Vermont ski resort
22 Rapper with the #1 hit "Money Maker"
24 Fly over the water
26 Arctic seabirds
27 Consoling words
28 Without ___ in the world
30 Take the prize
31 Fatty ___
33 River through Ann Arbor
34 Bar Harbor locale
35 Dark purple fruits
37 Thurman of "Pulp Fiction"
39 Org. with its HQ in Fort Meade
42 YouTube video preceders, often
45 Batman villain who makes decisions by flipping a coin
47 Acts despondent
50 Log-in info
53 Highest and lowest black key on a piano
55 Up to one's neck (in)
56 Unit of currency in the Harry Potter books
57 Oscar winner Blanchett
58 Point before "game"
59 Give up
60 Caffeine-yielding nut
62 "Now!"
63 Word that becomes its own synonym if the last letter is moved to the front
64 "NFL Live" airer
67 Safety measure

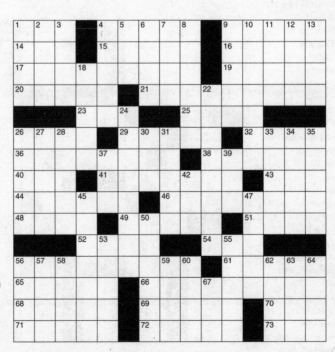

by Joel Fagliano

ACROSS

1 Belief system founded in China
7 Dessert wine . . . also what can fill the square at the crossing of 50-Across and 51-Down
11 Baseball Hall-of-Famer Roush
14 G.M. navigation system
15 Eins und zwei
16 Negative conjunction
17 Spark
18 ___ shui
19 Shade provider?
20 Relied (on)
21 "The Governator"
23 Explorer John
24 Shot out diffusely
27 Reds, for short
29 One putting off retirement as long as possible?
31 Bogotá bears
33 Warring, say
34 Not tacitly
38 Pie piece?
40 Emphatic confirmation
41 Brain tickler
42 Gush (over)
45 Critic Richard
46 Game with scouts and miners
49 Three-time Hart Trophy winner
50 Bumbled verbally
53 Standard
55 Biblical land
56 Kitchen gadgets
59 Furthermore
60 'Vette roof option
63 Maupassant's first novel
64 The Tigers of the N.C.A.A.
65 Western tribe
66 Gomez of "Ramona and Beezus"
67 Discernment

68 Comedian Sahl . . . also what can fill the square at the crossing of 1-Across and 1-Down
69 Downers, in brief

DOWN

1 Work hard
2 Actress Bancroft
3 Showbiz nominations
4 1986 rock autobiography
5 Glossy fabric
6 TV character who "will never speak unless he has something to say"
7 Sharable PC file
8 Resource in the game Settlers of Catan
9 Lead role in the film "La Cage aux Folles"
10 Scrooge
11 "Return of the Jedi" battle site
12 Watson's creator
13 Titular judge played by Stallone
22 Nervous one?
24 ___ Pepper
25 Fraternity letter
26 Bar fig.
27 N.Y.S.E. listing . . . also what can fill the square at the crossing of 24-Across and 25-Down
28 Golfer Aoki
30 Sir ___ Holm
32 Rest of the afternoon
35 Roulette choice
36 One at a keyboard
37 1841 rebellion leader . . . also what can fill the square at the crossing of 56-Across and 56-Down

39 Blind jazz piano virtuoso
40 ___ Group (Dutch banking giant)
42 Word repeated before "away"
43 Put away
44 Not single
47 Have as a tenant
48 View sharer
50 Union wage
51 Flowering plant
52 Excessive
54 What's on the fast track?
56 Sign of neglect
57 Milieu of 49-Across
58 Vast expanses
61 The Who's "Love, Reign ___ Me"
62 Sea-Tac setting: Abbr.

by Damon Gulczynski

ACROSS

1 "Aladdin" villain
6 Newton, e.g.
10 Ernie known as "The Big Easy"
13 "That's ___"
14 Make a point, perhaps
15 Word before dog or dance
16 Endothermic
18 Mike and ___ (candy)
19 Former Brit. Airways vehicle
20 Humorist Frazier frequently found in The New Yorker
21 Number of drummers drumming, in song
23 Birth place
28 "___ Place"
30 Free ticket
31 First-stringers
32 Rack-it game?
34 It may be attached to a windshield, in brief
37 Life-size likeness of Elvis, maybe
41 Start to sneeze?
42 Some are liberal
43 Devoutness
44 Resident of Riga
46 Carol kickoff
47 A fan might need one
52 Fragrance
53 Former Giant Robb ___
54 "Independence Day" vehicle
57 Utter
58 Unaffected by emotion
63 Feature atop the pyramid on the back of a dollar bill
64 Fontana di ___
65 Blade brand
66 "The Joyous Cosmology" subj.
67 Pit
68 Dr. Larch's drug in "The Cider House Rules"

DOWN

1 ___ of Life
2 Part of a Latin exercise
3 Popular retirement spot
4 Weaponize
5 One serving under Gen. 60-Down, informally
6 The Huskies of the N.C.A.A.
7 Affirmative action
8 Pique condition?
9 Roosevelt and Kennedy
10 'Enry's fair lady
11 Magic, e.g., once
12 Eschew frugality
14 Increase dramatically
17 Legal encumbrance
22 Punch lines?
24 Just slightly
25 Final "Romeo and Juliet" setting
26 Nanos, e.g.
27 Baby powder ingredient
28 Clip
29 Touchdown data, for short
32 Series opener
33 Leftover bit
34 Splits the tab
35 When repeated, miniature golf
36 Ocular malady
38 Part of a stable diet
39 High hairstyle
40 Level
44 The Eagle that landed, e.g.
45 Puts into law
46 Trouble spots?
47 Sitting stand
48 They can see right through you
49 Played (with)
50 How many bootlegs are sold
51 Fanta alternative
55 Grandly celebrate
56 Fragrance
59 Stibnite, for one
60 See 5-Down
61 Swinger in the woods?
62 Cellar dweller

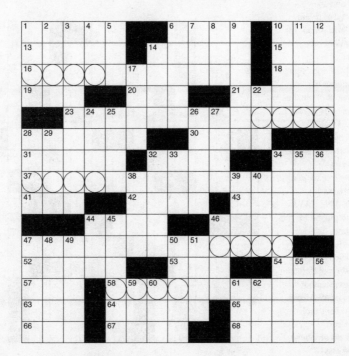

by Patrick Blindauer

ACROSS

1 Atlantic City hot spot, with "the"
4 Line out of N.Y.C.
8 Badge, maybe
13 ___ Nazir ("Homeland" character)
14 Lettuce
16 Black Sea getaway
17 Land on the Black Sea: Abbr.
18 Film lead character featured in a Disney World attraction
20 Dines
22 Put down
23 Pizazz
24 Remark about the end of 18-Across
26 Hamlet's parts
28 They're often seen with bows
29 By and by
30 Recoiled (from)
31 Kind of printer for home or office
36 Kit ___
37 School door sign
38 Mideast inits.
39 Remark about the end of 31-Across
42 1%, say
44 Bucolic settings
45 Short-story writer Munro
46 One that sucks at work?
49 2000 N.L. M.V.P. who played for the Giants
52 Kind of jacket
53 Politico Mo
55 Owner of Half.com
56 Remark about the end of 49-Across
59 Saddler's tool
60 Bar stock
61 "F" accompanier, perhaps
62 Arctic explorer John
63 XX
64 Was attractive
65 Turk. neighbor

DOWN

1 Tibia connections
2 "Er, yeah, regarding what happened . . ."
3 Things that zip up to go down?
4 Subj. of an Austin library and museum
5 Mosul residents
6 Appear over?
7 Did some garden work
8 Tube inits.
9 Where a photographer might take shots?
10 Unpleasantly pungent
11 View from Valence
12 Bros
15 Connecting inits.
19 Alternatives
21 ___-Coburg and Gotha (former British ruling family)
25 Soft spot
27 Land on one side of Lake Titicaca: Abbr.
29 Hardly inept
30 Item attached to a boot
31 Angle
32 Base for some Chinese art
33 Trendy features of some high-end gyms
34 Eroded
35 It may have a ring collar
37 Dress to wow
40 Four-time Indy 500 winner
41 Little, in Lille
42 Dobby, e.g., in the Harry Potter books
43 Modern verbal crutch
45 Blazing
46 They may accompany trains
47 Ghost story?
48 Certain cocktail, informally
49 Leto of "My So-Called Life"
50 Hunter who says "Be vewy vewy quiet"
51 Texas city named for a president
54 Notre-Dame-___-Champs (Paris Métro stop)
57 Ply
58 Fresh

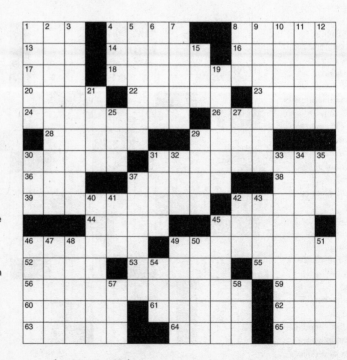

by Ian Livengood

ACROSS

1 Highly intelligent invertebrates
7 1970s–80s sketch comedy show
11 Josh
14 Brazen promoter
15 Hound's quarry
16 Veiled words?
17 Kingship
18 Shop door sign
19 Second-highest pinochle card
20 Get an ___ (ace)
21 Not showing much life
23 German greeting
25 Transcription, e.g.
27 ___ Millions (multistate lottery)
28 47, for Ag
29 Pick up on the innuendo
33 Yoga surface
36 Arctic ___ (migrating bird)
37 Vientiane native
38 Adage regarding skittishness
43 Prefix with cortex
44 Luxury hotel name
45 Private investigator, in old slang
46 "Charlotte's Web" rat
49 Pre-K song start
53 ___ fixe
54 A little less than 100%
57 Toes the line
59 Egyptian dam site
60 Discouraging words
61 Inventor's award
62 Fiber-yielding plant
64 Croupier's workplace
66 E-tailer's address
67 Watson who played Hermione Granger
68 "Hey"

69 "That inverted Bowl," per Edward FitzGerald
70 The "cetera" of "et cetera"
71 Heading on a baseball scoreboard

DOWN

1 Home of the Senators
2 Associate
3 Retire for the evening
4 Ear: Prefix
5 Atoner
6 Memorable hurricane of 2011
7 What a constant channel-surfer may have
8 Lt.'s superior
9 One less than quattro
10 "Ben-Hur" theme

11 Plant with fluffy flower spikes
12 Writer's block buster
13 End of a doorbell sound
22 Business card abbr.
24 "That's awful!"
26 Heavy reading?
27 ___ badge
30 London's ___ Gardens
31 Slangy turndown
32 Buzz Lightyear, for one
34 Does away with
35 "Takes a licking . . ." brand
38 Prov. on Hudson Bay
39 Bridal bio word
40 With skill
41 Block buster?
42 Green vehicle, briefly
47 Be inquisitive

48 Not the past or the future
50 Mexican hero Juárez
51 Worker with DNA, perhaps
52 Some vacuum cleaners
55 Arm of the sea?
56 Where to see "bombs bursting"
57 Great work
58 Dog's warning
59 Magazine filler
63 Punk rock subgenre
65 Belarus, until 1991: Abbr.

by Paul Hunsberger

ACROSS

1 Sports star who lent his name to a clothing line
8 Rental car extra, for short
11 Flipper, say
14 Culminations
15 Mauna ___
16 Bucolic setting
17 Ability to survive freezing temperatures?
19 Copier page size: Abbr.
20 Cette fille, e.g.
21 Con
22 "Shoo!"
23 ___ Bator
24 Selected a certain fabric softener?
27 911 maker
29 Roof window
30 Family pet name
31 Beauty
34 Tests that consist of five subjects, for short
35 Sprite who helps you find a shopping vehicle?
38 One shouldn't have a big head
41 Posthumous inductee into the Poker Hall of Fame, 1979
42 Lifesaver, briefly
45 Opposite (from)
48 Lose face
50 Super-choosy about timepieces?
53 English composer Thomas
54 Help for a do-it-yourselfer
55 ___ Pince, librarian at Hogwarts
56 Fill
57 Anesthesia option, for short
58 Like M&M's . . . or four words to describe 17-, 24-, 35- and 50-Across?

62 Grp. advising the president
63 "From ___ Zinc" (vitamin slogan)
64 FedEx form
65 Narcs' org.
66 S.F. hours
67 Basis of the Hanukkah story

DOWN

1 Sneakers, typically
2 Ill-fated mission of 1967
3 Arrests
4 "___ Nut Gone Flake," celebrated 1968 Small Faces album
5 You might get credit for this period of work: Abbr.
6 ___ rose
7 Series opener?
8 Secluded spots
9 Modified, as software for a different platform
10 Get hitched
11 "Here, you needn't do that"
12 Like pianos, periodically
13 Ones making sacrifices
18 Way of the East
24 Lead role in "Clueless"
25 Toffee bar brand
26 Bacchanalia
28 One concerned with co. money
32 One concerned with co. money
33 Salma of "Frida"
35 Swamp denizen, briefly
36 Bedtime prayer words after "Now"
37 Abbr. in many a military title
38 Caboose
39 Shadow maker

40 "Fifty Shades of Grey" genre
42 All over the place
43 R&B singer Jordan
44 Entice with music
46 Winter Olympics wear
47 Nursery rhyme couple
49 Certain melon
51 "___ Rappaport" (1986 Tony winner for Best Play)
52 Blackguard
59 Starchy vegetable
60 Early second-century year
61 Hockey's Bobby

by Michael Blake

ACROSS

1 Coastal backflows
9 Strongly criticize
15 Speed trap operators
16 Staunton of Harry Potter movies
17 *Deep trouble, informally
18 Prepare, as leftovers
19 Hobby farm creature
20 Girl in a ball gown
21 More often than not
22 M.Sgt. and others
24 Burst, as a pipe
26 Amiens's river
28 Directive repeated in an aerobics class
29 Recipe amt.
33 Work assignment
35 Dines
37 Luau instrument, informally
38 Hated to death, say?
41 Gets ready to use, an an appliance
43 Lion's place
44 Crash-probing agcy.
46 Thumbs-ups
47 Pop
49 Work on copy
51 Wintry mix
54 Made illicit
57 Puzzle inventor Rubik
58 Kittens come in them
61 ___ alai
63 Dyer's vessel
64 Arriver's announcement
65 *Felon's sentence, maybe
67 Aslan's home
68 School sound system
69 Radiated, as charm
70 F.B.I. files

DOWN

1 Frome and others
2 It's more useful when it's busted
3 *Low-lying acreage
4 Haul to an impound lot
5 Jobs announcement of 2010
6 Hold off
7 God of darkness
8 Pre-Yeltsin-era letters
9 *Deep-sea diver's concern
10 Campaigner's dirty trick
11 Under wraps
12 Name of three Giants outfielders in 1963
13 Kelly Clarkson was the first "American" one

14 The Caspian Sea, as often classified
21 Thoroughly enjoyed
23 Urban haze
25 Six for a TD
27 Yield as profit
30 *Campus transportation, maybe
31 One of a biathlete's pair
32 Where to do 65-Across
34 *Fruity loaf
36 Seeks damages
38 Some are personal
39 Intro to conservatism?
40 Early I.B.M. PC standard
42 Sayers portrayed in "Brian's Song"
45 Life sketch
48 Not skip

50 Selena's music style
52 Captivate
53 Tribal emblems
55 Hawk's home
56 Moves abruptly
58 Word that can follow each part of the answers to the six starred clues
59 Immersive film format
60 Drive-___
62 Midmonth day
65 Camouflaged
66 Prefix with centennial

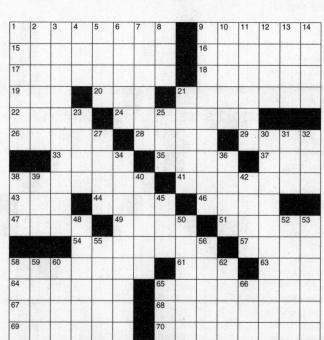

by Victor Fleming and Bonnie L. Gentry

ACROSS

1 It has a red stripe in pool
5 A gross
10 50%
14 Modern pentathlon event
15 Fuming
16 Potential solution
17 Blue-eyed pet
19 Former car-financing co.
20 It sticks out in some joints
21 Neat
23 See 18-Down
25 Not obvious
26 Earned
28 "Slow Churned" brand
31 "___ durn tootin'!"
32 With 29-Down, "golden treasure" in a Bilbo Baggins riddle
33 Wild scenes
35 Bob in the Rock and Roll Hall of Fame
39 Neatnik's opposite
41 Instrument that hints at the missing parts of certain answers in this puzzle
43 ___ Fayed, last romantic partner of Princess Diana
44 Kind of sax
46 Down Under climber
48 Certain shoe shade
49 Cutesy-wutesy affection
51 Oil container
52 Texter's exclamation
53 Part of the British Isles, poetically
56 Thickness measures
58 Darth Vader locale
61 Dance reminiscent of a horse's gait
64 Business opening?
65 Play that was the basis for "Cabaret"
67 Caroling time
68 "30 Rock" character, or the first name of his portrayer
69 Look intently
70 Sailors' domain
71 Like a die
72 Fin

DOWN

1 Annual Car and Driver list
2 ". . . baked in ___"
3 Using for support
4 Car that leaves you with a sour taste?
5 Slam
6 Some tram loads
7 Galifianakis of "The Hangover"
8 Amazon business
9 Take-home
10 Colleges and universities, informally
11 Marketing pro
12 Vaulted
13 Acid-burned Bat-villain
18 With 23-Across, sign, as a contract
22 Marie et Thérèse: Abbr.
24 Like much of Horace's poetry
26 Popular women's shoe seller
27 Check out
29 See 32-Across
30 Left the bench, say
34 Appendectomy memento
36 Drift off
37 Cheese with a red coat
38 Like some circuses
40 Western party wear
42 Model/TV host Heidi
45 "Whither thou goest, I will go" speaker
47 Guadalajara girlfriend
50 Calls on
53 Transition
54 Head nurse on "Scrubs"
55 Creator of Asteroids
57 Lanterns, e.g.
58 Length of a Beatles "week"
59 In ___ rush
60 Hustle
62 Twistable treat
63 Like barbershop harmony
66 Dancer Charisse

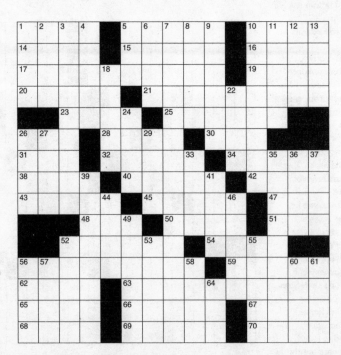

by Tom Pepper and Victor Barocas

ACROSS

1 Long part of a lance
6 Radar screen dot
10 ___-à-porter
14 Actor Quinn
15 Charlie Chaplin's last wife
16 Singsong syllables
17 What Ali Baba found on the treasure in the cave?
20 In the mail
21 Heart of the matter
22 Simple
23 Not supportin'
25 Down Under runners
27 Sign of a failed practice?
33 Baseball exec Bud
34 ___ trap
35 Honour bestowed by Queen Elizabeth: Abbr.
36 Sch. near Beverly Hills
37 Letter closing
39 Bar from Mars
40 Avril follower
41 Grammy-winning blues guitarist Jonny
42 In need of some manscaping, say
43 Puzzles as gifts?
47 Web site that users themselves may revise
48 Many a Rolling Stone cover subject
49 You'll need to take steps to get to it
52 ___ sci
54 Lerner/Loewe musical set in Paris
58 Be startled by singing monks?
61 Suit to ___
62 ___ dire (court examination)
63 Seat for a stand-up
64 Coloratura's practice
65 1990s compacts
66 What a verb ending may indicate

DOWN

1 Suckers
2 Employ
3 Deuce follower
4 1940 Disney film
5 Big bang letters
6 Sound of disgust
7 Digs in an old warehouse, maybe
8 Prevalent, as a rumor
9 Sound of disgust
10 When repeated several times, child's entreaty
11 Sitar master Shankar
12 Stat for 26-Down: Abbr.
13 Stun with a charge
18 Option on "Wheel of Fortune"
19 Arctic language
24 Booking
26 Cascades, e.g.: Abbr.
27 Old Renault
28 Stan's film partner
29 Toupee alternative
30 Lose-lose
31 Car mentioned in the Beach Boys' "Fun, Fun, Fun"
32 Hot, like a hunk
33 Cesspool
37 American, in England
38 Moving stealthily
39 Party in the parking lot
41 Classic shooter
42 Doc bloc
44 Acquires with sticky fingers
45 Crude fleet
46 Guarantor of financial accts.
49 Open a crack
50 Hippo's wear in 4-Down
51 Eliot Ness and others
53 Home of Miami University
55 Wise to
56 Classic muscle cars
57 Archipelago part
59 "The whole family can watch" program rating
60 33rd president's monogram

by Paula Gamache

ACROSS

1. ___ skirt
5. "The Tao of Pooh" author Benjamin
9. One with ergophobia
14. "Look what I found!" cries
15. Kind of tradition
16. "___ talk?"
17. "Good thing I don't have the same problem!"
19. Following
20. River of film
21. 1986 top 10 hit for Billy Idol
23. That's the point
24. Meal at which to drink four cups of wine
25. Part of a pickup line?
28. "___, boy!"
29. Earth goddess created by Chaos
33. Expanse
36. "Apparently"
38. What fell in the Fall
39. That is the question
41. Robert of "Quincy, M.E."
42. One who may need a shower?
44. Holder of a pair of queens
46. Shiner
47. Milk sources
49. N.B.A. Hall-of-Famer Walker
50. Belgian battleground during W.W. I
52. Letters in car ads
54. "Truthfully . . ."
57. Brought up to speed
61. Yokel, in slang
62. Classic rock song in "Easy Rider"
64. G.W. competitor
65. P.D.Q. Bach's "I'm the Village Idiot," e.g.
66. Rep. Darrell of California
67. Like the myth of Ragnarok
68. Luxury hotel name
69. Locale for a Village People hit, informally

DOWN

1. "Scrubs" locale: Abbr.
2. "Don't even think about it"
3. Bats
4. Showed politeness at the front door
5. Certain ring bearer
6. Relative of a gemsbok
7. ___ Schwarz
8. Fictional substance in a Disney film
9. Zodiac symbol
10. U.S.S. Enterprise chief engineer Geordi ___
11. Where reruns run
12. Overly precious
13. Mister, overseas
18. ___ Balls
22. Christmas hymn beginning
24. Events at which people are dead serious?
25. Some pyramids
26. In two, say
27. Ohio city WSW of Columbus
28. It's possessive
30. Some buggy drivers
31. Name on a bottle of Sensuous Nude perfume
32. Half of an old comedy team
34. Caen cleric
35. Butch Cassidy and the Sundance Kid, e.g.
37. Drifts away
40. Quaker product
43. Chardonnay feature
45. "Whatever!"
48. Fancy suite amenity
51. In and of itself
52. Ball mate
53. Mr. ___
54. What's not for big shots?
55. 38-Across's genus
56. "Ah, my Beloved, fill the Cup that clears" poet
57. "I say" sayer
58. Menu section
59. Threat ender
60. Time of 1944's Operation Neptune
63. ". . . goes, ___ go!"

by Evan Birnholz

ACROSS

1 Exposure units
5 Like many a superhero
10 Cheater's sound, maybe
14 Biblical twin
15 First in a line of Russian grand princes
16 Jazzy James
17 & 20 Story by 42-Across on which the movie "Blade Runner" is based
21 Best-suited for a job
22 Kind of lily
23 Cold war foe, slangily
26 Cause of a dramatic death in Shakespeare
27 Go ballistic
28 Displace
31 Music magazine founded by Bob Guccione Jr.
35 Disloyal sort
36 Like bits of old music in some new music
39 Keats creation
40 One going for a little bite?
42 Author Philip K. ___
43 XXX
45 Cleanse
47 Auctioned investments, in brief
48 Affright
51 Eat, eat, eat
54 & 59 Story by 42-Across on which the movie "Total Recall" is based
60 Together, in Toulouse
61 Swiss miss of fiction
62 African antelope
63 "Shane" star Alan
64 Put back in the fold
65 "Gnarly!"

DOWN

1 Request after a failure, sometimes
2 Since
3 Christine ___, heroine of "The Phantom of the Opera"
4 Light that darkens
5 Club
6 "Let's take ___"
7 Competition category in bridge and skating
8 Break off a relationship
9 Kind of brake
10 Noncommittal response
11 Andrew Carnegie's industry
12 Author Madame de ___
13 Home of the N.H.L.'s Lightning
18 Accountants put them on the left
19 Mil. awards
23 Humorist Bennett
24 Like some contraceptives
25 Remote button
26 Bruiser
28 Ascap rival
29 It's scanned in a store, for short
30 U2 song paying tribute to an American icon
32 Sulk
33 Run while standing still
34 Takes home
37 Throw in
38 View from Budapest
41 Ready for battle
44 Cares for maybe too much
46 "___ expert, but . . ."
47 "One ringy-dingy" comic
48 Ghastly
49 "Bleeding Love" singer Lewis
50 Astringent
51 Bird that's as small as it sounds
52 Beatnik's "gotcha"
53 Sparkly rock
55 Essen's river
56 Like hurricanes in January
57 Three-time N.H.L. All-Star Kovalchuk
58 "u r so funny . . . lmao," e.g.

by Jason Flinn

ACROSS

1 Full of tears, say
4 Thanksgiving song
9 Behind
13 Name that's one syllable in English, two syllables in Japanese
14 Sister of Melpomene
15 Copy, briefly
16 "Was ist ___?"
17 Custodial tool
19 Put out
20 Literary March
21 Comic Meadows formerly of "S.N.L."
22 "___ to Apollo"
23 Needed
25 Basic process of genetics
28 Keenly awaiting
29 Currency superseded by the euro
30 Actor McShane
31 Some keep waiting for them
32 "Listen, ___ the sound be fled": Longfellow
33 "Phooey!"
35 Abbr. at the bottom of a letter
36 All the time?: Abbr.
39 Prefix with week
41 Rapper ___-E
43 Repetitive inits.?
44 Dweller in ancient Persepolis
45 Clover locale
46 Self-titled platinum album of 1986
47 Eligible to be called up
48 Like many breakfast cereals
51 Oxygen's electrons, e.g.
52 Cousin
53 Relative of Mme.

54 Global economic org.
56 Tie one on at dinner, maybe
57 Inconceivable
60 Spanish bear
61 Singer Rimes
62 Lycée attendee
63 Traditional
64 Constellation next to Hercules
65 The hare, notably
66 G, e.g.

DOWN

1 Show eager anticipation
2 Native
3 Common site for 36-Across
4 Brake, e.g.
5 ___ lily
6 Noël Coward play

7 Football stat.
8 Cosa ___
9 Nectar detector
10 Common site for 36-Across
11 Inscription on stained glass, maybe
12 "The New Yorker" cartoonist Ed
15 Doesn't leave
18 Xbox competitor
24 Some legal bigwigs: Abbr.
26 "Anything else that you require?"
27 Leader of ancient Troy?
29 It may leave a sour taste in your mouth
34 Peripheral basilica feature
36 Revered Chinese figure

37 Athenian general who wrote "History of the Peloponnesian War"
38 2002 Salma Hayek film or its title role
40 Nonspeaking role on "CSI"
42 Last of 26
44 Comfy footwear, briefly
46 Paint type
48 Halloween prop
49 Like some fancy sauces
50 Procter & Gamble brand
51 Tender
55 "Gangway!"
58 Chain in biology
59 Band with the '79 album "Discovery"

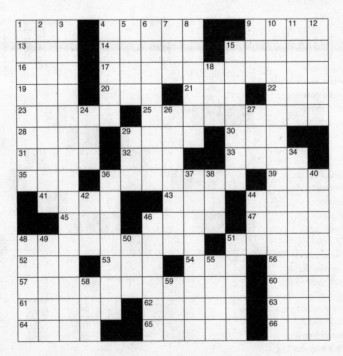

by Jeffrey Wechsler

ACROSS

1 Creator of Fearless Fosdick
7 "This is bad"
11 Word part: Abbr.
14 Kind of pork on a Chinese menu
15 What's to eat
16 Cedar Rapids college
17 Blow away singer Johnny?
19 National Dog Day mo.
20 Navigational aid
21 Name on some euros
22 Mountain goat's perch
23 Boars?
27 "In the end the pressure got to me"
30 Bluffer's words
31 What may precede one
32 "You wish!"
33 Sounds of relief
35 Call it quits . . . with a hint to 17-, 23-, 48- and 56-Across
40 Western treaty grp.
41 First Chinese dynasty
42 Inspiration for a "Jackass" stunt, maybe
43 "No acting up!"
45 Ticked off
48 Sala?
50 Salt Lake City athletes
51 Zwei cubed
52 Bub
55 "Jeez Louise!"
56 Toddler raised on chocolate?
60 Slip-__ (some shoes)
61 Removal from harm's way, for short

62 Hotelier Helmsley and others
63 Hwy.
64 Warrior princess of TV
65 J.F.K.'s W.W. II craft

DOWN

1 Like most car radios
2 Showgirl in the song "Copacabana"
3 Many a city dwelling
4 Volcano on Kyushu
5 Telephone system hacker
6 Rock that may float
7 End of a lame pickup line
8 "You wish!"
9 Med. scan
10 Cry that may accompany fist-pumping
11 Frightens off
12 Words on a 20-Across at a mall
13 Hosiery brand that sponsored women-only 10K races
18 Biogenesis scandal nickname
22 Hellenic X
23 U2's frontman
24 Shore dinner entree
25 Indy racer Luyendyk
26 Ex-president who swore in President Hoover
27 Digging, so to speak
28 One sharing living space
29 Practical smarts
32 One-time link
34 Anchorage-to-Nome racer
36 "Hang on a sec!"

37 Currently airs
38 Spiders' nests
39 Lamar who married a Kardashian
44 Navigational aid, for short
45 Angel or enemy preceder
46 Totally useless
47 "Give me a sec"
48 Bookstore section
49 First to stab Caesar
52 Ranchero's hand
53 Simple quatrain form
54 Dermatologist's concern
56 Put the whammy on
57 Time to revel
58 Sought office
59 Go for apples

by Samuel A. Donaldson

ACROSS

1 Z3 maker
4 Onetime N.F.L. star nicknamed Joe Willie
10 Challenge in "Legally Blonde," for short
14 "Phooey!"
15 San ___, Argentina
16 D-Day objective
17 Distance at St. Andrews golf course?
20 Org. of which 18 U.S. presidents have been members
21 Hindu life lesson
22 Base figs.
23 Cost of mail from Manhattan?
27 Statue in the Parthenon
28 Itching
29 "___ Nature, red in tooth and claw . . .": Tennyson
30 Arcturus, e.g., spectrally
34 Places docs wear smocks
35 Wing, e.g. . . . or a hint to answering 17-, 23-, 49- and 56-Across
38 White House fiscal grp.
40 Stuffed animal option
41 "The Beverly Hillbillies" dad
44 One way to play something
47 One on a Facebook News Feed
49 First-aid supply for Springsteen?
53 Morsel
54 Summer camp sight
55 Aunt in "Bambi"
56 Top-secret proverb?
61 Drain
62 Actor Martin of 1960s–70s TV
63 "___, non verba" (Latin proverb)
64 Vase handle
65 Looks bad?
66 Forerunner of Bach?

DOWN

1 Shot from a certain gun
2 Source of the line "Something wicked this way comes"
3 Elite group
4 Zip
5 "___ reminder . . ."
6 Capital whose main street is Nezavisimosti
7 Tally
8 "___ Remember"
9 Like a speaker with a 25-Down
10 Trip inits.
11 Reel
12 Locale of a 1956 fight for independence
13 Low digits
18 Diggs of "Rent"
19 Pro ___
23 Writer Hentoff
24 Like a private peeling potatoes
25 See 9-Down
26 Pulitzer winner James
31 William Shatner's sci-fi drug
32 Year abroad
33 Dietary std.
35 Aid in a scam, e.g.
36 ___ Romeo
37 Only U.S. senator with a unit of measure named after him
38 Noted Ohio conservatory
39 "Good heavens!"
41 Dada pioneer
42 Listening, say
43 Onetime White House inits.
45 Slow pitches have them
46 Adjusts one's sights
48 Picked out of a lineup
50 In conclusion, in Cannes
51 Decorative fabric
52 Designer Geoffrey
53 Numerical prefix
57 One of two possibilities to Paul Revere
58 German article
59 "___ Poetica"
60 Abbr. after some professionals' names

by Gary J. Whitehead

ACROSS

1 Keystone place
5 Some vacation spots
10 Uttered, as a farewell
14 Carnaby Street's locale
15 Brown, in a way
16 Gershwin's "Summertime" is one
17 Tornado monitors?
20 AOL or MSN
21 Like Mao's "little" book
22 Tito, the King of Latin Music
23 Deg. from M.I.T. Sloan
25 Note in a poker pot
28 Cafeteria stack
29 What the only detective on a case has?
33 "It ___ over till . . ."
34 Improve, as one's manners
35 Prefix with classical
38 What a bouncer may confiscate
40 Makes tough
42 Medevac destinations, briefly
43 New British royal of 2013
47 Smelling salts holder
48 What a remorseful Iago might have said?
50 Send as payment
53 Classic car whose name is a monogram
54 ___ Antiqua
55 Draw out
57 Get into
59 Wash. neighbor
62 Doubleheader . . . or what 17-, 29- and 48-Across are?
66 To be, to Béatrice
67 Make blond, maybe
68 Primordial ___
69 Spanish province or its capital
70 Fraternity letter
71 Band with the 1987 hit "Need You Tonight"

DOWN

1 Sparkling Italian export
2 Toils on a trireme
3 High-pitched group with a 1958 #1 hit, with "the"
4 Yuletide interjections
5 "Point taken"
6 Rush-hour subway rider, metaphorically
7 Director Jean-___ Godard
8 Ordinal suffix
9 Flow slowly
10 Business with an enticing aroma
11 Fight site
12 Like some looks and laundry
13 Slacks off
18 Disneyland vehicle
19 Often-breaded piece of meat
24 ___ noire
26 Shot-to-the-solar-plexus sound
27 Reuters alternative
29 It may have outdoor seating
30 "That is so not true!"
31 Happy Meal with a Sprite, e.g.
32 Beginning
35 "Lost in Yonkers" playwright
36 Airline that doesn't fly on the Sabbath
37 Kon-Tiki Museum city
39 Outfielder's cry
41 In perpetuum
44 Legendary Boston Garden skater
45 Part of a Reuben
46 Half a police interrogation team, maybe
48 Make queasy
49 Pend
50 Revolting sort
51 Make up?
52 Prefix with brewery
56 Clock sound
58 Gumbo need
60 Pierre's pair
61 Deadly snakes
63 Deadly snake
64 Peak next to a glacier, maybe
65 "Just ___ suspected"

by Robyn Weintraub

ACROSS

1 Become comfortable with
8 Spots for dipping, once
15 Bought more Time?
16 Reads with effort
17 Danced to Julio Sosa music, say
18 One-third of a French revolutionary's cry
19 She who says "si": Abbr.
20 QB targets
21 Like the women in a famous Rubens painting
22 Hepster
23 QB goals
24 Investment house employee
28 Trap
32 Either of two N.F.L. coaches named Jim
33 Lift
35 One vote in Vichy
36 Unwelcome reversal . . . or a title for this puzzle?
40 It might come after sex
41 Singer/actress Lenya
42 "This guy walks into ___ . . ."
43 China collections
45 What the Beatles had but Wings didn't?
48 Actress Gardner
49 Flotsam or Jetsam in "The Little Mermaid"
50 Blazing
53 Nasdaq unit: Abbr.
54 Prefix with color
57 Contemptuous one
58 Bridge type
60 Uranium 235, e.g.
61 Chenoweth of Broadway's "Wicked"
62 Some slow dances
63 Necessitates

DOWN

1 Field of many nonprofits
2 Prayer starter, often
3 Karina in many a Jean-Luc Godard film
4 Square ___
5 & 6 Mutual relationship
7 Track figures
8 Dangerous time
9 & 10 Critical comments
11 Shoe shiner
12 Asgard ruler
13 Head of the Seine?
14 Green Bay-to-Greenville dir.
22 Paella ingredient, perhaps
24 Scope
25 Prop for many a western
26 Something made in a chocolate factory?
27 "___ life"
28 ___-day calendar
29 End of an era?
30 What pulls out all the stops?
31 ___ nous
34 Tinnitus treater: Abbr.
37 & 38 One who may give you a lift
39 Bomb
44 Pay tribute to
46 & 47 Means of getting home, maybe
50 To boot
51 Dupe
52 "___ Tu" (1974 hit)
53 Benefit
54 New World monkey
55 Churn
56 Sights at many interstate exits
57 Small story
59 LAX patrollers

by Peter A. Collins

ACROSS

1 Derby features
6 James who wrote "The Postman Always Rings Twice"
10 Golden Fleece transporter
14 State-named avenues in Washington, essentially
15 Plot part
16 Zig or zag
17 First-stringers
18 Obits, basically
19 A penny is a small one
20 Start of a quizzical Bob Seger lyric
23 "___ chance!"
24 Employed pols
25 Pin holders
27 Hams it up for the camera
29 With 46-Across, song containing the lyric in this puzzle
31 Dowdy one
34 Venomous snake
35 Mark of mediocrity
36 Spy novelist Deighton
37 Lyric, part 2
41 H, to Homer
42 Interject
43 "Scream" director Craven
44 Performed satisfactorily
46 See 29-Across
49 Buttinsky, e.g.
51 Wrap brand
52 Submit to gravity
53 Bawls
57 End of the lyric
61 Race pace
62 Watched warily
63 Good and steamed
64 Clinton's attorney general
65 Stage solo
66 Lorelei, notably
67 Mideast port
68 Plenty
69 Passed out

DOWN

1 Muscles
2 Pi, for one
3 Latin clarifier
4 Soccer superstar
5 California's ___ Valley
6 Cruise ship accommodations
7 Tums' targets
8 Monopoly token
9 Site for brooding
10 Sporty Studebaker
11 Gave up
12 Figure out
13 Load from a lode
21 Go after 13-Down
22 Mauna ___ Observatory
26 Fajita filler
28 Original "America's Next Top Model" airer
29 Shade of blond
30 Student no.
31 Heels alternative
32 Like Lucille Ball
33 Too pink, say
34 Sympathetic sounds
38 Fess (up)
39 Made one
40 Passing thoughts, for short?
45 "I swear!"
47 Be a servant to
48 Neither Rep. nor Dem.
49 Bamboo lovers
50 Teamwork spoiler
52 Yarn unit
54 "Butterfield 8" author
55 Some kind of nut
56 Hägar's dog, in the funnies
58 Shipshape
59 Newbie
60 Feral
61 ___-la-la

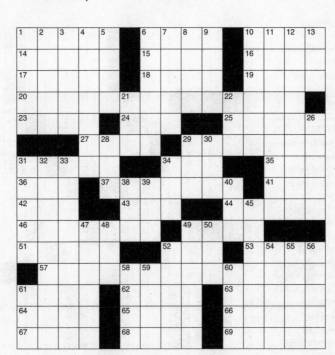

by Nancy Salomon

ACROSS

1 Pepperdine University site
7 "___ little spice to your life"
11 Rotund
14 1950 Asimov classic
15 You name it
16 Blood-type letters
17 Each animal has one in "Old MacDonald Had a Farm"
18 Crux
19 Excessively
20 Shakespearean bird call
23 Devils and Angels, e.g.
27 Highest score in baccarat
28 Many an office has one
29 Forearm part
30 Learns
32 "Laughed myself silly!"
34 National Poetry Month
38 Set of advantages
39 National airline of Afghanistan
40 Request on a memo from the boss
41 Advice of patience
44 Like some chest pain
46 X ___ xylophone
47 Engrave
50 Ones making pantry raids?
51 They usually have two runners on
52 Radar's hometown, in "M*A*S*H"
55 Kind of tax
56 Been in bed
57 Officially choose
62 Epilogue
63 Prong
64 Item literally useful in reading the answers to 20-, 32-, 41- and 52-Across
65 Late July birth
66 Linear
67 Nutso

DOWN

1 Start to take?
2 ___ nouveau
3 Mauna ___
4 ___ Saud, founder of Saudi Arabia
5 Yahoos
6 Jazz venue
7 Worry
8 "Stop procrastinating!"
9 Close pitch
10 No pro
11 Islamic declaration
12 "It's ___ time!"
13 Kind of fairy
21 N.Y. Liberty's org.
22 Ward site
23 Ballet apparel
24 Sneak off
25 Win by ___
26 Dolphinfish
30 Grazed
31 Italian port
33 Yemeni port
35 Bring up
36 Grants-___
37 Many yards
39 Azores locale: Abbr.
41 Bolivian underground?
42 Off-key
43 Kiln
45 "Sir ___ and the Green Knight"
47 Oil holder
48 Rope
49 Unit in a multiunit building
51 Seattle athlete, briefly
53 Low woman
54 Scot's tops
58 Legendary stick figure
59 Eng. neighbor
60 Feminist org. since 1966
61 "___ me!"

by Daniel C. Bryant

ACROSS

1 Fudge maker?
5 Iowa's ___ Society
10 Asian nation suffix
14 A lot?
15 Like early PC graphics
16 Mall aid
17 Start of a quip
20 Big bird
21 Source of iron
22 Pound sound
23 Some are famous
27 Unearthly
30 Elvis trademark
31 Induce rain from
33 Claimer's cry
34 Grant-in-___
36 Milky Way and others
38 City, state, ___
39 Quip, part 2
43 "Yo!"
44 Times to revel, maybe
45 Not the handsomest dog
46 Surface figure
48 Ones who've gone splitsville
50 Circus Maximus attire
54 Vas deferens and others
56 Place for carved initials
58 Top guns
60 Circus Maximus greeting
61 MP3 player maker
62 End of the quip
67 ___ of the earth
68 "You've got mail" hearer
69 Lily family member
70 Four-time Indy winner
71 Rotten
72 Uncool sort

DOWN

1 Boutonnieres' places
2 One found just around the block?
3 Pique
4 Account overseer, for short
5 Car discontinued in 2004
6 Grounds crew
7 "Exodus" hero
8 Bring home
9 Pasty-faced
10 Like hair at salons
11 Gold medal, e.g.
12 Lunched
13 Opposite of paleo-
18 Like some women's jeans
19 ___ time (course slot)
24 Hotfoot it
25 Demeaning one
26 Use wax on
28 Egyptian sacred bird
29 Empath's skill
32 Coffeemaker style
35 Went off the deep end?
37 Sing "K-K-K-Katy," say
39 Big silver exporter
40 Nice things to look at
41 Counter call
42 1974 Marty Feldman comic-horror role
43 Took to the cleaners
47 For no profit
49 Ready for dinner
51 Fountain sound
52 Hold fast
53 Did toe loops, say
55 "Quiet!" locale
57 Part of the mnemonic for EGBDF
59 Started a triathlon
62 Hip-hop "cool"
63 Noted resident of the Dakota
64 Milne marsupial
65 Off one's feed
66 Actor McKellen

by Paul Guttormsson

ACROSS

1 One born near the Butt of Lewis
5 Dish eaten with a spork
9 Dark-skinned fruit
13 One-sixth of an inch
14 Lose power
15 Football Hall-of-Famer Ronnie
16 Helpful multiple-choice answer
19 "I think we should"
20 "Later"
21 Important licensing org.
22 Chums
23 Helpful multiple-choice answer
30 Much of suburbia
31 Bit of butter
32 Nomadic warrior of the Old West
33 Sugar suffix
34 Darn
35 Swiss Alp
37 Helpful multiple-choice answer
41 Life instinct, to Freud
42 Aves.
43 Echevarría who played Santa Ana in 2004's "The Alamo"
46 Prepare for a wild ride
50 Helpful multiple-choice answer . . . or is it?
52 "True!"
53 Inventor, of a sort
54 Cheers
55 Opening for peace talks
56 Trees used to make archery bows
57 Baseball's Eddie, 1952 All-Star for the Senators

DOWN

1 Fix, in a way
2 Formally honor
3 Newspaperman Arthur ___ Sulzberger
4 Car brake light holder, once
5 It's often flipped
6 Sweetheart
7 Arbor leader
8 Diver's duds
9 Least straightforward
10 Mentally sluggish
11 Roman emperor for just three months
12 Accusatory words
17 Divisions
18 Cold war enemy
22 Muscle
23 Like-minded individuals
24 Creator of the Tammany Hall tiger
25 The America's Cup trophy, e.g.
26 They're guarded at the Olympics
27 Boss of fashion
28 Calif.-Fla. route
29 Like the Sahara
34 Kind of pie
35 Seconds
36 Printing on some cigar wrappers
38 Chicken
39 Charlie's Angels, e.g.
40 Fragrant compounds
43 Computer menu option
44 Whiskey fermenter
45 Requester of "As Time Goes By"
46 Writer of "Saint Joan"
47 Word before field or shirt
48 Name on many prints
49 Diet of worms locale?
51 Draw

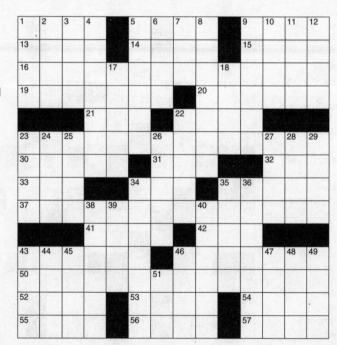

by Patrick Merrell

ACROSS

1 Flipper, e.g.
5 Butting heads
11 W.W. II spy org.
14 Fit to serve
15 Stick together
16 Some drops
17 Spot in the top tier
19 ___ de France
20 Hot spot
21 "Nova" network
22 Not fresh
23 Without support
24 Up to, quickly
26 Rope fiber
27 "Ben-___"
28 When wadis fill
32 Pellets, e.g.
34 Speed (up)
35 Accidental occurrence
36 1941 Cary Grant tearjerker
41 It may have periods
42 Capek play
43 Church part
45 Letterhead feature
50 Burden
51 Hoodwink
52 Poetic contraction
53 Ill-suited
55 Cabinet dept. since 1965
56 Host of an annual convention attended by publishers: Abbr.
58 Hut material
59 Public-house offering
60 Measure of a company's dominance (and a literal hint to 17-, 28-, 36- and 45-Across)
64 Circle meas.
65 Cause of weird weather
66 "The heat ___!"
67 Master hand
68 Lie atop
69 Backpack item, maybe

DOWN

1 Court ploy
2 Struggling, as a pitcher
3 The Velvet Fog
4 He said "Knowledge is power"
5 Retin-A treats it
6 Poodle, perhaps
7 Startled cries
8 With all one's heart
9 Evoking an "eh"
10 Lot sights
11 Rotten to the core
12 Deal with commercially
13 It touches the Gulf of Bothnia
18 Recovered from
23 Brainstormer's cry
24 Haberdashery stock
25 2, to ½
26 Where "besuboru" is played
29 Indo-___ languages
30 He-Man's toon sister
31 Caesar's end?
33 Time to get back to work, maybe
37 Big D.C. lobby
38 One kicking oneself
39 Record collection
40 1996 Madonna role
44 Tel. no. add-on
45 Black key
46 Eyepiece
47 Got by
48 Pines
49 Spending restraints
54 Like a rare baseball game
56 Part of VISTA: Abbr.
57 Bundle up
58 Oodles
61 Emergency ___
62 Musician Brian
63 Tolkien creature

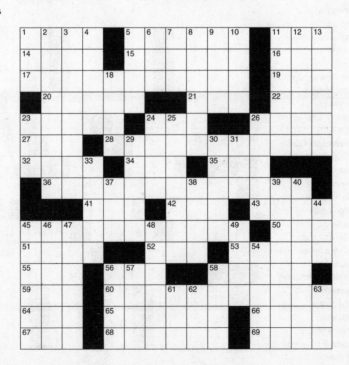

by Levi Denham

ACROSS
1 Pixels
5 Jaguars, e.g.
9 1942 movie with the song "Love Is a Song"
14 Setting for "The Plague"
15 Popular cookie
16 Each
17 Slayer of Ravana in Hindu myth
18 ___ ball
19 Aches
20 "Star Trek" genre
23 Refers (to)
24 Herald reader
28 Private line?
29 Bottom line
30 "But, ___ was ambitious, I slew him": Brutus
31 Literary oceans
33 Swinger's opportunity
34 Turntable, speakers, etc.
38 Lightly maul
39 "I've had enough!"
40 Slang expert Partridge
41 Hoosier cabinet wood
42 Lie alongside of
47 All-purpose
49 One way to win
50 Places to get online without plugging in
52 Finger ___
55 Tribe associated with the Seven Cities of Cíbola
56 "That'll be the day!"
57 Zippy
58 Kind of sch.
59 Pool path
60 Breakwater
61 ___ as a blue rose
62 Mythology anthology

DOWN
1 Quai ___ (French foreign office locale)
2 Magic 8 Ball, e.g.
3 Many Sri Lankans
4 Mix-ups
5 Degree recipient
6 Sectors
7 Coastal predator
8 Romantic notes
9 Raft material
10 Marine greeting
11 Door sign
12 Snare
13 Tags
21 "Hurray for me!"
22 Marksman's skill
25 Bibliophile's citation, for short
26 At the drop of ___
27 Bottom line
29 Precious mettle?
32 Pistol, in slang
33 Early zoology topic
34 One leading a chase
35 Victor's cry
36 Turn toward sunset
37 Break for games
38 Dowel
41 Ox
43 Get up after a multiplayer football tackle
44 "Aww"
45 Largest city on Belgium's coast
46 Coca-Cola product
48 Unsafe
49 Faux pas
51 Hip activity?
52 Presidential inits.
53 Make, altogether
54 Box with a manual

by Manny Nosowsky

ACROSS

1 Auto parts giant
5 They may be vaulted
10 Sharp or flat, say
13 Does in
14 Timely benefits
15 Cap-___ (from head to foot)
16 Bureaus
19 It may have electroreceptors
20 Dances with chairs
21 Rhinestone feature
22 Gooey stuff
23 Co. that offers I.M.'s
24 It usually starts "How many . . . ?"
31 Puts out of work
32 Like "Green Acres"
33 Bushy 'do
36 Appear
37 Glass ingredient
38 "Dracula" author Stoker
39 Gunpowder, e.g.
40 Navy elite
41 Assault on Troy, e.g.
42 2003 Nicolas Cage film
45 Hood's piece
46 Sr.'s exam
47 Barely enough
50 Liquid-Plumr competitor
53 Red-white-and-blue inits.
56 Their initials can be found consecutively in 16-, 24- and 42-Across
59 Diner sign
60 1978 Peace Nobelist
61 Some mayhem
62 Common title
63 It may be skipped
64 Fair

DOWN

1 "Good one!"
2 Have a hankering
3 Floor it, with "out"
4 Long-eared equine
5 Take in
6 D
7 Soft seat
8 There are two in a loaf
9 Part of an empire up to 1991: Abbr.
10 Crude group?
11 Send packing
12 Suffix with slug
15 Win in ___ (triumph easily)
17 "___ Amore"
18 "What ___ Believes" (Doobie Brothers hit)
22 Classic 1954 sci-fi film
23 Comet competitor
24 Telephone book, essentially
25 ___ fixe
26 Flash of light
27 Husband of Bathsheba
28 Slow times
29 City of Brittany
30 Violinist Zimbalist
34 Fury
35 Straw in the wind
37 Sunnis, e.g.
38 Hog, so to speak
40 Condoleezza Rice's department
41 New England catch
43 A de Mille
44 Set off
47 ___ cell research
48 Reduce to carbon
49 Word with fine or visual
50 "Dang!"
51 Make over
52 "___ example . . ."
53 Popular computer operating system
54 "Hold everything!"
55 Concerning
57 Ltr. addenda
58 "But I heard him exclaim, ___ . . ."

by Adam G. Perl

ACROSS

1 Orenburg's river
5 Untouched?
9 Pond dross
13 Red Cross headquarters site
14 "Some Like ___"
15 Cry of dread
16 Gulf state royalty
17 Mount Whitney's home
19 Nancy, in Nancy
20 Formicide: ant :: pulicide : ___
21 ___ Hirsch of "Lords of Dogtown"
22 1950s–60s twangy guitarist
25 Skating competition
27 Name in a Shakespearean title
28 Responses to tattooers
30 Something that's bruisable
31 Started (off)
32 Item at center stage
34 Hudson River city
35 Singer with a 1962 #1 hit that started a dance craze (and a hint to this puzzle's theme)
38 Stain blockers
41 It may be free for philosophers
42 "Dream on!"
45 "Ti ___" (Casanova's declaration)
46 Stay-at-home ___
47 Head of a flock
49 Froth
51 Aft
54 "The Brady Bunch" housekeeper
56 Extirpate, with "out"
57 1983 Indy winner Tom
58 Button holders
60 Much of Us Weekly

61 Smart
62 Come (from)
63 Long, long time
64 Interjects
65 Concert highlight
66 Something that's bruisable

DOWN

1 Where the shilling is money
2 Get back on
3 Enliven
4 Actor Burton
5 Kept in a pen
6 Each
7 Postal motto conjunction
8 To be, overseas
9 The merry widow, in the 1934 musical "The Merry Widow"
10 "Gigi" co-star

11 Experience
12 Bygone bird
14 The ___ Brothers of R&B
18 Hearing aids?
20 Gucci rival
23 Seasonal songs
24 Hayseed
26 ___ sauce
29 Prekindergarten
32 Crete's highest peak: Abbr.
33 "___ wait"
34 Electric dart shooter
36 Its slogan used to be "One mission. Yours."
37 Restaurant employee
38 What hist. majors pursue
39 Stuck
40 Broad way

43 "Take this job and shove it!"
44 Betrothed
46 Art style, informally
47 Went with
48 Deep fissure
50 Hands, slangily
52 Come in second
53 Classic sculpture
55 Spanish form of "to be" after "tú"
58 Test-conducting org.
59 ___-Magnon
60 Neighbor of Iran: Abbr.

by Bonnie L. Gentry

ACROSS

1 Crop up
6 Service leader
11 Cricket club
14 Like some eclipses
15 Detective Pinkerton
16 "___ you sure?"
17 Amphitheater cover?
19 Contest of sorts
20 Sharp as a tack
21 Macadam ingredient
22 O'Neal of "Peyton Place"
23 Temperamental sort
25 Pitchfork features
27 Gore and Hirt
30 Coins found at a dig?
34 Takes off
36 Genetic letters
37 Engine unit
38 Swarm member
39 Spa offering
42 Lee of Marvel Comics
43 Packed away
45 Prospector's need
46 Julia's role in "Ocean's Twelve"
47 Prefight ceremony?
51 A.A.R.P. part: Abbr.
52 Overthrow, e.g.
53 Dirty look
55 Deimos orbits it
57 ___ Irvin, who designed the first cover for The New Yorker
59 On the hook
63 William Tell's canton
64 Calm at a wrestling match?
66 Pewter, in part
67 "___ World Turns"
68 Children's refrain
69 Put out
70 Questionnaire category
71 Played over

DOWN

1 Thomas ___ Edison
2 Wishes undone
3 J., F. or K.: Abbr.
4 Tijuana toast
5 Like the Kama Sutra
6 Na-goodnik
7 Came to rest on a wire, e.g.
8 Sounds during wool-shearing
9 East Los Angeles, e.g.
10 Helpful contacts
11 Saturday night hire, often
12 Field
13 11-Down, frequently
18 They're dangerous when they're high
22 Stand up to
24 Ballerina Pavlova
26 Pro Bowl org.
27 Tattered Tom's creator
28 Maui neighbor
29 Little bit
31 Hose shade
32 Get on
33 Surrealist Max
35 Has the tiller
40 Picture holder
41 San ___, Tex.
44 Bergen's locale: Abbr.
48 Ranger's domain
49 Year-end decoration
50 Cow that hasn't had a cow
54 Flaxlike fiber
55 Kennel club rejectee
56 Star turn
58 Need an ice bag
60 Schooner filler
61 Luke Skywalker's sister
62 School on the Thames
64 Kung ___ chicken
65 Suffix with auction

by Randall J. Hartman

ACROSS

1. Kind of gun
4. Catalyzing subatomic particles
9. Singe
13. Father of octuplets on "The Simpsons"
14. Picture to carry around?
16. Knock over
17. Clowns' wear
18. Pipe fitting
19. O.T. book
20. It has many pages
21. Skull and Bones member, e.g.
22. Receivers of manumission
25. Dobbin's "right"
26. Cape ___, Portugal (continental Europe's westernmost point)
28. Pocket filler
30. Link
31. Flashlight backup
36. Title for this puzzle
40. Brunch option
41. About
44. "___ I Can Make It on My Own" (Tammy Wynette #1 hit)
45. Grade schooler's reward
46. German pronoun
47. Animal that can be ridden
51. Soprano Marton
52. Not tied up, as funds
56. Ring of plumerias
57. Like Duroc hogs
58. Leader in sports
61. Put the kibosh on
62. Makeup carrier
63. Set
64. CPR deliverers
65. Wedding reception party?
66. Emerson's "___ to Beauty"

DOWN

1. Rushed headlong
2. Mission commemorated on the back of the Eisenhower dollar coin
3. Subject of annual Congressional budget debate
4. ___-Argonne offensive of W.W. I
5. Open, in a way
6. Gambling inits.
7. Highlands negative
8. Camera types, for short
9. "Shake a leg!"
10. Takes one's turn
11. Threshold for the Vienna Boys' Choir
12. Switch in the tournament schedule, maybe
14. Scans ordered by M.D.'s
15. Suffix with glass
23. Adipocyte
24. Fretted instrument
27. Words with thumb or bum
29. Car making a return trip?
30. Storage units
32. Sweet drink
33. Like staples
34. Tylenol alternative
35. Canyon area
37. Holmes to Conan Doyle, e.g.
38. Like soda crackers
39. Not choose one side or the other
41. Lead-in to a questionable opinion
42. Two bells in the forenoon watch
43. Freshly worded
48. Pool problem
49. Reagan attorney general
50. Leeds's river
53. Gremlins and others, for short
54. Little, in Leith
55. "A Wild ___" (cartoon in which Bugs Bunny first says "What's up, Doc?")
59. 60s war zone
60. U. of Md. is in it

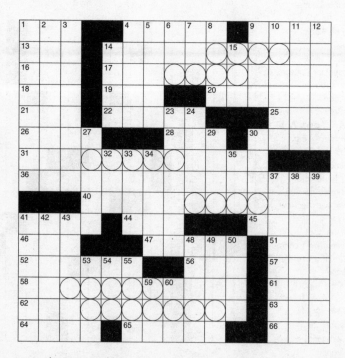

by Byron Walden

ACROSS

1 See 24-Down
5 Easy ___
10 Mental keenness
14 Nebraska native
15 Unlikely to defect
16 "The Plague" city
17 Bandleader known for 55-Down
19 Seine feeder
20 Many Tyson finishes
21 Capek play
22 "Gullible's Travels" writer
24 URL ending
25 Cemetery, informally
26 Up
29 Judd of "Taxi"
30 Vestments, e.g.
31 Big jerk
32 1926 Channel swimmer
36 Suffix with psych-
37 Open, in a way
39 Start of many Hope/Crosby film titles
40 Philippine locale in W.W. II
42 ___ Gratia Artis
43 A bunch of
44 Absorbed, in a way
46 Krone spenders
47 Zigged and zagged
50 Door sign
51 Conestoga driver
52 Guff
53 Atlantic City mecca, with "the"
56 "Vidi," translated
57 Bandleader known for 47-Down
60 St. Petersburg's river
61 Kegger wear, maybe
62 "Mockingbird" singer Foxx
63 Colored like a certain hound

64 Blow hard
65 Daimler partner

DOWN

1 Varsity letter earner
2 Words of agreement
3 Part of R.S.V.P.
4 Poetic contraction
5 Vinyl collectible
6 Go parasailing
7 Cries of regret
8 Entruster of property
9 Under-the-sink items
10 Bandleader known for 25-Down
11 "Three Sisters" sister
12 Stun gun
13 Bergen dummy
18 Fox or turkey follower
23 Invoice abbr.
24 Bandleader known for 1-Across

25 See 10-Down
26 "A Girl, A Guy and ___" (1941 Ball movie)
27 "Later"
28 Old chap, say
29 Barbarous one
31 Lunch counter orders
33 Horse coloring
34 Pool path
35 Breyers rival
38 Verb with thou
41 Interminable time
45 Transplant
46 Johnny who played Willy Wonka
47 See 57-Across
48 Surgery tool
49 Tequila source
50 The "Divine" Bette
52 Cry in a mudslinging contest
53 Trident part

54 Call from the flock
55 See 17-Across
58 Actor Tognazzi
59 Thorax protector

by Ed Early

ACROSS

1 With 71-Across, breakfast choice . . . or a punny hint to this puzzle's theme
6 River in a 1957 hit movie
10 SALT topic
14 Singer/actress Luft
15 Boss Tweed lampooner
16 ___ avis
17 Midwest hub
18 Eye
19 Words after "come" or "go"
20 Mark down for a sale, say
22 Model's path
24 "Lawrence of Arabia" figure
27 Spotted
28 Angel dust, briefly
30 Ore tester
32 "Amo, amas, I love ___"
34 Cut crosswise
38 Slangy affirmative
39 Make scents of?
42 Cry of derision
43 Hot desert wind
45 Yankees manager before Girardi
47 F.D.A.-banned diet pill ingredient
50 Thrice, on an Rx
51 With 35-Down, fictional heroine who says "I am no bird; and no net ensnares me"
53 Augustus ___
55 Hit for Guy Lombardo in 1937 and Jimmy Dorsey in 1957
57 Jewish or Iranian, e.g.
61 Make
62 Auden or Aiken
65 [Bo-o-oring!]

66 Swarm member
67 Layer of the eye
68 Singers James and Jones
69 Hard thing to carry
70 Meal for a weevil
71 See 1-Across

DOWN

1 Dona ___ (1976 Sonia Braga role)
2 Architect Mies van der ___
3 Like much folklore
4 Things that lead to mergers?
5 Billy Blanks fitness system
6 Small hills
7 Tail movement
8 Talking with one's hands: Abbr.
9 Roman road

10 Laundry staff
11 Request for group permission
12 Jones once of the Stones
13 Oodles
21 Tikkanen of hockey
23 Newsgroup system since 1980
25 Erik of "CHiPs"
26 Husband, in France
28 "No more!," e.g.
29 ___ Crunch
31 Bosox nickname of old
32 Sorrowful cries
33 Melodramatic series, in slang
35 See 51-Across
36 Mystery author John Dickson ___
37 Everyday article
40 Morse unit

41 10 sawbucks
44 The Ricardos, to the Mertzes
46 Italian city that is the title setting of a Walpole novel
48 Prom tux, usually
49 Japan's largest active volcano
51 Actress Pflug
52 Pianist Claudio
54 Photographer Adams
55 ___ lily
56 Digital book file extension
58 ___-Rooter
59 Give ___ (care)
60 Gershwin opera heroine
63 Egg head?
64 Fish contained in unadon

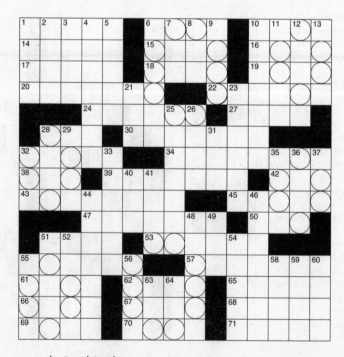

by David Steinberg

ACROSS

1 Spin doctor's concern
6 Mediterranean spewer
10 Sobriquet for Haydn
14 Gabbed away
15 Not fer
16 Drive away, as a thief?
17 With 21-Across, there's no . . .
19 Fall shade
20 Joanne of westerns
21 See 17-Across
23 Hard to miss
27 Sings in the Alps
28 Taters
29 It may be hard on a construction worker
32 Alley button
33 Dish served with a lemon wedge
34 Good source of potassium
36 There's no . . .
41 Brought up
42 "Little" boy of early comics
44 Bring a smile to
48 ___ Lingus
49 Take it off, take it all off
50 Shiny cotton fabric
52 "Told ya!"
54 With 59-Across, there's no . . .
57 "___ we there yet?"
58 School with King's Scholars
59 See 54-Across
64 Tabula ___
65 Asian princess
66 Company that took over Reynolds Metals in 2000
67 Lousy eggs?
68 Quartz type
69 Former Japanese capital

DOWN

1 Lyricist Gershwin
2 Raincoat, for short
3 Mandela's org.
4 "Sure, why not?!"
5 Accustoms
6 Bother, with "at"
7 Abbreviation said with a "Whew!"
8 Bogotá boy
9 Steamed
10 Memorial Day event
11 Takes advantage of, say
12 Mortar's partner
13 Swear (to)
18 Taker of vows
22 Service reading
23 Pressure cooker's sound
24 Each, slangily
25 Break in the action
26 Comedian's Muse
30 Licorice-scented herb
31 "Any ___ ?"
34 Arthur of "The Golden Girls"
35 ABC newsman Potter
37 Angler's basket
38 Sneakily
39 Trifling
40 Namer of a representative to OPEC, maybe
43 Unlock, to a poet
44 Rearward
45 Drink made with curaçao
46 Maximum
47 Interpreted to be
49 Run of luck
51 Funny-car fuel
53 Something that may be seen in a bank
55 Genghis ___
56 Start of a kid's counting rhyme
60 Fotos
61 Prefix with friendly
62 "___ so!"
63 The way of the Chinese

by Philip Thomson

ACROSS

1 Semifluid material
6 Enchantress, in Shakespeare
9 Put a belt on
13 Why and wherefore
15 Prefix with logical
16 "Old" ship's name
17 Big name in printers
18 2005 Samuel L. Jackson biopic
20 George who wrote "Fables in Slang"
21 De bene ___ (legal phrase)
22 Preoccupy
23 Controlled
24 Recording medium, for short
25 Humorist Shriner
26 Go through
28 Many a stained glass window
31 Eyelashes
32 Same old, same old
36 Without a break
37 Time in advertising
38 Knocked on the noggin
40 Mineral suffix
41 28-Across, e.g.
44 Some notes
45 Lap again
48 Foreign dignitary
49 "The Lord of the Rings" extra
50 Ones getting Secret Service protection
52 Acronym since 1941
54 Private talks
55 Bud protector
56 Uncover
57 Innocence locale
58 Some job hunters: Abbr.
59 University of Maryland, informally

DOWN

1 Going for, with "at"
2 "Domani" singer Julius
3 Wedding reception cry
4 Because
5 Do slam-dancing
6 Really enjoyed oneself
7 A's, e.g.
8 Beau ___
9 Dental problem
10 "Wow!"
11 Land that declared its independence on 11/11/1965
12 Words said before shaking hands
14 Ratatouille ___
15 Hound, say
19 "Reading" ability
25 Bang-up
27 Appear on the scene
28 Where Bob Dylan was born: Abbr.
29 Prefix with propyl
30 Kitchen containers
32 "Liza With a Z" Emmy winner
33 Like some income
34 1975 Edward Albee Pulitzer-winning play
35 Takes, as an exam
39 "Vox populi, vox ___"
41 Key of Mozart's "Odense" Symphony
42 Anger
43 Rendezvous
46 Leaders of class struggles?
47 Host Jules of E!
48 Not play subtly
51 Without ___ (dangerously)
53 Jersey wearer, maybe

by Brendan Emmett Quigley

ACROSS

1 One-liner, e.g.
5 Fighting
9 Fabrics for uniforms
14 Golden rule preposition
15 Canon creator
16 "That smarts!"
17 Depict a card game?
19 Hawke of film
20 "___ Fly Now" ("Rocky" theme)
21 Genesis locale
23 Believer's suffix
24 Sign-off
25 "CSI" airer
27 1976 Sally Field role
30 Depict an improv routine?
34 Rah-rah sort
36 Illusory works
37 James Brown's genre
38 Foul moods
41 Like centenarians
42 Scintillas
44 Holstein, e.g.
46 Depict part of the periodic table?
49 "Cool!"
50 "Concentration" pronoun
51 Lose zip
54 Down
56 One more time
58 Shaping tool
60 Confesses
63 Depict suds?
65 Site of Joan of Arc's demise
66 Hideous sort
67 Show one's teeth?
68 Chip maker
69 "Forget about it"
70 Christian Science founder

DOWN

1 Dog show V.I.P.
2 Ken Lay's company
3 Put up with
4 Crier's place
5 Blood typing system
6 Pauses
7 Knocked off, in a way
8 Beat, as wheat
9 Salon item
10 Raise a stink?
11 Way back when
12 Diagonal
13 Posted, say
18 Baseball card buys
22 Where B'way is
26 Track action
28 "You stink!"
29 Airbag activator
30 Comfort giver
31 It may be organized
32 Keene sleuth
33 Ongoing accounting fig.
34 Knuckle-dragger
35 Utter
37 Pose
39 Sci-fi subject, or a 1970s dance
40 Knocked off, in a way
43 Lunar plain
45 Kowtowed
47 Zeta follower
48 "White Fang" author
51 Knight's need
52 On top
53 Far from sterile
54 Delhi wrap
55 Doorbell-ringing company
57 "It follows that . . ."
59 French religious title
61 Minute
62 The Coneheads' show, for short
64 Ticket add-on

by Levi Denham

ACROSS

1 "Just ___"
5 Kodak rival
9 Put away
14 Vaquero's view
15 Show off, like Mr. America
16 Product first used commercially in toothbrush bristles
17 ___ Sea, outlet for the Amu Darya
18 Honest
19 Polish
20 See circles
23 Road hazard in Frankfurt
24 Doesn't bother
28 See circles
34 One of the sons on "My Three Sons"
35 Friedrich ___, first president of the German Republic
36 Univ. applicants, typically
37 Kitchen canful
38 U.S. military planes
39 Substitute position
40 "Lord, is ___?"
41 Subjects of research, e.g.
42 Sun block
43 See circles
46 Title words repeated in a 1974 song after "Como una promesa . . ."
47 Monte Leone, for one
48 See circles
55 "When it comes to . . ."
58 Leave
59 Prefix with knock or lock
60 "The Price Is Right" announcement
61 Indian melodic pattern
62 Poker declaration
63 Last-minute birthday recognition
64 Big name in theaters?
65 Lean

DOWN

1 Key of Beethoven's Symphony No. 7: Abbr.
2 Hospital fluids
3 Actor Morales
4 Modern means of character recognition?
5 From the top
6 Dale
7 Guinness entry
8 Toll unit
9 Minimal postage hike
10 M.L.B. team with a bridge in its logo
11 Land in un fleuve
12 Swindle
13 Dissolve
21 Part of the cyberworld
22 10-Down, e.g.
25 Affirmative in the lyrics of "Penny Serenade"
26 Concerned
27 Check again
28 One of five Spanish kings
29 Sen. Robert Byrd, for one
30 Green
31 Stop, perhaps
32 Steel bar
33 Mind-set?
38 Housewives, abroad
39 Female rocker with the 2003 hit "Why Can't I?"
41 Spayed
42 Actor Kilmer and others
44 What a B'way show might have
45 Big source of state revenue
49 Actress Austin
50 Final, say
51 Gulf of ___, arm of the Baltic
52 "Lean ___"
53 Certain Monopoly sq.
54 Peewee
55 Many a Monopoly sq.
56 Cyst
57 Its state flower is the orange blossom: Abbr.

by Michael Shteyman

ACROSS

1 1980s Chrysler product
5 Totally lost
10 No-goodniks
14 Coin tossed in the 15-Across fountain, nowadays
15 "Three coins . . ." fountain
16 Genesis victim
17 Unwelcome visitor
19 "Friends" spinoff
20 "My Cousin Vinny" star
21 Wavy design
22 Duplicates, for short
25 Totally crush
28 They may be pulled off
30 Blue-ribbon
31 Likewise
32 Good thing to be in
34 Some four-year degs.
37 Fellow in a 1944 Johnny Mercer song hinted at by 17-, 25-, 47- and 57-Across
41 Worker's check
42 Photo finish
43 ___ Domini
44 Jumbo, for one
45 Miscellaneous task
47 Tenacity
52 Treasury div.
53 Dodge 1-Across
54 V formation members
56 Rolling rock?
57 Like a bad apple
62 Highlight?
63 Fragrant resin
64 Maven
65 Fish caught in pots
66 Hem in
67 Fall locale

DOWN

1 Bud holder, maybe
2 Mangy mutt
3 ___ Ben Canaan, Leon Uris hero
4 Nail-biter's opposite
5 Bikini events
6 Tiny amount
7 Photo tone
8 67-Across figure
9 It's inspired
10 Wheedle
11 Bubbling
12 Combine name
13 More artful
18 Not play
21 Painter of haystacks
22 Rocky, twice
23 Salsa queen Cruz
24 Weenie
26 Weasel word
27 Reader's goal
29 Slurrer, perhaps
32 See 57-Down
33 Report letters?
34 1970s cinematic canine
35 ___ Wences
36 Hoity-toity sorts
38 Eastern V.I.P.'s
39 Bring down
40 Roll of dough
44 Drags through the mud
45 Moving on, say
46 1950s sitcom name
47 Like some starts
48 Ticked off
49 Ken-L Ration competitor
50 Cruel sorts
51 "C'mon, my turn!"
55 Rim . . . or trim
57 With 32-Down, places to browse
58 Cry of approval
59 Broadway nightmare
60 Before of yore
61 Wimple wearer

by Seth A. Abel

ACROSS

1 Watchdog org.?
6 Gets mushy
11 Nasdaq listings, for short
14 Horizon standout
15 Farm letters?
16 Squishee seller on "The Simpsons"
17 Where to home-shop for French couture?
19 Kauai keepsake
20 Bookbinding leather
21 "___ a date!"
22 Give the brush-off?
24 They can be hurled at people
26 Bloody Mary alternatives
27 Miss America Myerson and others
28 Dickens character with a metallic voice?
29 Old Tokyo
30 Some roulette bets
32 Alpine stream
33 Start of a British poet's card game?
36 Sailing
39 Positive end
40 Citrus ___, Calif.
43 Desk clerks, bellhops, maids, etc.?
46 Angry with
48 Turn into something else
49 Spanish island
50 Letter
51 "Frisco ___" (1945 crime drama)
52 Impend
53 Military org. that had roots in the Easter Rising
54 Nokia, in the telephone business?
57 L'Adriatique, par exemple

58 Great deal
59 Confrontation
60 Long introduction?
61 Answers, quickly
62 Proposal parameters

DOWN

1 Attribute
2 Acted amorously
3 Pioneering collagist
4 Titan dethroned by his son
5 Post-Manhattan Project org.
6 Supermarket section
7 One from Germany?
8 Quarterback Dawson
9 Connected (with)
10 Like some oaths
11 Flockhart of "Ally McBeal"
12 Alfresco

13 "No problem here"
18 Makes an unwanted pass at
23 Like a good subject
25 Big name in late-night
26 Botch
28 In thing
31 Left speechless
33 Russian summer retreat
34 Bombs produced in the 1950s
35 Almost eternity
36 TV Guide info
37 Not a good looker?
38 Catch
40 Scheherazade, for one
41 New York's ___ State Parkway
42 Filaments' structures
44 Sought, as office

45 Field of vision?
47 Amass
49 Principal pipes
51 Lose it
55 Sen. Reid's home: Abbr.
56 Big hits: Abbr.

by Randolph Ross

ACROSS

1 Busch Gardens locale
6 Enervates
10 Tête-à-tête
14 Modern source of pass-along jokes
15 Legal claim
16 Too smooth
17 For the ___
18 "Things are great for me"
20 Long march
21 Hotfooted it
22 Little laugh
23 #1 hit for the Crystals
25 Eerie ability
26 Pay, with "up"
27 Belief system
29 C.I.A. forerunner
32 Odds and ends
35 Serengeti sighting
36 Vitriol
37 "Quit cryin'"
40 Mailed
41 Whole lot
42 Does toe loops, e.g.
43 Army Corps of Engrs. supply
44 Source of an androgyne's confusion
45 Window ledge
46 Alley ___
48 Kipling's comment about "The Liner"
53 "Peter and the Wolf" bird's name
55 Suffragist Carrie Chapman ___
56 Award for Samuel Beckett
57 Track cry after "and"
59 "Absolutely Fabulous" mom
60 "Aha!"
61 Old Harper's Bazaar illustrator
62 Abacus wielder
63 Curtain holders
64 ___-majesté
65 Netizens

DOWN

1 Tithing fraction
2 Subject for an Italian aria
3 Prides of lions?
4 Criticize analytically
5 Happy hour order
6 Pass
7 Evangelist ___ Semple McPherson
8 Pitching, in a way
9 ___-Cat
10 Two-scoopers, e.g.
11 Acme
12 Lip balm ingredient
13 Little kid
19 Particular
21 Able to feel
24 One may be skipped
28 Get by (on)
30 Sour fruit
31 Finishes, with "up"
32 DOS part: Abbr.
33 "Fargo" director
34 Deteriorate
35 Martini ingredient
36 Undoubtedly
38 Game summary
39 Tulsa's locale: Abbr.
44 Butt heads
45 Fixed charge
47 "That's for sure"
49 Weapon handles
50 "___ With Me" (popular hymn)
51 Car on a train
52 A long time
53 Hurly-burly
54 "I get it now"
58 Fish lacking a pelvic fin
59 ___ de Cologne

by Manny Nosowsky

114 ⭐⭐

ACROSS
1 Hate or fear follower
5 Accra's land
10 Held up
14 Actress Skye
15 Like some beans
16 Golf club
17 Pen denizens
18 Jumped between electrodes
19 Retin-A treats it
20 Jungle crusher
22 Hostile incursion
24 Line C, maybe, in a voting booth: Abbr.
25 Bullet point
26 Quaint contraction
29 All there is
33 Fish in a John Cleese film
34 Inner: Prefix
35 It may follow a cut
36 Justice Fortas
37 Athrob
40 Badge issuer, for short
41 Kind of crime
43 Court statement
44 Phantom's haunt
46 Ready to freak out, maybe
48 Stable parents
49 Pencil-and-paper game
50 Brain scan: Abbr.
51 Response to "Gracias"
54 Brezhnev's successor
59 Scads
60 Busey and Coleman
62 Actress Conn
63 Bring under control
64 Excite
65 Maple genus
66 Caught some rays
67 Philosopher Georges
68 Miss Liberty, e.g.

DOWN
1 Santa ___
2 "Tell me more"
3 Sicilian city
4 Cancel
5 Thou
6 Source of a thundering sound
7 Chad's place
8 Family tree word
9 Ell, maybe
10 Moved like army ants
11 Bonkers
12 Mrs. Chaplin
13 Joined at the altar
21 Draft status?
23 Calif. neighbor
25 ___ rubber
26 Mop wielders
27 Something to kick
28 Lend ___ (listen)
29 Still not happy
30 Direct elsewhere
31 Buffalo skater
32 Walt Disney's middle name
34 Those girls, in Grenoble
38 Forces out of the spotlight
39 Stupid oaf
42 Gave a goofball
45 Asian shrines
47 Groundskeeper's supply
50 Bygone auto
51 Bygone auto
52 Pizazz
53 Iditarod terminus
54 1981 hit film with a 5'3" lead actor
55 Wall St. letters
56 Early Briton
57 Old music halls
58 Patience, e.g.
61 "I'll take that as ___"

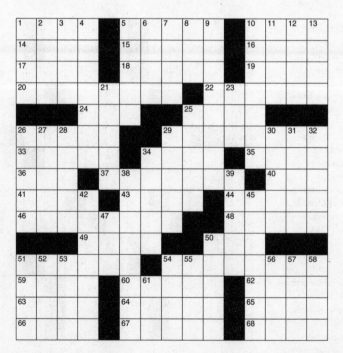

by David Pringle

ACROSS

1 Tear open
6 Made like
10 Take on
14 Composer Camille Saint-___
15 Farming community, e.g.
17 Camel
19 Legal matter
20 "Uh-oh"
21 Still in the game
22 Averse to
25 Made square
26 Embryonic sac
27 It may be rounded up in a roundup
29 Iona athletes
30 Postage purchase
31 End of another actor's line, maybe
34 Camel
38 W. Hemisphere group
39 A deadly sin
40 Tilter's tool
41 In accord (with)
43 Lewd
44 Stiff
47 It may be drawn
48 Quaking tree
49 NBC's "My Name Is ___"
51 Figs.
53 Camel
57 Elementary particles
58 Go leisurely
59 Wool caps
60 Night fliers
61 Jenny Lind, e.g.

DOWN

1 SALT party
2 Goya masterwork, with "The"
3 They make sense
4 Abbr. on a bank statement
5 Tire letters
6 It's inert
7 Heart, essentially
8 Big times
9 "Dapper" one
10 Semi, e.g.
11 Monte of Cooperstown
12 One of Chaucer's pilgrims
13 Like some seals
16 Split
18 Eight bells
23 Bit of trickery
24 ___ Parker
25 They're caught in pots
26 Soil: Prefix
27 Work out
28 Sizable
30 Hockey's ___ Smythe Trophy
31 Asian cuisine
32 Plain
33 Barbara who played a TV genie
35 It's inert
36 "Gil ___"
37 Go ballistic
41 Pros
42 Lowish voice
43 Uncontrolled
44 "It ___ me!"
45 "The Verdict" actor, 1982
46 It may be found in a den
47 Reporter's badge
49 Italy's Mt. ___
50 On ___ streak (winning)
52 Eye woe
54 Not be entirely truthful
55 Type widths
56 Scatter

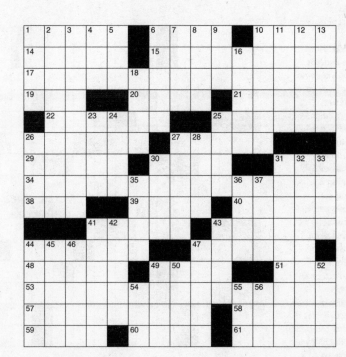

by James R. Leeds

116 ★★

ACROSS

1 Does battle
5 Name preceding "White Label"
11 Afore
14 Help hold up
15 They're often old and wise
16 Frame fillers in a perfect bowling game
17 Exhibited severe embarrassment
20 Latin stars
21 Enfant's dream
22 Hebrides tongue
23 Title role for Anne Baxter, 1950
25 Grimace maker, maybe
27 North Pole, for Santa
31 It might accompany a MS.
32 Stock ticker maker's inits.
33 Underclassman?
36 Dele undoers
40 Employees who once went up, up and away
44 Please, with "with"
45 "Your Future" sign displayer
46 Time unit in basketball: Abbr.
47 Hearing figs.
49 Cheapens
52 Uncommercial periodicals
57 Output of an arachnid
58 Testify
59 Essayist/novelist James
61 Relative of a bolt
65 Approximates the time of completion
68 The Eisenhower years, e.g.
69 Aquatic "grasses"
70 "Housewife" Longoria et al.
71 Teresa and Helena: Abbr.
72 Say forcefully
73 Rear end of a slug?

DOWN

1 Electric guitar effect
2 Tunic toppers
3 Take ten
4 Eyer
5 Ladies' org. since 1890
6 Ems-Weser Canal feeder
7 Had water up to one's ankles
8 Tequila source
9 You push these at bowling alleys and on VCR's
10 Lifeline for srs.
11 Nudge (oneself)
12 Originator of a popular peanut butter cup
13 Dimethyl sulfate, e.g.
18 Not spend
19 Assails
24 Start of North Carolina's motto
26 Relaxation
27 Encouraging start?
28 TV toon Deputy ___
29 Turtledove
30 Embroiders
34 Leachman replaced her on "The Facts of Life"
35 Ethel's sitcom husband
37 Honorifics for attys.
38 Tours head
39 Lith. and Ukr., once
41 Lighted-candle occasions
42 Animal milk source
43 Sketched
48 North and South Dakota
50 Informal letter closing
51 Alphabet start
52 Terrific times, slangily
53 Not let happen
54 Olympian Z's
55 "Criminy!"
56 Durable fabric
60 It flows to the Elbe
62 Rant
63 Guesstimates at J.F.K.
64 Early Hollywood sex symbol
66 High ___ kite
67 The Atl. Coast is on it

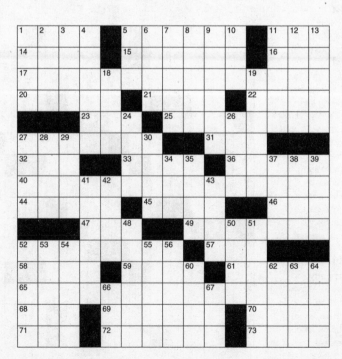

by Patrick Merrell

ACROSS

1 Corday's victim
6 Billiard shot
11 Convenience store sign
14 Classic game company
15 Like World Cup crowds
16 Charles X, e.g.
17 59-Across and others
19 Dispenser of 47-Across
20 Irritate
21 Where to spend kips
22 Mid fourth-century year
24 Results of ties: Abbr.
25 ___-Hawley Tariff Act of 1930
26 Cheer
27 Shelley's "___ Skylark"
28 Old Chevy
31 Professional grp.
34 Comment made while fanning oneself
37 Cyclades island
38 Classic Dickens title (from whose 10 letters this puzzle was constructed)
41 ___ polloi
42 Itsy bits
43 Must
44 Casual walk
46 Show
47 See 19-Across
48 Commandment word
51 ___ Poly
54 Wreck
56 Sail supporter
57 Colombian city
58 Coach Parseghian
59 Ebenezer Scrooge player in a 1951 movie version of 38-Across
62 ___ chi ch'uan
63 Conductor Georg
64 Portuguese colony until 1999
65 Entirely
66 Kind of energy
67 Pile up

DOWN

1 Introduction to economics?
2 On ___ (carousing)
3 "Groundhog Day" director
4 Seed covering
5 Start of a winning combination
6 Major export of Ivory Coast
7 Movie droid, familiarly
8 Perch
9 Stick in the water
10 Tiny Tim's mother in 38-Across
11 Places for theorizers?
12 Shed item
13 Rodolfo's love in "La Bohème"
18 ___ mater
23 Suffix with mini or Web
25 Working poor, e.g., in 38-Across
27 Rocky hill
28 1980s–90s TV nickname
29 Cheer (for)
30 Kon-Tiki Museum site
31 Cries of delight
32 59-Across, e.g.
33 It's usually tucked in
34 "Am ___ believe . . . ?"
35 "Dee-lish!"
36 Joke responses
39 Cards, on the scoreboard
40 Berne's river
45 Commercial suffix with Rock
46 Utah ski resort
48 Trivial
49 "___ mañana"
50 Moving
51 Conspirator against Caesar
52 Popular spy show
53 Line at an airport
54 "Bye now"
55 Spoken
57 Jampack
60 John
61 "Well, ___ monkey's uncle!"

by David J. Kahn

ACROSS

1 Cut closely
6 1970 Neil Diamond hit
11 "___ Adieux," a Beethoven 51-Across
14 Dog-___
15 Conundrum
16 Four-time Japanese prime minister
17 Start of a quote by jazz legend Miles Davis
19 Unlikely to raise one's hand in class
20 Prefix with technology
21 Quote, part 2
23 They may be part of a moving experience
25 Some people at nude beaches
27 So yesterday
28 ___-Cat
31 Medicinal shrub
32 Inscrutable one
35 Rate ___ (perform perfectly)
36 Quote, part 3
41 Villa ___, gold-mining center in 19th-century Georgia
42 Feeling that makes you go "hmm"
43 Appliance brand
45 Tennis ace Shriver
46 Some wampum
51 See 11-Across
53 End, after all is said and done
54 Quote, part 4
58 ___ Bora caves
59 Ewe, for one
60 End of the quote
62 "Thimble Theatre" name
63 ___ Bay, Philippines (site of 1944 fighting)
64 Designer Geoffrey
65 Recipe abbr.
66 Long baths
67 Isn't serious

DOWN

1 In stitches
2 "Oh, yeah, that's funny"
3 Play stations
4 Pertaining to blood vessels
5 Big name in ice cream
6 Side line
7 Alternative to a Twinkie
8 "Beauty ___ the eye . . ."
9 "Unhand me!"
10 Swinging set
11 Heed
12 Means of computer networking
13 ___ sauce
18 They may follow bee stings
22 City in upstate New York
24 "___ we forget . . ."
26 Court-appointed psychiatrist's ruling
28 Pen filler
29 Martial arts expert
30 Wee hour
33 Third degree, often
34 Super Bowl in which the Giants beat the Bills
36 Nest eggs, briefly
37 Hollywood's Dalton and Hutton
38 Good Samaritan's assurance
39 Yemen's capital
40 Part of the back of an orchestra
44 Web sites
47 Admission
48 Some desert homes
49 Historian Will
50 Ground breakers
52 "Are not!" response
53 Hallucinogen
55 Taj Mahal site
56 Nut case
57 Forever and a day
59 Martini guzzler
61 Kind of case, in gram.

by Elizabeth C. Gorski

ACROSS

1 Symbol of blackness
5 Stone of many Libras
9 Radio-active one?
13 Excessive indulgence
14 Monte __
15 Some learning
16 Take it on the lam
18 __ Barak, former Israeli P.M.
19 Sport fisherman's catch
20 Coffee-flavored liqueur
22 Dash
24 Toon's place
27 It's occasionally 5
28 Part of a stereo player
32 Dollar rival
34 Deviate
37 Hideous one
38 Bolt
41 Diuretic's target
42 Place to brood
43 Crate part
44 Make even deeper
45 Grp. formed in Bogotá
47 Cheer syllable
48 Scoot
53 Lamp filler
56 Yule scene
60 Lionel layout, maybe
61 Skedaddle
63 Building toy brand
64 John of the Broncos
65 Susan B. Anthony's goal
66 Give __ for one's money
67 Punta del __, Uruguay
68 River of Flanders

DOWN

1 Go for
2 Sea predator
3 Thickening agent
4 A serous fluid
5 Stroke's need
6 First: Prefix
7 "Cavalleria Rusticana" baritone
8 Lite
9 Some Halloween costumes
10 1922 Physics Nobelist
11 Place for pins
12 Hester Prynne's stigma
14 Chump change, abroad
17 Inside dope
21 Musical Miller
23 Aerosol gas
24 Handle the food for a party
25 Duck
26 Went for
29 Seasonal airs
30 China's Zhou __
31 Doesn't play
33 Pause indicator
35 Suffix with benz-
36 Surface anew
39 Lisbon's river
40 Like taro or sago
46 "No sweat"
49 [Titter]
50 Dye-yielding plants
51 Cereal box fig.
52 Having chutzpah
53 Stimulating nut
54 "Did you __?"
55 Prego competitor
57 __ Bay, Ore.
58 Kind of mail
59 Linda of Broadway
62 __ Bo (exercise system)

by Ernest Lampert

120

★ ★

ACROSS

1 Actress Birch of "American Beauty"
6 Skid row sound
9 Composer Siegmeister
13 Go from 11 to 12, say
14 Red-headed boy of '60s TV
16 Care
17 Classic paradox
20 Like bird flu, originally
21 Spicy condiment
22 An essayist's work is in it
25 Dotted line?
26 Argue forcefully
33 Keeps
34 Windmill part
35 Familiar place for a cat
36 Actress ___ Dawn Chong
37 Spectral
39 Abbr. in a baby announcement
40 Canada's Grand ___ National Historic Park
41 Sylvester's "Rocky" co-star
42 Farm feature
43 Disrespected
47 Like the hills
48 Winner of 2.7% of the 2000 presidential vote
49 Melancholy
53 Diamond and others
56 Is fine in the end
60 Turf
61 Role in "The Sign of the Cross"
62 Like premonitions
63 Goes off on a tangent?

64 Any of the four words hidden in 17-, 26-, 43- and 56-Across: Abbr.
65 Kind of queen

DOWN

1 Patient's need, briefly
2 "What a comic!"
3 Los Angeles's ___ College of Art and Design
4 File box contents
5 Modern capital of ancient Phrygia
6 Babe
7 Wall St. news
8 Magazine figure, for short
9 Ipecac, for one
10 Means of security
11 "Splendor in the Grass" writer

12 Nervous
15 Gas additive
18 1940s–50s All-Star ___ Slaughter
19 Needing to refuel
23 Perambulation
24 Bank problem
26 Change (into)
27 Sentient
28 Show subservience
29 Chief Pontiac's tribe
30 ___ Lowell, title character in a 1980s sitcom
31 Mercury model
32 ___ Downs
37 The only pieces there are exactly three of in Scrabble
38 Not just theoretical
42 Candy ___
44 Italian women
45 Author Ferber

46 Transuded
49 Dog command
50 Glow
51 Was attractive?
52 Pleaded
54 Coin collected by a numismatico
55 Slight
57 Prefix with lingual
58 Opposite of vert.
59 Voice vote

by David Pringle

ACROSS

1 Humble home
5 Software rerelease, e.g.
11 Plane with a machmeter: Abbr.
14 Protagonist
15 Meteor in a meteor shower
16 Spray-paint, maybe
17 Fly off the handle
18 Common computer feature
20 Chemical compound suffix
21 Hatcher of "Desperate Housewives"
22 Bulldog
23 German auto debut of 1974
27 Departed
28 Big name in stationery
29 Longoria of "Desperate Housewives"
31 Long, long ___
32 City near Saint-Exupéry International Airport
33 Frankie with the 1959 #1 hit "Why"
36 It's more than a pinch: Abbr.
37 First person to win a Smarties Prize, for children's books, three years in a row
40 "___ the season . . ."
43 Ohio city named for a mathematician
44 Lends a hand
48 1969 "bed-in" participant
49 Hoops org.
50 "Eat!"
51 Does in
53 Universal recipient type
57 Some game endings
59 Govt. org.
60 Neckline shape
61 Cause of some burns
64 Munich mister
65 Sting
66 Cropped up
67 Melpomene, e.g.
68 Units in a coll. curriculum
69 Least prominent
70 Hightailed it

DOWN

1 Turn from a grape into a raisin, e.g.
2 Progress
3 Automaker Maserati
4 One eye in ;-)
5 Peptic disorder
6 Los Angeles's San ___ Bay
7 Kind of column
8 "It's ___-brainer"
9 Curry of "The Rocky Horror Picture Show"
10 Drainage indicator
11 Show friendliness
12 Cash cache
13 "Rock-a-bye, baby" spot
19 Undeveloped
21 Shack roof material
24 If, and or but: Abbr.
25 They're part of the string section
26 Egg-shaped
30 "Raggedy" one
33 Dutch-speaking part of the West Indies
34 Words, informally
35 Spiked punch?
38 Novelist Kesey
39 Manner of going
40 An overdose of
41 Pro
42 Starts to melt
45 "You win"
46 Varied
47 Showed contempt
50 Like many a home improvement project, for short
52 Driver's license datum
54 Remote control button
55 Fairy tale baddies
56 Bloodhound's guide
58 It may be caught in a filter
62 Ida. neighbor
63 Round Table honorific
64 ___ Pinafore

by Steven Ginzburg

122 ⭐⭐

ACROSS

1 York successor
6 Country addresses, for short
10 Part of an Einstein equation
14 It might start "By the way . . ."
15 Lake ___, south of London
16 Word with black or fire
17 Twig broom
18 Turner of "Somewhere I'll Find You," 1942
19 Not yet final, in a way
20 "The X Factor" judge who wastes money?
23 ___-d'Oise (French department)
25 Directly
26 Eskimo-___ language family
27 Nodding picture?
32 The anesthetic lidocaine, e.g.
33 Obligation
34 Barely makes, with "out"
35 George who once led the C.I.A.
37 Part of the foot
41 Prefix with normal
42 ___ feed
43 Geologist?
48 D'___ (according to: Fr.)
49 Jon Stewart asset
50 Spanish 30-Down
51 Moment after a bad pun?
56 Affluent, in Acapulco
57 Poker cry . . . or an apt title for this puzzle
58 Some family histories

61 Quaint exclamation
62 "___ No Sunshine" (1971 Grammy-winning song)
63 Fraternity letter
64 Start of North Carolina's motto
65 Binge
66 "Lazy" one

DOWN

1 Pop-top feature
2 Consume
3 Bump
4 Cause for opening a window
5 Fix up
6 Late-inning pitching, maybe
7 Assault with a grenade, as a superior officer
8 Actress Merrill of "Desk Set"
9 Diploma feature
10 Crib plaything
11 Sci-fi figures
12 Didn't play
13 Italicize, say
21 Rap's OutKast, e.g.
22 Mouthing off
23 Reprehensible
24 Out of control
28 Empty talk
29 First name in late-night
30 Primary figure
31 Fruitcake
35 Mary Tyler Moore headwear
36 Poetic conjunction
37 Bullish order on Wall Street

38 Deems in court
39 Horoscope figure
40 Animal that howls
41 Home of Galileo Galilei International Airport
42 Some colony members
43 Small shoots
44 Heath plants
45 Out of fashion
46 "Jackson"
47 Draft contents
48 What nouns and verbs must do
52 Farewell in 41-Down
53 Ruler in a kaffiyeh
54 Pinball sound
55 Home of Pearl City
59 ___ loss
60 Start of many Latin American city names

by Pamela Amick Klawitter

ACROSS

1 Convenience store sign
4 "Coming soon" messages
10 Churls lack it
14 Constrictor
15 Convincing, as an argument
16 Confess openly
17 C
19 Cosmos legend
20 Celebrity biographer Hawes
21 Charlotte of "The Facts of Life"
23 Canapé topping
24 Coleridge, for one
27 Curved motorcycle part
29 Criticizes harshly
30 Concluding appearance
32 Clive Cussler's "___ Gold"
33 Coal scuttle
34 Conked out for good
37 Completely wowed
38 Columnist Hopper
41 Comedy series award, maybe
42 Con ___ (animatedly, in music)
43 Countless years
44 Commuter's choice
45 Collects one's winnings
49 Creature at SeaWorld
50 Clarify
52 Closely related
53 Comic strip prince's son
54 Civil rights org. that became a governing party
55 Clerk, to a bus. owner

58 Cole Porter's "___ Do It"
60 C
65 Critic James
66 Come aboard, in a way
67 Comfy retreat
68 Cartoon explorer
69 Cowley and Keats
70 Coach in Little League, often

DOWN

1 "Charlie's Angels" airer
2 Come ___ head
3 Cause damage to
4 Cuts for agts.
5 Circumambulate
6 Cruel person
7 Coloratura's home, with "the"

8 Consequence of a solo homer
9 Cremona collectibles, for short
10 Choose
11 C
12 Crayon choice
13 Coarse wool fabric
18 Concentrates on specific achievement
22 Conceit
24 Cassandra's father
25 "Capitalism" rock group ___ Boingo
26 C
27 Crossest
28 Committed to the truth, in court
30 "Can it!"
31 Cry of grief
35 Capua friends
36 "Chimes of Freedom" songwriter

39 Crosby's "So ___"
40 Cape ___
46 Captors of Patty Hearst: Abbr.
47 Chief
48 City near Cleveland
50 Course before an entree
51 Competitor of Ragú
55 C.I.A. betrayer Aldrich
56 Catch sight of
57 Credit application figs.
59 Coral ___
61 Cardinals, on scoreboards
62 Count up
63 Casserole morsel
64 Close

by Larry Shearer

ACROSS

1 Factory seconds: Abbr.
5 Sights
9 Support
13 "Cool!"
15 Starting fare, often
16 Shield border
17 "Scram!"
18 Practice area, of a sort
20 Get out of a bind?
22 Way to the top
23 ___ Snider, frontman for rock's Twisted Sister
24 Once-in-a-lifetime traveler
27 Figure usu. in hundreds or thousands of feet
28 "Black rat" as opposed to "Rattus rattus"
30 Org. established by Nixon
33 Sorry sort
35 Loudness unit
36 Biblical patriarch whose name means "he will laugh"
37 "What a ___!"
39 Catch
41 Radical Hoffman
42 Low-grade?: Abbr.
44 Hipsters
45 Abridged, for short: Abbr.
46 Northeast, on a map
48 Ditto
50 Delhi wrap
51 Here, in Toledo
54 Silk fabric for scarves
57 Onetime Missouri natives
59 Directories
62 Bygone women's magazine
63 Sharp
64 Humdinger
65 Parade honoree, familiarly
66 Himmel und ___ (traditional German potato dish)
67 Lawless role
68 Sun. deliveries

DOWN

1 About to bloom
2 Catch up with old classmates
3 Half of a showy display?
4 Covered walkway
5 Symbol of power, to the pharaohs
6 Cash substitute
7 Kennel club rejects
8 Railroad track workers
9 Overwhelm
10 Reaches
11 Lee Van ___ (spaghetti western actor)
12 Cigarette brand that sponsored "The Dick Van Dyke Show"
14 Like some oil rigs
19 Egyptian lifeline
21 Eponym of a classic Minnesota-brewed beer
25 Bump
26 ___ time
28 Grammy winner Winans
29 Shortage of punch
31 TV's Jack and kin
32 Point of no return?
33 Robot in "Forbidden Planet"
34 Without protection
36 ___ the finish
37 Job for Hercule Poirot
38 Spice holder
40 Splits
43 Misses the mark
46 Amherst campus, briefly
47 Miracle-___
49 Coeur d'___
51 Visibly stunned
52 Last place
53 Seconds: Abbr.
54 Impostor
55 Less conventional
56 Blackmore heroine
58 Stops on a sales rep's rte.
60 Knowledge
61 Mme., across the Pyrenees

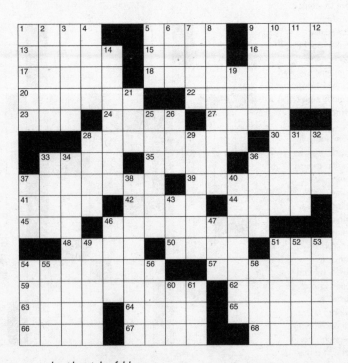

by Alan Arbesfeld

ACROSS

1   ___ and cheese (lunch dish)
4   Parasite's need
8   Too sentimental
13 Sporty Camaro
15 Cheese town
16 I.R.S. option
17 Wife of Jacob
18 It's handed down
19 1974 pardon recipient
20 Desktop publisher's need
23 Regards highly
24 Wild cat
28 Baseball rarity
29 Hawkeye's home
31 Acapulco gold
32 Company with a spokesduck
35 It may be upped
36 Fifth qtrs., so to speak
37 Commuter's woe
41 Turkish V.I.P.
42 Logical start?
43 Fountain spot, maybe
44 Except
45 Did a glissade
46 Tasman ___
47 Bagel choice
49 Like Duchamp's "Mona Lisa"
53 Def Leppard, for one
56 Deceptive talker
59 Fair-hiring org.
60 "At Last" singer James
61 Really bothered
62 Tracking ability
63 Fishing boat
64 Chocolatier's gear
65 River of Flanders
66 Super ___ (game system)

DOWN

1   ___ Bornes (card game)
2   Precincts
3   Take it easy
4   "S O S!"
5   Signs of decay
6   Bollywood costume
7   Some feds
8   Tutor of Nero
9   Full of ardor
10 Flicks
11 Mahmoud Abbas's org.
12 Nikkei currency
14 Spotted speedster
21 Clinton's first secretary of labor
22 Word with fire or water
25 Bath sponge
26 Baseball's Big Papi
27 "Vissi d'arte" opera
29 Way to indicate mistakes
30 "Beetle Bailey" dog
32 Most Al Jazeera viewers
33 Bach offering
34 Aspiring attys.' exams
35 Q7 maker
38 Crude carrier
39 More or less vertical, at sea
40 Tow truck type
45 Common sense
46 Game with a team of 11
48 On the horizon
49 The Cratchits' Christmas dinner
50 Stationery brand
51 ___ nous
52 Critical times
54 Turn down
55 Model T contemporaries
56 What 20-, 37- and 53-Across may do
57 "Am ___ believe . . . ?"
58 M.p.h., e.g.

by Gary J. Whitehead

ACROSS

1 Big kid?
5 Burns and Cowper
10 Sit heavily
14 Sch. of the Runnin' Rebels
15 Apply
16 Locale of the highways H1 and H2
17 Served to perfection?
18 Animal in the 2005 film "Madagascar"
19 Sound of silver striking crystal
20 South-of-the-border border town portmanteau
23 "___ certainly do not!"
24 Te-___ cigars
25 Plains border town portmanteau
33 Downed
34 Cellar stock
35 Cheerful, proud, powerful sort, it's said
36 Each state, symbolically
37 Displayed audacity
38 Fire starter?
39 Up to
40 Cattle-herding canine
41 Usher to the parlor
42 Mid-Atlantic border town portmanteau
45 Issue pikes and poleaxes, e.g.
46 Switzerland's ___ Léman
47 South-central border town portmanteau
55 Minestrone morsels
56 "The Big Trail" or "The Big Stampede"
57 Source for an outburst
58 The Putumayo River forms part of its northern border
59 Two bells, in a sailor's middle watch
60 Pressing need?
61 Milk dispenser
62 Encounters
63 Donkey ___

DOWN

1 Acquisition of the U.S. in the Spanish-American War
2 A while ago
3 Doonesbury's daughter in "Doonesbury"
4 Takeout alternative
5 1950s–70s Chevy
6 Jump and a twist
7 Do trailers?
8 Run (out of)
9 Like some poorly washed windows
10 Aphrodisiac, perhaps
11 Not of the cloth
12 "Horrors!"
13 Palooka
21 Nighttime scavenger, informally
22 $hopping season?
25 Holmes of "Dawson's Creek"
26 In the least
27 Bestow
28 Doleful air
29 Buck ___, first African-American coach in Major League Baseball
30 More foxy
31 Raptor's perch
32 "So ___?"
33 Abbr. before a date
37 Campus digs
38 Dove
40 Italian sweetie
41 Team letters
43 Hit the limit
44 Bells and whistles, say
47 Decision-making diagram
48 Fitch of Abercrombie & Fitch
49 Sugar ___, Marilyn Monroe's role in "Some Like It Hot"
50 To ___ (just so)
51 Straight up
52 Tic-tac-toe choice
53 Skin So Soft maker
54 Trolled
55 Make up one's mind

by Stephen Edward Anderson

ACROSS

1 Came down (on)
5 Word processing command
9 Off the wall
14 Word before luck or cluck
15 Cut, maybe
16 Studio sign
17 To boot
18 Ill-considered
19 Targets of some busts
20 Breakfast specialty of a rock singer?
23 First name in cosmetics
24 King of the stage
25 Spanks hard
29 Constant complainers
33 Relaxing place
36 Carry away, in a way
38 Zebra feature
39 Lunch specialty of an Emmy-winning actor?
43 Informed about
44 Popular online magazine
45 Part of B.Y.O.B.
46 Topple
49 Pass
51 Clinton cabinet member satirized by Will Ferrell
53 Arkansas River city
57 Dinner specialty of an R&B singer?
62 Spectrum part
63 Busy place
64 Docent's offering
65 Bicker
66 Basin go-with
67 A law ___ itself
68 Brute
69 Foreboding trouble
70 Freshman, most likely

DOWN

1 Bit of wisdom
2 Downtimes
3 "No more, thanks"
4 Butchers' offerings
5 Toiler of yore
6 Purim's month
7 Workbench attachment
8 ___ alcohol
9 Makeshift bookmark
10 Angered and enraged, e.g.
11 Dracula feature
12 Big Turkish export
13 Mos. and mos.
21 More recent
22 Wall St. watchdog
26 Priestly garment
27 Pueblo dweller
28 Topic for Vogue
30 Mil. alliance since 1949
31 Had down
32 Tailor-made
33 Tater
34 Le Pew of cartoons
35 Perched on
37 Pizazz
40 More than big
41 LAX posting
42 Religious offshoots
47 It may be under your hat
48 Brian of ambient music
50 Sound of rebuke
52 Expressed amazement
54 Director Sergio
55 Brown, perhaps
56 Rubber hub
57 Teed off
58 Bit of aquarium growth
59 Fuzzy fruit
60 "Did you ___?!"
61 Lacking moisture
62 Certain red wine, informally

by Michael Langwald

ACROSS

1 Basis of fries
6 A good breakfast, but a bad supper, according to Francis Bacon
10 Dumpsite pollutants, for short
14 ___ once
15 Robert of "The Sopranos"
16 Bloody, so to speak
17 Ton of
18 Federally guaranteed security
20 See 49-Down
22 Showy shrubs
23 Certain prayer starter
24 Special ties
25 Diamond setting
30 Arabian Peninsula port
33 Trickled (through)
35 "___ Cried" (1962 top 10 hit)
36 See 49-Down
39 Afore
40 It's often played before playing
41 Replies on the Enterprise
42 Cary Grant played a male one in 1949
44 Tin ___
46 "Donald's Cousin ___" (1939 Disney cartoon)
47 Back
51 See 49-Down
56 Private chats
57 Northeast airport
58 God, to Godard
59 Lead-in to meter
60 Spain's Princess ___
61 Lives no more

62 Unlikely valentine swappers
63 Skates on thin ice, e.g.

DOWN

1 Chip topper
2 Faint, in slang
3 Commercial prefix with suede
4 Start of many a story
5 ___ Island, N.Y.
6 Weather map numbers
7 Assortment
8 Ivy League choice
9 Marine eagle
10 Engagement agreement
11 Hard to take?
12 Bric-a-___
13 Dig for
19 Wagner princess

21 Designer for Jackie Kennedy
25 "This must ___ place"
26 Place for prayer
27 What "knock knock" may mean
28 Korea's Syngman ___
29 Understands
30 From the top
31 Celebrated Sigmund Freud patient
32 Oscar-winning song from "A Star Is Born"
34 Abbr. accompanying a college name
37 Perfect-game pitcher Don
38 Graph of the equation $y = ax2 + bx + c$

43 Leave in a hurry, slangily
45 Maneuvered
47 Dukes
48 Land that's more than 90% desert
49 Word defined by 20-, 36- and 51-Across
50 Best and Ferber
51 City near Sacramento
52 Black cuckoos
53 Emulated Arachne
54 Strong as ___
55 Strike out

by Joe Krozel

Turn the completed grid into a greeting card!

ACROSS

1 Indian music
5 12-time Pro Bowl pick Junior ___
9 N.F.L. game divs.
13 Close to closed
14 In debt
15 Europe/Asia boundary river
16 Step 1: Highlight this answer
19 Strainer
20 Sailor's "Stop!"
21 Wharf workers' org.
24 Little Rock-to-Birmingham dir.
25 Demolish
27 Step 2: With 43- and 55-Across, do this in the grid (scrambled or not) . . . it works for almost anyone!
33 How Santa dresses, mostly
34 Saturday worshipers
35 Electrical law maker
36 Diamond of note
37 Build ___ (settle down)
39 Canadian native
40 Fellow, in British slang
41 Co. figure
42 Belfry sound
43 See 27-Across
47 With 48-Across, ". . . and that ___!"
48 See 47-Across
49 End of a machine gun sound
50 "Star Wars" title
53 The heart in "I Love New York" signs, e.g.
55 See 27-Across
61 Big name in supercomputers
62 Set one's sights on
63 Sleep symbols

64 Prime coffee-growing area in Hawaii
65 Ferris wheel site
66 North Sea feeder

DOWN

1 Good cheer?
2 Steely Dan's best-selling album
3 Feature of Alfred E. Neuman's smile
4 Some Dada prints
5 Feature of many an office chair
6 Green land
7 Figure on a hill
8 Cry before or after sticking out the tongue
9 Eighth note
10 "___ Little Tenderness" (1960s hit)
11 "Darn it all!"
12 Part of a schedule
14 Overly large
17 End-of-ramp directive
18 Stuns
21 Bakers' coats
22 A suspect might appear in one
23 Make it
25 Sts. and rds.
26 Periodic table no.
28 Framable frame
29 Bounce
30 Irritated with
31 Louise's cinematic partner
32 Western ___
37 Nerve appendage
38 Like "das" in Ger.
39 King's former employer
41 Root who won the 1912 Nobel Peace Prize
42 Excite
44 One of the Jacksons
45 1977 James Brolin thriller with the tagline "What EVIL drives . . ."
46 Usually black garb
50 Where to tie one on?
51 Rounded hairdo
52 Meg of "You've Got Mail"
53 Do followers
54 Tag info
56 Part of Britain's mil.
57 Estuary
58 Reef dweller
59 Grain Belt state: Abbr.
60 "The Waste Land" poet's monogram

by Patrick Merrell

130 ★ ★

ACROSS
1. Benjamin Harrison's vice president, ___ P. Morton
5. Freaked out
10. Looks unhappy
14. Big pullers
15. Out
16. Soup or salad ingredient
17. Beloved film character with a tail
19. Car with an acronymic name
20. Cousin of the bald eagle
21. "___ precaution . . ."
22. "The White Horse ___" (operetta)
24. Holy man's title
25. One of the so-called Southern Ivies
27. Victor Nuñez title hero
28. Spike TV, once
29. Bit of force
30. Speaker's adjunct
32. Disqualify (oneself)
34. Drinks with a spoon, maybe
37. Mexican silver dollars
38. 1980s catchphrase
41. Baseball cover
42. Pens together
43. Whence the line "Whatever it is, I fear Greeks even when they bring gifts"
45. "Die Meistersinger" soprano
46. Spring break?
50. Rouge or noir, e.g.
51. ___ City, Fla.
53. "That's a ___!"
54. Diminutive suffix
55. With 52-Down, hangs out
56. Wall St. hire
58. Old Turkish title
59. Central point
61. Cry just before someone gets some big bucks?
64. W.W. II battleground
65. Pine
66. Catherine Deneuve was on its first U.S. cover
67. Court figs.
68. Battle site in "Animal Farm"
69. Range in lipsticks

DOWN
1. It makes livestock go crazy
2. Retired from a service
3. Mount ___
4. Pol. label
5. Robert of "Airplane!"
6. ___ prima (painting technique)
7. Midmillennium year
8. In a frenzy
9. One tied for first place
10. Barges
11. Place for grazing
12. Discovers
13. Group assimilated by the Romans
18. Be productive, as chickens
23. As required, after "if"
26. Go back
27. Stuck
30. It can never come back
31. Its coat of arms features a horseman spearing a dragon
33. Hill, in Spain
35. Food brand whose name is a portmanteau of two state names
36. Knife, slangily
38. Present, as a dessert tray
39. Made allusions to
40. ___ Kappa Nu (honor society)
41. Surfer's exclamation
44. It may be milked for all it's worth
47. Eye in the heavens
48. Ancient
49. "As a matter of fact, I do"
52. See 55-Across
53. Prison break, e.g.
56. Pond, in Liverpool
57. Crook
60. Accident letters
62. Morse T
63. Shrink

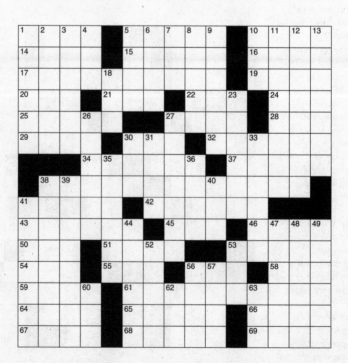

by Kevin G. Der

ACROSS

1 "The Divine Comedy," for one
5 Elisabeth of "Cocktail"
9 Housecat
14 It could be revolving
15 Mann of the Haus
16 High-end Honda
17 Windsor princess
18 Book of Mormon book
19 Dizzy Gillespie's jazz
20 "I asked for tomato bisque, not gazpacho!" (complaint #1)
23 Place for a housecat
24 ___ du Diable
25 Cousin of "aargh!"
28 "Has our waiter even made eye contact?" (complaint #2)
33 ___-Magnon
34 Shad ___
35 Sharpshooting Annie
36 Chart anew
39 14+
41 Zig and zag
42 Money for money
44 Au naturel
46 Something Elizabeth II has?
47 "What, are they growing the food?" (complaint #3)
51 Sevilla seasoning
52 Manhandle
53 Actor Stephen
54 Title of this puzzle
60 Place for a barbecue
63 Titan's place
64 A rock band's name often appears on it
65 Bikini, e.g.
66 Language of the Hindustan Express
67 Sci-fi sage
68 Al ___ (a bit firm)
69 Mulching material
70 10 C-notes

DOWN

1 Mild yellow cheese
2 My Little ___ (kids' toy line)
3 Charge holders
4 Spicy cuisine
5 Free local paper
6 Prefix with sphere
7 Mantel pieces
8 13th-century king of Denmark
9 Workshop fixture
10 Nailed, as a test
11 Pal
12 Pal
13 Pie hole
21 Motor City org.
22 Mishmash
25 On fire
26 Ingenious
27 Excited, with "up"
28 Queen of Soul, familiarly
29 German commander at the invasion of Normandy
30 Marker
31 ___ jacket
32 "South Park" boy
33 Sticking points?
37 It has a horn: Abbr.
38 Apartment security feature
40 Distant
43 Morales of "La Bamba"
45 Long past its prime
48 Confesses (to)
49 Bloodshot
50 Pops
54 Suffer from the heat
55 The Old Sod
56 Robert who won a Tony for "Guys and Dolls"
57 Fairway club
58 Like Michelangelo's David
59 Webzine
60 Crash site?
61 Had a bit
62 Won ___

by Daniel Kantor and Jay Kaskel

ACROSS

1 Diamond datum
4 Annual fashion award
8 Syrian city of 2.5+ million
14 Long interval
15 Long (for)
16 More 26-Across
17 Three short, three long, three short
18 University of Paris, familiarly
20 Curved molding
22 Fit for warehousing
23 Like some potatoes
25 Popped up
26 Lilliputian
29 Selects, as a racehorse, maybe
31 Spend the night
33 Everyday speech
37 ___-Rooter
38 Classic 1911 children's novel . . . with a hint to this puzzle's theme
44 Hesitate
45 ___ metabolism
46 Best players
48 Washed-out look
53 Essex competitor
54 Spot checkers?
59 River near 18-Across
60 Short-range club
63 Nos. for crowds
64 What you can find in the grid after completing this puzzle, looking up, down, left, right and diagonally, word-search style
67 Bleachers sound
68 Dumpling stuffed with cheese
69 Capital of Valais
70 "___ Town"
71 Carpentry and the like
72 Designer/architect Goldfinger
73 Oils, say

DOWN

1 Soak up again, as liquid
2 Dance energetically
3 Antenna holder, maybe
4 See 66-Down
5 Phil who sang "I Ain't Marching Anymore"
6 Sorority letter
7 "___ no?"
8 Gillette shavers
9 Women's ___
10 Certain alkene
11 Good floor material
12 What you might be doing this puzzle in
13 Tram contents
19 Río de ___, former Spanish territory in Africa
21 Some Caltech grads, for short
24 Skinny

27 Tivoli's Villa d'___
28 "The chief nurse of England's statesmen"
30 Creation of the Energy Reorg. Act of 1974
32 Three-time Hart Trophy winner
34 Ball
35 Hydrospace
36 Doctor Who and others, briefly
38 One way to get to the top
39 "Too great a burden to bear": Martin Luther King Jr.
40 Stage actress Duse
41 Forerunner of rocksteady
42 Hiatus
43 "___ the day!" (Shakespearean interjection)

47 Horse-training school
49 Dixie hero
50 Capital of República Portuguesa
51 Going from concert to concert
52 Vacation destination
55 Comic Leary
56 Peace, in Russian
57 Unevenly notched, as a leaf
58 Respectful reply
61 Big shirt maker
62 Light material?
64 Quick to pick up
65 Scorsese, e.g.: Abbr.
66 With 4-Down, tracked vehicle

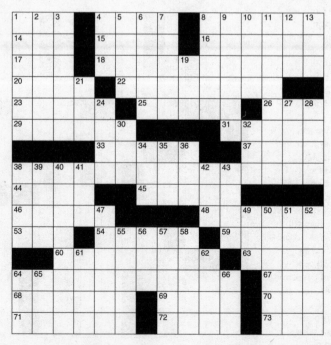

by David J. Kahn

ACROSS

1 First rock band whose members received Kennedy Center Honors
7 Jiffy
11 Shade of black
14 Fix, in carpentry
15 Undoubtedly
17 Dropped a line?
18 Olympians' food
19 Figures for investors
20 Animal that catches fish with its forepaws
21 Ward on a set
22 Shade of gray
24 Work ___
25 Annual with deep-pink flowers
28 Miles off
30 Tailor
33 Part of the Dept. of Labor
34 All-Star Martinez
35 "Guys and Dolls" composer/lyricist
37 Like dirty clothes, often
39 Secondary: Abbr.
40 The muscle of a muscle car, maybe
42 Soup scoop
43 Fill
44 Abba's genre
46 "Alice" actress Linda
48 Kyrgyzstan's second-largest city
49 Game discs
53 Uncopiable, say
55 Quick session for a band
57 Springsteen hit with the lyric "Only you can cool my desire"
58 Noted graffiti artist
59 Viking, e.g.
60 Philosophize, say
61 Strike leader?
62 Breather
63 Trained groups

DOWN

1 Sights at the dentist's office
2 Three-time Olympic skating gold medalist
3 Georgia of "The Mary Tyler Moore Show"
4 1955 Pulitzer-winning poet
5 Rushed
6 Maxim
7 Pot and porn magazines, typically
8 Norton Sound city
9 Diplomat who wrote "The Tide of Nationalism"
10 Reform Party founder
11 Legitimate
12 Construction project that began in Rome
13 Rush
16 "Yeah . . . anyway"
23 Ultra sound?
26 Boolean operators
27 Charging things?
29 Ensnare, with "in"
30 "It wasn't meant to be"
31 Literally, "the cottonwoods"
32 Those with will power?
36 Exactly 10 seconds, for the 100-yard dash
38 Spanish greeting
41 Tending to wear away
45 Illogically afraid
47 Draw (from)
50 Actor Werner of "The Spy Who Came in From the Cold"
51 Heroic tale
52 Lid afflictions
53 Cleaner fragrance
54 They're sometimes named after presidents
56 Squat

by Brendan Emmett Quigley

134 ★★★

ACROSS

1 Fictional amnesiac portrayer
10 Out
15 Mix and match?
16 Total
17 Identifies with
18 Old computing acronym
19 Head Start program service, briefly
20 Some drillers, for short
21 Prefix with gram
22 Stay (with)
23 Turned on a friend, maybe?
24 Painting surface
28 Proscribed
30 Destination in the "Odyssey"
32 "No need to go on"
37 Without embellishment
39 Vitamin in meat, milk and eggs
40 Resolve a bromance spat, say
42 Crime scene sight
43 Muscle Beach sights
45 Backs
46 Garden decorations
50 Evade
52 2007 horror sequel
53 It may be hard to reach
54 Fool
58 1970s subcompact
59 Member of a medical minority
61 British running great Steve
62 Start of a Dickensian request
63 Clipped
64 Emulate Ferris Bueller

DOWN

1 Dealer's amt.
2 Parrot
3 Communications leader?
4 Big Indonesian export
5 "Silent Spring" topic
6 Gland: Prefix
7 Costumed figure
8 Suleiman the Magnificent, for one
9 Modernists
10 Difficult sort
11 Addition
12 Common subject of medieval art
13 Blank ___
14 Title role for Charlton Heston
22 Election-related nonprofit since 1990
23 Cymbal sound
24 "Mystic Pizza" actress Annabeth
25 Dramatic accusation
26 Cut with more than one layer
27 Bit of Bollywood attire
29 Mac
31 Base for some incense
33 Dry
34 Tynan player in "The Seduction of Joe Tynan"
35 "Severn Meadows" poet Gurney
36 Retreats
38 "Delish!"
41 Presentation by Bill Clinton in 2007 or Bill Gates in 2010
44 Cores
46 Sensitive subject?
47 Green
48 Sports league V.I.P.
49 Paws
51 Tawdry
53 They're a handful
54 What might put you through your paces?
55 Minor opening?
56 Wave function symbols
57 Suffixes with mountain and cannon
60 Grp. involved in the Abbottabad raid

by John Lieb and David Quarfoot

ACROSS

1 Food item resembling an organ
11 Not long-departed
15 Question after a public shellacking
16 Plutoid just beyond the Kuiper Belt
17 Many a detective film cover-up
18 Squire
19 Lack of authorisation?
20 "Casablanca" carrier
22 It really stands out
25 Be loud at a funeral, say
26 Many 56-Across users
29 It may have check marks
30 General exercise?
31 Stretches out
35 "We're in trouble now!"
36 Abbr. on a sports ticker
37 Topics at some religious retreats
41 Cousin of a screwdriver
44 Largest city in the South Pacific
45 Go back on
46 Six bells in the morning watch
49 Prefix with geek
50 Hand picks?
52 Monogram of the author of "A Charge to Keep: My Journey to the White House"
55 Kind of block
56 It replaced the Indian rupee in 1932
60 Winnipeg's ___ Franko Museum

61 Ithaca is at its southern end
62 Be inclined
63 His Secret Service code name was Providence

DOWN

1 Classic name in New York delis
2 Subject precursor
3 Like some eggs
4 Intro to Euclidean geometry?
5 Letter abbr.
6 Casual assent
7 As
8 Weena's race, in fiction
9 Generally speaking
10 Big name in video streaming
11 Five and ten, e.g.

12 Ticketmaster info, maybe
13 Coloring
14 Compact first name?
21 Formation on 28-Down
22 About 186,282 miles
23 Marathoner Pippig
24 NASA's Aquarius, e.g.
26 Done some strokes
27 Routine reaction?
28 See 21-Down
32 Home of the Black Mts.
33 Crow relatives
34 Stock mover
38 Shrimp
39 Midas's undoing
40 Katana wielder

41 Curt
42 Beauregard follower
43 GPS abbr.
46 Cheerleader's move
47 Relative d'un étudiant
48 Many an animal rights activist
51 Baseball Hall-of-Famer who played for the Giants
52 Bother, with "at"
53 After-life gathering?
54 Backwoods relative
57 Starting device: Abbr.
58 Code word
59 Publisher of World of Work mag.

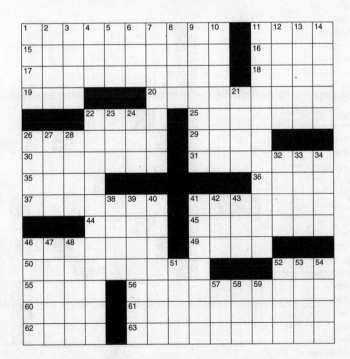

by Barry C. Silk

ACROSS

1 Bar fixture
4 Person who might suit you well?
15 Start of many a "Jeopardy!" response
16 Transported
17 Org. with an Office of Water
18 "Poor Little Fool" hitmaker, 1958
19 Danny who composed the theme music for "The Simpsons"
21 Eponymous Dr. Asperger
22 Onetime Michael Jackson bodyguard
23 Benders
24 Sight on a "Hee Haw" set
25 Hindu god often depicted with a bow and arrow
26 A choli may be worn under this
27 "Star Trek: T.N.G." role
28 Name on the cover of "Yosemite and the High Sierra"
29 Verb suffix?
30 Ancient scribe's work surface
32 Treadmill runners, maybe
34 "Sex is an emotion in motion" speaker
37 Not reliable
39 Empire State tech school
40 "Pride ___ before destruction": Proverbs
42 Be uncooperative
43 Showroom window no.
44 Discipline
45 European hub
46 Show stoppers?
47 Leipzig-to-Zurich dir.
48 Columnist Collins
49 Was triumphant in the end

50 Inventor's undoing?
53 Mineralogical appendage?
54 Avatar setting
55 Base man
56 Image on Utah's state quarter
57 Baker's dozen for the Beatles, for short

DOWN

1 Tree also known as a sugar apple
2 "You've got to be kidding!"
3 Perfectly
4 Wedding rings?
5 Have ___ (be advantageously networked)
6 Secret attachment, for short
7 South Bend neighbor

8 Court group
9 Dominick who wrote "A Season in Purgatory"
10 Some Snapple products
11 Conan O'Brien's employer from '88 to '91
12 1899 painting used to promote gramophones
13 Massive, as a massif
14 National service
20 Internal investigation, for short?
24 Hybrid menswear
25 Grasped
27 Texas Ranger Hall of Fame and Museum site
28 Many are blonde
30 Among
31 Enjoy the moment

33 Copier giant absorbed by the Kyocera Corporation
35 Appear suddenly
36 Track consultants
38 Banana Republic defender, maybe
40 Ersatz blazer
41 Speaker of Shakespeare's "If music be the food of love, play on"
43 Calculus calculation: Abbr.
45 Like some gruel
46 Pioneer in cool jazz
48 Mapped item
49 "Marjorie Morningstar" novelist
51 Got out of the way
52 Head of state?

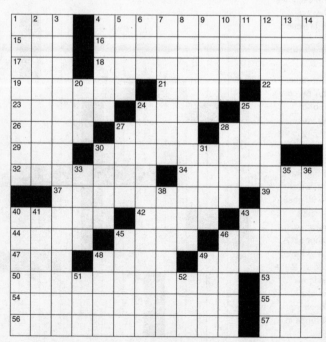

by Brad Wilber and Doug Peterson

ACROSS

1 Where Union Pacific is headquartered
6 Chinese ___ (popular bonsai trees)
10 Medieval drudge
14 Sister of Castor and Pollux
15 Fighter getting a leg up?
17 Site of Tiberius' Villa Jovis
18 Page on the stage
19 Comfortable
21 Taking place (in)
22 One-point throws
24 Appliance sound
25 Checkers, for instance
26 Play critic?
28 Hype
32 Onetime Arapaho foe
33 Grooming tool
36 Vietnamese holiday
37 O-shaped
38 Priest in I Samuel
39 Dread Zeppelin or the Fab Faux
41 Sports div. that awards the George Halas Trophy
42 Gold Cup venue
43 Quote qualification
44 Coin of many countries
45 Pretension
48 Get more inventory
50 Country whose flag is known as the Saltire
54 Bubble handler?
55 Foundation devoted to good works?
57 Uniform
58 Bag lady?

59 Less often seen
60 Deep black
61 Twist
62 America's Cup trophies, e.g.

DOWN

1 Broadway musical with two exclamation points in its name
2 They might have bones to pick
3 Like characters in a script
4 Some wetlands wildlife
5 Miyazaki film genre
6 Hosp. record
7 Creates an account?
8 Fast-food debut of 1981
9 Go along effortlessly
10 Vending machine drink
11 What to do when you have nothing left to say?
12 Peace Nobelist Cassin
13 Dance-pop trio Right Said ___
16 Symbol of happiness
20 Off the mark
23 English Channel feeder
27 Bad line readings
29 Launched the first round
30 Narcissistic one
31 Hand-held "Star Trek" devices
33 Sea creature whose name means "sailor"

34 Huxtable family mom
35 Surgical cutter
40 Gondoliers, e.g.
44 Like a poli sci major, maybe
46 Woodworking tools
47 Underhanded schemer
49 American Airlines hub
50 Drink served in a masu
51 Zodiac symbol
52 Palindromic man
53 "My man!"
56 Plaintive pet sound

by Patrick Berry

ACROSS

1 Title trio of a 1980 Pulitzer winner
16 One-on-one with a big shot
17 Gist
18 French preposition
19 "Just what I need"
20 Stamp purchases
23 "Cool dad" on "Modern Family"
24 Hill minority: Abbr.
28 Top honors for atletas olímpicos
29 They're often taken on horses
30 Happening
31 ". . . we'll ___ a cup o' kindness . . .": Burns
32 First name in Harlem Renaissance literature
33 Quail
34 Winged it
37 Napkin material
38 Son of 30-Down
39 "___ wise guy, eh?"
40 Very little (of)
41 A quarter of acht
42 Second-largest city in Nicaragua
43 Tree-hugger?
44 Youthful and fresh
45 Longtime late-night announcer
46 Breakout company of 1976
48 Spearfishing need
49 Moment's notice?
56 Vetoes
57 Some government checks

DOWN

1 It might tell you where to get off
2 Sch. founded by a Pentecostal preacher
3 Turn down
4 Dances around
5 Dangerous things to weave on
6 Ballparks at J.F.K.?
7 Her, to Henriette
8 Grabbed some sack time
9 Self-confidence to a fault
10 Vehicular bomb?
11 Romance novelist's award
12 Looking ecstatic
13 One of the Romneys
14 New Deal inits.
15 Snicker bit
20 Home of Sanssouci Palace
21 Wind River Reservation native
22 Hiawatha's grandmother in "The Song of Hiawatha"
23 Philatelist's concern, briefly
25 Clean type
26 Lab growth need
27 Designer Gabbana of Dolce & Gabbana
29 Stamp purchase
30 Father of 38-Across
32 Limoncello ingredient
33 K. J. ___, 2011 Players Championship champion
35 Univ. in Manhattan
36 Smaller cousin of a four-in-hand?
41 100 bits?
42 San Diego suburb
44 Russian retreat
45 One trying to avoid a banking crisis?
47 Loss from a guillotine
48 They're issued to cruisers, briefly
49 Little chances?
50 Fruitcake
51 It's H-shaped
52 First year of the Liang dynasty
53 "Kung Fu" actor Philip
54 Part of U.S.S.R.: Abbr.
55 Charlotte-to-Raleigh dir.

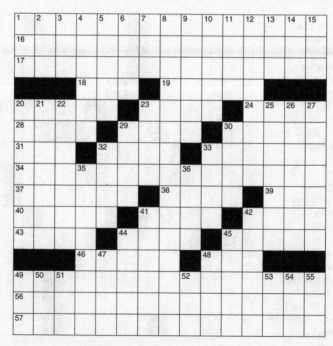

by Chris A. McGlothlin

ACROSS

1 Fighting
6 Amscray
10 They get taken easily
14 ___ Road (W.W. II supply route)
15 Hospital bed feature
16 Nail
17 Circular side?
19 Unisex name meaning "born again"
20 Many a security point
21 Straight
23 Form of "sum"
24 Sound name
25 Tom who won a Tony for "The Seven Year Itch"
26 Ones keeping on their toes?
29 The City of a Hundred Spires
31 Triage determination
32 Home of "NerdTV"
35 Line of rulers
37 Big game plans?
39 Argument-ending letters
40 Short distance
42 Occasions for bulldogging
43 Hot-and-cold menu item
45 Mathematician Cantor who founded set theory
48 Going without saying?
49 Aid in getting back on track
52 Means of reducing worker fatigue
54 Kraft Nabisco Championship org.
55 Color also known as endive blue
56 Classic Hitchcock set
58 Quiet place to fish
59 Suffixes of 61-Across
60 Rich of old films
61 Contents of some ledges
62 "___ Wedding" ("The Mary Tyler Moore Show" episode)
63 Occasioned

DOWN

1 Flat, e.g.
2 Fixes flats?
3 Hospital patient's wear
4 & 5 Lost control
6 Feature of some western wear
7 Pathfinder?
8 Reagan was seen a lot in them
9 Word after who, what or where, but rarely when
10 Things driven on construction sites
11 Anti-inflammatory product
12 Authorities might sit on one
13 Wonderful
18 Kind of wheel
22 One putting the pedal to the metal
24 Summer symbol?
27 One of the Eastern elite
28 Aviation safety statistic
29 Straightaway
30 Manhattan choice
32 Broken into on TV?
33 Kind of lab
34 Nemesis of some dodgers: Abbr.
36 Fellow chairperson?
38 Use a 24-Down
41 Like pigtails
43 Talks tediously
44 Hacker's achievement
45 American company whose mascot has a Cockney accent
46 Diamond flaw
47 Diagonal rib of a vault
50 One getting cuts
51 Early: Prefix
53 Exit lines?
54 Ethnologist's interest
57 254,000 angstroms

by Dana Motley

ACROSS

1 Baker's predecessor
5 "The Daily Rundown" carrier
10 Steinbeck siren
14 Vindaloo accompaniment
15 Admission about a story
16 Skillful, slangily
17 Brother's keeper?
20 In thing
21 In place
22 What one should take in: Abbr.
23 Engagement rings?
25 Muhammad, e.g.
27 Ready for another round
28 Packer in a bookstore
31 Young turkey
32 Strong order?
35 Compliment to the chef
36 Drawers hitting the pavement?
42 County whose seat is La Junta
43 Means of changing one's mind
44 One way to catch the game
45 Quaint letter-opening abbr.
47 Took the wrong way
48 13th Spanish letter
49 Ear plug?
53 Big inits. in power
54 Remark after holding someone up
57 War head?
58 Thrill
59 Strauss's "Tausend und ___ Nacht"
60 Backwoods agreement
61 Many a Madrileño
62 Walked all over

DOWN

1 Where to observe some workers
2 Napa Valley setting
3 Clipboard's relative
4 One way to fly: Abbr.
5 "Carota" and "Blue II," for two
6 Start of many an operation
7 Trivial objections
8 Blast from the passed?
9 Software box item
10 Peck, e.g.: Abbr.
11 Den mother's charge
12 Tony with an Emmy
13 Like many sonatas' second movements
18 Mad person's question
19 Leave to scrap, maybe
24 Indigent individuals
26 Numbered relations
28 "___ wind that bloweth . . ."
29 Bass parts
30 Legendary spring figure
33 Pier grp.
34 Bras ___ Lake (Canadian inland sea)
36 Rumor opener
37 Agenda opener
38 They're thirsty much of the time
39 What gobs take in
40 The Merry Mex of golf
41 Feeling no pain
46 Jewel cases?
47 Bill with barbs
50 Fruit giant
51 Home of the daily Hamshahri
52 Raiders Hall-of-Famer Jim
55 Coin feature
56 Unlike 38-Down

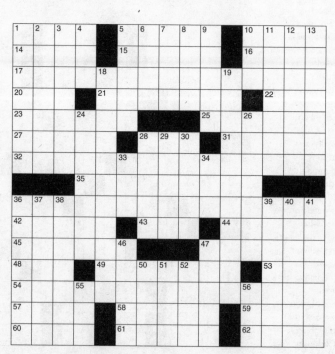

by Ed Sessa

ACROSS

1 Human-powered transport
8 Lingerie enhancements
15 Japanese "thanks"
16 Consumed
17 Like some Mideast ideology
18 Grammy-winning singer from Barbados
19 "___ me later"
20 Barrister's deg.
21 Belief opposed by Communists
22 Hammer and sickle
24 Small arms
25 "Be right there"
29 Labor outfits
30 Bubbly brand, for short
34 Oral reports?
35 Des Moines-to-Cedar Rapids dir.
36 It's known to locals as Cymraeg
37 "Money" novelist, 1984
38 Orange entree, informally
40 Not take a back seat to anyone?
41 Diner freebies
45 Fisherman's Wharf attraction
46 Young colleen, across the North Channel
48 Browns' home, for short
49 Bring to a boil?
52 By the boatload
53 Wastes
55 Cubs' home
56 Improbable victory, in slang
57 Potentially embarrassing video
58 Mezzo-soprano Troyanos

DOWN

1 Quebec preceder, to pilots
2 Meaningful stretches
3 Soft touch?
4 Supermarket inits.
5 Some bank offerings
6 Totally flummoxed
7 Spring figure?
8 Pitcher Blyleven with 3,701 strikeouts
9 Oatmeal topping
10 Close
11 Unit of wisdom?
12 "Little Girls" musical
13 Actress Kirsten
14 Hits with some trash
22 Sporty auto options
23 Torch carriers
25 Capital of South Sudan
26 Old one
27 Her voice was first heard in 2011
28 It's already out of the bag
30 Parts of a school athletic calendar
31 Designer Cassini
32 "Mi casa ___ casa"
33 Segue starter
36 Everything, with "the"
38 Trip
39 Fried tortilla dish
40 Landlocked African land
41 Collectors of DNA samples
42 Hides from Indians, maybe?
43 Chill
44 All-points bulletin, e.g.
47 Final word in a holiday tune
49 Locale for many political debates
50 Perdition
51 Site of the Bocca Nuova crater
54 Poli ___

by Ian Livengood

ACROSS

1 Start of a phobia?
5 All the best?
10 Five-time U.S. Open winner
14 Immensely
15 Leisurely
16 Sign of virtue
17 Malted alternatives
20 Be ruthless
21 Run-___
22 Pair of word processors?
23 Instinctive reaction
24 Verbal gem
25 Bygone country name or its currency
28 Safe to push off
34 It springs from Monte Falterona
35 Brush off
36 Place for tiger woods?
37 Get going
39 Not at all sharp, maybe
40 A shot
41 Plant production: Abbr.
42 "Go figure!"
48 One of the muskrats in the 1976 hit "Muskrat Love"
51 Play savior
53 Dual diner dish
54 Stickler's citation
55 "Or else ___ despiser of good manners": Shak.
56 Newton, e.g.
57 Event with body cords
58 Not at all sharp
59 Lands

DOWN

1 Brand of blades
2 Brand of literature
3 Where seekers may find hiders
4 Almost never
5 Go-for-broke
6 Proceeded precipitately
7 IV component
8 Chain of off-price department stores
9 Guzzle
10 Home of the world's largest artificial lake
11 Ground crew gear?
12 Like prairie dogs, notably
13 "Pippin" Tony winner
18 As if scripted
19 "Get the lead out!"
23 Get inside and out
25 Director/screenwriter Penn
26 "Exodus" character
27 Magazine with an annual "500|5000" conference
28 Likely result of excess 17- and 53-Across
29 Prefix with 36-Across
30 Seemed to be
31 Bit of chiding
32 Not dally
33 "That's fantastic news!"
35 One bound to hold notes?
38 Venom
39 Spot ___
41 Actress Matlin
42 Words of support
43 Do the final details on
44 Not coming up short
45 Frost, to François
46 Human Development Report publisher, in brief
47 About 50% of calls
48 Turnover alternative
49 Tax burden?
50 Measures up to
52 Like many a goody-goody

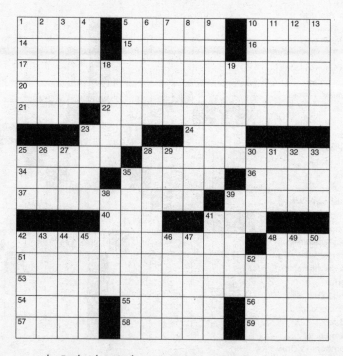

by Frederick J. Healy

ACROSS

1 First female candidate to win the Ames Straw Poll
16 War paths
17 It airs in the morning, ironically
18 Case builders: Abbr.
19 Copy from a CD
20 Understood
21 Show featuring special agents
22 Red Cloud, e.g.
24 Player of the bad teacher in "Bad Teacher"
26 Rear
27 Possible rank indicator
29 Overseas relig. title
30 Big name in car monitors
32 Beat it
34 "Keep dreaming!"
36 Word after a splat
37 Like some lovers' hearts
41 Strikes
45 She may be fawning
46 Colorful cover-ups
48 Brandy letters
49 Grilling test
51 Misses abroad: Abbr.
52 Newborn abroad
53 ___ Hedin, discoverer of the Trans-Himalaya
55 Folman who directed the 2013 film "The Congress"
56 Comcast Center hoopster
57 Alternative to a breakfast burrito

61 Big source for modern slang
62 Some critical comments from co-workers

DOWN

1 Yellowstone setting: Abbr.
2 Odysseus, e.g.
3 Dopes
4 Knocks off
5 Control tower info
6 Re-serve judgment?
7 Female adviser
8 Ill-humored
9 Norwegian Star port of call
10 Old oscilloscope part, briefly
11 Turns over in one's plot?
12 Was reflective

13 Its adherents are in disbelief
14 Formula one?
15 Neighbor of Victoria: Abbr.
21 Top kick, for one: Abbr.
22 Puck and others
23 Some exact likenesses
25 Part of Queen Elizabeth's makeup?
27 Certain league divisions
28 Forerunners of discs
31 Kind of cross
33 They may be returned with regrets: Abbr.
35 458 Spider and F12 Berlinetta
37 Production

38 Definitely
39 Give some space, say
40 Grind
42 Stormed
43 Modern mouse hole?
44 Ring bearer, maybe
47 Emulates Homer
50 Actor Burton
52 Competitor of Lauren and Klein
54 Numerical prefix
56 First name in footwear
57 "Two, three, four" lead-in
58 Org. with a clenched fist logo
59 Org. created right after the cold war
60 MS-DOS component: Abbr.

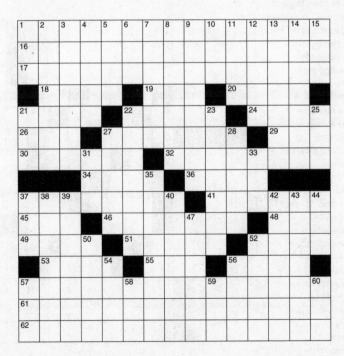

by David Steinberg

144 ★★★

ACROSS

1 TV host who won a Best Comedy Album Grammy
12 Vegan lunch option, informally
15 Cry used to pump up a crowd
16 Following
17 Fortune
18 Beast in a Marco Polo tale
19 Old station name
20 Abbr. in a birth announcement
21 Request in pool or beer pong
23 Hudson River school?
25 "Eww!"
27 Soundtrack to many a bomb-defusing scene
28 Prizes given to good docs?
31 "Kazaam" star, informally
32 Crying need?
36 A wedge might come out of it
37 Beast hunted by Hemingway in "Green Hills of Africa"
38 Work set mostly in Cyprus
40 Herbal quaff
42 Wilde wrote "De Profundis" in one
43 Lion runner
45 Unlike a showboat
46 Rash application
47 Reception opening
49 Hull sealer
51 1-Across's home, once: Abbr.
52 Resistance figure
57 Like pickle juice
59 Dated
61 Many a donor, in brief

62 Go around, but not quite go in
63 W.W. II defense
66 Sun ___
67 Fall fallout, some believe
68 Short agreement
69 Scorsese film before "Alice Doesn't Live Here Anymore"

DOWN

1 "The Two ___" ("Chinatown" sequel)
2 Like 1-Across, by descent
3 Quick set
4 "Oh no!"
5 His, modern-style?
6 Roll up and bind
7 Source of the word "alcohol"
8 Glass protector
9 Velázquez's "___ Meninas"
10 Repute
11 Orange and blue wearer, for short
12 It opens during the fall
13 Some trade barriers
14 Nada
22 On the line
24 Dangerous thing to sell
26 Humphries of the N.B.A.
29 Southern site of an 1865 battle
30 Weak spots
32 Wrap session?
33 Slant one's words, in a way
34 Picture with a lot of gunplay

35 Game controller button
39 Cholesterol-lowering food
41 First-choice
44 Hand over (to)
48 Self-titled debut album of 1991
50 Sign at a game
53 "Au Revoir, Les Enfants" writer/director
54 Sporty Lotus model
55 Put one's foot down, in a way?
56 Accord indicators
58 Protection
60 "I ___ tell"
64 1998 Angelina Jolie biopic
65 49-Across source

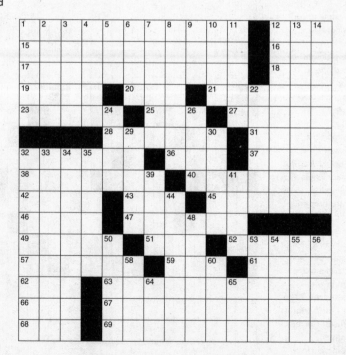

by Josh Knapp

ACROSS

1 Old Hollywood low-budget studios, collectively
11 "Oh, God!" actress
15 Wine bottle contents in Hitchcock's "Notorious"
16 Only event in which Venezuela medaled at the 2012 Olympics
17 Dessert often with cream cheese icing
18 Ironwoman org.?
19 Singer born Eithne Ní Bhraonáin
20 Map inits. created in the wake of the Suez Crisis
21 Now-rare connection method
23 Blather
25 Big name in markers
26 Nitroglycerin, for one
29 Director's alternative to a dolly
32 It was dissolved in 1991
34 Time in TV ads
35 Fused
36 Fortify
38 Domingo, e.g.
39 Onetime TV music vendor
41 Kind of community
43 Avocado relative
45 Ross Sea sights
46 Interrupts
47 Strike out
48 Excoriates
49 "Revolution 9" collaborator
51 It may slip in the back
55 L.B.J. biographer Robert ___
56 One-third of a triangle, maybe
59 Hindi relative
60 The goddess Kali appeared on its first cover
61 Bygone
62 New Jersey childhood home of Whitney Houston and Queen Latifah

DOWN

1 Brownish purple
2 Port where Camus set "The Plague"
3 Fluctuate
4 Brings to a boil
5 Rock in ___ (major music festival)
6 "Coppélia" attire
7 Hit from the 1978 disco album "Cruisin'"
8 More than chuckle
9 Planet first mentioned on "Happy Days"
10 It's used to define a border
11 Colorful dessert
12 Press production
13 Doing a government agency's job
14 Garner
22 Not the party type?: Abbr.
24 Part of 20-Across
25 Substance that citrus peels are rich in
26 Endor natives
27 Site of the last battle of the Cuban Revolution
28 Barriers used in urban renewal projects
29 Ire
30 Get a hint of
31 Party tray array
33 Vexing
37 Country name
40 Releases
42 Baseball's ___ Line (.200 batting average)
44 Prime meridian std.
47 Skip
48 Smallish lingerie spec
49 Electrical units
50 Ordered
52 "You can count on me"
53 Provided backup, in a way
54 Deep or high lead-in
57 Org. with inspectors
58 "A defeat for humanity," per Pope John Paul II

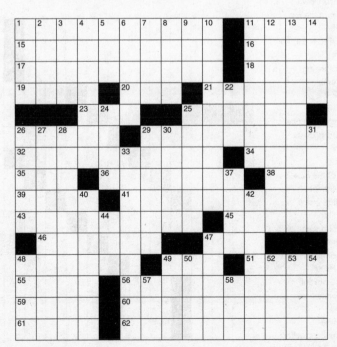

by Brad Wilber and Doug Peterson

146

★ ★ ★

ACROSS

1 World's tallest building
12 Instagram post
15 One way to cruise along
16 7 a.m. staple, briefly
17 They come out of many mouths
18 Protection from pirates: Abbr.
19 Sets forth thoroughly
20 Trite
22 Guitar maker Fender
23 She's beautiful, per a popular song
24 So-called "weekend pill"
28 Like some liquor stores
29 Like 30-Down
30 Room at the top, maybe
31 Spa treatment, for short
32 Unsurprising outcome
33 Radios, e.g.
34 "Sweet!"
35 Starz alternative
36 Belfast is on its shore
37 Mind
38 Site of the Sibelius Monument
40 Castle's place, initially
41 Took up some of
42 Big time
43 Trepanning targets
44 Some partial appointments
49 Blood
50 Big time
52 It may be cracked or packed
53 "C'est la vie"

54 Co. purchased by Wizards of the Coast
55 Hail Marys, e.g.

DOWN

1 Champion between Holyfield reigns
2 It has "batch" and "patch" commands
3 Not be smooth-talking?
4 Activity with holding and throwing
5 Singer of the 1987 #1 country hit "Do Ya"
6 Buds
7 "I shall not find myself so ___ die": Antony
8 Fictional accounts
9 Text attachment?
10 Bygone yellow-roofed kiosks
11 Forward, back or center
12 Like every Bond film since 1989
13 Virginal
14 Moor
21 Karate trainee in 2010's "The Karate Kid"
23 Agatha Christie's "There Is ___ . . ."
24 Is unable to cut the mustard
25 Form of strength training
26 It'll help you breathe easier
27 Fast flight
28 One in a religious majority
30 Brand on a face

33 Largest river of southern California
34 Norah Jones's "Tell ___ Mama"
36 Not amounting to much
37 "Holy" group in 17th-century literature
39 Something to beg pardon for
40 Ill-paid laborer
42 Something to beg pardon for
44 Not be gratuitous
45 ___ Sant'Gria (wine choice)
46 Servant in the "Discworld" novels
47 Kind of pudding
48 Whole bunch
51 Both Barack and Michelle Obama have them: Abbr.

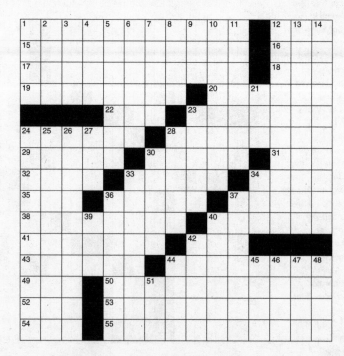

by Julian Lim

ACROSS

1 Holding
9 Way of looking at things
14 Reading light for an audiobook?
16 Detergent component
17 Going nowhere?
18 Pine for
19 Org. always headed by a U.S. general or admiral
20 Baltic native
22 "After ___"
23 Seat cushions?
25 Old airline name
28 Roofing choice
29 "According to reports . . ."
32 Wedded
33 They make a racket
34 Cell alternatives
35 Like each word from this clue
37 Many a time
40 Change places
41 White spread
42 Heavy and clumsy
43 White of the eye
45 The Dom is the third-highest one
46 A whole bunch
49 Blows a fuse
50 Nation with the most Unesco World Heritage Sites
53 Winner over Ohio State in 1935's so-called "Game of the Century"
55 Suez Crisis setting
56 Startling revelation
57 Xerox competitor
58 Buffalo Bill and Calamity Jane wore them

DOWN

1 Hold firmly, as opinions
2 Stuff used to soften baseball mitts
3 Generally
4 Hill house
5 "A whizzing rocket that would emulate a star," per Wordsworth
6 Big name in storage
7 Boortz of talk radio
8 Swinger?
9 Diane Sawyer's employer
10 Land on the Arctic Cir.
11 Most dismal
12 Mouthwash with the patented ingredient Zantrate
13 Shakespearean stage direction
15 Depression creator
21 Crab apple's quality
24 Old-fashioned respirator
26 Not as outgoing
27 Communist bloc news source
30 Experienced
31 Fountain drinks
33 Wrist bones
34 Lamebrain
35 It's not fair
36 Car collectors?
37 Greek salad ingredient
38 They arrive by the truckload
39 Movie trailers, e.g.
40 Carriage with a folding hood
41 Turbine parts
44 Advanced slowly
47 School door sign
48 Amendment to an amendment
51 Southeast Asian language
52 Dark side
54 Ikura or tobiko

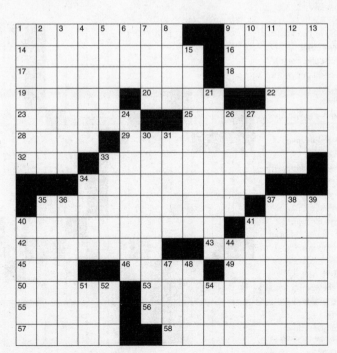

by Patrick Berry

ACROSS

1 Where a lot of dough gets thrown around
11 See 51-Across
15 Fuel for a warp drive engine on "Star Trek"
16 Resignation exclamation
17 Sleep aid, for some
18 BMW of North America and others: Abbr.
19 Zip around a field?
20 Makes happen
21 Assistant played by Bruce Lee
22 Wanting for nothing
24 "Celebrity Jeopardy!" show, briefly
25 Took revenge on
26 Broadview ___, O.
29 Become stiff
33 Get by force of will?
37 Punk's cousin
38 Info about a person's education and work history
39 Smooths
40 Follows a military order
41 Their habits give them away
42 Follows a military order
44 Time of long journées
45 Lets go through
46 Brief albums, in brief
48 Needing hand cream, maybe
51 With 11-Across, biblical woman who met a bad end
53 Board
56 "That gives me an idea . . ."
58 First spaceman's first name

59 Setting for "The Misfits"
61 Polo competitor
62 "My bad"
63 Musical production
64 Symbols of sharpness

DOWN

1 One with promotional potential
2 "___ Steps" (Christian best seller)
3 "10" is inscribed on it
4 Temple imperfection
5 Subject of the 2012 book "Circle of Treason"
6 Porter created by Burroughs
7 Winnebago relatives
8 "Incorrect!"
9 Babes in the woods?

10 Smartphone preceded by the Pre
11 Do the impossible, metaphorically
12 Anxious
13 It's never wrong
14 Standard breakup creation
23 Temptation for Luke Skywalker
25 Follow the sun?
27 Sniffs out
28 First capital of the Last Frontier
30 Like some fogs
31 Ham's handoff
32 Name associated with a mobster or a monster
33 Skyscraper component
34 Brief period of darkness?

35 Eager
36 Event with unmarked choices
43 Trial lawyer who wrote "O.J.: The Last Word"
47 Basidium-borne body
49 Adjective on taco truck menus
50 Crumple
51 "Can't Believe Your ___" (1988 Neil Young song)
52 Drink said to have originated on Lesbos
53 Titles for distinguished Indians
54 Main character in "The Paper Chase," e.g.
55 Cousin of a congo eel
57 Blabbers
60 See, in Santiago

by Jeff Chen

ACROSS

1 Offer to host
8 W.W. II vessels
15 Expressed slight surprise
17 "But really . . ."
18 ___ Empire
19 Deep-seated
20 What you might be overseas?
21 Part of A.M.A.: Abbr.
22 Principal
23 Leave in
24 Rx specification
25 Industry leader
26 Part of a place setting
27 Swelters
28 Absolutely correct
29 Relatives of spoonbills
31 Voyeur
32 Staggered
33 Many chains are found in them
34 Ticked off
35 Works at a museum, say
36 One of the girls
39 Going ___
40 Gnats and mosquitoes
41 Powerful engine
42 Pipe holder?
43 Watch brand once worn by 007
44 One of 24
45 1959 #5 hit with the B-side "I've Cried Before"
48 What a board may be against
49 Euripides tragedy
50 Satyrs, say

DOWN

1 Mountains of ___ (Genesis locale)
2 Strauss opera
3 "Trees" poet
4 Werner of "The Spy Who Came in From the Cold"
5 "In that ___ . . ."
6 Hall-of-Fame outfielder Roush
7 Throws off
8 Flag carried on a knight's lance
9 Blake's "burning bright" cat
10 Pessimist
11 Outmoded: Abbr.
12 Three-time Haitian president
13 Super-wonderful
14 Make more attractive
16 Warriors with supposed powers of invisibility and shapeshifting
22 Ready for an on-air interview
23 "Your mama wears army boots" and such
25 Put a charge into?
26 Leans precariously
27 "L'Arlésienne" composer
28 Workout targets, informally
29 Copycat
30 Long-haired cat breed
31 Simple and serene
32 Fox relative
33 Old arm
35 Pale shades
36 Fought
37 Shot-putter, e.g.
38 Puts in
40 "Positive thinking" pioneer
41 Grounds for a medal
43 Pet
44 Place for a jerk?
46 "Captain Video" figures, for short
47 '50s politico

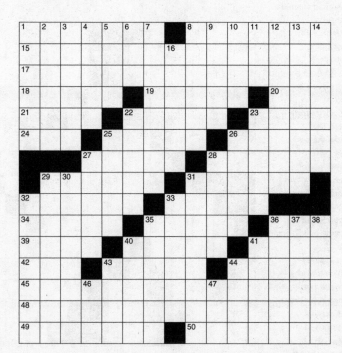

by Mangesh Ghogre and Doug Peterson

ACROSS

1 They aren't straight
6 "Aarrghh!"
13 Shove off
15 Lures
16 "Oo la la!" jeans, informally
18 Preceder of John Sebastian at Woodstock
19 Scott Joplin's "The Entertainer" and others
21 Chain
22 Heralds
24 Produces lush sounds?
25 Heavily populated areas, informally
26 They adhere to brains
28 Temple inits.
29 Lieutenant colonel's charge
30 Students with outstanding character?
31 See 48-Across
32 Its arms are not solid
35 Difficult journey
36 Gifted trio?
37 Follow the party line?
38 Round trip for one?
40 Direction givers, often
42 Superexcited
43 Delicate needlepoint lace
45 Is so inclined
46 Do some work between parties
47 Brings in for more tests, say
48 Fast parts of 31-Across
49 Meteorological probe

DOWN

1 Like wolves vis-à-vis foxes
2 Not at length
3 Takes up onto the surface
4 Susan's family on "Seinfeld"
5 The Father of the Historical Novel
6 Group of football games played at the beginning of Jan.
7 Dog it
8 Pardons
9 Choose in the end
10 Flawlessly
11 Areas next to bull's-eyes
12 Strongmen of old
14 Remedy for a bad leg

17 Fastballs that drop sharply near the plate
20 Durable cover
23 Wise sort
27 2002 Best Original Screenplay Oscar winner for "Talk to Her"
29 Spotted hybrid house pet
30 1980s Olympic star with the autobiography "Breaking the Surface"
31 Grant
32 Geisha's instrument
33 Expelled
34 Pressure gauge connection
35 Mechanic, say
36 Beyond that

37 Shop keeper?
39 "___ Lucy" (old sitcom)
41 Florida's De ___ National Monument
44 Wii ancestor, briefly

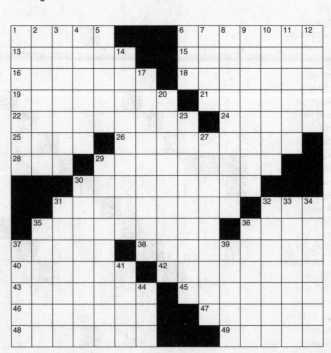

by Tim Croce

ACROSS

1 Begin
10 Donizetti heroine
15 Catches up to
16 Magnetron component
17 Relative of a spouse
19 "Just playin'"
20 Things often dropped in Harvard Yard?
21 Big name in winter vehicles
22 Fixer, perhaps
23 In the way of
24 Phony blazers
25 Birthplace of the Franciscan order
27 "Before My Birth" collagist, 1914
28 ___-yo (cold treat, briefly)
29 With 36- and 39-Across, go from 1- to 61-Across
31 10-year-old Best Supporting Actress
33 Robert W. Service's "The Cremation of Sam ___"
36 See 29-Across
37 Robert W. Service output
38 Soothing flora
39 See 29-Across
41 Bumped into
42 Bumped into
43 Razor target, maybe
47 Pack into a thick mass
50 Ottoman bigwig
51 Tan in a library
52 Anatomical ring
53 Direction de Paris à Nancy
54 Vegan gelatin substitute
55 Stopgap supervisor's duty

58 ___ Montoya, swordsman in "The Princess Bride"
59 Prefixes featured on some maps
60 Baden-Powell of the Girl Guides
61 End

DOWN

1 One known for riding out of gear?
2 Brings out
3 Sends in
4 He'll "talk 'til his voice is hoarse"
5 The Who's "___ Hard"
6 ___ Romanova, alter ego of Marvel's Black Widow
7 Landmark anime film of 1988
8 Many pulp heroes, in slang
9 Picking up skill?
10 Cheerful early risers
11 Preposition on a business-hours sign
12 Unit charge
13 "&" or "@," but not "and" or "at"
14 Restricted flight items
18 By yesterday, so to speak
23 Indication of some oxidation
24 Hug or kiss, maybe
26 Drink brand symbolized by a polar bear
27 39th vice president
30 "The Dark Knight Rises" director, 2012
31 Grammy category
32 What's typical

33 "Lordy!" in Lodi
34 Snow job?
35 Been chosen, as for office
40 One-two in the ring?
42 Pavlova portrayed one over 4,000 times
44 Storied place of worship
45 Eastern lodging
46 "2 Fast 2 Furious" co-star Gibson
48 Grand Caravan maker
49 Jumbles
50 One of Jacob's sons
53 Ser, across the Pyrenees
54 Loads
56 Piece of the street
57 ___-fi

by Peter A. Collins

152 ★★★

ACROSS

1 Clemson Tigers logo
9 Mistreating
15 Not left hanging, say
16 Draws
17 Mimosas and such
19 Toddler seats?
20 ___ Day (May 1)
21 ___ gratia
22 Become completely absorbed
23 Florida's ___ National Park
25 Rhone feeder
26 It can be found beneath the lower crust
27 "Look ___" (Vince Gill hit)
28 Sauce often served with oysters
32 See 43-Across
33 Beginning of time?
34 Mao's designated successor
35 Snoop Dogg, to Cameron Diaz [fun fact!]
37 Kind of check: Abbr.
38 Coeur ___
39 Capitale européenne
40 Angry Birds or Tetris, e.g.
43 With 32-Across, study of Hesse and Mann, informally
44 W.W. II battle site, for short
45 One might be a couple of years old
46 2013 women's singles champ at Wimbledon
47 Shows levelheadedness
50 Mobile advertising medium?
51 Hardly like the pick of the litter
52 "Oh man, that's bad"
53 Words after "say" or before "bad"

DOWN

1 Ring accompaniers
2 Like stunt pilots' stunts
3 Headed toward bankruptcy
4 Printer rollers
5 Release a claim to, legally
6 What the French think?
7 Marxist Andrés and writer Anaïs
8 Boom source
9 Centennial, e.g.
10 Good at drawing?
11 Continental abbr.
12 Attention-seeking, say
13 Woodenware
14 Davis of Hollywood
18 Put off
23 Occupy opponent
24 Suffix with hex-
26 Eyeshades?
28 Like a customer who may get special notice
29 Plastic that can be made permanently rigid
30 See red?
31 Corroded
33 Braggadocios
36 Inauguration recitation, maybe
37 Confirmed
39 Ones above military heads
40 Lists
41 "Would that it were!"
42 Former Israeli president Katsav
43 Adorned, per menus
46 Something with round parts?
48 Draw
49 Part of 8-Down

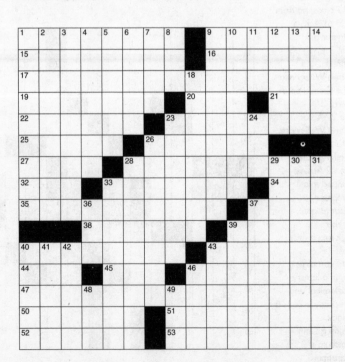

by Joe Krozel

ACROSS

1 Hall-of-Fame rock band or its lead musician
8 It sends out lots of streams
15 Very long European link
16 Rust or combust
17 It flies on demand
18 Skunk, at times
19 Some P.D. personnel
20 One who may be on your case
22 The Spanish I love?
23 What a couple of people can play
25 Stand-out performances
26 Chocolate bar with a long biscuit and caramel
27 Subject of the 2003 book "Power Failure"
29 Without hesitation
30 Subsist on field rations?
31 Its flowers are very short-lived
33 Like a sawhorse's legs
35 Critical
36 Party staple
37 Catered to Windows shoppers?
41 Noodle taxers?
45 Observes
46 Abbr. after 8-Across
48 Last band in the Rock and Roll Hall of Fame, alphabetically
49 "The Hudsucker Proxy" director, 1994
50 Columbia and the like
52 French river or department
53 "___ mentioned . . ."

54 Images on some lab slides
56 Lima-to-Bogotá dir.
57 Frankenstein, e.g.
59 Its passengers were revolting
61 Theodore Roosevelt Island setting
62 Destroyer destroyer
63 Colorful cooler
64 Makeover options

DOWN

1 Like some milk
2 Sashimi staple
3 Changing place
4 Blockbuster?
5 Mediums for dummies, say: Abbr.
6 Where it all comes together?
7 Ex amount?

8 Appointment disappointments
9 Nationals, at one time
10 Flag
11 Tablet banner, say, briefly
12 Reserve
13 Inventory
14 Duped
21 Gradual, in some product names
24 Giant in fantasy
26 Bar that's set very high
28 Physicist Bohr
30 Display on a red carpet
32 Basic solution
34 Without hesitation, in brief
37 Does some outdoor pitching?

38 "Don't joke about that yet"
39 Took away bit by bit
40 Event occasioning 7-Down
41 Cryotherapy choice
42 Artificially small
43 What might take up residence?
44 Truncated trunks?
47 Zero times, in Zwickau
50 Back-pedaler's words
51 About 7% of it is American
54 Vapor: Prefix
55 Apple assistant
58 Lib. arts major
60 Coral ___ (city near Oakland Pk., Fla.)

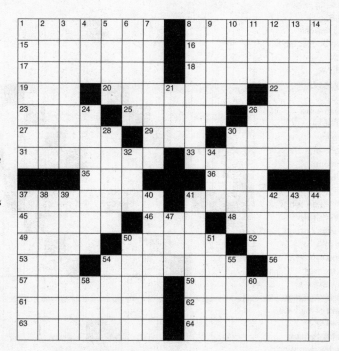

by Bruce R. Sutphin

ACROSS

1 It may provide closure in a tragedy
8 Discarded
15 City named for Theodore Roosevelt's vice president
17 Word search technique?
18 Webby Award winner who accepted saying "Please don't recount this vote"
19 With 11-Down, animal called "stubbin" by locals
20 Nascar stat that rises under caution flags
21 Diddly
22 Opening in the computer business?
23 Bad thing to lose
24 Flights
25 Taste makers?
26 Has it bad for, so to speak
27 -i relative
28 Largest city in Moravia
29 Mob member, informally
30 Morale
35 Second in command?
36 Cloverleaf section
37 Flat top
39 Blended dressing?
42 Shutter shutter
43 Literally, "I do not wish to"
44 Sauna exhalations
45 Solomonic
46 Chewed the fat
47 Watson's creator
48 Lowest of the low?
49 Prankery
50 1965 Beach Boys hit
53 Mission
54 Jason Mraz song that spent a record 76 weeks on Billboard's Hot 100
55 Outcries

DOWN

1 Outgoing
2 Lot arrangement
3 Draws
4 Some refrigerants
5 Reinforcement pieces
6 Mantel piece
7 Nissan bumpers?
8 Annual event since 1929, with "the"
9 Hard to pick up
10 Cigarette paper source
11 See 19-Across
12 Author of 1980's "The Annotated Gulliver's Travels"
13 Macedonia's capital
14 "El día que me quieras" and others
16 Large monitors
22 Abandon one's efforts, informally
23 "The Hound of the Baskervilles" backdrop
25 It's around a cup
26 1 Infinite ___ (address of Apple's headquarters)
28 Dover soul
29 Force in red uniforms: Abbr.
31 Course data
32 Palliate
33 Hit hard, as in an accident
34 Tip used for icing
38 They will be missed
39 Lightly hailed?
40 Major report
41 "Yowza!"
42 Hound
43 Dresden decimator of 1945
45 Something beyond the grate divide?
46 Herod's realm
48 1879's Anglo-___ War
49 "Fantastic Mr. Fox" author
51 War on Poverty agcy.
52 Advisory grp. that includes the drug czar

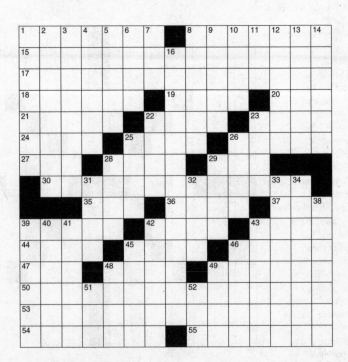

by Byron Walden

ACROSS

1 Forest newcomer
5 Group whose last Top 40 hit was "When All Is Said and Done"
9 To-do list
14 Sound after call waiting?
15 Sense, as a 14-Across
16 Nobel winner Joliot-Curie
17 Turkey sticker
20 "Everybody Is ___" (1970 hit)
21 Response to a threat
22 Old co. with overlapping globes in its logo
23 1960s civil rights leader ___ Brown
25 Katey who portrayed TV's Peg Bundy
27 Benchwarmer's plea
33 Drain
34 Bobby's follower?
35 Fibonacci, notably
36 Hockey Hall of Fame nickname
38 Alternative to ZzzQuil
40 Stat. for Re, La or Ti
41 "___ needed"
43 Papa ___ (Northeast pizza chain)
45 Now in
46 "That subject's off the table!"
49 Luster
50 They have edible shells
51 Whse. sight
53 "Philosophy will clip an angel's wings" writer
56 French class setting
59 Universal query?
62 Uncle Sam, say
63 One featuring a Maltese cross
64 Turkic word for "island"
65 Browser history list
66 Couldn't discard in crazy eights, say
67 Court suspensions

DOWN

1 Relief provider, for short
2 Blasts through
3 "And now?"
4 Sealing worker
5 "Per-r-rfect!"
6 ___-red
7 Alfred H. ___ Jr., founding director of MoMA
8 Like G.I.'s, per recruiting ads
9 Interval
10 Were present?
11 Gets payback
12 Sensed
13 They may be used in veins
18 They may be used around veins
19 All-Star Infante
24 Drone
26 1998 hit from the album "Surfacing"
27 False start?
28 Stockholder?
29 Like some hemoglobin
30 ___-A
31 Plantation habitation
32 Cybermemo
37 Something taken on the stand
39 Ring
42 They're on hunts
44 Revolving feature
47 Revolving features?
48 "Psst . . . buddy"
51 1/20 tons: Abbr.
52 Whence the word "bong"
54 Day of the week of Jul. 4, 1776
55 Wizened up
57 Indiana, e.g., to Lafayette
58 Some use electric organs
60 River Shannon's Lough ___
61 Sudoku segment

by Peter A. Collins

156 ★★★

ACROSS

1 Angry missive
10 Body parts often targeted by masseurs
15 Trailing
16 Hatch in the upper house
17 Chutes behind boats
18 Treaty of Sycamore Shoals negotiator, 1775
19 Taking forever
20 Antimissile plan, for short
21 Part of Duchamp's parody of the "Mona Lisa"
22 Octane booster brand
24 San ___, Calif, (border town opposite Tijuana)
26 Discount ticket letters
29 In the main
31 Stuffed bear voiced by Seth MacFarlane
34 Not likely to be a "cheese" lover?
36 Pens for tablets
38 Learn to live with
39 Like the sound holes of a cello
41 1986 Indy 500 champion
42 Champion
44 Venetian mapmaker ___ Mauro
45 Driver's license requirement
47 Portugal's Palácio de ___ Bento
48 What a movie villain often comes to
50 Faced
52 Enter as a mediator
54 Tribe whose sun symbol is on the New Mexico flag
56 Grandson of Abraham
60 Roadster from Japan
61 Sites for shark sightings
63 Gut trouble
64 Group in a star's orbit
65 Disney Hall architect
66 Sci-fi battle site

DOWN

1 Beats at the buzzer, say
2 Like a control freak
3 Houston ballplayer, in sports shorthand
4 Spring events
5 Word spoken 90 times in Molly Bloom's soliloquy
6 Desperately tries to get
7 "Criminal Minds" agent with an I.Q. of 187
8 Singer of the #1 single "Try Again," 2000
9 Half a couple
10 Vacancy clause?
11 Like the crowd at a campaign rally
12 Some mock-ups
13 One in a Kindergarten?
14 Three-time All-Pro guard Chris
21 Owen Wilson's "Midnight in Paris" role
23 Glenda Jackson/Ben Kingsley film scripted by Harold Pinter
25 Cunning one
26 Wolf (down)
27 ___ gun
28 Battle site of June 6, 1944
30 Grand Slam event
32 John Paul's successor
33 Inflicted on
35 Green org.
37 Shade that fades
40 Musical with a cow that's catapulted over a castle
43 Area inside the 20, in football
46 Appetite
49 More likely
51 Sadness symbolized
52 Complacent
53 Plaza square, maybe
55 Least bit
57 Blind strip
58 Morsel for a guppy
59 One with a password, say
61 Street crosser, briefly
62 "You wanna run that by me again?"

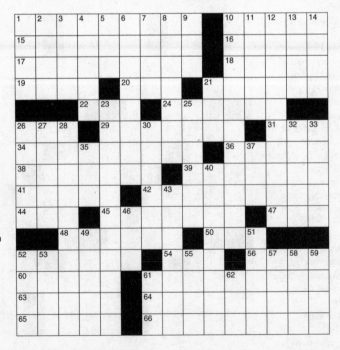

by John Farmer

ACROSS

1 1999 rap hit featuring Snoop Dogg
9 "Sin City" actress
13 Classic TV family
15 Represent
16 45 degrees, for 1
18 Wild things?
19 Puts on eBay again
20 Cuban province where Castro was born
22 Zoological groups
23 Diamond deal
24 Software plug-in
25 Mode of transportation in a 1969 #1 hit
26 Filmdom family name
27 Israel's Sea of ___
28 Silence fillers
29 Informal name of the 45th state
30 Softball question
33 Clean, now
34 Songbird Mitchell
35 Turkey ___, baseball Hall-of-Famer from the Negro leagues
37 Breaks
38 They get tested
39 ___ system, part of the brain that regulates emotion, behavior and long-term memory
40 2000s CBS sitcom
41 Sextet at Woodstock
42 "El Condor ___" (1970 Simon & Garfunkel hit)
43 Golda Meir and Yitzhak Rabin led it
45 Division d'une carte
46 Place of outdoor meditation
47 Mock words of understanding
48 Price of an opera?

DOWN

1 Gangster nickname
2 "Carmen" figure
3 Covers
4 Share a secret with
5 From the Forbidden City
6 Bad impressions?
7 Poverty, metaphorically
8 Dutch city ESE of Amsterdam
9 Shape shifters?
10 Try to hear better, maybe
11 Knock-down-drag-out
12 First name in shooting
14 Winter set
17 Didn't make it home, say
21 Arm
23 E-mail ancestors
25 "Wordplay" vocalist, 2005
27 "In your dreams!"
29 Mary ___ (doomed ship)
30 Italian region that's home to Milan
31 Chances that a year ends with any particular digit
32 Florida's Key ___
33 Musician who arranged the theme for "2001"
34 Fruit-filled pastry
35 Where to bury the hatchet?
36 Olympic ice dancing gold medalist Virtue and others
37 ___ Alley
38 Hypercompetitive
39 About 40–60 beats per minute
41 Volume measure
44 Volume measure

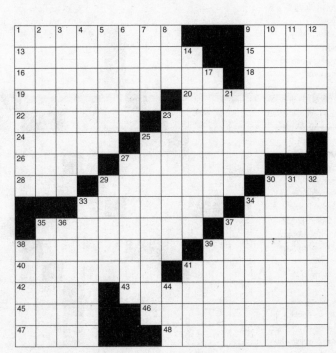

by David Steinberg

ACROSS

1 1980 new wave classic
7 1996 hybrid animation/live-action film
15 Cole ___, 2008 World Series M.V.P.
16 "Ahh" sloganeer
17 Juices
18 Hot numbers
19 "Bait Car" channel
20 Some hotels and old cars
21 Lays flat
22 It can precede masochism
23 Kind of mile: Abbr.
24 Location from which the phoenix rose
25 Ulan-___ (city in Siberia)
26 Biographer biographized in "Poison Pen"
29 Wear for Teddy Roosevelt
31 Amt. of copper, say
32 Surmounted
33 Dirty Harry fired them
37 Upstate N.Y. sch.
38 1985 #1 whose video won six MTV Video Music Awards
39 Rhode Island cuisine specialty
43 Rapper with the 2000 single "Party Up (Up in Here)"
44 "___ Story" (2007 Jenna Bush book)
45 Symbols of strength
46 Zales inventory
47 Give some juice
48 Benefits
50 Have thirds, say
51 Jockey competitor
53 Jin dynasty conqueror
54 Female novelist whose real first name was Howard

55 Rhyme for "drool" in a Dean Martin classic
56 Something between 49-Downs
57 Out of alignment

DOWN

1 "How's it goin', dawg?"
2 Hobby with Q codes
3 Fresh
4 Gnocchi topper
5 "___ It" (2006 Young Jeezy single)
6 100 metric drops: Abbr.
7 Dirt, in slang
8 Like the Simpson kids' hair
9 Dramatic opening
10 Lewis ___, loser to Zachary Taylor in 1848
11 Prefix with tourism

12 1995–2013 senator from Arizona
13 1985–93 senator from Tennessee
14 Raymond who played Abraham Lincoln
20 Cowboy feature
23 What a leadfoot may do
24 City that's headquarters for Pizza Hut and J. C. Penney
26 Former Australian prime minister Rudd
27 Supposed sighting off the coast of Norway
28 Where faces meet
30 Tight shoe wearer's woe
33 Mercury and Saturn, once
34 Follower of one nation?
35 Soup line

36 Marketing mantra
38 Return service
39 Sci-fi's ___ Binks
40 Many an early tie
41 Safe spots
42 First marketer of Cabbage Patch Kids
46 Outrageously freewheeling
48 ___ concours (unrivaled: Fr.)
49 Last file menu option, often
50 Bearded mountain dweller
52 Bit of action
53 Deg. from 37-Across

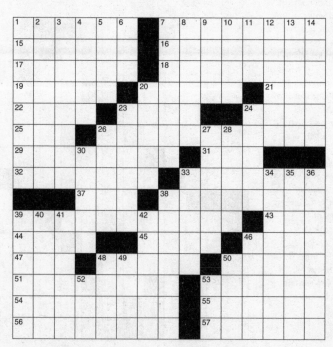

by Peter Wentz

ACROSS

1 Strip authority
8 Savanna bounders
15 Situation early in an inning
16 Target of some soccer kicks
17 Lipitor and such
18 State University of New York campus site
19 Like some glasses
20 1950s Dodgers pitcher ___ Labine
21 With 32-Down, end of an advertising pitch
22 Go-___ (certain motorized scooters)
23 Ink holder
24 French department that's home to the Chartreuse Mountains
26 G.I. hangout
27 Subject of a golf lesson
29 Pulitzer-winning historian Doris ___ Goodwin
30 Kennedyesque conquests
33 Player coached by Hank Stram
37 Mayor's introduction?
38 Wearer of a wraparound cloth called a lavalava
41 Like the hoi polloi
42 With 14-Down, part of a U.S. political map
43 Customary start for Wimbledon singles finals
44 Finish, with "up"
45 Kegger cry
46 Bender
47 "___ sir . . ."
49 Tub handle?

51 A musician might pick it
53 TNT ingredient?
54 Bouts of madness
55 Kindergarten admonition
56 Sealed
57 Rested

DOWN

1 Like the grunge rock movement
2 Where Neptune can be found
3 Level
4 "America the Beautiful" poet Katharine Lee ___
5 Boo-boo
6 Gear impediment
7 M.O.
8 "Too rich for my blood"
9 Place for a comb
10 Top Médoc classification
11 Certain mail destination: Abbr.
12 More strung out
13 Not ahead
14 See 42-Across
20 Underwritten?
23 Recipe amount
25 Slovenian-born N.B.A. guard Vujacic
27 The Galloping Gourmet
28 "Watership Down" director Martin
29 Defend with focus, in football
31 Setting numbered in multiples of the square root of 2
32 See 21-Across

34 Admission of clumsiness
35 Polish
36 Palestinian fighters
38 Hospital patron
39 Stimulate
40 Big wheels
44 Winner of a record 82 P.G.A. Tour events
45 Ventriloquist's prop
48 Tennis's Nastase
49 ___ adagio (score direction)
50 Word with flute or horn
52 "Lucky Number Slevin" actress, 2006
53 Reciprocal action

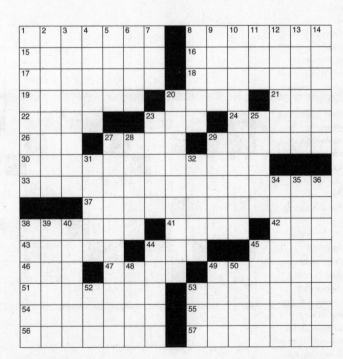

by Byron Walden

160 ★★★

ACROSS

1 Wiped the floor with
16 Use of blockades, say
17 Western daily
18 Lobby
19 Watch things
20 Limited edition?
21 Suffix with electr-
22 Blasting, musically
24 Bay, say . . . or bring to bay
28 Tempest, to Theodor
31 Bellyaches
33 ___ Rose
34 One may be tapped out
37 Brunch orders, briefly
38 McKinley's Ohio birthplace
39 Title priestess of opera
40 Aim
42 Setting of 10, maybe
43 Sony output
44 Bulldogs' sch.
46 Painter ___ della Francesca
48 Certain advertising medium
55 It's not word-for-word
56 Old French epics
57 Idolizes

DOWN

1 1970s–80s sitcom setting
2 "I'm ___" (Friday declaration)
3 Doctor's orders
4 Passing people
5 What Hamilton called the wealthy
6 "Sure, let's try"
7 ___ Arden Oplev, director of "The Girl With the Dragon Tattoo"
8 Mid third-century year
9 Gershwin biographer David
10 Guarders with droopy ears and pendulous lips
11 Some collectible lithographs
12 It hasn't happened before
13 Sans spice
14 Sought-after rock group?
15 Fun or laugh follower
22 Send quickly, in a way
23 Finders' keepers?
25 What stars may indicate
26 Cause of a class struggle?
27 Allure alternative
28 Sun blocker
29 Pearl Harbor attack initiator
30 Polaris bear
31 Limb-entangling weapon
32 Second-greatest period in the history of something
35 1931 Best Picture
36 Utility bill details
41 Light measures
43 Like much arable land
45 "I ___ Lonely" (1954 hit for the Four Knights)
46 Lead-in to deux or trois
47 Particular paean penner
48 Ozone destroyers, for short
49 "What's Hecuba to him, ___ to Hecuba": Hamlet
50 Sinatra's "Meet ___ the Copa"
51 Biblical miracle setting
52 Police dept. personage
53 Touch
54 Law school newbie

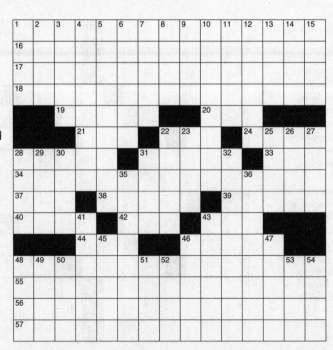

by Martin Ashwood-Smith

ACROSS

1 Domino's bottom?
11 Sing
15 Olympic Tower financier
16 Roman marketplaces
17 Lines to be cracked
18 Something to hold down
19 Asian silk center
20 Giving no performances
22 Aid in getting it together?
23 Off-limits
26 Al Bundy's garage, e.g.
28 Spot with a talking bear, maybe: Abbr.
31 XII, perhaps
33 Hailstorm, e.g.
34 Sarah Palin called herself an average one
37 How fresh paint glistens
38 "The Tourist" novelist Steinhauer
39 Best final result
41 Literary character who says "I'll chase him round Good Hope"
42 Kind of horoscope
44 Kids' party game
46 Bell heather and tree heath
48 Topic in a world religions course
49 Follower of Gore?
50 Like some laptop keyboards
52 Minable material
54 Part of un giorno
55 "I'll send for you ___": Othello
57 Record held for decades?

61 Swimmer featured in the 2013 film "Blackfish"
63 Important stud farm visitors
66 Ape's lack
67 Pre-Raphaelite ideal
68 Bad side of literature?
69 Sings

DOWN

1 Spotted South American mammal
2 The white surrounds it
3 99+ things in Alaska?
4 2008 title role for Adam Sandler
5 Buttercup family member
6 See 8-Down
7 Letter string
8 With 6-Down, old wheels
9 When hands are extended straight up and down
10 It may be over a foot
11 Closest bud, briefly
12 Head-turning cry
13 Make a fashionable entrance?
14 Its contents provide juice
21 Apprehended
24 Big name in Hispanic food
25 Juice
27 Sports stud
28 DC transformation location
29 Collection of green panels
30 CH3COOH
32 Some pleas, briefly

35 Flair
36 Like some colors and cornets
40 Grp. concerned with feeding the kitty
43 Karaoke stand-in?
45 Raiser of dogs?
47 Penalty box, to sports fans
51 Trattoria dessert
53 "32 Flavors" singer Davis, 1998
56 "Barney Miller" Emmy winner Pitlik
58 Armenia's basic monetary unit
59 French suffix with jardin
60 Proposal figs.
62 Draught ___
64 Jubilant cry
65 Trash

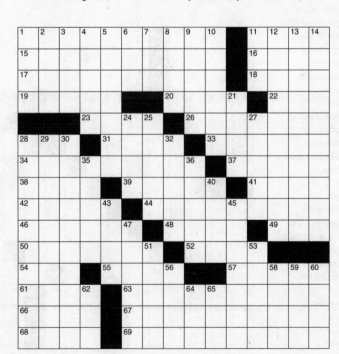

by Barry C. Silk

★ ★ ★

ACROSS
1 Sting, basically
5 Vera Miles, in 1948
15 City surrounded on two sides by Toiyabe National Forest
16 "Is this really my fault?"
17 About
18 House style
19 Video store section
21 It opens Letterman's "Viewer Mail"
22 Berkshire, e.g.
23 It might get busted
25 Wrestler Flair, multiple-time world heavyweight champion
26 Straight up
28 Jake's lover in "The Sun Also Rises"
30 Hearty meat dish
31 Bunch of sitcom characters
32 Fellahs
33 Stretched out
34 Calf muscle
37 Upset
41 Online greeting
42 Pontiff for just 26 days in 1605
43 Choice for un votant
44 ___ track
45 Drink that's stirred
46 Bird of the American Arctic that migrates south
49 Forger
51 Mistaken
53 Hard ___
54 Zip
55 More than a little off
56 Scooby-Doo and others
57 1979 revolution locale

DOWN
1 "Masterpiece Theatre" it ain't
2 Change from a hit to an error, say
3 West Indies island
4 Disappearing word
5 Humanities degs.
6 Entreats
7 Start to write?
8 Laugh maker
9 Actor Yaphet ___, of TV's "Homicide"
10 Equipped
11 What an A is not
12 Took pleasure in
13 Shower cap at a motel, maybe
14 Culls
20 1930s–50s Arab ruler
24 Univ. military programs
27 Hunter with a middle initial of J
28 Shows disdain
29 Indian dignitary
31 John Deere product
33 Los Angeles suburb
34 Picking up
35 Reagan Supreme Court nominee
36 1961 Michelangelo Antonioni film a k a "The Night"
37 Seasonal recurrence
38 Watch
39 Carnival displays
40 "You said it!"
42 Home of the Chiefs in minor-league baseball
44 Hooked up and left
47 "Now that's awesome!"
48 Chap
50 Landlocked land of 12 million
52 Bunch of fun

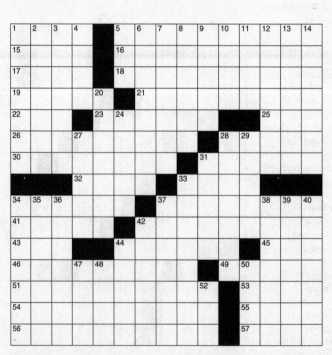

by Joe DiPietro

ACROSS

1 Refuse transportation?
5 Dust remover
15 One of a skeletal pair
16 Must
17 Spin
18 Uffizi collection
19 Engineering ring
21 Falling out
22 Derisive interjection
23 Put down
25 Hereditary ruler?
27 Inquisition target
29 Parlor pieces
33 Takes the wrong way?
34 "__ do you good"
36 Pillow padding
37 March word
38 Fraudulent acts
40 Greek letter spelled out at the start of a Beatles title?
41 Val d'__, France, 1992 Olympics skiing site
43 Astronomical effect
44 Faux pas
45 Propels, in a way
47 Insulting one
49 Way in or out
51 Folds
53 Swear words?
56 Air-freight, e.g.
58 Where Jehu ruled
59 Citrus-y drink
62 Oompah-paher
63 Emptied
64 Subj. with graphs
65 Alarmist
66 Chapter 11 issue

DOWN

1 Coastal resident's hurricane worry
2 Completely replace the staff
3 Danced the milonga
4 Ones refusing transportation?
5 Formal requirement
6 Sou'wester, e.g.
7 Swedish monopolist Kreuger
8 Vincent's successor as baseball commissioner
9 Cut in a fight, maybe
10 Nonconformists
11 Nickelodeon Chihuahua
12 Jazz singer Anita
13 Not esa or esta
14 Armyworm, eventually
20 "Maid of Athens, __ We Part" (Byron poem)
24 Make an emergency landing
26 Spacewalk, for NASA
28 Traction enhancer
30 Bunk
31 Emphatic negative
32 LP problem
33 Antique damage
35 Amethyst shade
38 Misleading
39 Like resorts, typically
42 Awesome
44 Under way
46 Lug
48 Old Mario Bros. console
50 It's wavy in São Paulo
52 Partial approach?
53 Target for nails
54 Charity
55 Something wordless to read
57 Short-lived particle
60 Preserve
61 Parochial schoolteacher

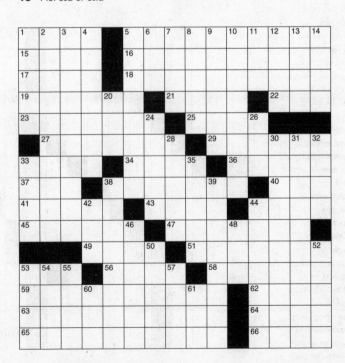

by Manny Nosowsky

164 ★★★

ACROSS
1 Some clowning around
11 Ancient Briton
15 Hotel amenity
16 Get ___ deal
17 Creep
18 Oil spot
19 Smarts
20 It may be given with a bow
22 Yellows or grays
23 Something hard to get nowadays by phone
24 1935 movie starring Helen Gahagan as Queen Hash-a-Mo-Tep of Kor
25 Jeweler's gadget
26 Bisque fleck
27 Appellate judge, often
28 Certain craft hobbyist
29 Circulated some winter airs
32 Kind of block
33 Equus hemionus
34 Places that serve O.J. beside the links?
35 "___ Out," 2003 Tony winner for Best Choreography
36 Fret over, slangily
37 10-4
40 Not a walk in the park
42 Closing bars
43 "'Deed I Do" singer
44 Lost all patience
45 ___ row
46 "May I interrupt you?"
48 Item component usually seen in threes or fours
49 "We're not getting back together"
50 Some hosp. records
51 Area of limited growth

DOWN
1 98 and 99, typically
2 "Knock it off!"
3 She played Musette to Gish's Mimi in "La Bohème," 1926
4 Things that are out of bounds
5 They knock back lots
6 Prefix with syllabic
7 Valued
8 "Ain't gonna happen"
9 Let
10 Time out?
11 Small favors that go to your head
12 Old TV drama set in San Francisco
13 Shroud of Torino?
14 Some middle-schoolers
21 Slip on a new piece of clothing?
23 Engine unit
25 Hourlong introduction?
27 Works the old bean
28 Like a liberal arts education
29 Consummate
30 Taking in too little
31 Wanting it all
32 Groggy query
34 "Gimme"
36 ___ Sunday a k a Quinquagesima
37 Jiver's greeting
38 Post operative?
39 Unmistakable
41 They're light-seeking
42 Staffs
44 Queen's domain
47 Up-to-date, informally

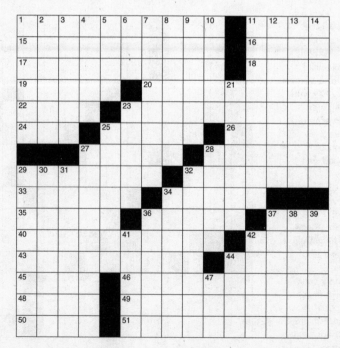

by Byron Walden

ACROSS
1 Historic trials
7 High-tech heart, for short
10 Somewhere over the rainbow
14 One affected by a strike
15 Like some devils?
17 Question upon hearing an accent
19 Host
20 Surface
21 Buck passer?
22 Particle stream
23 Possible penicillin target
25 Capital of Cambodia
28 It's not out of the ordinary
31 Put ___ (shove off)
33 Factor in some acad. probations
34 Starchy
36 Dramatic opening
38 Buck passer?
41 Kutcher who hosted TV's "Punk'd"
42 Horse-drawn vehicle
43 It may go for mi. and mi.
44 Sentencing request
46 A load
48 Point in the right direction?
50 Pageant put-on
52 Starter's aid
54 "Black" day in the stock market crash, 10/29/1929: Abbr.
56 "Don't be so shy!"
57 Ring sport
58 "Same thing, really"
62 Aged
63 Onetime Missouri natives
64 Corporeal canal
65 Sign of a crowd
66 With 9-Down, tops

DOWN
1 Not just bickering
2 Mehrabad International Airport site
3 Intelligence concern
4 Not at all lethargic
5 Windsor, for one
6 Comes (to)
7 Rally Sport, e.g.
8 Wage earners
9 See 66-Across
10 Concerning
11 Curriculum requirement, often
12 Te ___
13 Kind of sleep
16 Fizzle
18 Knocking noise
24 Topping for fish or meat
26 Thrusted thing
27 Nest
29 Etymologist's concern
30 Classic comedy film about gender-role reversal
32 Succeed in a big way
35 "Déjeuner sur l'herbe" artist
37 Nevada's second-largest county
38 Thun's river
39 Court org. since 1881
40 Wood problem
45 Comparatively creamy
47 Gordon ___ a k a Sting
49 Coach
51 It's negative
53 With 59-Down, unimpressive
55 Some aliens take it: Abbr.
57 Vulnerable gap
58 ___ Friday's
59 See 53-Down
60 Writing: Abbr.
61 East Lansing sch.

by Michael Shteyman

166 ★★★

ACROSS

1 Like some Old Masters
8 Epithets
14 Flop
16 Complete circuit
17 Runner's place
18 "Casablanca" words repeated before "as if it were the last time"
19 Not hard
20 Flexible fastener
22 Pickled
23 11-member grp.
24 Public debt instrument
25 18-Across speaker
26 Top
28 Amalfi articles
29 Chemical ending
30 Better than O.K.
32 Cantina request
37 Wilde and Yeats
38 ___-jongg
39 Trudge
42 Range rover
43 Shelter dug into a hillside
44 Itty bits
46 Geezers' grunts
47 "___ of the Times" (1966 Petula Clark hit)
48 Automated answering machine base
50 Petulance
51 "Likewise"
52 "Out of the question"
54 Cut
55 Sleeper, for one
56 Builds
57 Arch sites

DOWN

1 Hustle
2 Port from which the Spanish Armada departed in 1588
3 Goth's look enhancer
4 Like a brig
5 Final, as a deal
6 Penn name
7 Info request from a computer dating service: Abbr.
8 Evildoer of Asgard
9 Dill relative
10 Cronies
11 Catcher for Whitey in the 1960s Yankees
12 Veneer
13 Floors it
15 Becomes competitive
21 Military practice
23 Name
26 Pinned attire
27 Skin refresher
30 Org. whose first president general was first lady Caroline Harrison
31 Suffix with ball
33 Walloping
34 Atmosphere
35 Fund designation
36 Dilutants
39 Float like a butterfly, say
40 Construction machine
41 Indolent
43 Not on the level
45 Utah senator who lent his name to a 1930 tariff act
47 Prey for a ladybug
49 Time immemorial
50 View by computer tomography
53 ". . . ___ quit!"

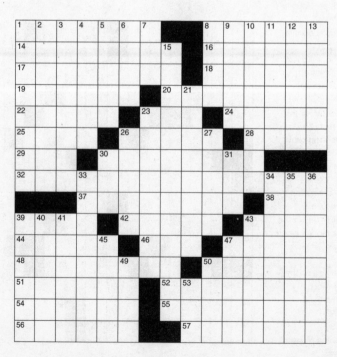

by Paula Gamache

ACROSS

1 Lummox
8 He prophesied the destruction of Jerusalem
13 Draw
15 Its chief town is Scarborough
16 Come before
17 El Alamein battle commander
18 Cuts off the back
19 Ireland's ___ De Valera
21 Seat of White Pine County, Nev.
22 One beginning?
23 Illegal firing
24 Free of excess matter
25 Cone head?
26 Opening words of the Beatles' "We Can Work It Out"
27 Patisserie output
28 "Ditto"
29 Unlikely loser
30 Reflexologist's target
33 Ramshackle residence
34 Bombs
35 Stowe slave
36 Checked out
37 Run smoothly
40 "___ sign!"
41 Quinces, e.g.
42 It has 720 hrs.
43 You can bet on it
44 Sphere, say
45 Cry of accomplishment
46 Divider of Nebraska
48 Eh
50 Western ring
51 Pole, for one
52 Pa Clampett player on TV
53 Tile piece

DOWN

1 Book with 150 chapters
2 When two hands meet
3 Peruvian, e.g.
4 Brief bid
5 They're sometimes stacked
6 Org. that provides R.V. hookups
7 "I'll wait"
8 It has a bright side
9 Tech stock option
10 Highest peak on Africa's west coast
11 A casino may have one
12 Lama, e.g.
14 Fluctuating fortunes
15 Suffix associated with accelerators
20 Stampede sound
23 Dilettantish
24 A fifth of quinze
26 Cross
27 "Grab ___!"
28 Table in old Rome
29 Uses a tap, perhaps
30 Development area
31 50 Cent and others
32 Politely got rid of
33 Apply by repeated small touches
36 Newspaper div.
37 Impish expression of delight
38 Flap
39 Workshop of Hephaestus
41 One who handles stress effectively?
42 Galleria array
44 Novelist Barstow
45 General ___ chicken
47 Bond
49 24-Down, across the Alps

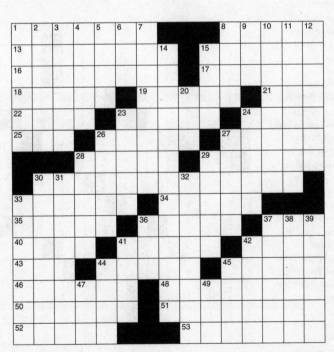

by Louis Hildebrand

ACROSS

1 Device used for film tracking shots
10 Cough up
15 "Lost in America" vehicle
16 Tickle
17 Key distributor
18 City near Dinosaur World
19 Work on a column
20 Early member of Clinton's cabinet
22 Places to serve slop
23 "The 39 Steps" star
24 Magritte's "The ___ of Man"
25 Putin foreign minister Igor ___
27 Banquet
28 Inveiglement
31 Donizetti's oeuvre
33 Wholehearted
34 Prefatory parts
35 Axes to grind
36 Straightaway
37 Pottery Barn purchases
38 1930s actress Farrell
40 ". . . ___ I again behold my Romeo!"
41 Sports Illustrated's first two-time Sportsman of the Year, 1996 and 2000
42 Plot anew
47 The two dots in "naïve"
49 Two-fisted
50 Little, bespectacled owl of the comics
51 Crossing them can affect you
53 Mote
54 Deleted
55 Grand ___
56 Says not for the first time

DOWN

1 It's full of holes
2 Add color to
3 "The scourge of the fashionable world": Schopenhauer
4 Where the malleolus is
5 Tossed over the side
6 "Oh yeah, uh-huh!"
7 Part of graduation attire
8 Everlasting
9 ___ Valley (Riverside neighbor)
10 Bother
11 Present time?
12 Does some heavy lifting
13 Plants engage in it
14 Meat quality
21 Didn't rush through
23 Kierkegaard, for one
26 Nags
27 Party platter preparer
28 Thin smoke
29 Short, of a sort
30 Juvenile outbreak
32 Sends to separate camps
33 Like some robbers' guns
34 They used to come from wells
36 Nurse's spot
39 Not leave
41 Best-seller list heading
43 Show signs of weakening
44 Hardly worth mentioning
45 Speaker of Yupik
46 Buttinskies
48 Pile of hay
49 Looks over
52 Lost, but not forgotten, in brief

by Patrick Berry

ACROSS

1 Where Patrick Ewing was born
8 Jalapeño-topped snack
14 Raising hell
15 Parry
16 Get out of shape?
17 Tranquilizer
18 Little butter?
19 Got a feel for, in a way
21 Counter offer
22 Denial
24 Wonder-full sounds
25 Kind of PC command
26 Pet dog at Camp Swampy
27 Giotto and others
29 Splitting words
31 Jacques Chirac and Grover Cleveland, once
32 Peripherals
34 Rosetta stone composition
38 Salt, sometimes
42 Desi's daughter
43 Portrays precisely
47 Grammy-nominated Franklin
48 An admission of guilt
49 Actor Willard of "The Color Purple"
50 ___ Canals
51 Shake alternative
52 Patterned fabrics
54 Certain dama: Abbr.
56 Staked out, say
58 Apt to snap back?
60 They may be required to get in
61 Supermarket checkout staple
62 Pickles
63 Soul-searching sessions?

DOWN

1 Enthusiast, informally
2 Divinely chosen
3 Ruled
4 Counselor: Abbr.
5 The "I" in I. M. Pei
6 Mailing label words
7 Medium
8 Sine qua non
9 The Titans were in it: Abbr.
10 Sociological study
11 Series of six
12 Leopardus pardalis
13 Cause of some fractures
15 Fancy
20 Hedda's schoolmate in "Hedda Gabler"
23 Frequent losers and gainers
25 Storybook ending, sometimes
26 Costa Rica's ___ Peninsula
28 Ear part
30 Put ___ to
33 Prussian pronoun
35 Psalm 119, e.g.
36 Trip in a tux, maybe
37 Picker-upper
39 Some roasters
40 Holder of notions
41 "Sorry!"
43 Chinatown chow choice
44 Go by
45 Monet subject
46 Table
52 Fashionable group
53 It takes quite a while to tell
55 Components of good deals
57 Randomizer
59 Star

by Elizabeth C. Gorski

170

★ ★ ☆

ACROSS

1 Agape, say
5 Poor
15 ___ room
16 Comment after a setup
17 See 57-Across
18 Features of standardized tests
19 Farm area
20 Long
21 Farm area
22 Like some injuries
24 Sweet drink
27 Takes in
28 Song in "The Sound of Music"
29 Lucky ones, it's said
30 NBC Sports personality
34 Front
35 Musician's better half
36 Golfer Michelle
37 Scrambler's aid
40 Place for old get-togethers
42 Terror's opposite
43 Like some traffic
44 Heat-seeking missile
47 Vacate a position, informally
48 Wait in line
49 Belted
50 A little birdie
51 Foreglimpse
55 Missing the boat
56 Movement explainer
57 With 17-Across, big name in international news
58 Watched
59 Rocky peaks

DOWN

1 Plays the innocent one
2 "Bo-o-oring"
3 Relaxing
4 Shakes
5 Protests
6 Catcher Buck ___, elected to baseball's Hall of Fame in its first year
7 Amounted (to)
8 Full of: Suffix
9 Patriots' org.
10 Soft & ___
11 Shelters on the beach
12 Firenze friends
13 Prefix with fluoride
14 Big flop
20 Core
23 H.M.O. listings
24 Log tossed in competition
25 Sea predator
26 "Notorious" setting, 1946
28 Tahoe or Monterey
30 Canine, e.g.
31 Words said while clapping
32 Wannabe rocker's instrument
33 Abalone eaters
35 Learned
38 Old western villain
39 University dept.
40 Having words
41 Right-thinking grp.
43 Slick
44 Goes over
45 Belief
46 Bisected
47 Instrument accompanying a tambura
49 Festive
52 Post office letters
53 Having one sharp
54 Sch. in the Big Ten
55 Wasted

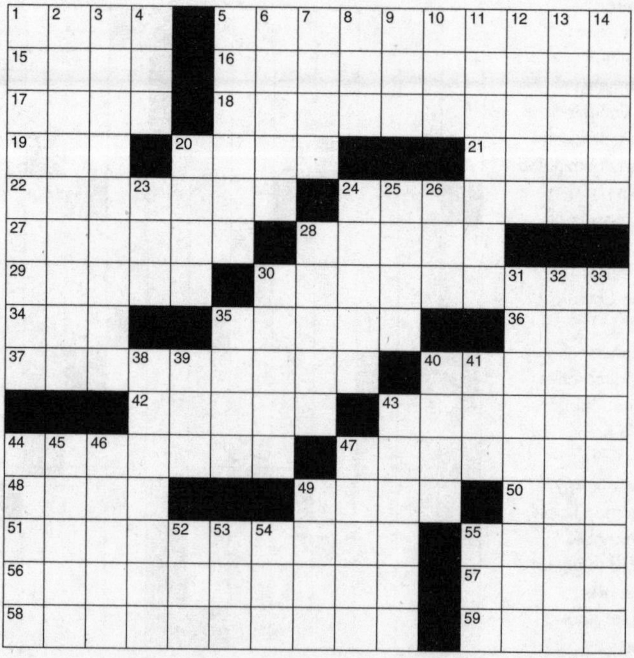

by Joe DiPietro

ACROSS

1 Sing, in a way
10 ___ Court (London district)
15 How campers may sit
16 Blocks
17 Say something personally embarrassing
19 Commemorative piece
20 Concerts
21 Suffix with señor
23 Mole
24 Scottish Peace Nobelist John Boyd ___
27 Seine tributary
29 Bones, anatomically
33 It's written with acid
38 Popular Florida amusement park
39 Let hang
40 Oxford foundation?
41 Over the hill, maybe
42 Film director Russell
43 African capital
47 Darn
49 Power structure
52 Bag carrier
56 Got in
60 Chosen
61 Second class, perhaps
62 Jag
63 Do-or-die effort

DOWN

1 Barely catches
2 "Sometimes you feel like ___ . . ."
3 Pal
4 Digestive bacteria
5 Long odds
6 Not just look
7 Intro providers
8 ___-locks (tangled hair)

9 1988 Olympics site
10 Like some kitchens
11 Originator of the maxim "One swallow does not make a summer"
12 Civil War general Jesse
13 Rested
14 Retired fleet
18 ___ hunch
22 Reply to "You're a stinker!"
23 Eyes
24 Girasols
25 Megabucks event?
26 Try to beat
28 Had a quick turn
30 Was really awful
31 Smarts
32 "As You Like It" setting

34 Kind of package
35 Dix preceder
36 Old Apple computers
37 Strong brews
44 Rocky ridge
45 Nonfunctioning
46 Ever
48 "Rome ___ . . ."
49 Gets on
50 Insect organ
51 Brighton landmark
53 Actress Talbot
54 Hamlet's big brother
55 Give ___ to (acknowledge)
57 Goddess, to Gaius
58 Workload for eds.
59 Suffix with special

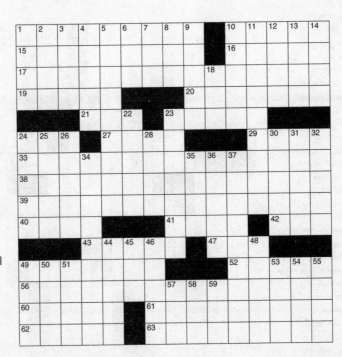

by Martin Ashwood-Smith

ACROSS

1 Superman feature
9 Wood work
15 Tiny openings
16 Designate
17 Petition for again
18 Teacher at TV's James Buchanan High
19 Unmanly
20 Love handle?
21 Blueblood line
22 Classic 1950 film presented mostly in flashback
23 Like some knots
26 Adlai Stevenson's middle name
27 N.H.L. defenseman who twice led the league in scoring
29 Aquarium implement
30 Exclamation added to the O.E.D. in 2001
33 One hanging around the kitchen
34 Grill refuse
35 Game whose name players yell during play
36 Daniel who played Furillo
39 Place for a needle
41 Period following Rome's fall
44 It has hooks
46 Like the sun god Inti
48 Stops daydreaming
49 1950s–60s sex symbol's nickname
51 Time on a marquee
52 Wrigglers, e.g.
53 Menu option
54 Invitation for a radio call-in
55 Prepare for a second crop
56 Was a neighbor of

DOWN

1 Bout of indulgence
2 Tin, maybe
3 First name in Indian politics
4 Antitheft device
5 Returns after being out
6 ___-Ude (Asian capital)
7 Physician Laënnec, who invented the stethoscope
8 The U.S. banned it in 1967
9 Babas and babkas
10 Unsatisfied person's request
11 "I'm busy!"
12 Something a pumpkin can provide
13 Radially symmetric sea creatures
14 Head count of an army
20 California observatory
22 Duracell rival
24 Structural support
25 Medium that uses ten-codes
28 Row
30 Parking lot sight
31 Private meeting
32 Roller derby wear
36 Museum official
37 Concluding part
38 Base
40 Business magnate's holdings
42 Iced treat
43 Liquid in a drip
45 Cowboy's companion
47 Illustrious
49 T'ang dynasty poet
50 State categorically
52 High ball

by Patrick Berry

ACROSS

1 Journalist's get
6 South extension
9 Jerk
14 Participants get a kick out of it
15 Eastern path
16 Worcester university
17 Last word?
18 Workout follower
20 Alpha Orionis
22 Stamp of approval?
23 Like some potatoes or oysters
25 112.5°
28 Commuting choices
29 Bloody Mary sings it
33 $10,000,000 award won in 2004 for successful private space flight
35 Old treasure transporters
36 "Alias" character Derevko
37 Taken
38 "Behold, the people ___": Genesis 11:6
39 Officially approved
41 R&B singer Phillips
42 C2H5OH
43 ___ juris
44 Dismiss
45 Indemnify
48 Neighbor of Slough
51 "A Confession" author
55 Very big one
57 Bracketed material
58 Very big
59 Temporal stretch
60 Air Force Ones, e.g.
61 Canonized Catalan
62 One with drill skill: Abbr.
63 Voltaire's faith

DOWN

1 Evidence of injury
2 Computer programmer's work
3 Tending to the matter
4 Some moldings
5 Pablo Picasso's "one and only master"
6 A Rosenberg and others
7 "The Thief of Baghdad" director Walsh
8 Fair
9 Jr.'s place
10 Most gray, in a way
11 Equivocates
12 Noted member of a Hollywood stable
13 Food that may be pickled
19 Perianth part
21 It might make waves
24 Ferry destination from Liberty State Park
25 Drive out, in a way
26 Sail extender
27 Novelist Remarque
30 Flutter
31 Incorporate
32 River near Albertville
34 Seriously
35 Flit
37 Ready for battle, say
40 Agronomists' study
41 Prefix with pop
43 Hindu precepts
46 Word after cutting and running
47 "Ah, Wilderness!" mother
48 Those caballeros
49 One with a big bell
50 Crack ___
52 Polynesian carving
53 Some tributes
54 Backwoods assent
56 Hudson contemporary

by Eric Berlin

174

★ ★ ★

ACROSS

1 Part of a French court
4 Drift
8 Scattered
14 "___ Box" (1992 six-disc set)
15 Hit man
16 Hot
17 Russian news source
19 "A Man Must Fight" author Gene
20 Couples
21 Starter: Abbr.
22 Kitchen gadgets
23 Kinship
26 Govt. loan agency
27 Looking up
28 When "77 Sunset Strip" aired: Abbr.
31 What a prosecutor may try to prove
34 ___ for iron
35 Presidential middle name
36 Locale called Minnahannock by the Algonquin Indians, bought by the Dutch in 1637
39 Popular syrup
40 Make tracks?
41 Loquacious
42 Short
43 Leaves alone
45 River connected to a 165-mile long European canal
46 Psyched about going
49 Military craft
52 Slutty
53 Villain at Crab Key fortress
55 The only royal palace in the U.S.
56 "My view is . . ."
58 Big name in oil
59 Opposite of "No, no"
60 Little wriggler
61 Hit list?
62 Abbr. before a date
63 "The Matrix" hero

DOWN

1 That's an order
2 Expand, as a compressed file
3 Alibi
4 Mich. neighbor
5 When to hear "O Romeo, Romeo! wherefore art thou Romeo?"
6 Puts on a show
7 Eagle's place
8 Nonessential
9 Like a mai tai
10 Picture
11 "A Different Read on Life" magazine
12 One holding a ball, maybe
13 ___ Grand (supermarket brand)
18 1962 hit with the lyric "Kiss me mucho"
24 Wainscot section
25 Newton, for one
28 Computer option
29 Bluster
30 1981 adventure film hero
31 Bugs
32 Ancient mariner?
33 Broadcaster
35 Dessert style
37 Squeezed
38 "Fer ___!"
43 Occult practice
44 Sci-fi preservation technique
46 Outdoor party
47 Percy Bysshe Shelley, e.g.
48 Airport no-no
49 Pre-Celtic person
50 Deere competitor
51 Brief interruption
54 One of the Ringling Brothers
57 Naughty boy, in "Toy Story"

by Karen M. Tracey

ACROSS

1 Alpha particle emitter
7 Admitted guilt for
13 Slips
14 Not for real
16 Fenced-in area
17 Mrs. Lovett's pastries in "Sweeney Todd"
18 Letters at a launch
19 Jelly Roll Morton genre
21 "Gimme ___!"
22 First name in spydom
24 Big wheel at a supermarket?
25 1970s baseball All-Star ___ Colbert
26 "I Still See ___" ("Paint Your Wagon" song)
28 Wall St. market, briefly
29 Broadcast network
30 B team
33 Unattached
34 Jitters
40 Mode of travel pointed in two directions
41 New Testament book: Abbr.
42 Be still, at sea
43 Sticking point?
44 Cornball
46 Organ teacher's field: Abbr.
47 It's tied in back
48 They're made by running water
50 Tognazzi of "La Cage aux Folles"
51 Headphone wearers
53 Tries to get the hard-to-get
55 It may be French or Italian, but not German
56 Latin word usually abbreviated with a single letter
57 Whipper-snapper?
58 Admiral at Guadalcanal, 1943

DOWN

1 A lot of copy shop business
2 Discount oil source
3 Far-reaching
4 Suffix with different
5 Where I-15 and I-70 cross
6 Land with a cavalry in Ezekiel
7 Fountain locale
8 Leap for Lipinski
9 Special gift
10 Hesitant question
11 Popular diner
12 Bar offerings
14 Response to a sales clerk
15 Take-charge kind of guy
20 Handy kitchen cooker
23 Currently
25 Home of Literature Nobelist Wole Soyinka
27 Cell part
29 An Adams
31 Currency board abbr.
32 One may get bonded
34 Agreements
35 English novelist Pym
36 Without help
37 Beautiful women
38 Knickknack holder
39 In other words
44 Emote, with "up"
45 "That's disgusting!"
48 Famed sewer
49 Big Apple park, once
52 "Woe ___" (classic book for "grammarphobes")
54 Natl. League city

by Manny Nosowsky

ACROSS

1 Pudding content?
9 Unlikeliest to be bought
15 Smoothly added throughout
16 Emmy winner for "Tuesdays With Morrie"
17 Costume party comment
18 Houses named for a house
19 Medieval fighter
20 Prepares the board
21 Relig. title
22 Former Argentine president Carlos
24 Ribbonlike marine plant
28 Place close to Sundance
32 Decorate, as a pumpkin
34 Employ
35 One vote in the European Union
36 Inflatable exercise aid
38 Y beneficiary
39 Where the Germans sank their own freighter, the Antilla, in W.W. II
41 Signals
43 Latin for "scraped"
44 ___ Springfield (town eponym on "The Simpsons")
45 Heavy footsteps
47 O and W, e.g.
50 Mustang braking system?
53 Stymie the feds, in a way
57 "How could you say such a thing?!"
58 Its capital was once Gondar
59 System of continuous revolution
60 From the bottom of one's heart
61 Prince Siegfried's love, in ballet
62 Unchains

DOWN

1 Soap slot, maybe
2 Rolled snacks
3 Professor Moriarty, for one
4 Diminished, with "out"
5 Laughter, in La Mancha
6 It might make a cameo appearance
7 Oklahoma people
8 Vehicles used by pushers
9 Gets dark
10 "Main" color in "Rule, Britannia"
11 1966 Lana Turner melodrama
12 London statue originally called the Shaftesbury Monument
13 Beget
14 Red ink source?
23 It may be planned
25 Evian Masters org.
26 John who wrote "She who has never lov'd, has never liv'd"
27 Having an edge
29 "Tender Mercies" actress
30 Bring (out)
31 Chem. datum
32 Cold cover
33 A celebrity might be bathed in one
34 Vegetarian people of fiction
37 Maximum
40 Wayne duds
42 Enumerate
44 "No one else"
46 German president Köhler
48 Trait of Iago
49 Rush
50 Bar locale
51 "Diary of ___ Black Woman" (2005 film)
52 Dealing box, in blackjack
54 Have down to ___
55 Stimulate
56 Sounds at pounds

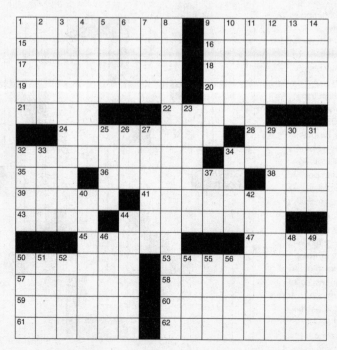

by Byron Walden

ACROSS

1 Israel's Arens
6 Focus of an annual Fort Worth event
15 Have ___ for
16 Where Brits drive
17 Passed out
18 Examined, as another's affairs
19 "Silent Spring" subj.
20 Certain nobility
21 Per ___
22 Reporter's item
24 Half a comedy duo
25 Left in the dust
26 Apple computers introduced in 1983
29 Embitterment
30 Draft choice
32 Photo ___
35 Former empire abbr.
36 Cooling-off periods
37 DDT banner
38 Some Caltech grads, for short
39 Try to find
40 Broadcast inits.
41 1999 Stanley Cup winner
42 More and more?
44 It's kind of corny
47 Narrow-width mortar tile installation
48 Tie up
49 Round of four
52 Shopper's convenience
53 For the time being
55 They may be super
56 Powder used in paint pigment and matches
57 Sitting around
58 Pitch
59 Train crash site?

DOWN

1 Wasn't silent
2 Short, as a meal
3 Abalone eaters
4 "God Knows" author
5 Setting for a Wash. Nats game
6 Alternative to a Segway
7 About
8 Hullabaloo
9 "___ All That" (1999 comedy)
10 Clarinetist Lewis
11 Shortens, in a way
12 City near Dayton
13 Following
14 Botanical opening
20 Nostrum
23 Old Church of England opponents
24 Toscanini and others
26 Security issue
27 A "Spartan dog," according to Lodovico
28 Investigators
31 Look of prurience
32 Hurdles
33 Pastry shop treat
34 Kids always lose them
41 Fetor
43 Chant
44 Sugarcoating
45 They have a central meeting place
46 Sugarcoating
47 Citizen rival
49 Very hot
50 Twin sister of Ares
51 Late-'60s fashion item
54 Kid
55 Point

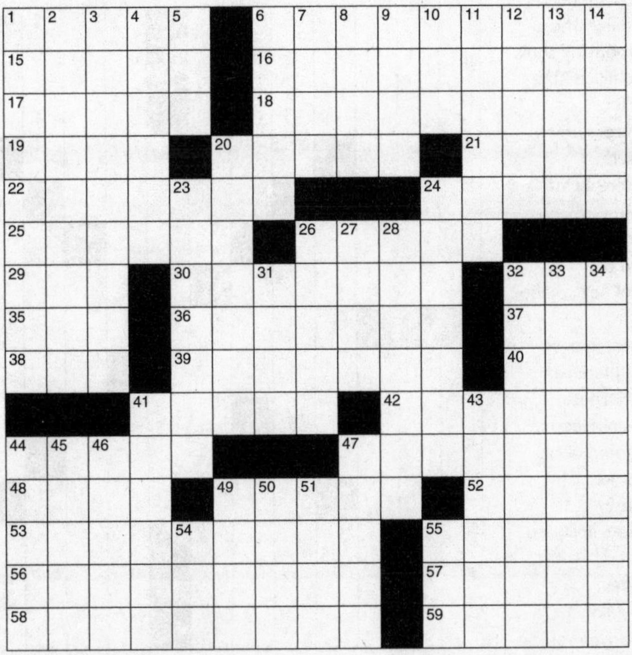

by Joe DiPietro

178

★ ★ ★

ACROSS

1 Intro interruption
8 Title character who dies before the novel begins
15 Struggling
16 Exceeded
17 Words to a skeptic
18 Ends, as a class
19 Organization functionary
20 "Hah!"
22 Suffix with Capri
23 Bewildered utterances
25 Champs Élysées features
26 Title professor in a 1957 novel
27 Some commerce nowadays
29 Pipe fitting
30 Antigone's cruel uncle
31 Medicinal plants
33 Entertainer whose first Broadway show was subtitled "The Royal Tour"
35 Biological series
37 Released
40 Civic competitor
44 Having entanglements
45 Cavern end
47 "Borstal Boy" author
48 Soaks
49 Sharpen, in a way
51 Jiang's predecessor as Chinese Communist leader
52 Flightboard abbr.
53 Two seater, perhaps?
55 G.I. chow in Desert Storm
56 Intensifies
58 Yacht outing
60 Wind-driven vehicle with runners
61 Words of discovery
62 Pontiac's followers
63 Coup targets

DOWN

1 Good spellers?
2 Neither here nor there
3 1982 Grammy-winning singer for "Gershwin Live!"
4 Requests to speak up
5 Zingers
6 "___ World," segment on "Sesame Street"
7 Need a ring, maybe
8 Not be oneself?
9 Civil rights leader portrayed in "For Us, the Living"
10 "La Belle et la ___"
11 Defibrillator locales: Abbr.
12 Sang
13 It may be exercised
14 Wave catcher
21 Be the center of attention
24 Impeccable
26 Tried to look smart
28 Flock
30 Star
32 It's about 375 miles NW of LAX
34 They may start affairs
36 Deflation targets?
37 Stereo sound source
38 Raise anew
39 Boss's address?
41 A waiter may be asked to hold it
42 Cut loose
43 Christian devotion
46 Rotten
49 Capital east of Asmara
50 ___ pudding
53 Request for attention, maybe
54 Colors
57 Keglers' grp.
59 Michaelmas mo.

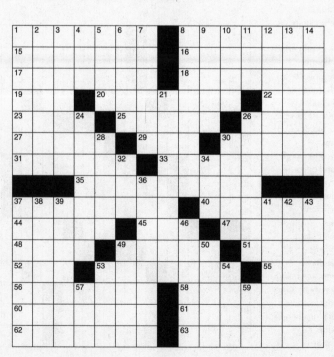

by Rich Norris

ACROSS

1 No. for Na or Ni
5 Give ___ of the hat
9 Symbols of masculinity
14 Shows no one comes to see
17 Takes the wrong way
18 Opening
19 Relatively common letters
20 Popular writers
21 It's unresolved
22 "Ah"
24 Center in a state's center
26 "No kidding"
28 Thompson of "Family"
30 Org. to which eight U.S. presidents have belonged
32 Footed receptacles
33 Conductor seen at night
35 Change one's focus
37 Beans
39 Product with three heads
41 "___ come to that"
42 Boom
44 Takes a course
45 Limb's end
46 Anatomical passage
48 Confectioner's raw material
50 Caballero's locale
52 King ___ II known as "The Stout"
54 It might expose rings
56 Went after
57 Something folded before a meal
59 Mucho
61 Kinsey report topic
64 John le Carré characters
65 Takes an alternate course
66 Adopted son of Claudius
67 Anhydrous

DOWN

1 Not hide
2 Boom producer
3 Brunch order
4 Anticommunist leader
5 Early Surrealist
6 Clipped
7 Wishful words
8 Salt's partner
9 Dr.'s order
10 How easy things might be
11 Source of pop-ups?
12 Source of pop-ups?
13 Bacon sizzle
15 Pamper
16 Carrying
23 End of a Scottish title sung at many parties
25 Catherine of history
27 Big employer of inspectors: Abbr.
29 A Freud
31 Old radio title character
32 Soldier's group
34 Start of North Carolina's motto
36 Color-conscious grp.
38 "___ Eyes" by the Eagles
40 Relative of a bottlenose
43 One being brought along
47 Famous player of a milkman with many daughters
49 Big name in insurance
51 Run like ___
53 Not so hard
55 Detroit's county
56 Knife
58 Hasn't left
60 They ring out in rings
62 Literary inits.
63 Game with a Wild Draw Four card

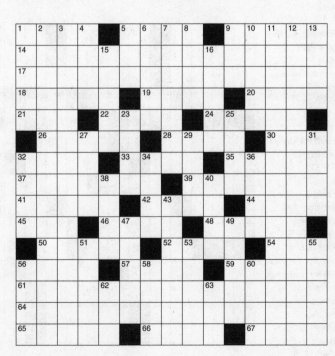

by Patrick Merrell

180

★ ★ ★

ACROSS

1 Sinclair Lewis's ___ Timberlane
5 Bad tads
9 Forest issue
14 "___ Hora" (Ezra Pound poem)
15 "Dutch Interior" painter
16 Dull type
17 Wealthy, as a dueña
18 Lies, perhaps
20 Sports affiliate
22 Ham
23 Kind of column
24 The Arc feeds it
26 Region between the Vosges and the Rhine
28 Career pitcher
32 Lixiviate
33 One bottled up
34 TV debut of 1972
35 Red distributor, say
37 Grocery store suppliers
39 Abbr. in the Yellow Pages
40 Composition of some towers
42 Kind
43 High-tech company with a landmark 1995 I.P.O.
45 Some are fit for a king
46 Walked from one bank to another
47 Balance providers
48 Steamed dish
51 Certain doo-wopper
55 Norton Anthology focus, for short
57 Outback critters
58 Fen resident
59 "Suddenly, as ___ things will, it vanished": E. B. Browning

60 White-bearded Africans
61 Hard to settle
62 Hungarian city near Miskolc
63 Innovative furniture designer Aarnio

DOWN

1 Old "What's My Line?" panelist
2 Cantatrice's offering
3 Beyond criticism
4 Quickly repealed statute
5 Block
6 Red giant in Cetus
7 Indication of future success
8 Conciliatory gesture
9 Graceful loops
10 Gnomes
11 Prayer partner?
12 Orbital point
13 Play a big part
19 1751 Henry Fielding novel
21 Specialist's point
25 Light-colored
26 Sgt. York
27 Hanover's river
29 Cheap substitute, of sorts
30 1975 Pulitzer-winning critic
31 Puts forward
33 Get a feel for things?
36 Shakes
38 Make a comeback
41 Mark for a particular purpose
44 Moist lowlands
45 One who might get a pinch
48 Be prolific
49 Parisian protector

50 Some hirers: Abbr.
52 Ending with some very large numbers
53 Museum offering
54 Benito's bone
56 Its spiritual head was the pope: Abbr.

by Dana Motley

ACROSS

1 Pizza order
7 It may be used to put on a brave face
15 Bewitch
16 1955 Gloria Grahame musical role
17 Paternal kinsman
18 Forgathers
19 Not let run wild
20 1973 Toni Morrison novel
21 Well-put
22 Splits
24 Distinctly representative
26 19th-century urban transportation
28 Betel palm
29 Ones who'd like to get the goods on you
32 Former U.N. Secretary-General Kofi ___ Annan
36 Smooth over
37 It may be used for many unhappy returns: Abbr.
38 Indirect object?
41 Textile trademark
42 Feeling one's oats
47 Winning words?
50 They whistle while they work
51 Church matters: Abbr.
52 Let off steam, maybe
54 "You ___ kidding!"
55 Famous last words?
57 Go up, up and away
58 Raspberries
59 Missile datum
60 Snail feature
61 Logs

DOWN

1 "___ me!"
2 "Measure for Measure" villain
3 N.F.L. Hall-of-Famer Willie
4 Some kitchen appliances
5 Whys and wherefores
6 Singer/actress with an Oscar, two Grammys and a Golden Globe
7 W.W. II group
8 Deuce follower
9 ___ Martins, main character in Graham Greene's "The Third Man"
10 Like the "y" sound in "yes"
11 See 30-Down
12 Privately
13 Has little to complain about
14 It may be unprecedented
23 Hawthorne's home
25 Start of a Cockney toast
27 Lower the price of, maybe
30 Popular TV host, seller of many 11-Down
31 Concern for Batman
32 Not for free
33 Like some weekends
34 Vintage toy material
35 Without ___ (dangerously)
39 Give a look that could kill
40 Wipe out an old score
43 Absolute
44 Ingredient in some soaps
45 Lead by the hand
46 Perfumery compounds
48 1972 top 10 hit that was over 7 minutes long
49 Mound
53 Mammoth growth
56 Pops in the fridge?

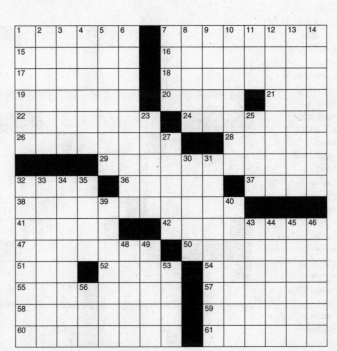

by Sherry O. Blackard

ACROSS

1 Didn't get nothing
7 North Carolina river
10 Telekinesis, e.g.
13 British royal house for nearly two centuries
15 Sound from a speaker
17 Busy
18 Champagne concoctions
19 Now
21 Can
22 Speedy steed
26 Florida's Saint ___ University
27 Head of ___
32 Impregnable stronghold
35 Ball carrier, at times
37 Shoulder pad
38 It may be overhead
40 Teen of TV lore
41 Off
43 Vice-presidential middle name
45 Resembling
46 Concert souvenirs
47 Pony Express segments
50 Unimprovable situation
57 One who's been seeing things
58 Acetaminophen brand
60 Part of his body was famously insured for $100,000 by Lloyd's of London
61 Not a complete amateur
62 Full-house indication
63 Homophone of 50-Down
64 Some after-dinner quaffs

DOWN

1 Cable guide abbr.
2 Beat
3 Airing
4 End of an architect's name
5 It's what's happening
6 European air hub
7 Actress in "Anger Management," 2003
8 Springs
9 Increase quickly, with "up"
10 Its biggest attraction is on a list
11 Impregnate
12 Half the portals
14 "Who has seen the wind?" poet
16 Water temperature gauge
20 Horse's halter
22 Got on
23 Harass and insult, slangily
24 Half a world capital
25 Pauley Pavilion athlete
28 Welcome sight for a marathoner
29 Not decumbent
30 1977 Tony-winning musical
31 Tactic in rotation
33 The spy in "The Spy Who Came In From the Cold"
34 Moves to a new bed
36 Puzzle's center
39 Ones providing insights?
42 Bad, in Bogotá
44 1970s song subtitled "Touch the Wind"
48 Make a note of
49 Hayek of "Wild Wild West"
50 Twelve to one
51 Mark's replacement
52 Constellation next to Norma
53 Veritas provider?
54 Check
55 Expy.
56 It's done while holding hands
57 Field stats
59 Section of L.A.

by Henry Hook

ACROSS

1 Expire
9 Top removed by attendants
15 Be in concert
16 Library feature
17 Cormorants, e.g.
18 Suddenly arose
19 Barely move?
20 Cinderella's clothes
21 Sister of Selene
22 Wanes
25 Destructive 1999 Florida hurricane
26 Glower
29 Glower, maybe
32 Aid in creating an idealized figure
34 Former lakeshore tribe
35 Not rot
37 Seed structure
38 Locale of the Bocca Nuova crater
39 Fix
40 Camel alternatives
42 Alluring
43 Thinking ___
45 "Walk Away ___" (1966 hit)
46 Good vantage point
48 You can burn it
51 Fairy tale figures
53 Cousin of a capillary
55 Restaurant cry
56 Member of a historical trio
58 Agreement
59 Exhausted
60 Mite-sized
61 Start attacking

DOWN

1 So last year
2 Prefix with phenetidin
3 Cancer components
4 "Quién ___?"
5 Like many elephants
6 Glad-hand, as politicians are wont to do
7 What's more
8 "I knew it!"
9 Balls
10 Much
11 Without even a warning
12 Emerge
13 Maintain
14 Xers?
20 Fringe of the green?
23 Misapplies
24 Guarantees
27 Lush
28 Trim
29 Some pods
30 A line winds in and out of it
31 Fish might go over it
33 Powwow
36 Go all out
41 Attack
44 Grandparents, typically
47 Square
48 Things not wanted in locker rooms
49 Sacrificial site
50 Flirt
51 Hit hard
52 Clip
54 Son of Willy Loman
56 "You ___?"
57 One in the Army

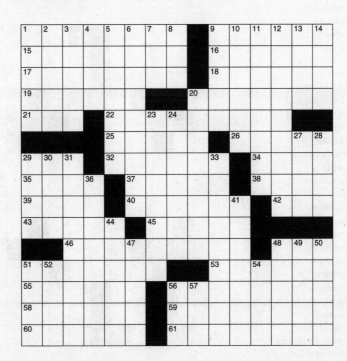

by Joe DiPietro

ACROSS

1 More inclined
8 Longfellow's Hiawatha, e.g.
14 Uninterrupted space
15 Anthony Trollope's "___ Finn"
16 Saves every penny
17 Some lefties
18 Lotus car model
19 Word of greeting and parting
21 Natural
22 Language of Indochina
23 Build up
25 Red on a fire truck
26 Turkey tip?
28 Signal box controls
30 House builder's purchase
31 Literary flubs
34 Glow
35 As luck would have it
40 Friend of Tigger
41 Not at a distance
42 Focaccia topping
44 Isn't going anywhere
46 Piano bar
48 One of the "Magnificent Seven"
49 "___, danke"
50 Director of "The Ladykillers," 2004
51 Wine-tasting consideration
53 Entertainer nicknamed "The Abdominal Showman"
55 Covers
57 Phased-out Toyotas
58 French word for "kitchen"
59 "Livin' With the Blues" singer
60 Rough place to grow up, with "the"

DOWN

1 Scalp
2 Cry out
3 Nonanalytic
4 It may be a step up
5 Gravestone abbr.
6 Medium power
7 Life-saving operations
8 One of the rivers near Three Rivers Stadium
9 Headsail
10 Out of favor (with)
11 Bovine hybrid
12 Brave
13 Groups
15 Theory to explain seafloor spreading
20 Totally making stuff up
24 Buzzards
25 Org. that battled P. T. Barnum
27 Roll bar?
29 Oscar Mayer unit
32 New money
33 They're inclined to brood
35 Revive
36 Sang à la Jimmie Rodgers
37 "Les Femmes Savantes" playwright
38 4.19 joules
39 Normal habitat
43 Plays with
45 Pass
47 First name in Mideast politics
50 Cuba libre ingredient
52 Put-up job
54 Content between intermissions
56 Crank

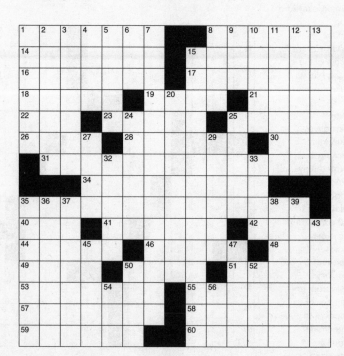

by Patrick Berry

ACROSS

1 Mideast leader?
5 Dropped by
15 Take the bait
16 Be mature
17 Iowa kin
18 Something politicians are loath to do
19 Part of A.S.T.: Abbr.
20 TiVo forerunners
21 "Kate & Allie" actress
22 Neckwear for SpongeBob SquarePants
24 "___ one . . ." (opiner's opening)
26 Not permanently wet
28 Stymied
33 Treat with Graham crackers
34 Verse site
36 ___ Rhin (French department)
37 Outstanding issues
38 Modern pentathlon event
39 "Easy as pie!"
41 Dress shirt feature
42 Some wedding arrangements
43 Accept
45 Convertible alternative
47 Obviously enjoy, as a joke
48 Impersonated at a party
52 Tennis score
54 H
55 Stays too long at the gym, say
57 Acclaim
58 Attended to a detail
59 Model born Melissa Miller

60 Group f/64 co-founder
61 Battle of the ___, opened on 10/16/1914

DOWN

1 Cruising, say
2 One puppy to another
3 "See?" follower
4 Cost of doing business
5 Lot for sale
6 Rent-___
7 Reply to "Who's there?"
8 Pageboys, e.g.
9 Pasqueflowers, e.g.
10 Practiced
11 Watson's "___ Holmes . . ."

12 ___-Altenburg (old German duchy)
13 Entertainment exec Robert
14 Hardy soul
20 Part of an aura
23 Parade pattern
25 Foul-mouthed
27 Still
29 See 57-Down
30 Fantastic notions
31 How to shoot ducks at a shooting gallery
32 One destined to pass the bar
35 Fox competitor
37 Weight-watcher's drink
40 The Acropolis, once
41 Hacienda hand, maybe
44 Red eye cause
46 Ottoman honorific

48 It ends with two bars
49 Literary stream
50 Team since 1962
51 One-named artist
53 Per ___
56 SFO posting
57 With 29-Down, greeting for Mrs. Kowalski in "A Streetcar Named Desire"

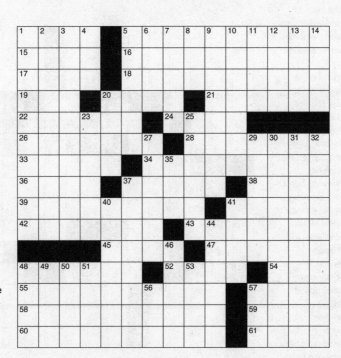

by Manny Nosowsky

ACROSS

1 1906 novel that helped produce widespread social reforms
10 Certain League members
15 Troubling
16 Canon rival
17 Post production?
18 Ellen who won three Emmys between 1973 and 1976
19 Fit
20 Thousands, slangily
22 Old intelligence org.
23 Part of a modern soldier's address
24 Floor exercise, in Britain
27 Chiropterologist's interest
28 Gloomy thistle-eater of children's lit
30 French writer who coined the phrase "Facts are stubborn things"
32 Hinge of a palindrome
36 Henry Higgins and others
39 Demonizing, with "of"
40 First ___ (title for Napoleon)
41 "I'm dying, Egypt, dying" speaker
45 Word of support
46 Chromium use
50 It has some crust
51 Apt. specs
52 Gob
53 First star ever photographed, 1850
54 They greet each other by pressing their noses together
57 Scrapbook fodder
60 Needle holders

61 Nobelist who proposed a League of Peace
62 Can
63 Ends of the earth

DOWN

1 It may be blacked out
2 Bug with red and blue stripes
3 Germany to Russia, in W.W. II
4 Joke
5 Endangered Great Basin language
6 "The Four-Chambered Heart" novelist
7 Soak
8 Pegbox holders
9 Some driving tests
10 Cissoid segment

11 Blanco or Negro
12 Ones seeking steady work?
13 Star of two of 1990's top 15 Nielsen-rated shows
14 Ambulance chasers
21 Heavyweight champ, 1882–92
24 Raise attentively
25 Prairie region in Kansas rich in gypsum and iron
26 Pounding, in a way
29 Auspices
31 Relative of an avocet
33 Degree in martial arts
34 Schlep
35 Christmas ___

36 Where Elijah defeated the prophets of Baal
37 Salty hail
38 Hits hard, to no effect
42 Spread out
43 Pettifog
44 Froth producers
47 Capital served by Kotoka International Airport
48 Clutch performer?
49 Dip
53 Lively, on scores
55 Shell asset
56 Metric prefix
58 23rd of 24 letters
59 Vinegar

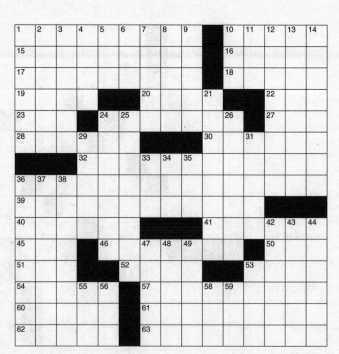

by Byron Walden

ACROSS

1 Where one might be rushed
10 Engages in violent practices?
15 Getting there
16 Like some currents
17 Elite military group
18 Legend, e.g.
19 Intensely excited
20 It's just above a foot
21 Bank abbr.
24 Union land: Abbr.
25 Sugar and salt, commonly
26 Service collection
28 Possible antibiotic target
29 "Hit it!"
30 Part of a sultry look
34 "Flash Gordon" cartoonist ___ Raymond
35 ___ profit
36 Subject preceder
37 Banking assessor, perhaps
39 One way to microwave
40 Long-distance calls?
41 Record-keeping aid
42 Science students' costs
45 Lord's Prayer adjective
46 Director Demme
47 Debuggers' discoveries
48 Does some curling
50 "Do ___?"
51 Extraordinary communicators
55 Some change
56 Supped
57 Some male dolls
58 Hot shots?

DOWN

1 Ray extension
2 Stranded messenger?
3 Safari transport, briefly
4 ___ sample
5 Dinosaur, so to speak
6 "Two to go" situation
7 Major company renamed in 1997
8 Place for a house-plant
9 G.R.E. distributor
10 Cup of ice?
11 Wolf's delivery
12 Like 58-Across
13 ___ show, at a carnival
14 Blind parts
20 Outbound vessel
21 Up
22 "The Arraignment of Paris" playwright
23 Blows up
25 Double execution?
27 Almost even
28 George who wrote "The Bubble of American Supremacy"
30 Withdraws
31 Arm
32 Show
33 Wrapped (up)
35 Some game pieces
38 Lady, e.g.
39 Kind of gold
41 Tattered condition
42 Big maker of binoculars
43 "As You Like It" setting
44 A store might have its own
45 Old message system
48 Ex-governor of California ___ Wilson
49 Undisturbed?
51 Classroom assignments?: Abbr.
52 Spike TV, once
53 Snicker part
54 Namesakes, sometimes: Abbr.

by David Liben-Nowell

188

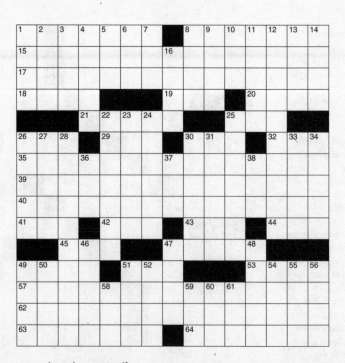

ACROSS

1 Some bait
8 Best-selling novel featuring lawyer Mitch McDeere
15 Central Vermont, e.g.
17 Element of irony
18 Ship, to a poet
19 Not separate
20 Possessive on a Chinese menu
21 Semidome sites
25 Cry of disbelief
26 Son of Prince Valiant
29 Far from welcoming
30 ___-Mex
32 Cut
35 Not take risks
39 Neighbor of a Prussian
40 Unsentimental practicality
41 F1 neighbor
42 He played Sam on "Cheers"
43 Expert finish?
44 Rob Roy's rejection
45 Movie inits.
47 Related Nobel-winning physicists
49 Film critic Balázs
51 "I get it!"
53 They have no grace
57 1994 Christopher Walken comedy
62 Townsman
63 Dry, in a way
64 Sail

DOWN

1 Comment after an accident
2 Informal rejection
3 Apartment V.I.P.
4 Col. Paul Tibbets's mother
5 Pieces of bread?: Abbr.
6 Popular sushi fish
7 Host's invitation
8 Substantial volume
9 In color
10 Spanish pronoun
11 Coca-Cola Company brand
12 Material for tablecloths and doilies
13 City named for a Civil War general
14 They're often sold with papers
16 Intelligence
22 Target
23 Project
24 Shadow site
25 One before a tribunal, maybe
26 Moderate
27 Slangy moves
28 "It didn't work out"
30 Part of many workouts, informally
31 From the top
33 Ukrainian port, to natives
34 As such
36 Peck at
37 Many a delivery
38 Anger, e.g.
46 Primary
47 Big do
48 Movable type
49 Part of Indonesia
50 Dark, in verse
51 French cordial flavoring
52 Natural incubators
54 Some batteries
55 Something to be slapped with
56 Abbr. on Mexican mail
58 Part of l'Indonésie
59 Decline in price
60 Typing system
61 Inconsequential invention

by Robert H. Wolfe

ACROSS

1 Event in which teams may drink rounds during rounds
8 Comb
15 Minimal, with "of"
16 Broke out
17 Conditioning system
18 Dumpling dish
19 Defeats easily
20 Doesn't stick around
21 1920s birth control advocate Russell
22 Author of "Save Your Job, Save Our Country: Why Nafta Must Be Stopped—Now!"
24 Name on some euros
25 They may be found in sneakers
27 "___ vindice" (Confederacy motto)
28 Chairperson?
29 Big name in flight
31 Place on a game board?
33 A.L. home run champ of 1950 and '53
35 Mop holder?
38 Often-minimized thing
43 1966 Grammy winner for "If He Walked Into My Life"
44 Focus of some ball-handlers?
46 Spanish mistress
47 Samoan capital
48 Cuts into a pie, often
50 Field fare, briefly
51 Distribution slip
53 Ostensible composer of "The Abduction of Figaro" and "Oedipus Tex"
55 Summit goal
56 Bennett of the Ronettes
57 Worker doing a desk job?
58 Bright planet, sometimes
59 "First . . ."
60 Information technology subject

DOWN

1 Leader who claimed to have put a fatal curse on J.F.K.
2 Cousin of Ascii
3 Dances in waltz time
4 Some radio sources
5 "'___ Me?' I do not know you" (Emily Dickinson poem)
6 Get slippery, in a way
7 Zipped up
8 Boho-chic footwear
9 Big combo
10 Old marketplace surrounder
11 Saints, e.g.
12 Function whose domain is between -1 and 1
13 Not-so-new work crew
14 First pitcher to have defeated all 30 major-league teams
23 Having a better bottom?
26 Part of a certain kit
28 Wolf, e.g.
30 H.S. subject
32 Faster, maybe
34 "Danger!"
35 Enter for a spin
36 Bristly appendages
37 Words after "Whew!"
39 Least sensible
40 20th-century German leader's moniker
41 Part of a fin?
42 Load-bearing things?
43 Most intrepid
45 Man and others
48 Zagat contributor
49 Opinion opener
52 Italian province or its capital
54 Amts.

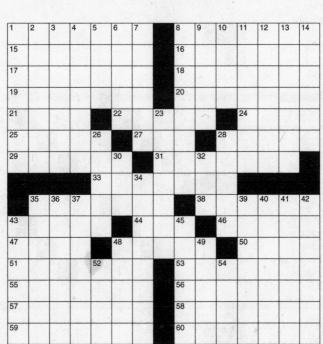

by Brendan Emmett Quigley

ACROSS

1 Climbing Mt. Everest, for Sir Edmund Hillary
12 1937 Paul Muni drama
14 Art, metaphorically
16 History
17 Probe
18 Manfred ___ Earth Band
19 Roman well
20 Basic verse option
21 Whacked
22 Drum containers
23 Site of the siege of Candia
24 Feaster on frogs
25 Legato indicator
26 Coast Guard boat
27 It's hard to recall
29 Cowboys, but not Indians
32 Fitting decision?
33 Clued in, once
36 Stains
37 Delicate
38 Singer who is part owner of Forbes magazine
39 First name in fragrances
40 "In that area"
41 Cousin in a Balzac title
42 Cut across
44 Reminiscent of the 1890s
45 Census Bureau data
47 Only if it's worth the trade-off
48 London Zoo locale

DOWN

1 Remote access?
2 Stanford of Stanford University
3 Base runners?
4 Evidence that one is short
5 A foot has 305 of these: Abbr.
6 Like most medicine bottles
7 Things in rings
8 Big name in college guides
9 Old one, along the Oder
10 Holmes fought him
11 50–50 proposition
12 Hand holding
13 Passing subject?
14 Artist Wyeth
15 Not lit
19 Princess Ozma's creator
22 Nine ___ (London district)
23 Bug zapper?
25 "Dear" ones
26 Under a quilt, say
27 Set off
28 "Blue II" painter, 1961
29 It's headquartered in the G.E. Building
30 Sacramento suburb
31 Global positioning system, e.g.
33 Bit of jazz improvisation
34 Bait
35 Meter makers
37 Certain inverse function
38 Get going
40 Honduras-to-Guatemala dirección
41 City bombed in the gulf war
43 Waste
44 Rockne protégé
46 Country singers England and Herndon

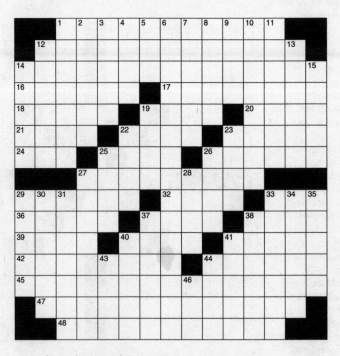

by Paula Gamache

ACROSS

1 Big flap on the road?
12 Yearbook div.
15 Song sung by Mehitabel in Broadway's "Shinbone Alley"
16 Treaty of Rome org.
17 Traitorous
18 First Fiesta Bowl winner: Abbr.
19 Since
20 Algorithm component
21 Forgoes a cab, say
23 Nickelodeon nut
24 Rijksmuseum subject
26 Ready to be driven
30 Poetry Out Loud contest org.
31 Vandals' target
32 Tennis's Ivanovic
33 Est., once
34 ___-Ball
35 Sketching
39 She's entertaining
41 Abba's "___ the Music Speak"
42 Subj. of the 2006 film "The Good Shepherd"
44 Identification aid in an obituary
45 Original sponsoring publication of TV's "Project Runway"
46 Prefix with culture
47 The Danube flows through it
51 People in a rush
54 Host and winner of the 1966 World Cup: Abbr.
55 With 59-Across, it lasted from about 3500 to 1000 B.C.
56 Defeater of Schmeling in 1933
59 See 55-Across
60 Slogan ending
61 Dedicatee of "The Muppet Movie"
64 Flow checker
65 Dish with coddled egg
66 ___-Mère-Église (D-Day town)
67 Order of ants

DOWN

1 Prolific suspense novelist Woods
2 Soft, thin silk cloth
3 2006 Tony-nominated "Sweeney Todd" actress
4 1977 Steely Dan title track
5 They're often fried
6 Offended
7 Member of the 1960s Rams' Fearsome Foursome
8 Sports biggies
9 Insurance fig.
10 Cornelius Vanderbilt and Jay Gould
11 Cook, at times
12 Dangerous swimmer with an oarlike tail
13 Bathtub rings, e.g.
14 Deep-sixes
22 Card
25 Be in harmony
27 Bizarrely hellish
28 Aussie's place of higher learning
29 Mardi Gras, in the U.K.
35 Early-birds' opposites
36 Ride roughshod over
37 "Born to Be Blue" singer
38 Yield some
40 Lead-in to a sheepish excuse
43 Home to some fighters
48 Charles Darwin's ship H.M.S. ___
49 Ready to be driven
50 Steering committee's creation
52 Language in which "k" and "v" are the words for "to" and "in"
53 Kitchen gripper
57 It rises in the Cantabrian Mountains
58 Plaintiff's opposite: Abbr.
62 Beauty
63 Turncoat

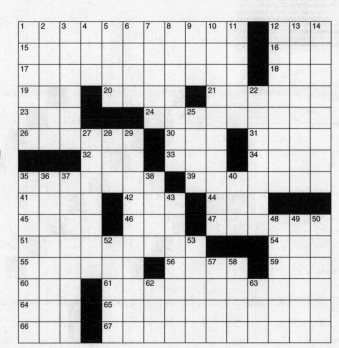

by Brad Wilber

ACROSS

1 Los Angeles's ___ Tower
7 They're seen around some cakes
15 Alaska's ___ Sound
16 Mom's partner?
17 What a toaster may hold
19 Un article défini
20 Modern greeting
21 Plays intensely, in jazz slang
22 It often follows something
24 Doesn't toss
26 Fictional upper class
27 One who doesn't chew the fat?
29 Find ___ for (match)
31 TV's Spike, once
32 Bygone explosive
34 Dungeons & Dragons race
36 "The White House," for "the presidency," e.g.
38 Abba's style
42 Rootless sort
44 Lombardia's capital
45 Game with sticks
48 Got on
50 Dog-___
51 It's mild and a bit nutty
53 Racket string material
55 Coll. elective program
56 Serenade, as the moon
58 Noted fifth-century invaders
60 Regrettable E.R. status
61 Refrain from eating pasta?
64 Where to find Nancy
65 Ready to receive visitors, say
66 Held
67 Beguiles

DOWN

1 One known for finger-pointing
2 "It's the truth"
3 M.I.T.'s class ring, familiarly
4 Long green box?
5 Informal demurral
6 Touch
7 Post-W.W. I conference site
8 Setting for some columns
9 It's issued to several stations, briefly
10 Caterpillar product
11 Caterpillar hairs
12 Raise, as a steering wheel
13 Long Branch Saloon visitor
14 Escorts after greeting
18 Earth personified
23 Bond girl player Shirley
25 Choose not to pick?
28 ___ bricks
30 Like some similarities
33 Preacher Beecher
35 Like the Julian calendar
37 Small, round sponge cake topped with fruit and whipped cream
39 Takeoffs
40 Direct
41 They may be received by free subscriptions
43 In up to one's neck
45 Interstellar matter
46 Some spuds
47 LaGuardia and others
49 "How then ___ he now see?": John 9:19
52 Twins' name at the 1984 Olympics
54 "I ___ Lover" (1979 John Cougar hit)
57 Bygone crown
59 Brain component
62 Gambler's place
63 Fort Worth sch.

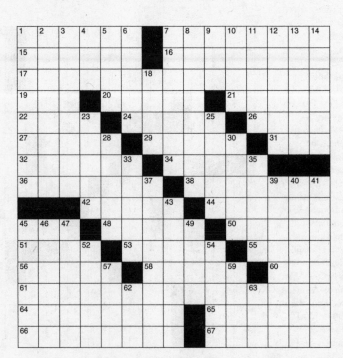

by Kevin G. Der

ACROSS
1 Judy Garland or Liza Minnelli
8 Sushi covering
15 It began in 1968, for tennis
16 Targetable
17 "Family Ties" family
18 Football coaching figures
19 Combustion product
20 Slice, say
22 An end to peace?
23 Behind
25 Bashkir's close cousin
26 Station
27 Weapon for Wonder Woman
29 TV shopper's option
30 Undertake
31 Dancer's guider, for short
33 Shallow
35 Big name in notebooks
37 Chips-in-a-can brand from Lay's
38 Silicon Valley city
42 Top of a slope?
46 Hill of law
47 Milieu for Katarina Witt
49 Old Testament patriarch
50 Romance, e.g.
51 Female demon
53 People's 1999 Sexiest Man Alive
54 City ESE of Utrecht
55 Botched salon job
57 OB, e.g.
58 Lagged
60 1970 western named for a fictional Texas city
62 Virtuoso
63 Ethnic conflict
64 Jacket option
65 Banderas's "The Mambo Kings" co-star, 1992

DOWN
1 Some four-wheelers
2 Popular costume party costume
3 "Groovy"
4 Undesirable result of making a pass?: Abbr.
5 High-ranking suits
6 ". . . then again, maybe I'm wrong"
7 Market for Microsoft
8 Bodybuilders' prides
9 "Scandalized Masks" painter, 1883
10 "But hark! __ comes gently to the door": Robert Burns
11 Weak
12 What a superscript in a text might refer one to
13 Chanel fragrance for men
14 Place for a trash can
21 Some four-wheelers, for short
24 Episcopal leader
26 Warning about people moving from side to side?
28 Speedy express
30 Wind
32 Piece of a candy bar?
34 "__ O.K."
36 Rodgers and Hammerstein refrain starter
38 Side
39 One way to do something stupid
40 Bit of cocoa?
41 Fool
43 55-Down with fiddles
44 Flipper
45 2003 sci-fi disaster film featuring a subterranean team of "terranauts"
48 Bimonthly magazine for environmentalists
51 Stimulating order
52 Met's lineup?
55 Blowout
56 Casual footwear, briefly
59 Bombed
61 Setting for an idyll

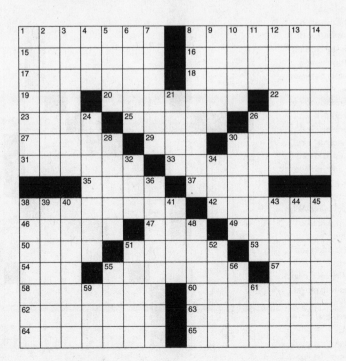

by David Quarfoot

ACROSS

1 They have many sticking points
11 Falcons' grp.
15 1978 cult film with a mutant child
16 Gazetteer meas.
17 Sealing fans?
18 Oscar-nominated "My Man Godfrey" actor, 1936
19 One of four directions in 5-Down
20 Goes on
21 Mathematician ___ Henrik Abel
22 Brown and others
23 Hit the big time
24 Not too far away
27 Football Hall-of-Famer Huff
28 Where many pens are found
29 Corrida sticker
30 Pessimist in a Disney cartoon
33 Drop the ball
34 Letters between two names
35 One way to get through a wall
36 Severe
37 Checkers, e.g.
38 Uses as a bed
39 End of many a race
40 It involves many unknowns: Abbr.
41 Sched. maker, often
42 One using soft soap
44 "Michael Collins" title role player, 1996
46 Here and there
48 Fogs
49 Desk tray labels
50 Eye of the tigre?
53 At any point
54 Choice for intercontinental travel
56 Endow
57 Student activity
58 It is in Peru
59 Doll that was once a going thing

DOWN

1 Credit report damager, briefly
2 Prizes for top atletas
3 Curer
4 Tikkanen of hockey
5 It's no longer divided
6 Architectural subdiscipline
7 "___ Lady" (1971 hit song)
8 Meet preliminaries
9 Roadside stand units
10 Old sit-in org.
11 Lend-Lease Act provision
12 Zydeco instrument
13 Ease
14 Simplest, in math and logic
21 When doubled, what a rat does
22 Sound of disapproval
23 Home to San Quentin State Prison
24 Opening pair?
25 Tidy up the lawn, in a way
26 Marmalade ingredient
27 "I've been better"
31 Like some profs.
32 Cries for attention
35 "Stand and Deliver" Oscar nominee, 1988
39 Brewery fixture
43 Ban
45 Perfect Day maker
46 "___ of traitors!": Shak.
47 Gravy holders
49 Summer cooler
50 Taking care of business
51 Former Norwegian P.M. Stoltenberg
52 Immoderate indulgence
54 Where races are screened?: Abbr.
55 "They Like ___" (song from "Call Me Madam")

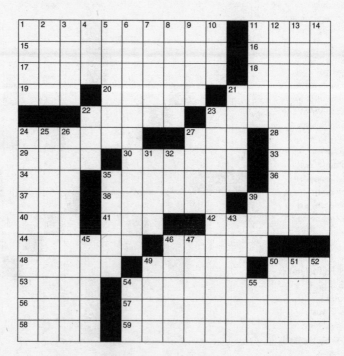

by Peter A. Collins

ACROSS

1 Yak
7 Nurses, say
15 Zebralike
16 Like anchors
17 Kept one's own counsel, online
18 Geographic feature depicted in the Armenian coat of arms
19 Some pointers
20 Big numismatic news
21 Steps away from
23 Forced, in a way
24 See 22-Down
25 "Obviously, Einstein!"
27 ___ legomenon (word or phrase used only once in a document or corpus)
29 Salt with the maximum proportion of element #53
35 Common soccer score
37 Star of "London After Midnight," 1927
38 1991 conflict between Slovenia and Yugoslavia
42 Western Australia, for example
43 Brawn
45 Compound with a double bond
46 Soft leather used in wallets, whose name derives from a place in California
51 Volkswagen Polo, for one
53 Shrub also known as Russian olive
55 One suspended in adolescence
56 Light mixer
57 Split personality?
58 As time expires, in a football game
59 Street lighting specialist?
60 Roller skate features
61 Claim of convenience, in ads or otherwise

DOWN

1 Jigger that jiggles?
2 Alternative to a water ski
3 Begin to blossom
4 Lance Armstrong foundation?
5 Hot month in Chile
6 Notable distinction for the planet Krypton
7 Where to go
8 Like some animal rights campaigns
9 Some DVR's
10 Legendary brothers in law
11 Sting
12 Spanish festival
13 Animal in Poe's "The Murders in the Rue Morgue"
14 Run-down
22 With 24-Across, number one position
26 Minute Maid drink brand
28 Earliest recorded Chinese dynasty
30 Quaker cereal
31 MTV reality show
32 Lifeless
33 Sets off
34 Parts of makeup kits
36 Flower of Pâques
39 Saw the light
40 Frogs and toads
41 One who stands for something
44 Composer of "Das Augenlicht," 1935
46 Tacitly acknowledge
47 First justice alphabetically in the history of the Supreme Court
48 First African-American golfer with 12 P.G.A. Tour wins
49 They go places
50 Plus
52 CD-burning software company that bought Napster
54 Neighbor of Ghana

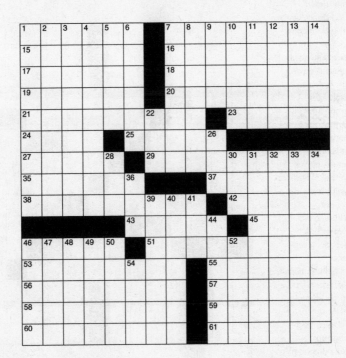

by Byron Walden

ACROSS

1 Pick up
8 Not as consequential
15 What seeds may be found in
16 A mouse may help you get there
17 Sprint competitor
18 Setting for TV's "Matlock"
19 Layer that scratches
20 Stadium snack
22 She, overseas
24 Time to burn?
25 Winter Olympics equipment
27 ___ Highway, old auto route from New York City to San Francisco
28 Overwhelms, with "down"
32 ___ Pacific Airways
34 Drag during the day?
37 Petroleum gases
39 Legalese adverb
40 Part of some complexes
42 Person lifting
43 "Symphony in Black" artist
44 Strike marks
46 Comics canine
47 Symbol of limpness
50 Symbols of authority
51 Where to order a cheesesteak "wit" or "witout"
56 Bully
57 Six bells, nautically
58 Reprimand lead-in
60 Patron saint of Palermo
61 Aid in picking things up
62 Make a point of
63 Brandy holder

DOWN

1 Where it's happening
2 Follows
3 W.W. II shelter
4 City area, briefly
5 "Last one ___ . . ."
6 Job-related moves, for short
7 Spectacle
8 Cousin of a flea market
9 Reading rhythm
10 Less error-prone
11 Its scores range from 120 to 180: Abbr.
12 Capital of Upper Austria
13 Major conclusion?
14 Coin on the Spanish Main
21 Ringleaders' nemeses
23 Be glued (to)
26 Not loco
28 His #13 was retired in 2000 by the Miami Dolphins
29 How much of genius is inspiration, according to Edison
30 Like typhoid bacteria, often
31 Gym shoes, e.g.
33 Referendum choice
35 Lukewarm reviews
36 Mountain ___ (Pepsi products)
38 Best substitute on the court
41 Bandar ___ Begawan, capital of Brunei
45 Some dips
47 Whippersnapper
48 "Silas Marner" girl
49 One of the Mercury Seven
51 Orch. section
52 Eager cry
53 Major start?
54 Tendon trouble
55 Subject of Nepalese legend
59 Mag founder of 1953

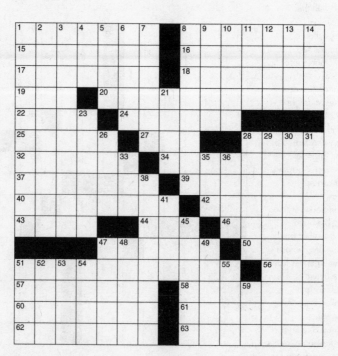

by Barry C. Silk

ACROSS

1 Scornful dismissals
7 Cause of temporary blindness
14 Symptom of nervous system impairment
15 Linebacker Brian banned from the 1987 Orange Bowl for steroid use
16 Sports stats specification
17 Current
18 They're often moved back in airports: Abbr.
19 It might help you dress in a shop
21 Ally's roommate on "Ally McBeal"
22 This, in Toulouse
23 Small wonder?
25 It begins near the end of winter: Abbr.
26 Associate of Thomas
28 Kind of rock
29 Mounts in a frame
30 Son and successor of Seti I
32 Relative of -ish
34 Very worried
39 Claptrap
40 Form of intimidation
41 Calls in the field
44 Warholian
46 "___ ask . . ."
47 Neighbor of Telescopium
48 Brand in the freezer section
50 1/192 qt.
51 Point and click, e.g.
53 Cab opener?
54 Places
55 Series finale?
57 Affix, in a way
59 Caped combatant

60 Amusement park vehicle
61 Children's Bargain Town, today
62 Tuner's place

DOWN

1 Indy sights since 1911
2 Governor's guide
3 It's done in the slammer
4 Lines on planes
5 Youngest golfer ever to win a U.S.G.A. adult event (age 13)
6 Grandmother of Jacob
7 Seat of Shawnee County
8 Record finish?
9 In ___ (briefly)
10 Hounded
11 It's big in Rio
12 Swear
13 It may rain in these
15 Cinematic captain of Star Command
20 Start putting stuff away?
23 "___ him who believes in nothing": Victor Hugo
24 Words said when one's hand is shaky?
27 Old dynasty members
29 1965 march setting
31 It's heard on the Beatles' "Rubber Soul"
33 Runners' locations
35 Howled
36 Very wide, in a way
37 Result of getting even with someone?

38 Enter on the sly
41 Gov. Lester Maddox walked off his show in 1970
42 Reply to someone in denial
43 Fighting words?
45 Dupes
48 Rigel or Spica
49 1939 Wimbledon winner
52 Producers of some storage cells
54 The prodigal son is found in it
56 Part of many schools' addresses
58 Auction offering

by Mike Nothnagel

★ ★ ★

ACROSS

1 Abstainer's order
9 Ranger rival
14 Linden
15 Like some cubs
16 Accidental in the key of B or E
17 Olympic event since 1988
18 Call letters?
19 Retreats
20 Three-ingredient treats
21 Producer/director ___ MacNaughton of Monty Python
22 Peck parts: Abbr.
23 Beethoven's "Pastoral" Symphony is in it
27 Noted centenarian of 2000, familiarly
32 Chocolate snacks
33 Parent's ruse to hush noisy kids
34 Job preceder: Abbr.
35 Silence
36 Silk Road locale
37 Burger replacement
39 Key
40 One way to wax
41 Stands in line at an airport?
42 Member of an "ooky" sitcom family
43 Take in tentatively
44 Dash
48 Betray horror
49 Yamaha product, briefly
52 Title woman of a film that won the 1985 Camera d'Or
53 Dodger's dread?
55 Do borderline work?
56 Sleuth who "looked rather pleasantly like a blond satan"
57 Small pieces
58 Spellbinding "Batman" villainess played by Joan Collins

DOWN

1 Tynan player in "The Seduction of Joe Tynan"
2 Force
3 End of a loving trio
4 Huddled (with)
5 Places to make tracks
6 Unfulfilled duty
7 Rimes with "Blue"
8 Catch in pots
9 Band ensemble
10 1969 and 1974 Hart Trophy winner, familiarly
11 Number between drei and funf
12 About
13 Staying power
15 Largest tenant of Pittsburgh's tallest skyscraper
22 It often gets down
23 Réunion reunion attendee
24 German wine region
25 Poetic conjunction
26 2002 Denzel Washington drama
27 Pursuit
28 Contemporary of Agatha and Erle
29 Pair from a deck, maybe
30 Literally, "women's boat"
31 Board
33 Rare delivery
35 Guatemala's national bird
38 "Mmmm . . . Toasty!" sloganeer
39 It might get you backstage
41 Pecking order?
43 Miles of film
44 Old man
45 Modern home of ancient Medes
46 Feeding tubes?
47 Powerful D.C. lobby
48 Meat
49 When the Feast of Lots is observed
50 Periodic riser
51 Powerful engine
54 News inits.

by David Quarfoot

ACROSS

1 Not a very good drawing
11 Cache
15 A little red
16 Da capo ___ (Baroque piece)
17 Band with the 1982 platinum album "The Number of the Beast"
18 Fade
19 Honors
20 Thai relative
21 View from the back seat?
22 Wings
23 Certain code
25 Choreographer Lubovitch
26 Meas. of progress, at times
27 Labor secretary under the first George Bush
28 River past the ruins of Nineveh
30 Martin Luther's crime
32 Pluck
33 Get ready to take off
36 Singer whose 2002 song "Foolish" was #1 for 10 weeks
38 Runway topper
39 Cakes often made with ground nuts
41 Like some sires
43 Modern info holders
44 When Arbor Day is observed: Abbr.
47 Pound sound
48 Recent developments
50 Nebraska City's county
51 Cleaning target
53 Inclination
54 Central Florida Community College site

55 The other shoe, e.g.
56 Bean product?
58 Mordant
59 10th-century exile from Iceland
60 Rosencrantz or Guildenstern
61 Upsetting types

DOWN

1 Joke indicator
2 Bygone New York daily, with "the"
3 Nonalcoholic beer brand
4 Twist things
5 Rolaids alternative
6 "An' singin there, an' dancin here, / Wi' great and ___": Burns
7 Like some chromium and arsenic
8 Base numbers, in math
9 Experiencing drunkenness
10 Charged
11 Cut
12 Test
13 Medium in a tube
14 It's hard to do this barefoot
23 Inner tubes, e.g.
24 Fountain requests
27 The Blue Demons of the N.C.A.A.'s Big East
29 Ranking nos.
30 "Pal Joey" lyricist
31 Standard
33 Burns overnight?
34 Two-part lake connected by the Strait of Tiquina

35 1996 Emmy-winning role for Alan Rickman
37 Saves, e.g.
40 Unprotected, in a way
42 Put (on) gently
44 Connecting flight
45 Question answerer
46 Checks, as checks
49 Land in the Colosseum
50 Cousin of rust
52 Ancient denizen along the Caspian
54 ___ Rios Bay
57 Last in a series

by Rich Norris

ACROSS

1 Is blessed with many assets, before "him" or "her"
16 Have cosmetic surgery, for example
17 Sources of government waste
18 Old Turkish title
19 Significant advancement
20 Excess
21 Awards for J. K. Rowling and P. L. Travers: Abbr.
23 Gulf of Aqaba city
24 Traps
25 Like an "eh," maybe
27 Something that shouldn't be left open
28 Three-time Masters winner Nick
29 Sensitivity
31 One of the Jackson 5
32 "___ votre permission"
33 Fix
34 Sounded smooth
37 1954 title role for Ava Gardner
41 Singer Jamie with the 2001 #1 country song "When I Think About Angels"
42 John
43 It's negative
44 D-Day sights: Abbr.
45 Heads of a tribe?
47 Turkish title
48 Onetime Bowie collaborator
49 Fired pitcher?
51 Void, in Vichy
52 Gross domestic product producer
55 Some bank offerings
56 At every point

DOWN

1 Connector in a song
2 Studied under a microscope
3 Most agile
4 Ham's place
5 Hardly hard questions
6 Roundish
7 Tops
8 Thug
9 Sometime ahead
10 Buzzards Bay, e.g.
11 Bags
12 Popular Volkswagen model
13 Carry out
14 "As You Like It" romantic
15 Leans against
22 Vast arid wastes
24 California city with a horticultural name
26 Carpenter's tool
28 Coca-Cola brand
30 But, to Brutus
31 See 38-Down
33 Progress in negotiations
34 Alternative to pasta
35 Straighten out
36 Double-check, as figures
37 Put in a bibliography, e.g.
38 Titles for Italian 31-Down
39 Words before "a Brain" and "an Animal" in book titles
40 Examine, in Exeter
42 Ohio city on Lake Erie
45 Nearing the hour
46 Book containing a prediction of the coming of the Messiah
49 Spring
50 Thomas ___, artist of the Hudson River School
53 Home of the Salmon River Mtns.
54 No score

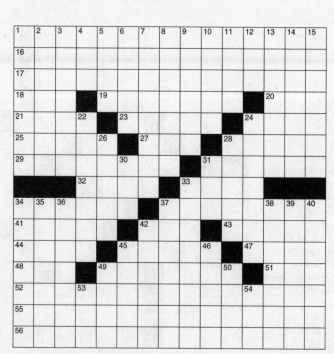

by Manny Nosowsky

The New York Times
SMART PUZZLES
Presented with Style

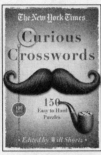

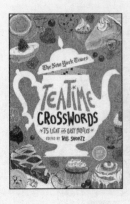

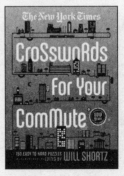

Available at your local bookstore or online at www.nytimes.com/nytstore

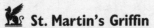 St. Martin's Griffin

1

```
J A D E   · M A C A W   · A P E D
I B E X   · O S S I E   · C A G E
B E A C O N H I L L   · · T U R K
· S T L U K E   · S T A N L E E
· · S A Y A H   · S H O R T S ·
A B B E Y   · G E T   · A W E ·
M A A M   · T H E H U B   · V E G
Ⓜ I K E   · H A L E R   · M E T Ⓐ
O L E   · B O S T O N   · O R A L
· D E L   · T A R   · F U E L S
H O B N O B   · P Y R O S · ·
O N E T W O S   · E X E R T S
R E A R   · F E N W A Y P A R K
S A N E   · F R E E D   · A R I A
E L S E   · O B O E S   · D E B T
```

2

```
I S P S   · D O G S   · H E L M S
N E R O   · S H O O   · E C A S H
F L I P F L O P S   · L O D G E
L E M U R   · H O M I N Y · ·
O N E P I E C E   · C O O L E R
W A R   · C O R K S   · L U L U
· L A R O S A   · N I C K S
C O V E R U P   · B L A N K E T
E T A T S   · E L O I S E · ·
L O G S   · A R O O M   · A C T
S H A D E S   · U M B R E L L A
· B A S H E S   · A N G E R ·
I C O N S   · B E A C H G O E R
M I N C E   · B U R N   · E R S E
F E D E X   · S P I N   · L E E R
```

3

```
A C M E   · L A P A Z   · C A G E
B O O T   · A B A B A   · L U L L
E P I C   · N O D O Z   · I D E E
· · H E A R T W A R M I N G ·
N S C   · S I T H   · E B O N Y
T A R O T   · A S I F · · ·
E Y E R O L L I N G   · D I A M
S H A M P O O   · O L E A N N A
T I M E   · G U T B U S T I N G
· · T O D O   · S A T I N ·
S U S H I   · R O S E   · S E A
K N E E S L A P P I N G · ·
I T E M   · I C E A X   · A J A X
M I M E   · C A D R E   · Z O N E
P E E N   · K N O T S   · E G G S
```

4

```
D A M A S K S   · J A G   · M A O
I C E B L U E   · A B U S E R S
P E R S O N A   · R E S P E C T
· · E G G O   · T I T H E · ·
S A T I S F A C T I O N · ·
O P A L   · U L C E R   · E B B S
L I K E A   · U R A L   · E R A
V E E   · R O L L I N G   · L O T
E C U   · B R I T   · S T O N E
D E P T   · C L I O S   · O N C E
· W H A T S G O I N G O N ·
B O W I E   · T R I P · · ·
I M A G I N E   · E R A S E R S
L E T S R I P   · S E D A L I A
E N T   · S T A   · S E S S I O N
```

5

```
A G I T A   · C L O C K   · S R A
R O G E R   · R O C H E   · H E N
C O U N T R Y S T A R   · A L A
A G A S S I   · E A R   · E L A L
D O N E   · F O R D G A L A X Y
E L A S T I C   · S E T T L E S
S S S   · I F A T   · C O A S T
· · K E I T H M O O N · · ·
C A S A S   · Y E P S   · P S A
A S C R I B E   · N E T G A I N
P H O E N I X S U N   · I R A N
S T U N   · G P A   · U P T I M E
I R R   · D A I L Y P L A N E T
Z A G   · S P R E E   · A N G S T
E Y E   · T E E M S   · N O S E E
```

6

```
A S S   · D I S C   · S W I S S
D A K   · S E R T A   · P I N T A
D Y E   · T A K E C H A N C E S
U N T I E   · I T A   · D A M S
P O C K E T K N I V E S · ·
· H E R O N   · E R O D E S
E L B A   · T O R E   · A R E N A
B O O   · C O P C A R S   · M V P
A L O H A   · F A T E   · B O Y S
Y A K I M A   · U N I O N · ·
· P I N C H P E N N I E S
I R I S   · N R A   · U N Z I P
L I F T W E I G H T S   · I D A
L O S E R   · M A M I E   · N E T
S T O R Y   · P R O P   · G R E
```

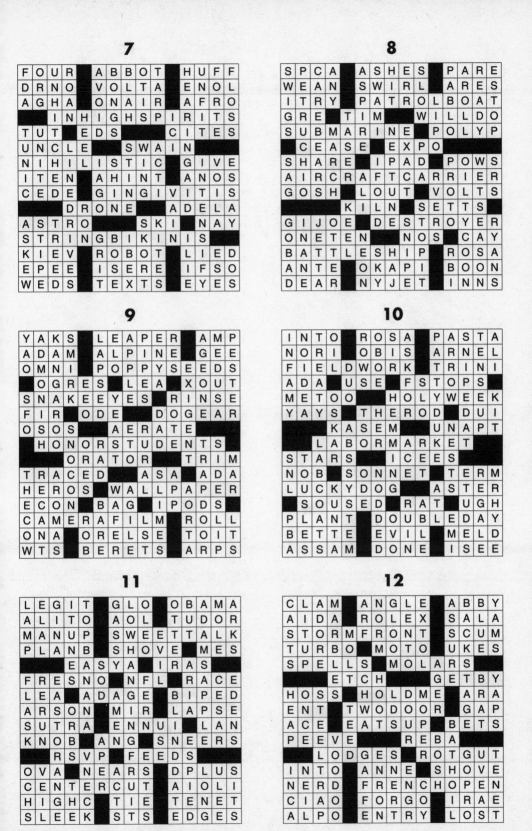

7

```
FOUR   ABBOT   HUFF
DRNO   VOLTA   ENOL
AGHA   ONAIR   AFRO
    INHIGHSPIRITS
TUT  EDS     CITES
UNCLE    SWAIN
NIHILISTIC   GIVE
ITEN   AHINT   ANOS
CEDE   GINGIVITIS
    DRONE    ADELA
ASTRO    SKI   NAY
STRINGBIKINIS
KIEV   ROBOT   LIED
EPEE   ISERE   IFSO
WEDS   TEXTS   EYES
```

8

```
SPCA   ASHES   PARE
WEAN   SWIRL   ARES
ITRY   PATROLBOAT
GRE  TIM    WILLDO
SUBMARINE   POLYP
   CEASE   EXPO
SHARE   IPAD   POWS
AIRCRAFTCARRIER
GOSH   LOUT   VOLTS
      KILN   SETTS
GIJOE   DESTROYER
ONETEN    NOS   CAY
BATTLESHIP   ROSA
ANTE   OKAPI   BOON
DEAR   NYJET   INNS
```

9

```
YAKS   LEAPER   AMP
ADAM   ALPINE   GEE
OMNI   POPPYSEEDS
 OGRES   LEA   XOUT
SNAKEEYES   RINSE
FIR   ODE   DOGEAR
OSOS    AERATE
 HONORSTUDENTS
   ORATOR    TRIM
TRACED   ASA   ADA
HEROS   WALLPAPER
ECON   BAG   IPODS
CAMERAFILM   ROLL
ONA   ORELSE   TOIT
WTS   BERETS   ARPS
```

10

```
INTO   ROSA   PASTA
NORI   OBIS   ARNEL
FIELDWORK   TRINI
ADA   USE   FSTOPS
METOO   HOLYWEEK
YAYS   THEROD   DUI
    KASEM   UNAPT
   LABORMARKET
STARS    ICEES
NOB   SONNET   TERM
LUCKYDOG   ASTER
 SOUSED   RAT   UGH
PLANT   DOUBLEDAY
BETTE   EVIL   MELD
ASSAM   DONE   ISEE
```

11

```
LEGIT   GLO   OBAMA
ALITO   AOL   TUDOR
MANUP   SWEETTALK
PLANB   SHOVE   MES
    EASYA   IRAS
FRESNO   NFL   RACE
LEA   ADAGE   BIPED
ARSON   MIR   LAPSE
SUTRA   ENNUI   LAN
KNOB   ANG   SNEERS
   RSVP   FEEDS
OVA   NEARS   DPLUS
CENTERCUT   AIOLI
HIGHC   TIE   TENET
SLEEK   STS   EDGES
```

12

```
CLAM   ANGLE   ABBY
AIDA   ROLEX   SALA
STORMFRONT   SCUM
TURBO   MOTO   UKES
SPELLS   MOLARS
    ETCH   GETBY
HOSS   HOLDME   ARA
ENT   TWODOOR   GAP
ACE   EATSUP   BETS
PEEVE    REBA
   LODGES   ROTGUT
INTO   ANNE   SHOVE
NERD   FRENCHOPEN
CIAO   FORGO   IRAE
ALPO   ENTRY   LOST
```

13

```
A P A I N . E B O N . B O S S
L A P S E . T A P E . R A K E
I S A A C H A Y E S . A K I N
S T R I K E . O R T O . L E S
T A T A . F I N A L P H A S E
. H E N C E . E T O N . . .
U G H . M E E T S . E D A M
S T A T U R E . P U L S A T E
S O P H . S W I N E . S E T
. P E S O . A N V I L .
M A Y O N N A I S E . E L L E
O L D . L E S T . I M D E A D
N O A H . S T E E L Y G A Z E
E N Y A . E R R S . S E V E N
T E S T . C O S T . T R E S S
```

14

```
W H A T . S R A . C A R T E
A O N E . L A S E . A V A I L
X B O X R I V A L . M I N T S
Y O N . A M E B A . E A G L E
. . F R E N C H F O R Y E S
T A H O E S . A N Y . .
A G O G . R E M I T . N B A
P E R S O N A L P R O N O U N
S E N . L E E K S . A S S T
. . C D E . A S S E T S
C R Y O F D E L I G H T .
L E O N I . R E N E E . Q E D
U S U A L . M I N I A T U R E
E E R I E . A C E S . W I S E
S T E R S . A R T . O P T S
```

15

```
A C T S . B L A C K . W O R D
S L O T . U L T R A . A L A I
K E R R . S A L A R Y H I K E
. A R E A . M A P L E . V E T
P R E S S P A S S . R A I S E
G U N S H Y . M E I R
A P T . T R A I T . E A R N S
. G O O D C A T C H .
S H E E N . S E O U L . A R T
T E L L . B A M B O O
E L A T E . R A B B I T R U N
A L P . S I E G E . R E A L
M U S I C S C O R E . T H A W
E V E R . P A R E R . N A D A
D A D A . S P A T E . A M E N
```

16

```
K U M Q U A T . T Y P H O O N
A T E I N T O . H O R M O N E
L E T D O W N . E D A S N E R
E R A . S T E A M E D . A G O
S I L K . R E L A Y .
. . S A I N T S . O A T S
. H Y U N D A I . K O W T O W
A A A . K E T C H U P . O D E
G U N G H O . H O R A T I O
E L K O . B O T T L E .
. . B A R A K . C H O W
E B B . B O R E D O M . I M O
M A R C O N I . C H A T T E R
A L A D D I N . C O L U M N S
G I N S E N G . C H I N E S E
```

17

```
P A N . A S A P . D A P P E R
U P I . G A L S . E L A I N E
M A M M A M I A . C A N N O T
A R O A R . L E O . A T R A
S T Y X . M U M M Y S T O M B
. . I B I D . I S L E .
A H A . A R O O . I L O S T
M I L L I O N M O M M A R C H
I M P E L . B A A L . S H Y
. . T E M P . H A Y S .
M A M M Y Y O K U M . L A M A
A T I E . N T H . A A R O N
C E S S N A . M M M M G O O D
H I T E C H . E X A M . M E R
U N S E R S . R I C O . A D E
```

18

```
L A B E L . E S C A P E . P S A
I N A N E . E R A S E R . A W N
D A N C E S W I T H W O L V E S
. G O R E . N O I S E L A W
W I L D A T H E A R T . V O T E
S W E E T . A L P E . F E V E R
J O S . A V E . M O L A R S
. D A T E M O V I E S .
U M L A U T . R E X . W A R
G O E R S . P L I E . E J E C T
A L O T . T H E G R A D U A T E
N I N E I R O N . P I N K .
D E A D P O E T S S O C I E T Y
A R R . S O B E I T . T O S E E
N E D . O P E N L Y . S R T A S
```

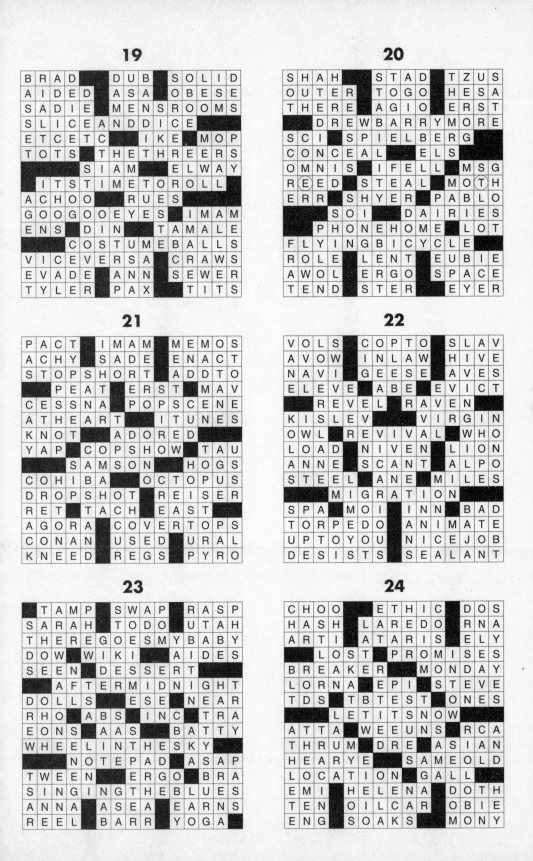

19

B R A D ■ D U B ■ S O L I D
A I D E D ■ A S A ■ O B E S E
S A D I E ■ M E N S R O O M S
S L I C E A N D D I C E ■ ■
E T C E T C ■ I K E ■ M O P
T O T S ■ T H E T H R E E R S
■ ■ S I A M ■ E L W A Y
■ I T S T I M E T O R O L L
A C H O O ■ R U E S ■ ■
G O O G O O E Y E S ■ I M A M
E N S ■ D I N ■ T A M A L E
■ C O S T U M E B A L L S
V I C E V E R S A ■ C R A W S
E V A D E ■ A N N ■ S E W E R
T Y L E R ■ P A X ■ T I T S

20

S H A H ■ S T A D ■ T Z U S
O U T E R ■ T O G O ■ H E S A
T H E R E ■ A G I O ■ E R S T
■ D R E W B A R R Y M O R E ■
S C I ■ S P I E L B E R G ■
C O N C E A L ■ ■ E L S ■
O M N I S ■ I F E L L ■ M S G
R E E D ■ S T E A L ■ M O T H
E R R ■ S H Y E R ■ P A B L O
■ ■ S O I ■ D A I R I E S
■ P H O N E H O M E ■ L O T
F L Y I N G B I C Y C L E ■
R O L E ■ L E N T ■ E U B I E
A W O L ■ E R G O ■ S P A C E
T E N D ■ S T E R ■ E Y E R

21

P A C T ■ I M A M ■ M E M O S
A C H Y ■ S A D E ■ E N A C T
S T O P S H O R T ■ A D D T O
■ P E A T ■ E R S T ■ M A V
C E S S N A ■ P O P S C E N E
A T H E A R T ■ I T U N E S
K N O T ■ A D O R E D ■ ■
Y A P ■ C O P S H O W ■ T A U
■ S A M S O N ■ H O G S
C O H I B A ■ O C T O P U S
D R O P S H O T ■ R E I S E R
R E T ■ T A C H ■ E A S T ■
A G O R A ■ C O V E R T O P S
C O N A N ■ U S E D ■ U R A L
K N E E D ■ R E G S ■ P Y R O

22

V O L S ■ C O P T O ■ S L A V
A V O W ■ I N L A W ■ H I V E
N A V I ■ G E E S E ■ A V E S
E L E V E ■ A B E ■ E V I C T
■ R E V E L ■ R A V E N ■
K I S L E V ■ V I R G I N
O W L ■ R E V I V A L ■ W H O
L O A D ■ N I V E N ■ L I O N
A N N E ■ S C A N T ■ A L P O
S T E E L ■ A N E ■ M I L E S
■ M I G R A T I O N ■
S P A ■ M O I ■ I N N ■ B A D
T O R P E D O ■ A N I M A T E
U P T O Y O U ■ N I C E J O B
D E S I S T S ■ S E A L A N T

23

■ T A M P ■ S W A P ■ R A S P
S A R A H ■ T O D O ■ U T A H
T H E R E G O E S M Y B A B Y
D O W ■ W I K I ■ A I D E S
S E E N ■ D E S S E R T ■
■ A F T E R M I D N I G H T
D O L L S ■ E S E ■ N E A R
R H O ■ A B S ■ I N C ■ T R A
E O N S ■ A A S ■ B A T T Y
W H E E L I N T H E S K Y ■
■ N O T E P A D ■ A S A P
T W E E N ■ E R G O ■ B R A
S I N G I N G T H E B L U E S
A N N A ■ A S E A ■ E A R N S
R E E L ■ B A R R ■ Y O G A

24

C H O O ■ E T H I C ■ D O S
H A S H ■ L A R E D O ■ R N A
A R T I ■ A T A R I S ■ E L Y
■ L O S T ■ P R O M I S E S
B R E A K E R ■ M O N D A Y
L O R N A ■ E P I ■ S T E V E
T D S ■ T B T E S T ■ O N E S
■ L E T I T S N O W ■
A T T A ■ W E E U N S ■ R C A
T H R U M ■ D R E ■ A S I A N
H E A R Y E ■ S A M E O L D
L O C A T I O N ■ G A L L
E M I ■ H E L E N A ■ D O T H
T E N ■ O I L C A R ■ O B I E
E N G ■ S O A K S ■ M O N Y

25

```
T A P E   G A P E     N A L A
N E I N   A L O T   M O T O R
U S A I N B O L T   A T T I C
T O N G A   U S U A L F A R E
  P O M P S     B L A R E D
  B A S I N   S A R I
S E A S   B O S C   A R T S Y
P A R   U S B P O R T   A T E
A R S O N   L Y L E   U L E E
  I R A E   D A N S K
M I L L E R     M O O R E
U S E R S F E E S   I P A D S
G E T I T   U S H E R E D I N
G R O G S   R A I L   N I N A
Y E N S   O I N K   S O A P
```

26

```
G R U B   A I L S   J I H A D
L I S A   K N E E   O N O N E
A T M S   I F A T   S T A T E
M A C I N T O S H   H E X E D
  L I A R     C U R
T O X I C   M E C H A N I C
A D A S H   N R A   G L O
M I C K E Y M O U S E C L U B
P U T   E E K   N A O M I
  M O C C A S I N   T R O P E
  H U H   U S E S
S E D E R   M U C K R A K E R
E V I C T   E L L E   L O V E
G E E K S   A N E W   E K E D
A N T S Y   D A I S   S O L O
```

27

```
C A T T Y   D R I V E   P A P
O M A H A   R A D A R   O N E
R U N A W A Y J U R Y   G E E
A S K I N G   A N I   D O W N
L E S   E L F   N O S E S
  B R E A K O U T S T A R
S E T A   T I N   S U P I N E
A X O N S   L E A   D I C T A
F E U D E D   E S Q   S K I D
E S C A P E C L A U S E
  H I T C H   P A T   S H E
L A U D   L O G   F A T H O M
A L P   T A K E O F F R A M P
Z O O   A R E N A   F U M E T
Y E N   B E R E T   S E E D Y
```

28

```
A H O R A   B A S I C   D L I
R A T E R   E T H N O   O I D
C L E A R T H E A I R   O C T
O A R   M A I   O S H E A
  L I N E A R T H I N K I N G
  C N N   I S A A C S
S T P A T   S O T O   K E V
I H E A R T H U C K A B E E S
B R A   W I T H   S A Y S O
  A N C H O R   C T R
A C U T E A R T H R I T I S
S I T A R   U A E   N U T
S A O   M I D D L E E A R T H
A N I   E R R O L   S H E R A
Y S L   S E E R S   A I M A T
```

29

```
A C M E   A E R   T S E T S E
N O I R   J L O   O P E R A S
D O N A D A M S   R O G E R S
R E D S O X   S P A R   A D E
E D S E L   E I G H T Y S I X
  S L U R   A S Y O U
T N T   E E N Y   G R I T
W O U L D Y O U B E L I E V E
A W R Y   M O N A   R Y E
  B R U S H   R O S A
S H O E P H O N E   S N I F F
T A J   L A N E   S O I R E E
O N E C A R   G E T S M A R T
R O T A T E   E L O   A T M E
M I S T E R   V F W   L E I S
```

30

```
C U R S   A M B E R   A W A Y
O L E O   W I L M A   F E T A
S C R O L L L O C K   F L O W
M E A N Y   K N E E   A L P S
O R N E R Y   D E R A I L
  S E E S     B R I N E
J E S T   A P A C H E   K E G
O N T   T R I P L E L   E R G
L V I   A N N E A L   O D D S
T Y L E R     M E S H
  L A P S E S   N O M O R E
P A L S   A S A P   I S L A M
E X I T   S Q U A L L L I N E
R I F E   S U N N I   A V O N
U S E R   Y E A S T   W E N D
```

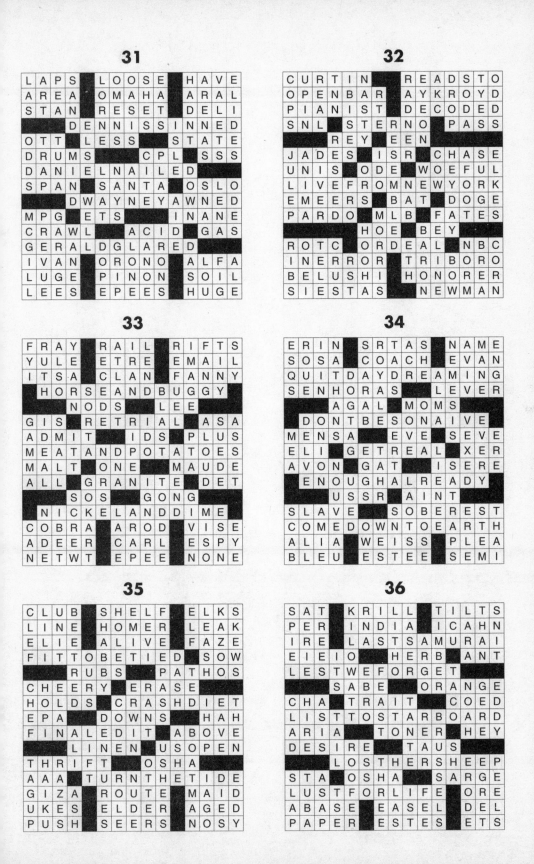

31 · 32 · 33 · 34 · 35 · 36

37

```
H A N G   E P S O M   I H O P
O N E A   P O P P A   G U L L
S T A R   I C E I N   U R G E
S I T B A C K A N D R E L A X
      L P S   K E Y E S
M I M E O   P O D   L S A T S
E W E   R E F   M I S C U E
D O W N F O R T H E C O U N T
I N L A I D   H A G   R E A
A T S I X   R E D   B L A S T
      L I M E D   O O O
C O M E T O T E R M S W I T H
A X E D   L I V E N   E D A M
S E M I   T R I N I   N I N O
K N O T   S E L E S   D O G S
```

38

```
L E N O   D F L A T   A S T I
E V I L   A R O M A   M E I R
S A G E   M E T E R   B R A E
    H O U S E T R A I L E R S
A C T   R E O     M E N A T
F A C I A L F E A T U R E S
A T A L L   R U B S
R O P E   P A R K S   A T R A
        E A S E   S T R E P
  C A R T R I D G E C L I P S
T R E A T   O V A   E S O
B E R M U D A S H O R T S
S W A M   E B O O K   O O P S
P E T E   F L U M E   G U R U
S L E D   T Y P E D   A T O P
```

39

```
S P A T   S A I L   M I R E D
I O T A   E B R O   Y O U R E
N U T C R A C K E R S U I T E
A N Y H O W   S W A T   N E D
I D S   W A C   S P I T
      A S T R O   S Q U A T S
A M A T   E E L S   U R I A H
B O L T F R O M T H E B L U E
R A T I O   N O R A   A S T A
A T O L L S   S A T I N
      A L A S   Y R S   A C C
A S A   O A T S   A N I M A L
S C R E W B A L L C O M E D Y
P A N A M   R O O K   A B E D
S N O R E   E G O S   M A T E
```

40

```
S U M A C S   C B S   S T A T
A T O N A L   O L E   L E A R
W I N D T U N N E L   E S A U
I C E R   S E A N   S E T
N A T E   H A N D P U P P E T
      T R Y   U P S I Z E
A G A T E   G R A S P   L I N
F I N I S H I N G S E C O N D
R A T   P A S S E   R O T E S
O N E T O N   E S P
S T R I N G B E A N   A D A M
    O D D   L A R D   P E L E
B L O B   B E S T S E L L E R
M I M I   R A Y   U S E F U L
W E S T   A K A   P L A T T E
```

41

```
A G O G   U P S E T   N E W T
L O B E   G O T T I   I S E E
P R O A T H L E T E   G A P E
O P E R A   S M A S H H I T S
      U R L   O U T
  S U P P O R T I N G C A S T
S H H   S C O R N   S A N T A
A A H S   H O U N D   P I E D
A M U C K   S T I E S   S E A
B E H I N D T H E W H E E L
      S I R   Y O N
C A B S T A N D S   V A L U E
O S L O   F O R T H E B E S T
S T I R   T O N E R   L E N A
T O P S   S N O W S   E R A S
```

42

```
F L O   L E A R   R E D C A P
L O U   O R N E   I N A R U T
O C T   C L E F   N O M A D S
P A P A H E M I N G W A Y
P L U M S   I L E   T O F U
Y E T I   M A M A L E O N E S
      S T A   S T A N   E T E
B A S S I S T   O N O R D E R
O H O   P O O H   E S O
B A B Y S N O O K S   G U S T
O S S A   T R E   O U N C E
    T H E T H R E E B E A R S
S H O O T S   O N M E   B E T
A U R O R A   R E M Y   L E E
G E Y S E R   S R A S   E N D
```

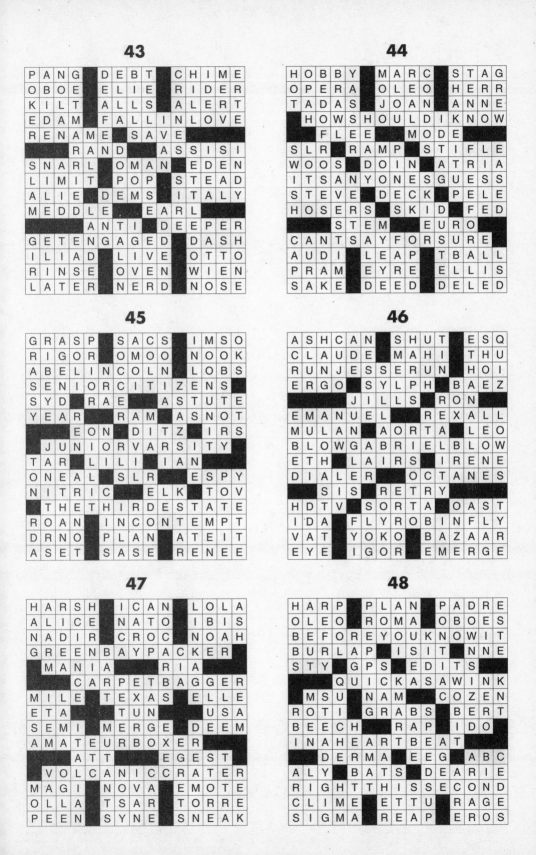

43

```
P A N G _ D E B T _ C H I M E
O B O E _ E L I E _ R I D E R
K I L T _ A L L S _ A L E R T
E D A M _ F A L L I N L O V E
R E N A M E _ S A V E _ _ _ _
_ _ _ R A N D _ A S S I S I
S N A R L _ O M A N _ E D E N
L I M I T _ P O P _ S T E A D
A L I E _ D E M S _ I T A L Y
M E D D L E _ E A R L _ _ _ _
_ _ _ A N T I _ D E E P E R
G E T E N G A G E D _ D A S H
I L I A D _ L I V E _ O T T O
R I N S E _ O V E N _ W I E N
L A T E R _ N E R D _ N O S E
```

44

```
H O B B Y _ M A R C _ S T A G
O P E R A _ O L E O _ H E R R
T A D A S _ J O A N _ A N N E
_ H O W S H O U L D I K N O W
_ F L E E _ M O D E _ _ _ _
S L R _ R A M P _ S T I F L E
W O O S _ D O I N _ A T R I A
I T S A N Y O N E S G U E S S
S T E V E _ D E C K _ P E L E
H O S E R S _ S K I D _ F E D
_ _ S T E M _ E U R O _ _
C A N T S A Y F O R S U R E
A U D I _ L E A P _ T B A L L
P R A M _ E Y R E _ E L L I S
S A K E _ D E E D _ D E L E D
```

45

```
G R A S P _ S A C S _ I M S O
R I G O R _ O M O O _ N O O K
A B E L I N C O L N _ L O B S
S E N I O R C I T I Z E N S _
S Y D _ R A E _ A S T U T E
Y E A R _ R A M _ A S N O T
_ E O N _ D I T Z _ I R S
J U N I O R V A R S I T Y
T A R _ L I L I _ I A N
O N E A L _ S L R _ E S P Y
N I T R I C _ E L K _ T O V
_ T H E T H I R D E S T A T E
R O A N _ I N C O N T E M P T
D R N O _ P L A N _ A T E I T
A S E T _ S A S E _ R E N E E
```

46

```
A S H C A N _ S H U T _ E S Q
C L A U D E _ M A H I _ T H U
R U N J E S S E R U N _ H O I
E R G O _ S Y L P H _ B A E Z
_ _ J I L L S _ R O N _
E M A N U E L _ R E X A L L
M U L A N _ A O R T A _ L E O
B L O W G A B R I E L B L O W
E T H _ L A I R S _ I R E N E
D I A L E R _ O C T A N E S
_ S I S _ R E T R Y _
H D T V _ S O R T A _ O A S T
I D A _ F L Y R O B I N F L Y
V A T _ Y O K O _ B A Z A A R
E Y E _ I G O R _ E M E R G E
```

47

```
H A R S H _ I C A N _ L O L A
A L I C E _ N A T O _ I B I S
N A D I R _ C R O C _ N O A H
G R E E N B A Y P A C K E R _
_ M A N I A _ R I A _
_ C A R P E T B A G G E R
M I L E _ T E X A S _ E L L E
E T A _ T U N _ U S A
S E M I _ M E R G E _ D E E M
A M A T E U R B O X E R _
_ A T T _ E G E S T
_ V O L C A N I C C R A T E R
M A G I _ N O V A _ E M O T E
O L L A _ T S A R _ T O R R E
P E E N _ S Y N E _ S N E A K
```

48

```
H A R P _ P L A N _ P A D R E
O L E O _ R O M A _ O B O E S
B E F O R E Y O U K N O W I T
B U R L A P _ I S I T _ N N E
S T Y _ G P S _ E D I T S _
_ Q U I C K A S A W I N K
_ M S U _ N A M _ C O Z E N
R O T I _ G R A B S _ B E R T
B E E C H _ R A P _ I D O
I N A H E A R T B E A T
_ D E R M A _ E E G _ A B C
A L Y _ B A T S _ D E A R I E
R I G H T T H I S S E C O N D
C L I M E _ E T T U _ R A G E
S I G M A _ R E A P _ E R O S
```

49

```
S T U T Z   I M A M   P A V E
P O L E S   G I N O   U S E R
O N C E A M O N T H   R H E A
I K E   Z E R O   A L P E R T
L A R O S A   T R I A L
    R A G A   O R D E A L S
I R M A   E G G O   S H R E K
M O A N   R H Y M E   E B A Y
A M I G O   A M E X   A S K S
C A M E R A S   R O A R
    J E S T S   D I T T O S
T H R U S T   P L U M   A B O
M A U I   H I Y O S I L V E R
A L E C   M O O G   N O I S E
N O S E   A N N E   G A S E S
```

50

```
S M O G   S T A G E   M E S A
L A V A   H O V E R   U S P S
A X E R   O R I O N   E S A U
G I N G E R R O G E R S
    O F T E N   A L P E N
P A P Y R U S   G A L I L E O
A M I L E   O M S   A L T
R O S E M A R Y C L O O N E Y
R E C   N F L   S P A R E
O B E L I S K   A M H E R S T
T A S E R   G O R E N
    P E P P E R M A R T I N
B O D E   A I R T O   O U Z O
M U I R   S T R A T   A T O P
W I N S   S A Y S O   D U D E
```

51

```
C A D G E   D E A N   A R C H
A C O R N   R E N O   L U A U
G R E A T   E R O S   I N C A
Y E S V I R G I N I A   I A N
    E R A S E   E G G N O G
T I N S E L   D R N O
R O O T   P L I E   E B B E D
I T I   T H E R E I S   A A R
P A R S E   A E R O   A L V A
    A S A P   N U T M E G
C A R O L S   S E I N E
A B A   A S A N T A C L A U S
D I V A   U H O H   L I L L E
I T E M   M O R E   A E T N A
Z E N O   E Y E R   D R E A M
```

52

```
H E E L   F I E F   H A M E L
A L A I   O N T O   A M U L E
H M S B O U N T Y   S O F I A
A S T R A L   A T T H E T O P
    E R S T   H A B I T S
D O L T S   E S P A N A
A L I T   P A P A Y A   F U R
F A M O U S R A C E H O R S E
T V A   N E A R E R   N A M E
    N E U T E R   P E N A L
E N N E A D   S E R F
M A I L R O O M   L A I D U P
I D E S T   J E L L Y F I S H
R I C O H   A L O E   T R E Y
S A E N S   I S B N   H E R S
```

53

```
B A R   A E T N A   D E G A S
A T O   S Q U A T   E N O L A
S O B   P U L P F I C T I O N
S P E C I A L   D A R N E D
    R U N T   T E L L Y
M A T T   O Z O N E   F E S T
A L P   T R A P S   S E A T O
T E E T H   P S I   R E S I N
E V E R Y   A E G I S   T N T
S E L A   S T E N S   L O G O
    S T E A D   O M A R
A R C H I E   S T E W A R D
J U I C E N E W T O N   N O R
A L T A R   S H O P S   G T O
R E I N S   T Y P E A   E S P
```

54

```
M A G I   T E L L   A R M O R
A M E N   E X I T   D O O N E
J O E J E T T E R   L O T S A
    A F R O S   D I T H E R
A D M I R A L   S O B   E T S
D O Y L E   C E N S O R
O R S   M I N U E T   A J A R
B A T S   S O F T G   F U S E
E L E C   O N F O O T   I S A
    R I F L E S   A R C E D
B E Y   A D S   A N X I E T Y
I N J O K E   T R E E S
B R E V E   J U N E S Q U A D
L O S E R   A T A D   U R G E
E N T R Y   S U Z Y   E L A N
```

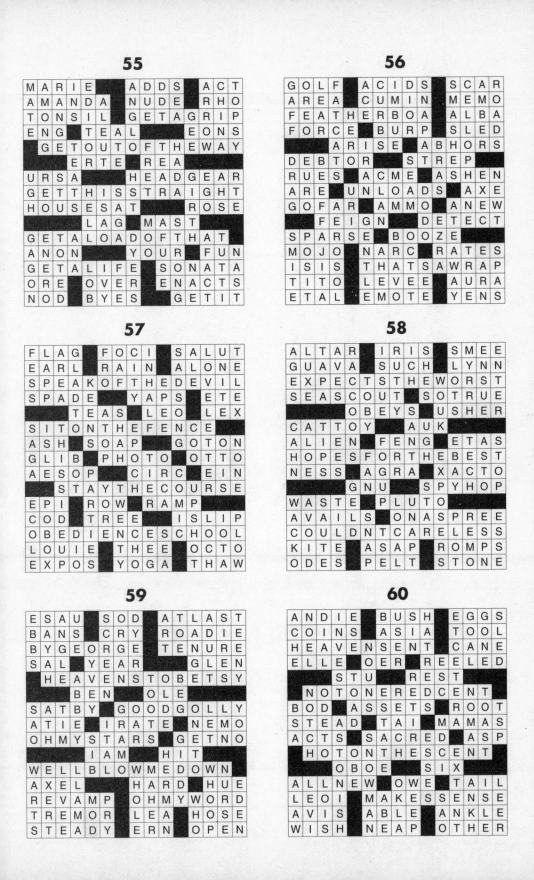

55

```
M A R I E ■ ■ A D D S ■ ■ A C T
A M A N D A ■ N U D E ■ ■ R H O
T O N S I L ■ G E T A G R I P ■
E N G ■ T E A L ■ ■ ■ E O N S ■
■ G E T O U T O F T H E W A Y ■
■ ■ E R T E ■ R E A ■ ■ ■ ■ ■ ■
U R S A ■ ■ H E A D G E A R ■ ■
G E T T H I S S T R A I G H T ■
H O U S E S A T ■ ■ R O S E ■ ■
■ ■ L A G ■ M A S T ■ ■ ■ ■ ■ ■
G E T A L O A D O F T H A T ■ ■
A N O N ■ ■ Y O U R ■ F U N ■ ■
G E T A L I F E ■ S O N A T A ■
O R E ■ O V E R ■ E N A C T S ■
N O D ■ B Y E S ■ ■ G E T I T ■
```

56

```
G O L F ■ A C I D S ■ ■ S C A R
A R E A ■ C U M I N ■ ■ M E M O
F E A T H E R B O A ■ A L B A ■
F O R C E ■ B U R P ■ S L E D ■
■ ■ ■ A R I S E ■ A B H O R S ■
D E B T O R ■ S T R E P ■ ■ ■ ■
R U E S ■ A C M E ■ A S H E N ■
A R E ■ U N L O A D S ■ A X E ■
G O F A R ■ A M M O ■ A N E W ■
■ F E I G N ■ D E T E C T ■ ■ ■
S P A R S E ■ B O O Z E ■ ■ ■ ■
M O J O ■ N A R C ■ R A T E S ■
I S I S ■ T H A T S A W R A P ■
T I T O ■ L E V E E ■ A U R A ■
E T A L ■ E M O T E ■ Y E N S ■
```

57

```
F L A G ■ F O C I ■ ■ S A L U T
E A R L ■ R A I N ■ A L O N E ■
S P E A K O F T H E D E V I L ■
S P A D E ■ ■ Y A P S ■ E T E ■
■ ■ T E A S ■ L E O ■ L E X ■ ■
S I T O N T H E F E N C E ■ ■ ■
A S H ■ S O A P ■ ■ G O T O N ■
G L I B ■ P H O T O ■ O T T O ■
A E S O P ■ C I R C ■ E I N ■ ■
■ S T A Y T H E C O U R S E ■ ■
E P I ■ R O W ■ R A M P ■ ■ ■ ■
C O D ■ T R E E ■ ■ I S L I P ■
O B E D I E N C E S C H O O L ■
L O U I E ■ T H E E ■ O C T O ■
E X P O S ■ Y O G A ■ T H A W ■
```

58

```
A L T A R ■ I R I S ■ ■ S M E E
G U A V A ■ S U C H ■ ■ L Y N N
E X P E C T S T H E W O R S T ■
S E A S C O U T ■ S O T R U E ■
■ ■ O B E Y S ■ U S H E R ■ ■ ■
C A T T O Y ■ A U K ■ ■ ■ ■ ■ ■
A L I E N ■ F E N G ■ E T A S ■
H O P E S F O R T H E B E S T ■
N E S S ■ A G R A ■ X A C T O ■
■ ■ G N U ■ S P Y H O P ■ ■ ■ ■
W A S T E ■ P L U T O ■ ■ ■ ■ ■
A V A I L S ■ O N A S P R E E ■
C O U L D N T C A R E L E S S ■
K I T E ■ A S A P ■ R O M P S ■
O D E S ■ P E L T ■ S T O N E ■
```

59

```
E S A U ■ S O D ■ A T L A S T ■
B A N S ■ C R Y ■ R O A D I E ■
B Y G E O R G E ■ T E N U R E ■
S A L ■ Y E A R ■ ■ G L E N ■ ■
■ H E A V E N S T O B E T S Y ■
■ ■ B E N ■ ■ O L E ■ ■ ■ ■ ■ ■
S A T B Y ■ G O O D G O L L Y ■
A T I E ■ I R A T E ■ N E M O ■
O H M Y S T A R S ■ G E T N O ■
■ ■ I A M ■ ■ H I T ■ ■ ■ ■ ■ ■
W E L L B L O W M E D O W N ■ ■
A X E L ■ H A R D ■ H U E ■ ■ ■
R E V A M P ■ O H M Y W O R D ■
T R E M O R ■ L E A ■ H O S E ■
S T E A D Y ■ E R N ■ O P E N ■
```

60

```
A N D I E ■ B U S H ■ E G G S ■
C O I N S ■ A S I A ■ T O O L ■
H E A V E N S E N T ■ C A N E ■
E L L E ■ O E R ■ R E E L E D ■
■ ■ ■ S T U ■ ■ R E S T ■ ■ ■ ■
■ N O T O N E R E D C E N T ■ ■
B O D ■ A S S E T S ■ R O O T ■
S T E A D ■ T A I ■ M A M A S ■
A C T S ■ S A C R E D ■ A S P ■
■ H O T O N T H E S C E N T ■ ■
■ ■ O B O E ■ ■ S I X ■ ■ ■ ■ ■
A L L N E W ■ O W E ■ T A I L ■
L E O I ■ M A K E S S E N S E ■
A V I S ■ A B L E ■ A N K L E ■
W I S H ■ N E A P ■ O T H E R ■
```

61

S	E	E	P		S	C	A	L	A		A	C	E	S
P	L	E	A		P	E	R	I	L		F	O	G	G
A	L	L	S	H	O	O	K	U	P		A	L	O	T
			S	I	T	S			H	A	R	I		
H	A	W	K	S			P	S	A	T		N	A	G
A	L	E	E		S	T	R	A	T	A		P	S	I
I	T	S	Y		H	A	I	L	E	D		O	T	B
R	O	T	S		E	L	V	I	S		A	W	O	L
C	O	G		P	L	I	A	N	T		P	E	R	U
U	N	E		E	L	A	T	E	S		P	L	I	E
T	A	R		E	A	S	E			H	A	L	A	S
		M	A	R	C			A	P	E	R			
R	E	A	R		K	I	N	G	C	R	E	O	L	E
C	O	N	E		E	V	E	R	T		N	A	I	L
A	N	Y	A		D	E	G	A	S		T	R	E	K

62

I	S	M	S		T	E	M	P	E		W	R	A	P
R	E	A	P		A	C	O	R	N		H	I	Y	A
A	M	I	E		B	O	R	E	D	B	O	A	R	D
S	I	Z	E	S		N	N	E		A	L	T	E	R
	M	E	D	I	A		I	N	C	R	E	A	S	E
G	E	M		S	C	A	N		A	S	H			
U	T	A	H		E	L	G	A	R		O	I	L	S
L	A	Z	E		T	E	M	P	O		L	S	A	T
F	L	E	A		A	F	O	O	T		E	L	S	A
			R	I	T		U	P	I	N		E	E	G
H	E	A	D	G	E	A	R		D	E	B	A	R	
A	L	T	H	O		R	N	A		B	R	I	B	E
S	W	E	E	T	S	U	I	T	E		U	S	E	R
T	E	A	R		A	B	N	E	R		S	L	A	G
E	S	T	D		P	A	G	E	R		H	E	M	S

63

C	R	A	B		O	C	T	E	T		P	L	O	T
H	O	L	A		A	R	I	S	E		L	E	G	O
A	M	O	S		F	O	R	C	E	F	I	E	L	D
D	A	T	E	L	I	N	E		S	L	A	K	E	D
			B	O	S	E		C	H	A	N			
S	P	L	A	S	H		S	H	O	W	T	I	M	E
L	U	L	L	S		S	L	A	T			S	O	D
O	R	A	L			A	I	R		S	A	N	G	
T	E	M		H	U	N	T		S	P	A	T	E	
H	E	A	D	L	O	C	K		M	E	E	K	E	R
			O	I	L	Y		W	A	L	E			
P	A	L	T	R	Y		M	A	I	L	D	R	O	P
S	P	A	C	E	C	R	A	F	T		W	A	K	E
A	S	T	O		O	A	T	E	R		A	C	R	E
T	E	E	M		W	H	E	R	E		Y	E	A	R

64

	S	T	U	D		Q	I	D		N	O	M	A	D
	W	O	R	E		U	N	A		O	P	I	N	E
F	O	O	L	F	A	I	N	T		B	I	L	G	E
A	R	K	S		E	R	I	E		O	U	T	E	R
R	E	N		F	R	E	E		A	D	M	I	R	E
G	O	O	G	O	O		P	R	Y		E	S	S	
O	F	T	W	O		P	U	R	I	S	T			
	F	E	E	L	L	I	K	E	A	F	O	O	L	
			N	I	E	C	E	S		E	R	V	I	N
M	I	T		N	I	K		G	E	N	E	V	A	
I	N	R	A	G	S		I	D	O	L		R	E	V
A	C	E	T	O		K	N	O	B		A	S	W	E
S	H	A	R	K		A	P	R	I	L	F	E	E	L
M	E	D	I	A		Y	U	M		I	T	L	L	
A	S	S	A	Y		O	T	S		T	A	L	L	

65

A	M	I	N		C	R	A	W		Z	A	P	P	A
S	A	N	E		A	N	N	A		A	D	O	R	N
F	I	R	S	T	L	A	D	Y		N	O	S	E	D
O	N	E	T	O			S	A	S	E		S	S	E
R	E	S		S	E	C	O	N	D	G	U	E	S	S
		E	D	S	E	L		S	I	R	S			
A	C	R	E		L	U	X		E	A	S	E	L	
C	O	V	E	R	S	E	V	E	R	Y	B	A	S	E
C	R	E	P	E		I	D	O		L	I	S	A	
			E	D	I	T		E	L	L	E	N		
T	H	I	R	D	D	E	G	R	E	E		T	S	K
O	A	R		W	I	N	O		D	I	J	O	N	
G	R	E	T	A		H	O	M	E	A	L	O	N	E
A	S	N	E	R		U	N	I	T		S	A	I	L
S	H	E	L	F		T	Y	R	A		A	N	A	T

66

G	A	B	E		A	D	D	U	P		Z	O	L	A
O	W	E	S		I	R	A	T	E		O	M	I	T
B	E	D	T	I	M	E	F	O	R	B	O	N	Z	O
I	D	E	A	S		S	T	P		E	L	I	A	N
			T	H	U	S		I	M	H	O			
A	R	N	E		P	A	J	A	M	A	G	A	M	E
S	A	O		S	A	G	A		E	V	I	G	A	N
C	I	V	I	C		E	B	B		E	C	O	L	I
A	M	E	L	I	E		B	I	R	D		R	E	A
P	I	L	L	O	W	T	A	L	K		M	A	S	C
			T	R	E	Y		L	O	C	O			
T	O	E	R	R		C	A	Y		I	R	I	S	H
I	D	R	E	A	M	O	F	J	E	A	N	N	I	E
E	D	N	A		R	O	T	O	S		I	F	F	Y
A	S	S	T		I	N	S	E	T		N	O	T	S

67

```
F I B   A T T N     E M P L O Y
I D I   T A R O     S A L I N E
N E Z   I R I S     P L A N E T
D A K O T A F A N N I N G      
S L I M     L I I     C U K E  
  S T E P H E N H A W K I N G  
    G E E   T I V O     S E A  
P A L A T A L     L I M I T E D
E V A     E R I C     E E L    
R O B E R T B R O W N I N G    
K N O X     B A R     A C U E  
    H E N R Y F I E L D I N G  
S T E R E O   T O M E     S S R
I A M T O O   E L M O     L I E
D O E S N T   D E A N     A T T
```

68

```
L E N[GT]H     P S A     S P A
B E A[RH]U G   D E P P   T A B
S O S[UE]M E   O P E R   A N Y
   [MA]S H   U S E  [OG]R E S
T R A[PP]  R A B I D  [CU]R L S
E A S[YA]  I L L    O B[EY]
A S T[OR]  G O E S   O[AS]I S
S T I[LT]S   U F O  S[NA]T C H
  A N[DM]Y   D E N S  SN[ARE]
  [ME]M O   A N T   ED[GAR]
K A R[EN]  S A T Y R  LD[OPA]
A G E[NT]  C P U   OR[EO]
P A M   F A R R   H O[VL]A N E
U Z I   B R I E   S T[EL]L A R
T E X   I S L       I[NS]E T S
```

69

```
M A A M   S U R F S     I C E S
A T N O   C R E A K     R O T E
S H A D   H I N D I     K A H N
S W E E T W A T E R T E X A S  
I A M   A A H     M E D I N A  
F R I S K S   T R I M   N O T  
S T A L E   M O O S   O G L E  
    U N I O N O H I O          
T R A M   S T E M   T H A W S  
H E R   C L O D   L A S S I E  
R U S S I A     A I L   P E A  
O N E H A N D E D T Y P I N G  
N I N E   D A R E R   A R E A  
E T A L   E L O P E   P E R T  
S E L F   R E S T S   A R S E  
```

70

```
O B S   A F I R S T     T W I G
R A T   S L O O P S   H O N E
C R A C K U N D E R(F O R C E)
A C T A   E S S A  (A R E A)
S A U R O N     K O S        
  R E D U C E(D I S T A N C E)
    T Y R A N T    (T I M E)
H A Z E S   E R G   C E C I L
E G A D   I C E T E A        
P O P U L A T I O N(M A S S)
    O N O  (V O L U M E)
  T H U D   R A N I   O L E S
P H Y S I C S F O R M U L A S
C O M E   D E T R O P   E R E
P U N S   S T A I N S   N Y X
```

71

```
S E I S   A B J E C T   A R E
C Y S T   P R A G U E   T A R
A R L O   R I N G E D   S I N
R E A L M O N E Y   I T E M S
    E E N Y   K U W A I T
C H I N A   U M A M I      
Z O O M L E N S E S   S T N S
A L T O   L O O S E   T O U T
R E A M   I N N A M E O N L Y
    E S T E E   X F I L E
S C O N C E   P E A L      
Q U I T E   K I L L M E N O W
U R N   N E W D A D   M A C H
A S K   E L A I N E   O S H A
D E S   S I N G E R   N A S T
```

72

```
D O G G Y B A G   P A W S A T
E R A S A B L E   A X I O M S
F I S H H O O K   L E S S E E
L O L A   Y U K S   S H O R T
A L A R M   O O H   B R I S
T E M P E S T   D I V O R C E
E S P   S O I L   T O N Y A S
    H O R S E S H O E        
S H R U N K   D I E D   M A A
M A I L S I N   P R O F E S S
U S D A   N O R   O I N K S
S H A H S   T O L D   R O S A
H O B O E S   T I R E I R O N
E U L O G Y   C L E A N C U T
S T E P O N   S T A R G A T E
```

73

```
C O S T A ■ H E X A D ■ N S A
O C T E T ■ A M I C I ■ O E R
N E A L E ■ V E N D S ■ D I S
J A R L S B E R G C H E E S E
O N T ■ T A T ■ ■ ■ D A M N
B I O S ■ G O L F C O U R S E
S A F E R ■ A R O D ■ ■ ■ ■
■ F L I M S Y A L I B I ■ ■
■ ■ E M I L ■ ■ N O N P C
W I F F L E B A L L ■ B A I L
E P E E ■ ■ O A S ■ S L O
T H I N G S W I T H H O L E S
B O G ■ A L I A S ■ I N U S E
A N N ■ B O N G O ■ L E M U R
R E S ■ S P O O F ■ L A P P S
```

74

```
W I P E ■ D M V ■ ■ U S E D
A D A M ■ C R U E T ■ N E A R
R O T C ■ R A N T O ■ P I T Y
■ ■ S E A O F C O R T E Z ■
■ E Y E O F T H E T I G E R
C F C ■ R T S ■ D E B ■ D E A
E F L A T S ■ ■ S E R U M S
L E I C A ■ M U D ■ R E P O S
E T N A ■ B A N J O ■ H O T E
B E E I N O N E S B O N N E T
■ ■ B A S ■ ■ S E Q ■ ■
■ S E E Y O U I N C O U R T
M A W R ■ M C G E E ■ I O U S
I G O R ■ E L G I N ■ S A N E
C A K Y ■ D A Y N E ■ T R E X
```

75

```
S T A N D ■ A N A T ■ O W N S
S I N E W ■ D E C O ■ W A A C
W A I T A N D S E E ■ I S T O
■ ■ ■ R E O ■ ■ ■ U N H A T
G O O F F O N A T A N G E N T
M A R A ■ S U R F S ■ S T Y
C H A C H A ■ S U R A L ■ ■
S U L T A N A T E O F O M A N
■ ■ A R D O R ■ S E N O R A
G I A ■ L O U I S ■ G E A R
I N S T A N T A N E O U S L Y
J A P A N ■ ■ A N N ■ ■
O T I S ■ U N A T T E S T E D
E I R E ■ Z I N C ■ I C A R E
S E E D ■ I T C H ■ L I N E S
```

76

```
(1) T H E D O G S O F F ■ B A (5)
I H A V E N O I D E A ■ A P B
O R I O L E S N E S T ■ T H O
P O L ■ A T S E A ■ C R O I X
E W E S ■ W I S ■ C A A N S
■ ■ P R O P ■ H T T P ■ ■
A L G A E ■ O R R ■ S E T A
D O N T (3) U S W E L L (4) Y O U
S O U L ■ R O E ■ T I E R S
■ ■ E M I T ■ D O D O ■ ■
A P S O S ■ H E T ■ N C A R
C H I E N ■ C A P E S ■ A M O
A O L ■ G U A D A L C A N A L
T R E ■ S T P A U L I G I R L
(2) A S ■ T O O C L O S E T O (6)
```

(1) CALL (2) CALL (3) CALL (4) CALL (5) CALL (6) CALL

77

```
B A B E ■ E M I T S ■ I T C H
I C E S ■ N A S A L ■ S O L O
T H E S U L T A N O F S W A T
S E R E N I T Y ■ W O U N D S
■ ■ ■ S I S ■ ■ P A R E ■ ■
H A T ■ S T A T U T E ■ H S T
O A H U ■ E T O N ■ G R A T E
P R E S I D E N T H O O V E R
E G R E T ■ A G E E ■ D R I P
S H E ■ A R M A D A S ■ E N S
■ ■ A L E S ■ ■ R U B ■ ■
H O R R I D ■ M A K E U P T O
I H A D A B E T T E R Y E A R
T I T O ■ A R G O N ■ E R I C
S O A R ■ T E E M S ■ R U T H
```

78

```
T T A ■ D R O L ■ D E M Y H R
Y H T ■ N A M O ■ E L I O T E
R E T R A C E N A C I R R U H
O S H O ■ E R D N A ■ L O C
■ A E L ■ S T O T ■ S T I M O
E U G E S ■ A N I R T A K ■
K R Y P T O ■ ■ A I G ■ ■
G I M L E T ■ EYE ■ O F N E W T
■ ■ A P O ■ S E I N E S
■ T Y P H O O N ■ B R I D E
R E U S E ■ I P U T ■ E L Y
A N T ■ G L E N S ■ E W E S
B R O O K L Y N C Y C L O N E
B O R N E O ■ E I R E ■ H O V
I N S E A M ■ R O T S ■ C H E
```

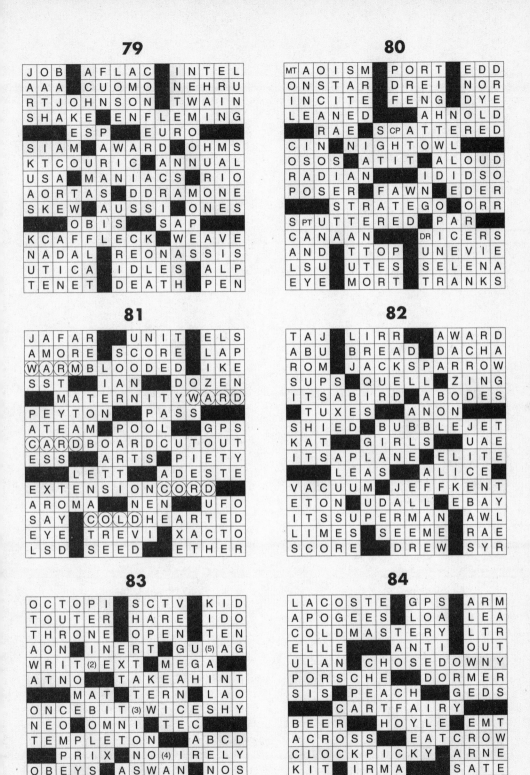

79 **80**

81 **82**

83 **84**

(1) TENT (2) TENT (3) TENT (4) TENT (5) TENT

85

```
E B B T I D E S   A S S A I L
T R O O P E R S   I M E L D A
H O T W A T E R   R E C O O K
A N T   D E B   A S A R U L E
N C O S   R U P T U R E
S O M M E   S T E P   T B S P
    L O A D   S U P S   U K E
A N A G R A M   P L U G S I N
D E N   N T S B   Y E A S
S O D A   E D I T   S L E E T
    T A B O O E D   E R N O
L I T T E R S   J A I   V A T
I M H E R E   H A R D T I M E
N A R N I A   I N T E R C O M
E X U D E D   D O S S I E R S
```

86

```
B A L L   D O Z E N   H A L F
E P E E   I R A T E   I D E A
S I A M E S E C A T   G M A C
T E N O N   S H I P S H A P E
    I N T O   L A T E N T
W O N   E D Y S   Y E R
E G G   R I O T S   S E G E R
S L O B   C L O C K   D O D I
T E N O R   K O A L A   T A N
    L U V   D R U M   O M G
    S C O T I A   M I L S
D E A T H S T A R   G A L O P
A G R I   I A M A C A M E R A
Y U L E   T R A C Y   P E E R
S E A S   S I D E D   S P O T
```

87

```
S H A F T   B L I P   P R E T
A I D A N   O O N A   L A L A
P R I N T S O F T H I E V E S
S E N T   P I T H   N A I V E
    A G I N   E M U S
  L O S I N G P A T I E N T S
S E L I G   L I N T   O B E
U C L A   Y O U R S   T W I X
M A I   L A N G   H A I R Y
P R E S E N T S O F M I N D
    W I K I   I D O L
A T T I C   P O L I   G I G I
J U M P A T T H E C H A N T S
A T E E   V O I R   S T O O L
R U N S   G E O S   T E N S E
```

88

```
H U L A   H O F F   S L O T H
O H O S   O R A L   C A N W E
S U C K S BB Y O U   A F T E R
P H O E N I X   BB A L O V E R
    D O T   S E D E R
T A X I   H E R E   G A E A
O P E N A R E A   S E E M S BB
M A N BB O R N O T BB   I T O
B R I D E BB   C H E S S S E T
S T A R   E W E S   C H E T
    Y P R E S   A P R
BB H O N E S T   B R I E F E D
G O M E R   B O R N BB W I L D
U M A S S   A R I A   I S S A
N O R S E   R I T Z   T H E Y
```

89

```
R A D S   C A P E D   P S S T
E S A U   I V A N I   E T T A
D O A N D R O I D S D R E A M
O F E L E C T R I C S H E E P
    A B L E S T   C A L L A
C O M M I E   A S P
E R U P T   B U M P   S P I N
R A T   S A M P L E D   O D E
F L E A   D I C K   A D U L T
    R I D   T N O T E S
A L A R M   P I G O U T
W E C A N R E M E M B E R I T
F O R Y O U W H O L E S A L E
U N I E   H E I D I   O R Y X
L A D D   R E P E N   N E A T
```

90

```
S A D   P A E A N   B A C K
A B E   E R A T O   R E P R O
L O S   D U S T S W E E P E R
I R K   A M Y   T I M   O D E
V I T A L   V A R I A T I O N
A G O G   L I R A   I A N
T I P S   E R E   N U T S
E N C  SUN MON TUE WED THU FRI SAT  M I D
  E A Z Y   O C D   M E D E
    L E A   E N Y A   O N E A
S W E E T E N E D   O C T A D
K I N   S R A   I M F   B I B
U N D R E A M E D O F   O S O
L E A N N   E L E V E   O L D
L Y R A   L O S E R   K E Y
```

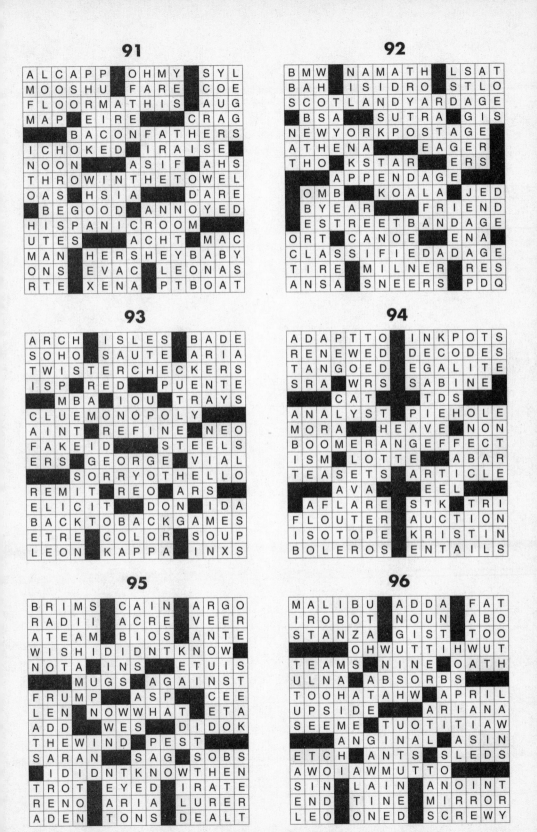

91

```
A L C A P P   O H M Y   S Y L
M O O S H U   F A R E   C O E
F L O O R M A T H I S   A U G
M A P   E I R E     C R A G
    B A C O N F A T H E R S
I C H O K E D   I R A I S E
N O O N     A S I F   A H S
T H R O W I N T H E T O W E L
O A S   H S I A     D A R E
  B E G O O D   A N N O Y E D
H I S P A N I C R O O M
U T E S     A C H T   M A C
M A N   H E R S H E Y B A B Y
O N S   E V A C   L E O N A S
R T E   X E N A   P T B O A T
```

92

```
B M W   N A M A T H   L S A T
B A H   I S I D R O   S T L O
S C O T L A N D Y A R D A G E
  B S A   S U T R A   G I S
N E W Y O R K P O S T A G E
A T H E N A     E A G E R
T H O   K S T A R   E R S
  A P P E N D A G E
O M B   K O A L A   J E D
B Y E A R     F R I E N D
E S T R E E T B A N D A G E
O R T   C A N O E   E N A
C L A S S I F I E D A D A G E
T I R E   M I L N E R   R E S
A N S A   S N E E R S   P D Q
```

93

```
A R C H   I S L E S   B A D E
S O H O   S A U T E   A R I A
T W I S T E R C H E C K E R S
I S P   R E D   P U E N T E
  M B A   I O U   T R A Y S
C L U E M O N O P O L Y
A I N T   R E F I N E   N E O
F A K E I D   S T E E L S
E R S   G E O R G E   V I A L
  S O R R Y O T H E L L O
R E M I T   R E O   A R S
E L I C I T   D O N   I D A
B A C K T O B A C K G A M E S
E T R E   C O L O R   S O U P
L E O N   K A P P A   I N X S
```

94

```
A D A P T T O   I N K P O T S
R E N E W E D   D E C O D E S
T A N G O E D   E G A L I T E
S R A   W R S   S A B I N E
    C A T   T D S
A N A L Y S T   P I E H O L E
M O R A   H E A V E   N O N
B O O M E R A N G E F F E C T
I S M   L O T T E   A B A R
T E A S E T S   A R T I C L E
    A V A   E E L
  A F L A R E   S T K   T R I
F L O U T E R   A U C T I O N
I S O T O P E   K R I S T I N
B O L E R O S   E N T A I L S
```

95

```
B R I M S   C A I N   A R G O
R A D I I   A C R E   V E E R
A T E A M   B I O S   A N T E
W I S H I D I D N T K N O W
N O T A   I N S   E T U I S
  M U G S   A G A I N S T
F R U M P   A S P   C E E
L E N   N O W W H A T   E T A
A D D   W E S   D I D O K
T H E W I N D   P E S T
S A R A N   S A G   S O B S
  I D I D N T K N O W T H E N
T R O T   E Y E D   I R A T E
R E N O   A R I A   L U R E R
A D E N   T O N S   D E A L T
```

96

```
M A L I B U   A D D A   F A T
I R O B O T   N O U N   A B O
S T A N Z A   G I S T   T O O
    O H W U T T I H W U T
T E A M S   N I N E   O A T H
U L N A   A B S O R B S
T O O H A T A H W   A P R I L
U P S I D E   A R I A N A
S E E M E   T U O T I T I A W
  A N G I N A L   A S I N
E T C H   A N T S   S L E D S
A W O I A W M U T T O
S I N   L A I N   A N O I N T
E N D   T I N E   M I R R O R
L E O   O N E D   S C R E W Y
```

97

```
L I A R   A M A N A   S T A N
A C R E   L O R E S   T O T E
P E O P L E W I T H T Y P E O
E M U   O R E   Y E L P
L A S T W O R D S   E E R I E
S N E E R   S E E D   D I B S
    A I D   B A R S   Z I P
  P E R S O N A L I T I E S
H E Y   E V E S   P U G
A R E A   E X E S   T O G A S
D U C T S   T R E E T R U N K
    A C E S   A V E   R C A
D O N O T W R I T E R I G H T
E N D S   A O L E R   A L O E
F O Y T   M O L D Y   N E R D
```

98

```
S C O T   S L A W   S L O E
P I C A   W A N E   L O T T
A T H I S I S N T R I G H T
Y E S L E T S   S E E Y O U
      F C C   B U D S
B N E I T H E R I S T H I S
L A W N S   P A T   U T E
O S E   S E W   E I G E R
C T R Y T H E N E X T O N E
      E R O S   S T S
E M I L I O   S T R A P I N
D A L L O F T H E A B O V E
I S S O   L I A R   O L E S
T H A W   Y E W S   Y O S T
```

99

```
L I M B   A T O D D S   O S S
O N E A   C O H E R E   D E W
B A L C O N Y S E A T   I L E
  S T O V E   P B S   O L D
A L O N E   T I L   J U T E
H U R   R A I N Y S E A S O N
A M M O   R E V   H A P
  P E N N Y S E R E N A D E
    E R A   R U R   N A V E
C O M P A N Y S E A L   T A X
S C A M   E E R   I N A P T
H U D   A B A   A D O B E
A L E   M A R K E T S H A R E
R A D   E L N I N O   I S O N
P R O   R E S T O N   T E N T
```

100

```
D O T S   C A T S   B A M B I
O R A N   O R E O   A H E A D
R A M A   N E R F   L O N G S
S C I F I F A N T A S Y
A L L U D E S   M I A M I A N
Y E S S I R   S U M   A S H E
    D E E P S   A T B A T
  H I F I E Q U I P M E N T
P A W A T   U N C L E
E R I C   O A K   A B U T O N
G E N E R A L   B Y A N O S E
  W I F I H O T S P O T S
L A K E S   Z U N I   I B E T
B R I S K   E L E M   L A N E
J E T T Y   R A R E   E D D A
```

101

```
N A P A   A P S E S   O F F
I C E S   B O O N S   A P I E
C H E S T S O F D R A W E R S
E E L   H O R A S   F A C E T
    T A R   A O L
L I G H T B U L B J O K E
I D L E S   R U R A L   F R O
S E E M   S I L E X   B R A M
T E A   S E A L S   S I E G E
  M A T C H S T I C K M E N
  G A T   G R E
S C A N T   D R A N O   U S A
T H R E E P R E S I D E N T S
E A T S   S A D A T   R I O T
M R S   S T O N E   E X P O
```

102

```
U R A L      S A N E   S C U M
G E N[EVA]   I T H O T  O H N O
A M I R      S I E R R A N[EVA]D A
N O M   F L E A   E M I L E
D U A N E E D D Y   P A I R S
A N T O N Y   O W S   E G O
  T E E D   M I K E   T R O Y
    L I T T L E E V A
B I B S   W I L L   A S I F
A M O   D A D   C L E R I C
S P U M E   A T T H E R E A R
  A L I C E   R O O T  S N[EVA]
E L[EVA]T O R C A R S   P I C S
P E R T   A R I S E   A G E S
A D D S   S O L O   K N E E
```

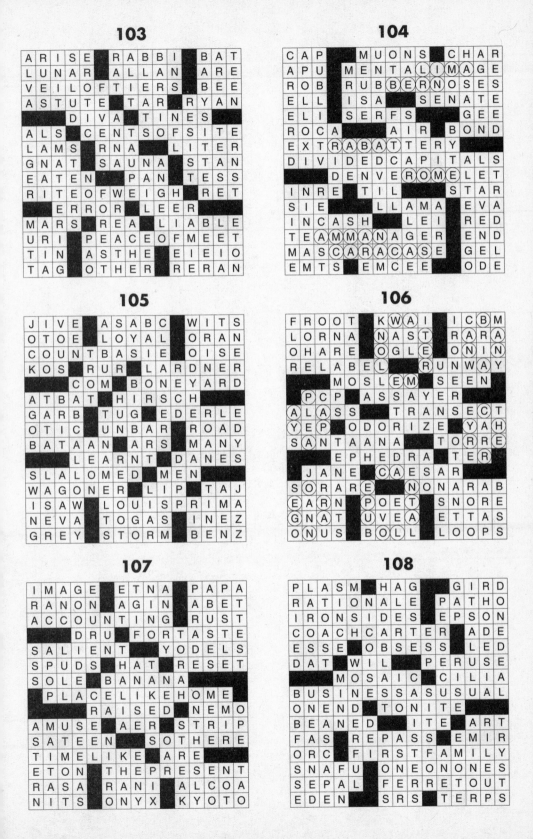

103

```
A R I S E ■ R A B B I ■ B A T
L U N A R ■ A L L A N ■ A R E
V E I L O F T I E R S ■ B E E
A S T U T E ■ T A R ■ R Y A N
■ ■ D I V A ■ T I N E S ■ ■
A L S ■ C E N T S O F S I T E
L A M S ■ R N A ■ ■ L I T E R
G N A T ■ S A U N A ■ S T A N
E A T E N ■ P A N ■ T E S S ■
R I T E O F W E I G H ■ R E T
■ E R R O R ■ L E E R ■ ■
M A R S ■ R E A ■ L I A B L E
U R I ■ P E A C E O F M E E T
T I N ■ A S T H E ■ E I E I O
T A G ■ O T H E R ■ R E R A N
```

104

```
C A P ■ M U O N S ■ C H A R
A P U ■ M E N T A L I M A G E
R O B ■ R U B B E R N O S E S
E L L ■ I S A ■ S E N A T E
E L I ■ S E R F S ■ G E E
R O C A ■ A I R ■ B O N D
E X T R A B A T T E R Y ■
D I V I D E D C A P I T A L S
■ D E N V E R O M E L E T
I N R E ■ T I L ■ S T A R
S I E ■ L L A M A ■ E V A
I N C A S H ■ L E I ■ R E D
T E A M M A N A G E R ■ E N D
M A S C A R A C A S E ■ G E L
E M T S ■ E M C E E ■ O D E
```

105

```
J I V E ■ A S A B C ■ W I T S
O T O E ■ L O Y A L ■ O R A N
C O U N T B A S I E ■ O I S E
K O S ■ R U R ■ L A R D N E R
■ ■ C O M ■ B O N E Y A R D
A T B A T ■ H I R S C H ■ ■
G A R B ■ T U G ■ E D E R L E
O T I C ■ U N B A R ■ R O A D
B A T A A N ■ A R S ■ M A N Y
■ ■ L E A R N T ■ D A N E S
S L A L O M E D ■ M E N ■ ■
W A G O N E R ■ L I P ■ T A J
I S A W ■ L O U I S P R I M A
N E V A ■ T O G A S ■ I N E Z
G R E Y ■ S T O R M ■ B E N Z
```

106

```
F R O O T ■ K W A I ■ I C B M
L O R N A ■ N A S T ■ R A R A
O H A R E ■ O G L E ■ O N I N
R E L A B E L ■ R U N W A Y
■ M O S L E M ■ S E E N ■
P C P ■ A S S A Y E R ■ ■
A L A S S ■ T R A N S E C T
Y E P ■ O D O R I Z E ■ Y A H
S A N T A A N A ■ T O R R E
■ E P H E D R A ■ T E R ■
■ J A N E ■ C A E S A R ■
S O R A R E ■ N O N A R A B
E A R N ■ P O E T ■ S N O R E
G N A T ■ U V E A ■ E T T A S
O N U S ■ B O L L ■ L O O P S
```

107

```
I M A G E ■ E T N A ■ P A P A
R A N O N ■ A G I N ■ A B E T
A C C O U N T I N G ■ R U S T
■ ■ D R U ■ F O R T A S T E
S A L I E N T ■ Y O D E L S
S P U D S ■ H A T ■ R E S E T
S O L E ■ B A N A N A ■ ■
■ P L A C E L I K E H O M E
■ ■ R A I S E D ■ N E M O
A M U S E ■ A E R ■ S T R I P
S A T E E N ■ S O T H E R E
T I M E L I K E ■ A R E ■
E T O N ■ T H E P R E S E N T
R A S A ■ R A N I ■ A L C O A
N I T S ■ O N Y X ■ K Y O T O
```

108

```
P L A S M ■ H A G ■ G I R D
R A T I O N A L E ■ P A T H O
I R O N S I D E S ■ E P S O N
C O A C H C A R T E R ■ A D E
E S S E ■ O B S E S S ■ L E D
D A T ■ W I L ■ P E R U S E
■ M O S A I C ■ C I L I A
B U S I N E S S A S U S U A L
O N E N D ■ T O N I T E ■ ■
B E A N E D ■ I T E ■ A R T
F A S ■ R E P A S S ■ E M I R
O R C ■ F I R S T F A M I L Y
S N A F U ■ O N E O N O N E S
S E P A L ■ F E R R E T O U T
E D E N ■ S R S ■ T E R P S
```

109

```
J E S T ■ A T I T ■ D R A B S
U N T O ■ B A C H ■ Y O W I E
D R A W P O K E R ■ E T H A N
G O N N A ■ E D E N ■ I S T ■
E N D ■ C B S ■ S Y B I L ■
■ ■ S K E T C H C O M E D Y
■ B O O S T E R ■ O P A R T
S O U L ■ S N I T S ■ A G E D
I O T A S ■ ■ M I L K C O W
T R A C E E L E M E N T ■ ■
■ ■ N E A T O ■ E W E ■ S A G
S A D ■ A N E W ■ L A T H E
A V O W S ■ D R A F T B E E R
R O U E N ■ O G R E ■ B E A M
I N T E L ■ N O P E ■ E D D Y
```

110

```
A S E C ■ A G F A ■ O N I C E
M E S A ■ F L E X ■ N Y L O N
A R A L ■ R E A L ■ E M E N D
J A I L S E N T E(N)C E ■ ■
■ ■ ■ E I S ■ ■ L E T S B E
F O U R T H D I(M)E N S I O N
E R N I E ■ E B E R T ■ S R S
L A R D ■ F T E N S ■ L I E U
I T I ■ A R E A S ■ V I S O R
P O P U L A R M A(G)A Z I N E
E R E S T U ■ ■ A L P ■ ■
■ ■ T E S T E R S(E)S H O U T
A S F O R ■ E X I T ■ A N T I
V A L U E ■ R A G A ■ I M I N
E C A R D ■ I M A X ■ R E L Y
```

111

```
K C A R ■ A T S E A ■ C A D S
E U R O ■ T R E V I ■ A B E L
G R I M R E A P E R ■ J O E Y
■ ■ P E S C I ■ M O I R E
C C S ■ S T E A M R O L L E R
H E I S T S ■ A O N E ■ ■
A L S O ■ S T Y L E ■ B S S
M I S T E R I N B E T W E E N
P A Y ■ M A T T E ■ A N N O
■ ■ S I Z E ■ O D D J O B
F I R M R E S O L V E ■ I R S
A R I E S ■ ■ G E E S E ■ ■
L A V A ■ W O R M R I D D E N
S T A R ■ E L E M I ■ G U R U
E E L S ■ B E S E T ■ E D E N
```

112

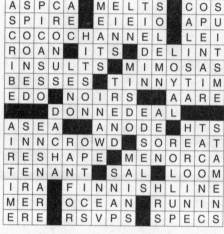

```
A S P C A ■ M E L T S ■ C O S
S P I R E ■ E I E I O ■ A P U
C O C O C H A N N E L ■ L E I
R O A N ■ I T S ■ D E L I N T
I N S U L T S ■ M I M O S A S
B E S S E S ■ T I N N Y T I M
E D O ■ N O I R S ■ A A R E
■ ■ D O N N E D E A L ■ ■
A S E A ■ A N O D E ■ H T S
I N N C R O W D ■ S O R E A T
R E S H A P E ■ M E N O R C A
T E N A N T ■ S A L ■ L O O M
I R A ■ F I N N I S H L I N E
M E R ■ O C E A N ■ R U N I N
E R E ■ R S V P S ■ S P E C S
```

113

```
T A M P A ■ S A P S ■ C H A T
E M A I L ■ L I E N ■ O I L Y
N O N C E ■ I M D O I N G O K
T R E K ■ S P E D ■ T E H E E
H E S A R E B E L ■ E S P ■
■ ■ P O N Y ■ I S M ■ O S S
S C R A P S ■ G N U ■ B I L E
Y O U R E A B I G B O Y N O W
S E N T ■ T O N ■ S K A T E S
T N T ■ S E X ■ S I L L ■
■ ■ O O P ■ S H E S A L A D Y
S A S H A ■ C A T T ■ O B I E
T H E Y R E O F F ■ E D I N A
I S E E ■ E R T E ■ A D D E R
R O D S ■ L E S E ■ U S E R S
```

114

```
[MON]G E R ■ G H A N A ■ S L O[WED]
I O N E ■ R E[FRI]E D ■ W O O D
C O N S ■ A R C E D ■ A C N E
A N A C O N D A ■ I N R O A D
■ ■ I N D ■ I T E M ■ ■
S H A N T ■ U N I V E R S E
W A N D A ■ E N D O ■ D E A L
A B E ■ P U L[SAT]I N G ■ F B I
B I A S ■ P L E A ■ O P E R A
S T R E S S E D ■ M A R E S
■ ■ D O T S ■ ■ E E G ■ ■
D E N A D A ■ A N D R O P O V
A L O T ■ G A R Y S ■ D I D I
T A M E ■ E N[THU]S E ■ A C E R
[SUN]N E D ■ S O R E L ■ S T A[TUE]
```

115

```
U N R I P ■ A P E D ■ H I R E
S A E N S ■ R U R A L A R E A
S K A T I N G M A N E U V E R
R E S ■ O O P S ■ A L I V E ■
■ D O W N O N ■ E V E N E D ■
A M N I O N ■ S T E E R ■ ■ ■
G A E L S ■ C O I L ■ C U E ■
R J R E Y N O L D S B R A N D
O A S ■ E N V Y ■ L A N C E ■
■ A T O N E ■ W A N T O N ■ ■
W O O D E N ■ P I S T O L ■ ■
A S P E N ■ E A R L ■ N O S ■
S H I P O F T H E D E S E R T
N E U T R I N O S ■ M O S E Y
T A M S ■ B A T S ■ S W E D E
```

116

```
W A R S ■ D E W A R S ■ E R E
A B E T ■ A D A G E S ■ X E S
W A S A S R E D A S A B E E T
A S T R A ■ R E V E ■ E R S E
■ ■ E V E ■ D E T E S T E R ■
A D D R E S S ■ ■ S A E ■ ■ ■
T A E ■ ■ S E R F ■ S T E T S
T W A S T E W A R D E S S E S
A G R E E ■ S E E R ■ Q T R ■
■ ■ D A S ■ ■ D E B A S E S ■
G A Z E T T E S ■ W E B ■ ■ ■
A V E R ■ A G E E ■ S C R E W
S E T S A T A R G E T D A T E
E R A ■ S E D G E S ■ E V A S
S T S ■ A S S E R T ■ F E S T
```

117

```
M A R A T ■ C A R O M ■ A T M
A T A R I ■ A R O A R ■ R O I
C O M I C A C T O R S ■ M O M
R O I L ■ L A O S ■ C C C L I
O T S ■ S M O O T ■ R A H ■ ■
■ ■ T O A ■ ■ C A M A R O ■ ■
A S S O C ■ I M H O T ■ I O S
A C H R I S T M A S C A R O L
H O I ■ A T O M S ■ H A S T O
S T R O L L ■ ■ A I R ■ ■ ■
■ T L C ■ S H A L T ■ C A L
T O T A L ■ M A S T ■ C A L I
A R A ■ A L A S T A I R S I M
T A I ■ S O L T I ■ M A C A O
A L L ■ S O L A R ■ A M A S S
```

118

```
S H A V E ■ S H I L O ■ L E S
E A R E D ■ P O S E R ■ I T O
W H E N Y O U H I T A ■ S H Y
N A N O ■ W R O N G N O T E ■
U H A U L S ■ O G L E R S ■ ■
P A S S E ■ S N O ■ S E N N A
■ ■ ■ S P H I N X ■ A T E N
I T I S T H E N E X T N O T E
R I C A ■ D E J A V U ■ ■ ■
A M A N A ■ P A M ■ B E A D S
S O N A T A ■ L A N D U P ■
■ T H A T M A K E S ■ T O R A
S H E ■ I T G O O D O R B A D
O Y L ■ C O R O N ■ B E E N E
T S P ■ S O A K S ■ J E S T S
```

119

```
C O A L ■ O P A L ■ C B E R
O R G Y ■ C A R L O ■ R O T E
S C A M P E R O F F ■ E H U D
T A R P O N ■ T I A M A R I A
■ H O T F O O T I T ■ ■ ■
C E L ■ P A R ■ T U N E R
A V I S ■ V E E R ■ C R O N E
T A K E T O O N E S H E E L S
E D E M A ■ N E S T ■ S L A T
R E D I G ■ O A S ■ S I S
■ ■ C U T A N D R U N ■ ■
K E R O S E N E ■ C R E C H E
O V A L ■ H I T T H E R O A D
L E G O ■ E L W A Y ■ V O T E
A R U N ■ E S T E ■ Y S E R
```

120

```
T H O R A ■ H I C ■ E L I E
L A T E N ■ O P I E ■ M I N D
C H I C K E N O R T H E E G G
■ A S I A N ■ C H U T N E Y
■ ■ P R O S E ■ A N I ■ ■
M A K E A S T R O N G C A S E
O W N S ■ R O T O R ■ L A P
R A E ■ G H O S T L Y ■ L B S
P R E ■ T A L I A ■ S I L O
H E L D I N L O W E S T E E M
■ ■ O L D ■ N A D E R ■ ■
S A D N E S S ■ N E I L S
T U R N S O U T H A P P I L Y
A R E A ■ N E R O ■ E E R I E
Y A W S ■ D I R ■ D R A M A
```

121

```
S H E D   U P D A T E   S S T
H E R O   L E O N I D   M A R
R A N T   C D R O M D R I V E
I D E   T E R I     Y A L I E
V W S C I R O C C O   W E N T
E A T O N     E V A   A G O
L Y O N   A V A L O N   T S P
      J K R O W L I N G
T I S   E U C L I D   A I D S
O N O   N B A     D I G I N
O F F S   A B P O S I T I V E
M A T E S   A G C Y   V E E
U V E X P O S U R E   H E R R
C O N   A R I S E N   M U S E
H R S   M E R E S T   S P E D
```

122

```
T U D O R   R F D S   M A S S
A S I D E   E R I E   O P A L
B E S O M   L A N A   B E T A
    P R O D I G A L S I M O N
V A L   D U E     A L E U T
I M A G E O F C O N S E N T
L O C A L   O N U S
E K E S   T E N E T   B A L L
      P A R A   A U D I O
  S E D I M E N T A R Y J O B
A P R E S     W I T   U N O
G R I M A C E P E R I O D
R I C O   I M I N   S A G A S
E G A D   A I N T   T H E T A
E S S E   O R G Y   S U S A N
```

123

```
A T M   P R O M O S   T A C T
B O A   C O G E N T   A V O W
C A R S T A R T E R   P E L E
    E S M E   R A E   R O E
P O E T   M U D G U A R D
R I P S   S W A N S O N G
I N C A   H O D   D E A D
A G O G   H E D D A   E M M Y
M O T O   E O N   R A I L
  C A S H E S I N   O R C A
S P E L L O U T   A K I N
A R N   A N C   A S S T
L E T S   C L A M P S H A P E
A G E E   H I R E O N   D E N
D O R A   O D I S T S   D A D
```

124

```
I R R S   A I M S   B A C K
N E A T O   S O U P   O R L E
B U Z Z O F F   P U T T I N G G R E E N
U N L A S H   S K I L I F T
D E E   H A J I   E L E V
    C O M M O N N A M E   E P A
  R U E R   S O N E   I S A A C
C O N C E P T   E N S N A R E
A B B I E   E L E M   C A T S
S Y N   U P P E R R I G H T
  S A M E   S A R I   A C A
F O U L A R D   O S A G E S
A D D R E S S B O O K S   M C C A L L S
K E E N   O N E R   S T P A T
E R D E   X E N A   S E R S
```

125

```
M A C   H O S T   S A P P Y
I R O C   E D A M   E F I L E
L E A H   L O R E   N I X O N
L A S E R P R I N T E R
E S T E E M S   O C E L O T
    T I E   I O W A   O R O
A F L A C   A N T E   O T S
R U S H H O U R T R A F F I C
A G A   I D E O   P L A Z A
B U T   S L I D   S E A
S E S A M E   G O A T E E D
    H A R D R O C K B A N D
J I V E R   E E O C   E T T A
A T E A T   N O S E   D O R Y
M O L D S   Y S E R   N E S
```

126

```
G O A T   B A R D S   P L O P
U N L V   E X E R T   O A H U
A C E D   L E M U R   T I N G
M E X I C A L I M E X I C O
    N O I     A M O
  K A N O R A D O K A N S A S
E A T E N   W I N E S   L E O
S T A R   D A R E D   P Y R O
T I L   C O R G I   S E E I N
D E L M A R D E L A W A R E
    A R M     L A C
  T E X A R K A N A T E X A S
O R Z O   O A T E R   N O V A
P E R U   O N E A M   I R O N
T E A T   M E E T S   K O N G
```

127

```
A L I T   S A V E   D A F F Y
D U M B   E D I T   O N A I R
A L S O   R A S H   G A N G S
G L E N N F R E Y S E G G S
E S T E E       L E A R
      S W A T S   C R A N K S
S P A   E L A T E   M A N E
P E T E R B O Y L E S S T E W
U P O N   S L A T E   O W N
D E P O S E   E N A C T
      R E N O   T U L S A
  S A M C O O K E S S T E A K
C O L O R   H I V E   T O U R
A R G U E   E W E R   U N T O
B E A S T   D I R E   T E E N
```

128

```
S P U D S   H O P E   P C B S
A L L A T   I L E R   R A R E
L O T T A   G I N N I E M A E
S T R E T C H O N E S N E C K
A Z A L E A S       O U R
      I N S   B A L L P A R K
A D E N   S E E P E D   S H E
N O V E L I S T S T E P H E N
E R E   A N T H E M   A Y E S
W A R B R I D E   E A R
    G U S   F I N A N C E
L A R G E W A D I N G B I R D
O N E O N O N E S   L O G A N
D I E U   V O L T   E L E N A
I S N T   E X E S   D A R E S
```

129

```
R A G A   S E A U   Q T R S
A J A R   O W I N G   U R A L
H A P P Y B I R T H D A Y T O
    S I E V E   A V A S T
I L A   E S E   R A Z E
C I R C L E L E T T E R S T O
I N R E D   J E W S   O H M
N E I L   A N E S T   C R E E
G U V   E X E C   K N E L L
S P E L L O U T T H E N A M E
  A I N T   H A Y   T A T
D A R T H   R E B U S
O F Y O U R R E C I P I E N T
C R A Y   A I M A T   Z E E S
K O N A   F A I R   E L B E
```

130

```
L E V I   H A D A [COW] S [COW] L S
O X E N   A L I B I   [COW]P E A
[COW]A R D L Y L I O N   S A A B
E R N   A S A   I N N   S R I
E M O R Y   U L E E   T N N
D Y N E   A M P   R E C U S E
    C O C O A S   D U R O S
W H E R E S T H E B E E F
[COW]H I D E   [COW]R I T E S
A E N E I D   E V A   T H A W
B E T   D A D E   L A U G H
U L E   A I R   M B A   B E Y
N O D E   R I D E E M[COW]B O Y
G U A M   Y E A R N   E L L E
A T T S   [COW]S H E D   R E D S
```

131

```
E P I C   S H U E   T A B B Y
D O O R   H E R R   A C U R A
A N N E   O M N I   B E B O P
M Y S O U P I S C O L D
    L A P   I L E   A C K
  A R E W E I N V I S I B L E
C R O   R O E   O A K L E Y
R E M A P   U H F   W E A V E
A T M F E E   R A W   Z E D
W H E R E S O U R O R D E R
S A L   P A W   R E A
    W H I N E A N D D I N E
P A T I O   S I L O   D R U M
A T O L L   U R D U   Y O D A
D E N T E   P E A T   O N E G
```

132

```
R B I   C O T Y   A L E P P O
E O N   A C H E   T I N I E R
S O S   T H E S O R B O N N E
O G E E   S T O R A B L E
R I C E D   A R O S E   W E E
B E T S O N       R O O S T
    P R O S E   R O T O
T H E S E C R E T G A R D E N
B A L K   B A S A L
A T E A M   P A L L O R
R E O   A D M E N   S E I N E
  N I N E I R O N   E S T S
A D O Z E N R O S E S   B O O
P I R O G I   S I O N   O U R
T R A D E S   E R N O   A R T
```

133

```
T H E W H O ■ S N A P ■ J E T
R E N A I L ■ T O B E S U R E
A N G L E D ■ A M B R O S I A
Y I E L D S ■ S E A O T T E R
S E L A ■ A S H ■ E T H I C ■
■ ■ C O W H E R B ■ A F A R
A L T E R ■ O S H A ■ T I N O
L O E S S E R ■ I N A H E A P
A S S T ■ V T E N ■ L A D L E
S A T E ■ E U R O P O P ■ ■
■ L A V I N ■ O S H ■ P O G S
P A T E N T E D ■ O N E S E T
I M O N F I R E ■ B A N K S Y
N O R S E M A N ■ I D E A T E
E S S ■ R E S T ■ C A D R E S
```

134

```
M A T T D A M O N ■ P A S S E
S P E E D D A T E ■ I N A L L
R E L A T E S T O ■ E N I A C
P R E K ■ N C O S ■ C E N T I
■ ■ ■ R O O M ■ S E X T E D
G E S S O ■ T A B O O ■ ■ ■
I T H A C A ■ N U F F S A I D
S T A R K L Y ■ B T W E L V E
H U G I T O U T ■ C O R D O N
■ ■ ■ H E M E N ■ R E A R S
G N O M E S ■ D U C K ■ ■ ■
S A W I V ■ I T C H ■ D U P E
P I N T O ■ M A L E N U R S E
O V E T T ■ P L E A S E S I R
T E R S E ■ S K I P C L A S S
```

135

```
K I D N E Y B E A N ■ L A T E
A N Y O N E E L S E ■ E R I S
T R E N C H C O A T ■ G E N T
Z E D ■ ■ A I R F R A N C E
■ ■ L U L U ■ U L U L A T E
S H I I T E S ■ L I S T ■ ■
W A R G A M E ■ E X T E N D S
U H O H ■ ■ ■ N C A A
M A N T R A S ■ B R A D A W L
■ ■ S U V A ■ R E V E R S E
S E V E N A M ■ U B E R ■ ■
P L E C T R U M S ■ ■ G W B
L E G O ■ I R A Q I D I N A R
I V A N ■ C A Y U G A L A K E
T E N D ■ E I S E N H O W E R
```

136

```
S O T ■ H A B E R D A S H E R
W H O ■ O N C L O U D N I N E
E P A ■ R I C K Y N E L S O N
E L F M A N ■ H A N S ■ M R T
T E A R S ■ B A L E ■ K A M A
S A R I ■ W O R F ■ A N S E L
O S E ■ W A X T A B L E T ■ ■
P E T M I C E ■ M A E W E S T
■ ■ H I T O R M I S S ■ R P I
G O E T H ■ B A L K ■ M S R P
A R E A ■ O R L Y ■ T I V O S
S S W ■ G A I L ■ W O N O U T
L I E D E T E C T O R ■ I T E
O N L I N E F O R U M ■ C U R
G O L D E N S P I K E ■ E P S
```

137

```
O M A H A ■ E L M S ■ S E R F
H E L E N ■ K I C K B O X E R
C A P R I ■ G E R A L D I N E
A T H O M E ■ S I T U A T E D
L E A N E R S ■ B E E P ■ ■
C A B S ■ R E F ■ B O O S T
U T E ■ N A I L C L I P P E R
T E T ■ A N N U L A R ■ E L I
T R I B U T E B A N D ■ N F C
A S C O T ■ S I C ■ P E S O
■ ■ A I R S ■ R E O R D E R
S C O T L A N D ■ T H E F E D
A R T M U S E U M ■ A L I K E
K A T E S P A D E ■ R A R E R
E B O N ■ S K E W ■ E W E R S
```

138

```
G O D E L E S C H E R B A C H
P R I V A T E A U D I E N C E
S U M A N D S U B S T A N C E
■ ■ ■ D E S ■ G R E A T ■ ■
P A N E S ■ P H I L ■ I N D S
O R O S ■ B E T S ■ A F O O T
T A K ■ Z O R A ■ C R I N G E
S P O K E O F F T H E C U F F
D A M A S K ■ E R O S ■ S O A
A H I N T ■ Z W E I ■ L E O N
M O S S ■ D E W Y ■ P A R D O
■ ■ A T A R I ■ A I M ■ ■
O N E S E C O N D P L E A S E
P U T S T H E K I B O S H O N
S T A T E A S S I S T A N C E
```

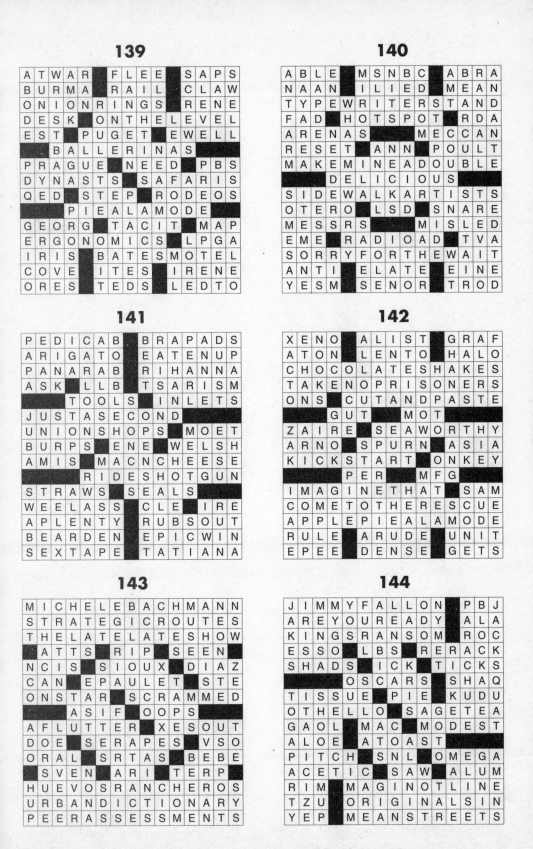

139

A	T	W	A	R		F	L	E	E		S	A	P	S
B	U	R	M	A		R	A	I	L		C	L	A	W
O	N	I	O	N	R	I	N	G	S		R	E	N	E
D	E	S	K		O	N	T	H	E	L	E	V	E	L
E	S	T		P	U	G	E	T		E	W	E	L	L
		B	A	L	L	E	R	I	N	A	S			
P	R	A	G	U	E		N	E	E	D		P	B	S
D	Y	N	A	S	T	S		S	A	F	A	R	I	S
Q	E	D		S	T	E	P		R	O	D	E	O	S
			P	I	E	A	L	A	M	O	D	E		
G	E	O	R	G		T	A	C	I	T		M	A	P
E	R	G	O	N	O	M	I	C	S		L	P	G	A
I	R	I	S		B	A	T	E	S	M	O	T	E	L
C	O	V	E		I	T	E	S		I	R	E	N	E
O	R	E	S		T	E	D	S		L	E	D	T	O

140

A	B	L	E		M	S	N	B	C		A	B	R	A
N	A	A	N		I	L	I	E	D		M	E	A	N
T	Y	P	E	W	R	I	T	E	R	S	T	A	N	D
F	A	D		H	O	T	S	P	O	T		R	D	A
A	R	E	N	A	S			M	E	C	C	A	N	
R	E	S	E	T		A	N	N		P	O	U	L	T
M	A	K	E	M	I	N	E	A	D	O	U	B	L	E
		D	E	L	I	C	I	O	U	S				
S	I	D	E	W	A	L	K	A	R	T	I	S	T	S
O	T	E	R	O		L	S	D		S	N	A	R	E
M	E	S	S	R	S			M	I	S	L	E	D	
E	M	E		R	A	D	I	O	A	D		T	V	A
S	O	R	R	Y	F	O	R	T	H	E	W	A	I	T
A	N	T	I		E	L	A	T	E		E	I	N	E
Y	E	S	M		S	E	N	O	R		T	R	O	D

141

P	E	D	I	C	A	B		B	R	A	P	A	D	S
A	R	I	G	A	T	O		E	A	T	E	N	U	P
P	A	N	A	R	A	B		R	I	H	A	N	N	A
A	S	K		L	L	B		T	S	A	R	I	S	M
			T	O	O	L	S		I	N	L	E	T	S
J	U	S	T	A	S	E	C	O	N	D				
U	N	I	O	N	S	H	O	P	S		M	O	E	T
B	U	R	P	S		E	N	E		W	E	L	S	H
A	M	I	S		M	A	C	N	C	H	E	E	S	E
			R	I	D	E	S	H	O	T	G	U	N	
S	T	R	A	W	S		S	E	A	L	S			
W	E	E	L	A	S	S		C	L	E		I	R	E
A	P	L	E	N	T	Y		R	U	B	S	O	U	T
B	E	A	R	D	E	N		E	P	I	C	W	I	N
S	E	X	T	A	P	E		T	A	T	I	A	N	A

142

X	E	N	O		A	L	I	S	T		G	R	A	F
A	T	O	N		L	E	N	T	O		H	A	L	O
C	H	O	C	O	L	A	T	E	S	H	A	K	E	S
T	A	K	E	N	O	P	R	I	S	O	N	E	R	S
O	N	S		C	U	T	A	N	D	P	A	S	T	E
			G	U	T			M	O	T				
Z	A	I	R	E		S	E	A	W	O	R	T	H	Y
A	R	N	O		S	P	U	R	N		A	S	I	A
K	I	C	K	S	T	A	R	T		O	N	K	E	Y
			P	E	R			M	F	G				
I	M	A	G	I	N	E	T	H	A	T		S	A	M
C	O	M	E	T	O	T	H	E	R	E	S	C	U	E
A	P	P	L	E	P	I	E	A	L	A	M	O	D	E
R	U	L	E		A	R	U	D	E		U	N	I	T
E	P	E	E		D	E	N	S	E		G	E	T	S

143

M	I	C	H	E	L	E	B	A	C	H	M	A	N	N
S	T	R	A	T	E	G	I	C	R	O	U	T	E	S
T	H	E	L	A	T	E	L	A	T	E	S	H	O	W
	A	T	T	S		R	I	P		S	E	E	N	
N	C	I	S		S	I	O	U	X		D	I	A	Z
C	A	N		E	P	A	U	L	E	T		S	T	E
O	N	S	T	A	R		S	C	R	A	M	M	E	D
		A	S	I	F		O	O	P	S				
A	F	L	U	T	T	E	R		X	E	S	O	U	T
D	O	E		S	E	R	A	P	E	S		V	S	O
O	R	A	L		S	R	T	A	S		B	E	B	E
	S	V	E	N		A	R	I		T	E	R	P	
H	U	E	V	O	S	R	A	N	C	H	E	R	O	S
U	R	B	A	N	D	I	C	T	I	O	N	A	R	Y
P	E	E	R	A	S	S	E	S	S	M	E	N	T	S

144

J	I	M	M	Y	F	A	L	L	O	N		P	B	J
A	R	E	Y	O	U	R	E	A	D	Y		A	L	A
K	I	N	G	S	R	A	N	S	O	M		R	O	C
E	S	S	O		L	B	S		R	E	R	A	C	K
S	H	A	D	S		I	C	K		T	I	C	K	S
			O	S	C	A	R	S			S	H	A	Q
T	I	S	S	U	E		P	I	E		K	U	D	U
O	T	H	E	L	L	O		S	A	G	E	T	E	A
G	A	O	L		M	A	C		M	O	D	E	S	T
A	L	O	E		A	T	O	A	S	T				
P	I	T	C	H		S	N	L		O	M	E	G	A
A	C	E	T	I	C		S	A	W		A	L	U	M
R	I	M		M	A	G	I	N	O	T	L	I	N	E
T	Z	U		O	R	I	G	I	N	A	L	S	I	N
Y	E	P		M	E	A	N	S	T	R	E	E	T	S

145

```
P O V E R T Y R O W ■ G A R R
U R A N I U M O R E ■ E P E E
C A R R O T C A K E ■ L P G A
E N Y A ■ U A R ■ D I A L U P
■ ■ G A S ■ ■ P E N T E L ■
E S T E R ■ S T E A D I C A M
W A R S A W P A C T ■ N I T E
O N E ■ B O L S T E R ■ D I A
K T E L ■ R E T I R E M E N T
S A G E G R E E N ■ B E R G S
■ C U T S I N ■ F A N ■ ■ ■
B L A S T S ■ O N O ■ D I S K
C A R O ■ O T H E R W O M A N
U R D U ■ M S M A G A Z I N E
P A S T ■ E A S T O R A N G E
```

146

```
B U R J K H A L I F A ■ P I C
O N A U T O P I L O T ■ G M A
W I S D O M T E E T H ■ T M S
E X P O S I T S ■ O L D H A T
■ ■ ■ L E O ■ A M E R I C A
C I A L I S ■ S T A T E R U N
A S I A N ■ S U I T E ■ T L C
N O R M ■ S E N D S ■ Y E A H
T M C ■ M A I N E ■ S E E T O
H E L S I N K I ■ C O R N E R
A T E I N T O ■ E O N ■ ■ ■
C R A N I A ■ C R O N Y I S M
K I N ■ M A J O R L E A G U E
I C E ■ A N D S O I T G O E S
T S R ■ L A S T R E S O R T S
```

147

```
C L A S P I N G ■ A N G L E
L A S E R B E A M ■ B O R A X
I N A N I M A T E ■ C R A V E
N O R A D ■ L E T T ■ Y O U
G L U T E I ■ E A S T E R N
T I L E ■ R U M O R H A S I T
O N E ■ C O N A R T I S T S ■
■ L A N D L I N E S ■ ■ ■
■ F O U R L E T T E R ■ O F T
C O I N P U R S E S ■ B R I E
H U L K I N G ■ S C L E R A
A L P ■ G O B S ■ R A G E S
I T A L Y ■ N O T R E D A M E
S I N A I ■ E Y E O P E N E R
E P S O N ■ S T E T S O N S
```

148

```
P I Z Z A J O I N T ■ W I F E
A N T I M A T T E R ■ A L A S
W H I T E N O I S E ■ L L C S
N I L ■ S E E S T O ■ K A T O
■ S E T ■ S N L ■ G O T ■
■ H T S ■ T I E O N E O N
I N H E R I T ■ N E W W A V E
B I O D A T A ■ G R E A S E S
A T T A C K S ■ S I S T E R S
R E T R E A T S ■ E T E ■
■ O K S ■ E P S ■ R A W
L O T S ■ S T E P O N ■ S A Y
Y U R I ■ R E N O N E V A D A
I Z O D ■ I S C R E W E D U P
N O T E ■ S T E E L T R A P S
```

149

```
A S K O V E R ■ P T B O A T S
R A I S E D A N E Y E B R O W
A L L K I D D I N G A S I D E
R O M A N ■ I N N E R ■ S I E
A M E R ■ M A J O R ■ S T E T
T E R ■ T I T A N ■ K N I F E
■ B A K E S ■ D E A D O N
■ I B I S E S ■ P E E P E R
A M A Z E D ■ M A L L S ■ ■
R I L E D ■ B U S T S ■ S H E
A T I T ■ P E S T S ■ V T E N
P A N ■ S E I K O ■ K A R A T
A T E E N A G E R I N L O V E
H O S T I L E T A K E O V E R
O R E S T E S ■ L E E R E R S
```

150

```
L I A R S ■ ■ B L A S T I T
U N D O C K ■ C O M E O N S
S A S S O N S ■ S A N T A N A
T W O S T E P S ■ F E T T E R
F O R E T E L L S ■ S L U R S
U R B S ■ P I A M A T E R S
L D S ■ B A T T A L I O N
■ L E T T E R M E N ■ ■
■ C O N C E R T O S ■ S E A
■ T O U G H R O A D ■ M A G I
C O N G A ■ S O L O H O M E R
L O C A L S ■ F E V E R I S H
A L E N C O N ■ C A R E S T O
M E D I A T E ■ R E S E E S
P R E S T O S ■ S O N D E
```

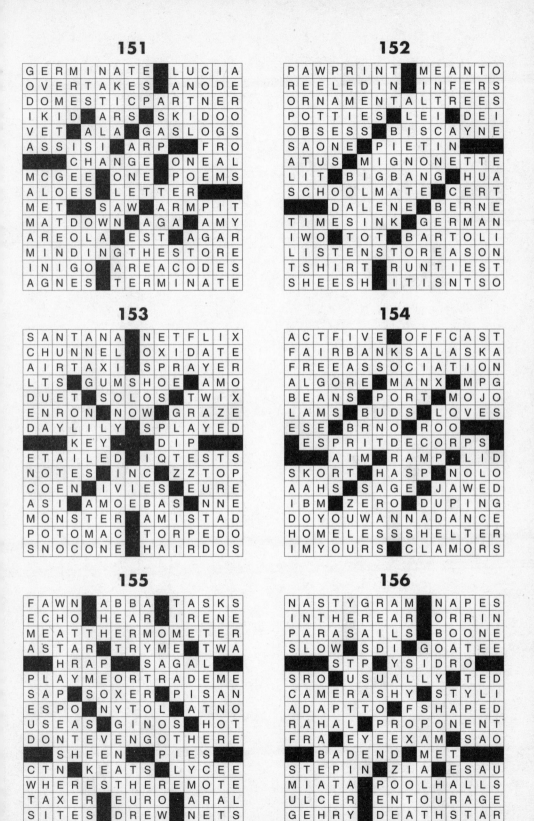

151

```
G E R M I N A T E ■ L U C I A
O V E R T A K E S ■ A N O D E
D O M E S T I C P A R T N E R
I K I D ■ A R S ■ S K I D O O
V E T ■ A L A ■ G A S L O G S
A S S I S I ■ A R P ■ F R O
■ C H A N G E ■ O N E A L
M C G E E ■ O N E ■ P O E M S
A L O E S ■ L E T T E R ■
M E T ■ S A W ■ A R M P I T
M A T D O W N ■ A G A ■ A M Y
A R E O L A ■ E S T ■ A G A R
M I N D I N G T H E S T O R E
I N I G O ■ A R E A C O D E S
A G N E S ■ T E R M I N A T E
```

152

```
P A W P R I N T ■ M E A N T O
R E E L E D I N ■ I N F E R S
O R N A M E N T A L T R E E S
P O T T I E S ■ L E I ■ D E I
O B S E S S ■ B I S C A Y N E
S A O N E ■ P I E T I N
A T U S ■ M I G N O N E T T E
L I T ■ B I G B A N G ■ H U A
S C H O O L M A T E ■ C E R T
■ D A L E N E ■ B E R N E
T I M E S I N K ■ G E R M A N
I W O ■ T O T ■ B A R T O L I
L I S T E N S T O R E A S O N
T S H I R T ■ R U N T I E S T
S H E E S H ■ I T I S N T S O
```

153

```
S A N T A N A ■ N E T F L I X
C H U N N E L ■ O X I D A T E
A I R T A X I ■ S P R A Y E R
L T S ■ G U M S H O E ■ A M O
D U E T ■ S O L O S ■ T W I X
E N R O N ■ N O W ■ G R A Z E
D A Y L I L Y ■ S P L A Y E D
■ K E Y ■ D I P ■
E T A I L E D ■ I Q T E S T S
N O T E S ■ I N C ■ Z Z T O P
C O E N ■ I V I E S ■ E U R E
A S I ■ A M O E B A S ■ N N E
M O N S T E R ■ A M I S T A D
P O T O M A C ■ T O R P E D O
S N O C O N E ■ H A I R D O S
```

154

```
A C T F I V E ■ O F F C A S T
F A I R B A N K S A L A S K A
F R E E A S S O C I A T I O N
A L G O R E ■ M A N X ■ M P G
B E A N S ■ P O R T ■ M O J O
L A M S ■ B U D S ■ L O V E S
E S E ■ B R N O ■ R O O
■ E S P R I T D E C O R P S ■
■ A I M ■ R A M P ■ L I D
S K O R T ■ H A S P ■ N O L O
A A H S ■ S A G E ■ J A W E D
I B M ■ Z E R O ■ D U P I N G
D O Y O U W A N N A D A N C E
H O M E L E S S S H E L T E R
I M Y O U R S ■ C L A M O R S
```

155

```
F A W N ■ A B B A ■ T A S K S
E C H O ■ H E A R ■ I R E N E
M E A T T H E R M O M E T E R
A S T A R ■ T R Y M E ■ T W A
■ H R A P ■ S A G A L ■
P L A Y M E O R T R A D E M E
S A P ■ S O X E R ■ P I S A N
E S P O ■ N Y T O L ■ A T N O
U S E A S ■ G I N O S ■ H O T
D O N T E V E N G O T H E R E
■ S H E E N ■ P I E S ■
C T N ■ K E A T S ■ L Y C E E
W H E R E S T H E R E M O T E
T A X E R ■ E U R O ■ A R A L
S I T E S ■ D R E W ■ N E T S
```

156

```
N A S T Y G R A M ■ N A P E S
I N T H E R E A R ■ O R R I N
P A R A S A I L S ■ B O O N E
S L O W ■ S D I ■ G O A T E E
■ S T P ■ Y S I D R O
S R O ■ U S U A L L Y ■ T E D
C A M E R A S H Y ■ S T Y L I
A D A P T T O ■ F S H A P E D
R A H A L ■ P R O P O N E N T
F R A ■ E Y E E X A M ■ S A O
■ B A D E N D ■ M E T
S T E P I N ■ Z I A ■ E S A U
M I A T A ■ P O O L H A L L S
U L C E R ■ E N T O U R A G E
G E H R Y ■ D E A T H S T A R
```

157

```
S T I L L D R E ■ ■ A L B A
C O N E H E A D S ■ M E A N
A R C T A N G E N T ■ O A T S
R E L I S T S ■ O R I E N T E
F A U N A S ■ T W I N B I L L
A D D O N ■ J E T P L A N E ■
C O E N ■ G A L I L E E ■ ■
E R S ■ D E S E R E T ■ L O B
■ ■ D E T O X E D ■ J O N I
■ S T E A R N E S ■ T A M E S
T H E O R E M S ■ L I M B I C
Y E S D E A R ■ S A N T A N A
P A S A ■ L A B O R P A R T Y
E T A T ■ ■ Z E N G A R D E N
A H S O ■ ■ L E O N T Y N E
```

158

```
W H I P I T ■ S P A C E J A M
H A M E L S ■ C O C A C O L A
A M P S U P ■ H I T S O N G S
T R U T V ■ O M N I S ■ K O S
S A D O ■ N A U T ■ P Y R E
U D E ■ K I T T Y K E L L E Y
P I N C E N E Z ■ R D A ■
G O T O V E R ■ M A G N U M S
■ ■ R I T ■ T A K E O N M E
J O H N N Y C A K E S ■ D M X
A N A S ■ O X E N ■ G E M S
R E V ■ H E L P S ■ G O R G E
J O E B O X E R ■ M O N G O L
A N N E R I C E ■ F A Z O O L
R E S T S T O P ■ A T O D D S
```

159

```
P I T B O S S ■ I M P A L A S
O N E A W A Y ■ F A R P O S T
S T A T I N S ■ O N E O N T A
T H R E E D ■ C L E M ■ G E T
P E D S ■ ■ P A D ■ I S E R E
U S O ■ G R I P ■ K E A R N S
N E W F R O N T I E R S ■ ■
K A N S A S C I T Y C H I E F
■ ■ T H E H O N O R A B L E
S A M O A N ■ N O N U ■ R E D
T W O P M ■ S E W ■ T O G A
J A G ■ K I N D ■ P A R K A Y
U K U L E L E ■ T O L U E N E
D E L I R I A ■ A C T N I C E
E N S U R E D ■ T O O K T E N
```

160

```
M A D E M I N C E M E A T O F
E C O N O M I C W A R F A R E
L O S A N G E L E S T I M E S
S P E C I A L I N T E R E S T
■ ■ S T E M S ■ ■ I S S ■
■ ■ O D E ■ F F F ■ T R E E
S T U R M ■ B E E F S ■ A X L
M O R S E C O D E S I G N A L
O J S ■ N I L E S ■ L A K M E
G O A L ■ M A X ■ T V S ■
■ ■ U G A ■ ■ P I E R O ■
C O M M E R C I A L R A D I O
F R E E T R A N S L A T I O N
C H A N S O N S D E G E S T E
S E T S O N A P E D E S T A L
```

161

```
P I Z Z A C R U S T ■ B L A B
A R I O N A S S I S ■ F O R A
C I P H E R T E X T ■ F O R T
A S S A M ■ ■ D A R K ■ K I T
■ ■ N O G O ■ M A N C A V E
P S A ■ N O O N ■ P E L T E R
H O C K E Y M O M ■ W E T L Y
O L E N ■ A P L U S ■ A H A B
N A T A L ■ H O T P O T A T O
E R I C A S ■ S E C T ■ T E X
B A C K L I T ■ D A T A ■ ■
O R A ■ A N O N ■ ■ O L D I E
O R C A ■ B R O O D M A R E S
T A I L ■ I T A L I A N A R T
H Y D E ■ N A M E S N A M E S
```

162

```
T R A P ■ M I S S K A N S A S
R E N O ■ A M I T O B L A M E
A S T O ■ S P L I T L E V E L
S C I F I ■ L E T T E R O N E
H O G ■ B R O N C O ■ R I C
T R U E N O R T H ■ B R E T T
V E A L S T E W ■ B R A D Y S
■ ■ M A C S ■ L A I N ■ ■
S O L E U S ■ M A L D E M E R
E C A R D ■ P O P E L E O X I
N O N ■ T E N U R E ■ N O G
S N O W G O O S E ■ S M I T H
I N T H E W R O N G ■ A T I T
N O T O N E I O T A ■ L O C O
G R E A T D A N E S ■ I R A N
```

163

S	C	O	W		W	H	I	S	K	B	R	O	O	M
U	L	N	A		H	A	V	E	N	E	E	D	T	O
R	E	E	L		I	T	A	L	I	A	N	A	R	T
G	A	S	K	E	T		R	I	F	T		Y	A	H
E	N	T	E	R	E	D		G	E	N	E			
	H	E	R	E	T	I	C		D	I	V	A	N	S
C	O	P	S		I	T	L	L		K	A	P	O	K
H	U	P		D	E	C	E	I	T	S		P	S	I
I	S	E	R	E		H	A	L	O		S	L	I	P
P	E	D	A	L	S		T	A	U	N	T	E	R	
		D	U	C	T		C	R	E	A	S	E	S	
I	D	O		S	H	I	P		I	S	R	A	E	L
T	O	M	C	O	L	L	I	N	S		T	U	B	A
C	L	E	A	R	E	D	O	U	T		E	C	O	N
H	E	N	N	Y	P	E	N	N	Y		D	E	B	T

164

H	E	A	D	S	T	A	N	D	S		P	I	C	T
I	N	D	O	O	R	P	O	O	L		A	R	A	W
G	O	O	N	T	I	P	T	O	E		P	O	R	E
H	U	R	T	S		R	E	V	E	R	E	N	C	E
A	G	E	S		L	I	V	E	P	E	R	S	O	N
S	H	E		S	I	Z	E	R		C	H	I	V	E
			C	I	T	E	R		B	E	A	D	E	R
C	A	R	O	L	E	D		W	R	I	T	E	R	S
O	N	A	G	E	R		I	H	O	P	S			
M	O	V	I	N		S	W	E	A	T		Y	E	P
P	R	E	T	T	Y	H	A	R	D		C	O	D	A
L	E	N	A	H	O	R	N	E		H	A	D	I	T
E	X	I	T		G	O	T	A	M	I	N	U	T	E
T	I	N	E		I	V	E	M	O	V	E	D	O	N
E	C	G	S		S	E	M	I	D	E	S	E	R	T

165

A	T	E	S	T	S		C	P	U		A	F	A	R
T	E	N	P	I	N		H	A	N	D	S	O	M	E
W	H	E	R	E	A	R	E	Y	O	U	F	R	O	M
A	R	M	Y		P	A	V	E		D	O	E		
R	A	Y		S	T	R	E	P		R	I	E	L	
	N	O	R	M		T	O	S	E	A		G	P	A
	F	O	R	M	A	L		S	C	E	N	E	I	
A	U	T	O	M	A	T	E	D	T	E	L	L	E	R
A	S	H	T	O	N		T	R	O	I	K	A		
R	T	E		M	E	R	C	Y		T	O	N	S	
E	A	S	T		T	I	A	R	A			G	U	N
		T	U	E		C	M	O	N		S	U	M	O
T	H	A	T	S	W	H	A	T	I	M	E	A	N	T
G	O	T	O	L	D	E	R		O	S	A	G	E	S
I	T	E	R		S	R	O		N	U	M	E	R	O

166

F	L	E	M	I	S	H			L	A	B	E	L	S
L	A	Y	A	N	E	G	G		O	N	E	L	A	P
I	C	E	S	K	A	T	E		K	I	S	S	M	E
M	O	L	T	E	N		T	W	I	S	T	T	I	E
F	R	I	E	D		C	S	A		E	B	O	N	D
L	U	N	D		S	H	I	R	T		U	N	A	S
A	N	E		D	A	R	N	G	O	O	D			
M	A	R	G	A	R	I	T	A	N	O	S	A	L	T
			I	R	I	S	H	M	E	N		M	A	H
S	L	O	G		S	T	E	E	R		A	B	R	I
I	O	T	A	S		E	H	S		A	S	I	G	N
M	A	I	N	M	E	N	U		S	P	L	E	E	N
I	D	O	T	O	O		N	O	C	H	A	N	C	E
L	E	S	I	O	N		T	R	A	I	N	C	A	R
E	R	E	C	T	S			I	N	S	T	E	P	S

167

P	A	L	O	O	K	A			M	I	C	A	H	
S	T	A	N	D	O	F	F		T	O	B	A	G	O
A	N	T	E	D	A	T	E		R	O	M	M	E	L
L	O	I	N	S		E	A	M	O	N		E	L	Y
M	O	N	O		A	R	S	O	N		T	R	I	M
S	N	O		T	R	Y	T	O		A	R	O	M	A
		M	E	T	O	O		S	H	O	O	I	N	
	P	R	E	S	S	U	R	E	P	O	I	N	T	
S	H	A	N	T	Y		F	A	I	L	S			
T	O	P	S	Y		C	A	S	E	D		H	U	M
I	T	S	A		P	O	M	E	S		S	E	P	T
P	O	T		S	O	L	I	D		T	H	E	R	E
P	L	A	T	T	E		N	O	T	S	O	H	O	T
L	A	R	I	A	T		E	U	R	O	P	E	A	N
E	B	S	E	N			T	E	S	S	E	R	A	

168

S	T	E	A	D	I	C	A	M		E	X	P	E	L
W	I	N	N	E	B	A	G	O		A	M	U	S	E
I	N	N	K	E	E	P	E	R		T	A	M	P	A
S	C	U	L	P	T		L	E	S	A	S	P	I	N
S	T	I	E	S		D	O	N	A	T		S	O	N
			I	V	A	N	O	V		D	I	N	E	
	C	O	A	X	I	N	G		O	P	E	R	A	S
S	I	N	C	E	R	E		P	R	O	L	O	G	S
A	G	E	N	D	A		B	E	E	L	I	N	E	
W	A	R	E		G	L	E	N	D	A				
E	R	E		W	O	O	D	S		R	E	M	A	P
D	I	E	R	E	S	I	S		V	I	R	I	L	E
O	L	L	I	E		T	I	M	E	Z	O	N	E	S
F	L	E	C	K		E	D	I	T	E	D	O	U	T
F	O	R	K	S		R	E	A	S	S	E	R	T	S

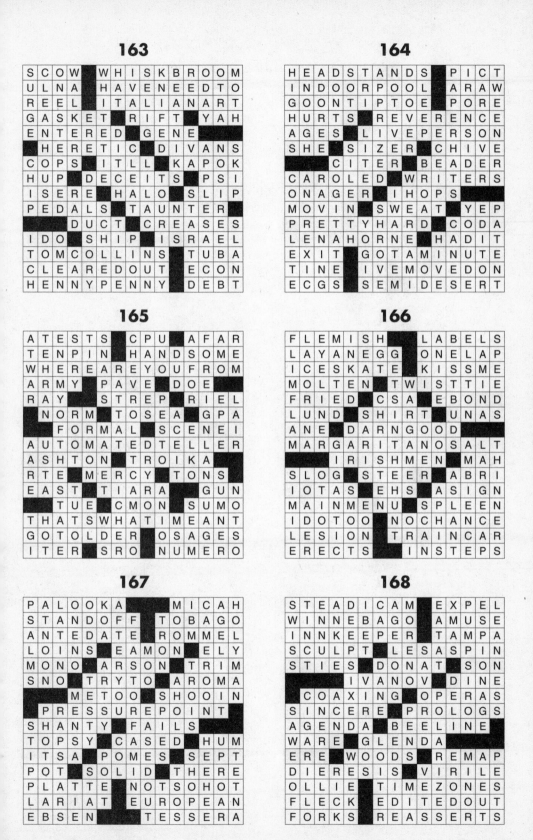

169

```
J A M A I C A █ N A C H O S
O N A T E A R █ D E F L E C T
C O N T O R T █ R E L A X E R
K I D █ H E F T E D █ S A L E
█ N A Y █ O O H S █ M S D O S
O T T O █ F R E S C O I S T S
S E E Y A █ M A Y O R S █ █ █
A D D O N S █ █ B A S A L T
█ █ D E I C E R █ L U C I E
D E L I N E A T E S █ E R M A
I L I E D █ P U G H █ S O O █
M A L T █ M O I R E S █ S R A
S P I E D O N █ E L A S T I C
U S E R I D S █ T V G U I D E
M E S S E S █ S E A N C E S
```

170

```
A W E D █ S E C O N D R A T E
C H A T █ I W A S F R A M E D
T A S S █ T I M E L I M I T S
S T Y █ P I N E █ A C R E
N A G G I N G █ C O R D I A L
A D O P T S █ M A R I A █ █ █
I R I S H █ B O B C O S T A S
V A N █ S I D E A █ █ W I E
E G G B E A T E R █ A G O R A
█ A N G E L █ S T O P G O
S T I N G E R █ S H I P O U T
P E N D █ G I R T █ T I T
A N T I C I P A T E █ L A T E
N E W T O N S L A W █ I T A R
S T O O D G U A R D █ T O R S
```

171

```
N A M E N A M E S █ E A R L S
I N A C I R C L E █ A R E A S
P U T O N E S F O O T I N I T
S T E L E █ █ U N I S O N S
█ █ █ I T A █ P L A N T
O R R █ O I S E █ █ O S S A
P O I S O N P E N L E T T E R
A D V E N T U R E I S L A N D
L E A V E I N S U S P E N S E
S O L E █ A F A R █ K E N
█ R A B A T █ S E W █
A P P A R A T █ S A N T A
G A I N E D A D M I S S I O N
E L E C T █ L E S S O N T W O
S P R E E █ L A S T S T A N D
```

172

```
S P I T C U R L █ C A N V A S
P I N H O L E S █ A N O I N T
R E D E M A N D █ K O T T E R
E P I C E N E █ P E T N A M E
E A R L S █ R A S H O M O N
█ N A U T I C A L █ E W I N G
█ B O B B Y O R R █ N E T
D O H █ A R O M A █ A S H
U N O █ T R A V A N T I
M E T E R █ D A R K A G E S
P O P M U S I C █ I N C A N
S N A P S T O █ L A L O L L O
T O N I T E █ L I V E B A I T
E N T R E E █ O P E N L I N E
R E S E E D █ B O R D E R E D
```

173

```
S C O O P █ E R N █ S C H M O
C O N G A █ T A O █ C L A R K
A D I E U █ H O T S H O W E R
B E T E L G E U S E █ U S D A
█ █ S C A L L O P E D
E S E █ E L S █ B A L I H A I
X P R I Z E █ G A L L E O N S
I R I N A █ H A D █ I S O N E
L I C E N S E D █ E S T H E R
E T H A N O L █ S U I █ A X E
█ █ R E I M B U R S E
E T O N █ L E O T O L S T O Y
S U P E R S T A R █ A S I D E
O B E S E █ E R A █ N I K E S
S A N T O █ D D S █ D E I S M
```

174

```
D U C █ W A F T █ E F F U S E
O N O █ I C E R █ X R A T E D
I Z V E S T I A █ T U N N E Y
T I E S █ I G N █ R I C E R S
█ P R O P I N Q U I T Y █
█ S B A █ S U N N Y █ F R I
I N T E N T █ I I S █ A L A N
R O O S E V E L T I S L A N D
K A R O █ S K I █ C H A T T Y
S H Y █ S T E T S █ E M S
█ R E A D Y T O R O C K
P T B O A T █ B A D █ D R N O
I O L A N I █ A S I S E E I T
C R I S C O █ S I S I █ E F T
T O P T E N █ E S T D █ N E O
```

175

```
R A D I U M ■ ■ ■ P L E D T O
E R R A T A ■ I L L U S O R Y
S T A L A G ■ M E A T P I E S
U S S ■ H O T J A Z Z ■ D A T
M A T A ■ G O U D A ■ N A T E
E L I S A ■ A S E ■ A I R E R
S E C O N D S T R I N G E R S
■ ■ F O O T L O O S E ■ ■
A B U N D L E O F N E R V E S
C A N O E ■ R O M ■ L I E T O
C R A W ■ H O K E Y ■ A N A T
O B I ■ R A V I N E S ■ U G O
R A D I O M E N ■ C H A S E S
D R E S S I N G ■ C E T E R A
S A D I S T ■ ■ H A L S E Y
```

176

```
T H E P R O O F ■ L A M E S T
W O V E I N T O ■ A Z A R I A
O H I T S Y O U ■ T U D O R S
P O L E A X E R ■ E R A S E S
M S G R ■ ■ M E N E M ■ ■
■ ■ E E L G R A S S ■ E T T A
H A N D P A I N T ■ E X E R T
O U I ■ G Y M B A L L ■ S O N
A R U B A ■ M O T I O N S T O
R A S A ■ J E B E D I A H ■
■ ■ T H U D S ■ ■ M A G S
L A S S O S ■ L A W Y E R U P
I M H U R T ■ E T H I O P I A
M A O I S M ■ D E E P F E L T
O D E T T E ■ S E T S F R E E
```

177

```
M O S H E ■ M I S S T E X A S
A N E E D ■ O N T H E L E F T
D E A L T ■ P R I E D I N T O
E C O L ■ P E E R S ■ D I E M
N O T E P A D ■ ■ M E A R A
O U T R A N ■ L I S A S ■
I R E ■ P A L E A L E ■ L A B
S S R ■ I C E A G E S ■ E P A
E E S ■ S E E K O U T ■ A P B
■ ■ S T A R S ■ T R I P L Y
G R I T S ■ ■ T H I N S E T
L A C E ■ S E M I S ■ T O T E
A D I N T E R I M ■ N O V A E
Z I N C O X I D E ■ I N E R T
E I G H T Y S I X ■ B E R T H
```

178

```
W E V E M E T ■ R E B E C C A
I N A H O L E ■ O V E R R A N
T R U S T M E ■ L E T S O U T
C O G ■ S O T H E R E ■ O T E
H U H S ■ S H O P S ■ P N I N
E T A I L ■ E L L ■ C R E O N
S E N N A S ■ D A M E E D N A
■ ■ L I F E C Y C L E ■ ■
F R E E T O G O ■ S E N T R A
M E S S Y ■ O U S ■ B E H A N
R E T S ■ S T R O P ■ D E N G
A R R ■ M A I T R E D ■ M R E
D E E P E N S ■ D A Y S A I L
I C E B O A T ■ I S E E Y O U
O T T A W A S ■ D E S P O T S
```

179

```
A T W T ■ A T I P ■ M A N E S
D R E S S R E H E A R S A L S
M I S A P P R O P R I A T E S
I N T R O ■ S P A M ■ B I C S
T I E ■ I S E E ■ E P C O T ■
■ T R U L Y ■ S A D A ■ N R A
U R N S ■ N E O N ■ R E A I M
N O O D L E S ■ N O R E L C O
I T M A Y ■ S P A R ■ O P T S
T O E ■ I T E R ■ C A C A O ■
■ L L A N O ■ O L A F ■ S A W
S U E D ■ P I T A ■ L O T S A
H E T E R O S E X U A L I T Y
I N T E L L I G E N C E M E N
V E E R S ■ N E R O ■ S E R E
```

180

```
C A S S ■ I M P S ■ F A W N S
E R A T ■ M I R O ■ I D I O T
R I C A ■ P R O P A G A N D A
F A R M T E A M ■ M U G G E R
■ ■ O P E D ■ I S E R E ■
A L S A C E ■ S A L E S R E P
L E A C H ■ G E N I E ■ H B O
V I N T N E R ■ D A I R I E S
I N C ■ I V O R Y ■ G E N R E
N E T S C A P E ■ S H E E T S
■ ■ W A D E D ■ A T M S ■
T A M A L E ■ F A L S E T T O
E N G L I S H L I T ■ R O O S
E G R E T ■ R A R E ■ G N U S
M E S S Y ■ E G E R ■ E E R O
```

181

```
S A L A M I ■ W A R P A I N T
E N A M O R ■ A D O A N N I E
A G N A T E ■ C O L L E C T S
R E I N I N ■ S U L A ■ A P T
C L E A V E S ■ T O T E M I C
H O R S E C A R ■ A R E C A ■
■ ■ S A L E S C L E R K S
A T T A ■ R E T A R ■ S A S E
T H I N G A M A J I G ■ ■
A R N E L ■ G A M E S O M E
P E P T A L K ■ K E T T L E S
R E L ■ R A N T ■ W E R E N T
I D A R E Y O U ■ A V I A T E
C A T C A L L S ■ V E C T O R
E Y E S T A L K ■ E N T E R S
```

182

```
S C O R E D ■ T A R ■ P S I
H A N O V E R ■ O R A T I O N
O N T H E G O ■ M I M O S A S
■ E V E N A S W E S P E A K ■
■ ■ ■ T U S H I E ■ ■ ■
A R A B ■ L E O ■ S T E A M
G I B R A L T A R ■ A R N A Z
E P A U L E T ■ E X P E N S E
D O B I E ■ I M P R E C I S E
■ N A N C E ■ A L A ■ T E E S
■ ■ ■ R E L A Y S ■ ■ ■
■ H E A V E N O N E A R T H ■
T O U R I S T ■ T Y L E N O L
D U R A N T E ■ S E M I P R O
S R O ■ O U R ■ S A N K A S
```

183

```
P A S S A W A Y ■ G A S C A P
A C T A S O N E ■ A L C O V E
S E A B I R D S ■ L O O M E D
S T R E A K ■ T A T T E R S
E O S ■ T A P E R S O F F ■
■ ■ I R E N E ■ F R O W N
O R B ■ C O R S E T ■ E R I E
K E E P ■ O V U L E ■ E T N A
R E D O ■ M E R I T S ■ H O T
A L O U D ■ R E N E E ■ ■
■ F R O N T S E A T ■ F A T
S P R I T E S ■ T U B U L E
W A I T E R ■ T H E P I N T A
A C C O R D ■ O U T O F G A S
T E E N S Y ■ O P E N F I R E
```

184

```
R E A D I E R ■ O J I B W A
E X P A N S E ■ P H I N E A S
S C R I M P S ■ L I B B E R S
E L I S E ■ C I A O ■ A F R O
L A O ■ M O U N T ■ A D A I R
L I R A ■ L E V E R S ■ L O T
■ M I X E D M E T A P H O R S
■ ■ L U M I N E S C E ■ ■
B Y M E R E S T C H A N C E ■
R O O ■ O N S I T E ■ S A L T
I D L E S ■ I V O R Y ■ L E E
N E I N ■ C O E N ■ A R O M A
G L E A S O N ■ I N S U R E S
T E R C E L S ■ C U I S I N E
O D E T T A ■ S T R E E T S
```

185

```
A L I F ■ P A I D A V I S I T
B I T E ■ A C T O N E S A G E
O T O E ■ R A I S E T A X E S
A T L ■ V C R S ■ M E Y E R S
R E D T I E ■ I F O R ■ ■
D R Y A B L E ■ I N A S P O T
S M O R E ■ V A L E N T I N E
H A U T ■ D E B T S ■ E P E E
I T S A C I N C H ■ P L E A T
P E O N I E S ■ Y I E L D T O
■ ■ T T O P ■ R O A R A T
C A M E A S ■ A D I N ■ E T A
O V E R D O E S I T ■ H A I L
D O T T E D T H E I ■ E M M E
A N S E L A D A M S ■ Y S E R
```

186

```
T H E J U N G L E ■ A R A B S
V E X A T I O U S ■ R I C O H
G R A P E N U T S ■ C O R B Y
A B L E ■ G E E S ■ O S S
M I L ■ P R E S S U P ■ B A T
E E Y O R E ■ ■ L E S A G E
■ ■ M I D D L E L E T T E R
M A L E C H A U V I N I S T S
T H I N K I N G E V I L ■ ■
C O N S U L ■ A N T O N Y
A Y E ■ P L A T I N G ■ P I E
R M S ■ S C A D ■ V E G A
M A O R I ■ C L I P P I N G S
E T U I S ■ R O O S E V E L T
L E T G O ■ A N T I P O D E S
```

187

```
F R A T H O U S E   S P A R S
I N T R A N S I T   T I D A L
N A V Y S E A L S   A C U R A
    A B O I L   A N K L E T
A P R   E U R   S O L U T E S
T E A S E T   S T R E P    
B E G I N   P O U T Y L I P S
A L E X   T U R N A   I N R E
T E S T P I L O T   O N L O W
    Y E L L S   S L E E V E
L A B F E E S   T H Y   T E D
E R R O R S   P E R M S    
I D A R E   T E L E P A T H S
C E N T S   A T E D I N N E R
A N D Y S   S E X S C E N E S
```

188

```
I N S E C T S     T H E F I R M
M O U N T A I N O U S A R E A
O P P O S I T E M E A N I N G
K E E L     W E D   T S O S  
      A P S E S     P A H    
A R N   I C Y   C A L   L O P
B E O N T H E S A F E S I D E
A L S A C E L O R R A I N E R
T O U G H M I N D E D N E S S
E S C   T E D   I S E   N A E
    H B O   B O H R S      
B E L A   A H A     O A F S
A B U S I N E S S A F F A I R
L O C A L I N H A B I T A N T
I N K L E S S   G O B Y S E A
```

189

```
P U B Q U I Z   U N S N A R L
A N O U N C E   G O T F R E E
P I L A T E S   G N O C C H I
A C E S O U T   B E A T S I T
D O R A   P E R O T   E I R E
O D O R S   D E O   C A N E R
C E S S N A   S T J A M E S  
      A L R O S E N        
  H A I R G E L   W I N D O W
G O R M E   D E B   D U E N A
A P I A   R A D I I   M R E S
M I S D E A L   P D Q B A C H
E N T E N T E   E S T E L L E
S T A I N E R   D A Y S T A R
T O S T A R T   S Y S T E M S
```

190

```
    C L A I M T O F A M E    
    T H E W O M A N I L O V E
J E A L O U S M I S T R E S S
A N N A L S   P O K E I N T O
M A N N S   B E N E   A B A B
I C E D   E A R S   C R E T E
E E L   S L U R   C U T T E R
    D I M M E M O R Y        
N F L E R S   S I Z E   H E P
B L O T S   A I R Y   B O N O
C O C O   O R S O   B E T T E
T R A N S E C T   G A S L I T
V I T A L S T A T I S T I C S
  N O T A T A N Y P R I C E  
    R E G E N T S P A R K    
```

191

```
S P L A S H G U A R D   S R S
T O U J O U R S G A I   E E C
U N P A T R I O T I C   A S U
A G O   S T E P   L E G S I T
R E N     R E M B R A N D T
T E E D U P   N E A   G A U L
    A N A   S S R   S K E E
L I M N I N G   H O S T E S S
I L E T   C I A   N E E    
E L L E   A V I   S E R B I A
A T T A C K E R S     E N G
B R O N Z E   B A E R   A G E
E E R   E D G A R B E R G E N
D A M   C A E S A R S A L A D
S T E   H Y M E N O P T E R A
```

192

```
U S B A N K   S O A P S U D S
N O R T O N   A P P L E P I E
C H A M P A G N E B O T T L E
L E S   E C A R D   W A I L S
E L S E   K E E P S   E L O I
S P R A T   A M A T E   T N N
A M A T O L   O G R E S    
M E T O N Y M   E U R O P O P
    N O M A D   M I L A N O
N I M   F A R E D   E A R E D
E D A M   N Y L O N   R O T C
B A Y A T   J U T E S   D O A
U H O H S P A G H E T T I O S
L O R R A I N E   D E C E N T
A S S E R T E D   A M U S E S
```

193

```
G A Y I C O N ▓ S E A W E E D
O P E N E R A ▓ I N R A N G E
K E A T O N S ▓ X S A N D O S
A S H ▓ S O D A P O P ▓ N I K
R U M P ▓ T A T A R ▓ P O S T
T I A R A ▓ Q V C ▓ S E T T O
S T N I C K ▓ S K I N D E E P
▓ M E A D ▓ S T A X ▓
L O S A L T O S ▓ S K I H A T
A N I T A ▓ E I S ▓ E N O C H
T A L E ▓ L A M I A ▓ G E R E
E D E ▓ B A D P E R M ▓ D O C
R A N L A T E ▓ R I O L O B O
A R T I S T E ▓ R A C E W A R
L E A T H E R ▓ A S S A N T E
```

194

```
R O S E B U S H E S ▓ U S A F
E R A S E R H E A D ▓ S Q M I
P O L A R B E A R S ▓ A U E R
O S T ▓ L A S T S ▓ N I E L S
▓ T I N A S ▓ M A D E I T
A R O U N D ▓ S A M ▓ Z O O
D A R T ▓ E E Y O R E ▓ E R R
A K A ▓ O S M O S I S ▓ B A D
M E N ▓ L I E S O N ▓ V O T E
A L G ▓ M G R ▓ C O A X E R
N E E S O N ▓ A B O U T ▓
D A Z E S ▓ I N O U T ▓ O J O
E V E R ▓ O C E A N L I N E R
V E S T ▓ T E S T T A K I N G
E S T A ▓ B E T S Y W E T S Y
```

195

```
J A B B E R ▓ C A R E S F O R
E Q U I N E ▓ O N C A M E R A
L U R K E D ▓ M T A R A R A T
L A S E R S ▓ M I S P R I N T
O P T S O U T O F ▓ S T A G Y
S L O T ▓ N O D U H ▓
H A P A X ▓ P E R I O D I D E
O N E N I L ▓ C H A N E Y
T E N D A Y W A R ▓ S T A T E
▓ S I N E W ▓ E N O L
N A P P A ▓ S U P E R M I N I
O L E A S T E R ▓ B O Y M A N
D I E T S O D A ▓ E X M A T E
A T T H E G U N ▓ R I O T E R
T O E S T O P S ▓ N O M E S S
```

196

```
A C Q U I R E ▓ S M A L L E R
T O U R N E Y ▓ W E B S I T E
T M O B I L E ▓ A T L A N T A
H E N ▓ S O F T P R E T Z E L
E S S A ▓ S U M M E R ▓
S L E D S ▓ L E E ▓ M O W S
C A T H A Y ▓ N E E D A N A P
E T H E N E S ▓ T H E R E T O
N E U R O S I S ▓ S W I P E R
E R T E ▓ X E S ▓ S N E R T
▓ W E T R A G ▓ O R B S
S O U T H P H I L L Y ▓ C O W
T H R E E P M ▓ S E E H E R E
R O S A L I A ▓ A N T E N N A
S H A R P E N ▓ S N I F T E R
```

197

```
P S H A W S ▓ T E A R G A S
A T A X I A ▓ B O S W O R T H
C A R E E R ▓ U P T O D A T E
E T D S ▓ A D Z E ▓ R E N E E
C E T ▓ W H I Z K I D ▓ D S T
A L I T O ▓ G L A M ▓ S E T S
R A M S E S I I ▓ O S E ▓
S W E A T I N G B U L L E T S
▓ R O T ▓ H A T E M A I L
C A W S ▓ A R T Y ▓ D A R E I
A R A ▓ B R E Y E R S ▓ T S P
V E R B S ▓ P E D I ▓ L O C I
E T C E T E R A ▓ G L U E O N
T O R E A D O R ▓ G O K A R T
T O Y S R U S ▓ S T E R E O
```

198

```
A D A M S A L E ▓ D E V I L
L I M E T R E E ▓ U R S I N E
D N A T U R A L ▓ S U P E R G
A T T ▓ D E N S ▓ S M O R E S
▓ I A N ▓ Q T S ▓
F M A J O R ▓ Q U E E N M U M
R O L O S ▓ Q U I E T G A M E
E S T H ▓ Q U E L L ▓ A S I A
R E H N Q U I S T ▓ V I T A L
E L O Q U E N T ▓ K I O S K S
▓ I T T ▓ S I P ▓
P I Z A Z Z ▓ G A S P ▓ A T V
O R I A N A ▓ I R S A U D I T
P A T R O L ▓ S A M S P A D E
S N I P S ▓ T H E S I R E N
```

199

S	H	O	R	T	S	T	R	A	W	■	S	T	O	W
M	E	D	I	U	M	R	A	R	E	■	A	R	I	A
I	R	O	N	M	A	I	D	E	N	■	W	I	L	T
L	A	U	D	S	■	V	I	E	T	■	N	A	P	E
E	L	L	S	■	T	A	X	L	A	W	■	L	A	R
Y	D	S	■	D	O	L	E	■	T	I	G	R	I	S
■	H	E	R	E	S	Y	■	S	P	U	N	K		
S	T	R	A	P	I	N	■	A	S	H	A	N	T	I
T	I	A	R	A	■	T	O	R	T	E	S	■		
A	T	S	T	U	D	■	P	D	A	S	■	S	P	R
Y	I	P	■	L	A	T	E	S	T	■	O	T	O	E
S	C	U	M	■	B	E	N	T	■	O	C	A	L	A
M	A	T	E	■	B	R	A	I	N	C	H	I	L	D
A	C	I	D	■	E	R	I	C	T	H	E	R	E	D
D	A	N	E	■	D	A	R	K	H	O	R	S	E	S

200

H	A	S	A	L	O	T	G	O	I	N	G	F	O	R
I	M	P	R	O	V	E	O	N	N	A	T	U	R	E
P	O	R	K	B	A	R	R	E	L	B	I	L	L	S
B	E	Y	■	S	T	R	I	D	E	S	■	F	A	T
O	B	E	S	■	E	I	L	A	T	■	G	I	N	S
N	A	S	A	L	■	F	L	Y	■	F	A	L	D	O
E	S	T	H	E	S	I	A	■	M	A	R	L	O	N
■	A	V	E	C	■	M	E	N	D	■				
P	U	R	R	E	D	■	C	O	N	T	E	S	S	A
O	N	E	A	L	■	L	A	V	■	A	N	I	O	N
L	S	T	S	■	T	O	T	E	M	■	A	G	H	A
E	N	O	■	C	E	R	A	M	I	C	■	N	U	L
N	A	T	I	O	N	A	L	E	C	O	N	O	M	Y
T	R	A	D	I	T	I	O	N	A	L	I	R	A	S
A	L	L	A	L	O	N	G	T	H	E	L	I	N	E

The New York Times

Crossword Puzzles

The #1 Name in Crosswords

Available at your local bookstore or online at nytimes.com/nytstore

St. Martin's Griffin